THE E   RCIAL

PROPERTY MARKETS

ONE WEEK LOAN

Co   icant sector   ues beyond
the   to provide a
rig   focuses on impor-
tan   the way in which the
bui   es that drive new com-
me   is divided into three main
sec

-                                s

-                        ial property

-                perty

Em   rawn from all around the world clearly illustrate the
the   es and issues discussed. Throughout, the emphasis is on making an
often complex area as accessible and readable as possible. This text will be
an invaluable resource for students of property economics and related subject areas, as well as to professionals working in the built environment.

Michael Ball is Professor of Urban Economics at the School of Urban
Development and Policy, South Bank University, London. **Colin Lizieri** is
Director of Postgraduate Research and Senior Lecturer in the Department of
Land Management and Development at the University of Reading. **Bryan D.
MacGregor** is the MacRobert Professor of Land Economy and Director of
the Centre for Property Research in the Department of Land Economy at the
University of Aberdeen.

THE ECONOMICS
OF COMMERCIAL
PROPERTY MARKETS

*Michael Ball, Colin Lizieri and
Bryan D. MacGregor*

London and New York

First published in 1998
by Routledge
11 New Fetter Lane, London EC4P 4EE

Simultaneously published in the USA and Canada
by Routledge
29 West 35th Street, New York, NY 10001

© 1998 Michael Ball, Colin Lizieri and Bryan D. MacGregor

The rights of Michael Ball, Colin Lizieri and Bryan D. MacGregor to
be identified as the Authors of this Work have been asserted by them
in accordance with the Copyright, Designs and Patent Act 1988

Typeset in Times by
J&L Composition Ltd, Filey, North Yorkshire
Printed and bound in Great Britain by
Clays Ltd, St. Ives PLC

British Library Cataloguing in Publication Data
A catalogue record for this book is available from the British Library

Library of Congress Cataloging in Publication Data
A catalog record for this book has been requested

ISBN 0–415–14992–4 (hbk)
ISBN 0–415–14993–2 (pbk)

DEDICATION

In the course of writing this book, the joys, tragedies and humdrum of life continued. Bryan's wife gave birth to twin daughters, Colin married and moved house and Michael's mother, at the start of the project, and father, towards its end, both died suddenly. These are supposed to be some of the most stressful things that can happen in normal life. Even for obsessive authors, pressed by deadlines, such relationships and events will always be most important. So, we should like to dedicate this book to:

Nicola, Catriona and Eilidh MacGregor
Michelle Lizieri
Muriel and John Ball

CONTENTS

CONTENTS

FIGURES

ix

TABLES

PREFACE

In the mid-1980s, many property market specialists saw little point in study-ing economics and its applications to commercial property. A good illustra-tion of this is the comment by a senior surveyor that surveying students should not waste time studying macroeconomics and finance but should, instead, learn about the property market. The academic view was no less encouraging. Property economics and finance were seen by many as, at best, a backwater.

Things have changed dramatically since then. It is now an axiom in the property professions that an understanding of the wider context within which commercial property markets operate is essential; and professionals and academics in other disciplines – such as, economics, finance, planning and geography – accept the importance of the study of commercial property markets. There is also a rapidly expanding literature, and growing academic status for the leading property journals.

Commercial markets are characterised by boom–bust periods of over and then under supply, with consequences for the wider economy. The built environment in which we live is shaped by forces that drive new commercial building and redevelopment. These forces are complex and are moderated by institutional contexts. Some are transmitted to property from the macro-economy and from the capital markets, each of which must increasingly be considered within a global context. Others arise from within the property market itself, in the behavioural responses of the thousands of individuals to the constraints and opportunities existing for them at particular times. Whatever their origin and the feedback effects such forces may generate, there are locally specific outcomes. The roles and functioning of towns and cities are strongly influenced by property market processes. This book sets out to explain those processes and their effects.

When this book was conceived, we thought the task would be easier than it turned out to be. Each of us felt we had a reasonable grasp of the literature, particularly as together we could claim over 50 years' teaching experience of the subject, or parts of it, to undergraduates and post-graduates from all of the relevant academic disciplines. The initial optimism was soon replaced by a sense of the magnitude of the task as we began to piece the book together. Substantial differences in the level of development of theory in the various sub-areas became far more apparent than any of us had earlier been prepared to recognise.

There has, for example, been much attention over the last ten years to the application of financial economics to the analysis of property investment. While the vocabulary is a mixture of finance and traditional surveying terms, the area is reasonably well developed. In contrast, the influence of commercial property markets on the macroeconomy is poorly understood. No other property text that we know of tries to put property in the context of macroeconomic theory. Yet issues such as the property cycle cannot be properly investigated without incorporating understandings of their relationship to the business cycle.

Surprisingly, the area that we had all expected to be the one of the easiest, the microeconomics of commercial property, proved to be the most difficult to draw together. Despite the extensive literature in urban economics and economic geography, there simply does not exist an adequate and complete general microeconomic theory of urban property markets. There are long running debates about the impacts of the fixed location and long life of buildings, the interrelationships among buildings, and the resultant effects on the behaviour of agents. These, we feel, remain unresolved, even though there are many important insights available from the existing body of theory.

The book is aimed at those with a basic understanding (roughly equivalent to first year undergraduate level) of economics (both micro and macro), statistics and financial mathematics. This is not to suggest that a detailed understanding of these subjects is essential but it helps. The size and scope of the book means that it may not all be relevant to every reader. The unifying theme is the application of standard economic principles to the analysis of commercial property markets.

The book should be of value to students, both undergraduate and postgraduate, in a wide range of subjects, including economics, surveying, planning, geography, construction and finance. We hope it will also be of use to practitioners, especially those involved in research.

ACKNOWLEDGEMENTS

Many people contributed, some knowingly, most unknowingly, to the production of this book. In the course of collaborations, conferences, seminars and informal discussions, we have learned a lot from many people and they have helped us develop our ideas. It is always difficult to single out particular individuals but we have to try in the knowledge that we will miss out someone important. The following probably constitute a sub-set of those who have contributed to the academic content of this book: Andrew Baum, Steven Bourassa, Gerald Brown, Neil Crosby, Maurizio Grilli, Foort Hamelink, Pat Hendershott, Martin Hoesli, George Matysiak, Paul McNamara, Tanya Morrison, Nanda Nanthakumaran, Steve Satchell, David Sunderland, Greg Schwann, Charles Ward and Elaine Worzala.

The support and tolerance of families, friends and work colleagues was much appreciated but probably insufficiently acknowledged. The quiet and professional patience and encouragement of the publishers, particularly Alison Kirk, helped considerably.

We should like to thank these and many more, although we accept full responsibility for any remaining errors and for any confusion or misunderstanding in our presentation of ideas.

Finally, we should acknowledge each other's inputs. We tolerated and were tolerated, and learned much from working with each other.

1

INTRODUCTION

THE IMPORTANCE OF COMMERCIAL PROPERTY MARKET ECONOMICS

This book seeks to provide a rigorous analysis of the economics of commercial property markets. Conventional economics texts neglect property as a sector. By contrast the majority of the existing (UK) texts in the property field are rooted in an urban economics tradition or are little more than introductory economics texts with housing and property examples pasted on. A limited number of other texts concentrate on finance and investment, neglecting wider economic factors. There is, thus, a clear need for a book that examines the economics of commercial property markets in detail, drawing on the growing body of economic research in both space and financial markets, and which provides readers with a clear overview of developments in the field.

An understanding of the economics of commercial property markets is important since there are many property-related issues that affect everyone and shape the built environment. Some of these issues and themes are highlighted below. In the research literature, these issues have been examined from the perspectives of a variety of academic disciplines and professions. These include, economics, finance, geography, sociology, urban economics, law, planning, surveying and construction management. This book integrates those analyses within a formal economics framework.

Before setting out the approach adopted in the book and outlining the content, some of the key economic issues in commercial property are now considered. These are divided into microeconomic, macroeconomic and financial issues, following the three-part structure of the text.

Microeconomic issues in commercial property

In examining micro themes, the text focuses on the structure of demand for commercial property, changing locational needs and the response of land and

1

property markets to those changing patterns. Relevant contemporary issues include:

- the large areas of vacant industrial properties and of vacant land in the centres of major urban areas in the early 1980s following closure of many manufacturing firms and factories;
- the pressures for the development of out-of-town shopping centres and retail warehouses and grocery superstores in the later 1980s; in some areas this led to major declines in city centre shopping and had environmental impacts;
- the expansion of high technology industrial activities along motorway corridors in the late 1970s and early 1980s; and
- decentralisation of many office-using activities from city centres to suburban, peripheral and satellite locations in the 1970s and 1980s and the development of call centres in the 1990s.

An understanding of market adjustment processes in commercial property markets is critical in analysing these events. Demographic and economic changes create new patterns of demand for property but the response of developers, investors and land owners determines the spatial outcomes and affects the competitiveness and profitability of sectors of industry in a city, a region or a country.

Macroeconomic issues in commercial property

The macro themes investigated in the book include the role of commercial property in the economy, the possibility of 'crowding out' or overinvestment in property, property cycles and the need to model property market behaviour. These are topics of great importance:

- in property booms capital switches from other parts of the economy; in busts, company asset values fall as property prices tumble;
- the property crash of the mid-1970s had a dramatic effect on the UK secondary banking sector with economic – and political – consequences;
- the property crash of the late 1980s led to many company failures and resulted in much high quality but vacant office space, particularly in the City of London; and
- the turmoil in South East Asian financial markets in the late 1990s is linked to the very large amounts of capital tied up in land and buildings and the contribution of property loans to debt in those countries.

The world-wide boom and bust property cycle of the late 1980s and early 1990s raised the awareness of the important links between the macroeconomy and commercial property markets. Generally, in the property literature

2

these links are only tangentially incorporated into analysis and discussion. There are a number of widely held beliefs concerning property that need detailed examination. For example, the common beliefs that there is over-investment in property and that the volume of property development is subject to marked cyclical fluctuations are not supported by the available UK data. Economic modelling of property market behaviour is of great importance in analysing the linkage between key economic and financial variables and the behaviour of commercial property.

Financial issues in commercial property

Commercial property has different (and difficult) financial features when compared to other asset classes. Nonetheless, there are increasing trends to integrate property asset management with that of other financial assets. Other key trends include the growth of cross-border investment and the development of indirect investment vehicles. Topics of importance and interest are listed below:

- The types and formats of financial analyses practised by property professionals are very different from those of other asset markets. This causes problems as property must compete with shares and bonds for a place in the investment portfolio.
- A number of well-publicised valuation 'disasters', particularly in the aftermath of the late 1980s and early 1990s property crash, reinforced suspicions about the adequacy of traditional valuation techniques and performance measures based on those techniques.
- Over the last two decades, the major pension funds and insurance companies have decreased the proportion of commercial property held in their investment portfolios.
- In many markets, notably in the United States with Real Estate Investment Trusts (REITs), there has been rapid growth in securitised or unitised property investment vehicles.
- Following financial liberalisation and deregulation in the mid-1980s, there have been large flows of overseas capital into commercial property; a substantial proportion of the office stock in the City of London is now owned by non-UK firms, while UK investors hold large portfolios of mainland European and North American property.

Insights drawn from financial economics help to explain these trends and provide a framework for analysis of investment issues. This is vital in breaking down the isolation of much existing property research.

THE PURPOSE

The purpose of the book, then, is to provide an economic framework within which to explain and understand these and related commercial property issues. The text should prove valuable for property researchers and practitioners in many ways. We hope that it will clarify and deepen understanding of:

- the likely behaviour of economic agents in the property markets;
- the implications for property of new business and social trends;
- the place of property and the development process in the wider economy;
- the causes and significance of property cycles;
- forecasting and modelling property markets;
- financial principles applied to property; and
- the role and consequences of valuation and other asset pricing models.

THE APPROACH

The book is divided into three broad parts covering microeconomics, macroeconomics and financial economics. The first two are standard divisions within economics. Microeconomic analysis investigates individual production and consumption decisions and their influence on the allocation of resources within an economy, while macroeconomic theory deals with interactions in the economy as a whole. The third area, financial economics, examines investment decision-making. This is an important but often neglected perspective from which to understand the economics of commercial property markets.

There has been a vast increase in the amount of research into commercial property over the last decade. Much of this research has drawn on applications from the more developed fields of financial and housing economics. This makes it difficult to write a definitive textbook. Rather, it has been necessary to order and survey the literature, to impose a structure and to set out the main themes of research. While property research related to financial economics has become more developed and complete in recent years, there are major gaps in the literature in other fields. These include the inadequate micro foundations for the modelling of property market supply and demand and the need to establish a formal theoretical link between the macroeconomy and the property market. The book attempts to develop these areas.

The approach adopted is based upon demand and supply interactions in four interlinked submarkets, using a simple competitive model with the assumption of rational economic agents. The remainder of the book is built upon this foundation. This perspective forms a valuable starting point for analysing the relationships and adjustment processes in property markets and has empirical backing. This does not mean that the model is expected to apply in all situations, rather, it is an 'ideal form' model. Property markets have specific characteristics, including heterogeneity, lumpiness, lack of information and externalities that make simplistic application of the competitive model problematic. The book explores these characteristics and examines modifications and extensions to, and critiques of, the competitive model.

The general principles outlined in the text apply to all commercial property markets. The perspective adopted is largely that of the UK and, to a lesser extent, of the US. European, Far Eastern and Australasian perspectives are used where appropriate. This reflects both the experience and knowledge of the authors and the importance of the UK and the US in the development of these subject areas.

Commercial property is generally divided into broad sectors: offices, shops and industrial property. This division underpins much commercial property research. The categories broadly relate to sectors of employment. Offices serve business and professional services, administrative and government activity; industrial space is utilised by manufacturing industry and warehousing; and shops are the retail outlets for consumption activity. The book does not consider residential property except in passing. Housing economics is the subject of other texts. While residential property is an important real estate investment sector in the US, it has yet to be established as such in the UK. Other classifications of commercial property are possible and new sectors, such as leisure property, are emerging.

In illustrating the economic principles discussed, offices are used more frequently than other sectors. This reflects three main factors. First, much of the published research literature deals with office markets. Second, offices are the most important investment sector by value. Finally, they offer the clearest illustration of many of the issues raised, including location, overbuilding, modelling and forecasting and internationalisation. Since offices remain strongly clustered in the centres of major cities, this leads to a strong urban focus in the text.

The academic development of different areas covered in the book varies. As a result, the form of the material in the book varies too, reflecting the current state of knowledge and the scope of the literature. In some areas, particularly in macroeconomics, a well-developed theoretical framework exists and, hence, discussion focuses on the role of property within existing models. In others, such as urban location, there are a variety of partial explanations drawn from different academic disciplines which must be set into some coherent framework. In areas such as property market forecasting, the field is still developing and material is best presented as a critical review of the research literature with identification of the broad themes. The need to interlink the themes and to cross-reference has led to long chapters. Practical examples and equations have been kept to a minimum to ensure that the focus is on the economic principles.

The book covers such diverse areas that it is unlikely that any one reader could be expected to have the same level of prior knowledge across all topics. However some assumptions have had to be made. It is assumed that readers will have studied micro- and macroeconomics to at least first year undergraduate level; that they will understand the basic principles of probability and statistical inference and that they understand the fundamentals of financial mathematics.

Some clarifications are required as to how certain key terms are used throughout the text. Different parts of the literature use the same terms in distinct ways, which can be confusing. Three that are worth highlighting are the concepts of *efficiency*, *institutions* and *investment*.

Economic efficiency in much of the economic literature refers to situations where resources are allocated optimally, so that the goods desired in the market place are produced in the cheapest possible way, given current technical knowledge. Consequently, efficiency in this sense is about making the best use of inputs to produce the maximum amount of output. In financial economics, *the efficient market hypothesis* defines price efficiency in terms of the amount of available information that is utilised. Weak form efficiency holds where an investor cannot profit from patterns in historic price series, strong form efficiency holds that prices reflect all available information at a particular time. This results in a more specific definition of price efficiency. This should be borne in mind in reading the financial economics sections.

Institutions in the financial economics literature generally refer to the major investor groups including pension funds, life insurance and general insurance companies. Institutional investors are highly significant in all investment markets including the commercial property markets. They hold a considerable proportion of investment property. In other areas of economics, *institutional analysis* refers to the behaviour of individuals and organisations as market agents and the role of market and social structures, rules and regulations in affecting market processes. This may entail relaxing some of the assumptions of economic rationality in the competitive model. The institutional framework determines how supply and demand adjustment processes take place. Although the particular usage of the term should be clear from the context an upper case I is used to refer to the investing Institutions and a lower case i to refer to institutional analysis and market structure.

In financial economics, *investment* means the acquisition of the title to some asset. Property investment, then, refers to the purchase of land or buildings and the right to receive rent as income and capital value growth. In macroeconomics, investment refers to investment in real goods as inventories or fixed capital. In the macroeconomic sense, property investment refers only to allocation of resources to create new structures – the development process. By contrast, financial investment could involve acquisition of existing property from another investor. Which definition is meant should be clear from the context.

Finally, different parts of the literature use different notations. Where appropriate, these have been standardised. However, to change long-standing notations in economics and property investment would only serve to confuse. Accordingly, in such cases both versions are presented, the notation chosen in a chapter being dependent on the context and the theoretical origins of the research.

THE CONTENTS

Part 1 of the book deals with the microeconomics of commercial property. Chapter 2 sets out *four interconnected property markets*: the *user* market, the *development* market, the *financial asset* market and the *land* market. In the user market, businesses demand space for their economic activities and are prepared to pay a price to occupy that space in the form of rent. The rental level acts as a signal for developers to supply new space and to bid for land held by land owners. The rent is a cash flow for investors in the financial asset market, who acquire property as an investment asset. In the model, equilibrium between supply and demand is established through the *price mechanism*.

Chapter 3 examines the nature of *occupational demand* more closely. Changes in the nature of demand for business space, associated with the growth of services and the decline of manufacturing in developed economies are considered. Next, a framework for understanding *spatial variations in demand* is set out. The chapter concludes with a discussion of the impact of demand on rent and the *response to demand signals* from developers and landowners.

Chapter 4 focuses on the *locational decisions* of firms and the impact of these decisions on the geographical distribution of commercial property. The theories examined will be familiar to those who have studied urban economics or economic geography. It is argued that there is no single satisfactory theory of urban location. Many of the models are deficient in their failure to represent adequately supply-side responses or the role of the financial asset market – a theme developed throughout the book.

Chapter 5 considers the role of *actors and institutions* in the property market in more depth, relaxing the assumptions of perfect competition, economically rational behaviour and the absence of scale effects. The chapter emphasises the importance of individual behaviour and institutional context in the land, development and financial asset markets and hence its importance in the supply of space in the user market. There are a wide variety of approaches to the analysis of individual and *institutional behaviour* in markets including historical approaches, conflict theory, the structure and agency approach and the concept of structures of provision. The chapter considers these various approaches and assesses their strengths and weaknesses in explaining development, land-supply and investment in property markets.

As is evident from this outline, analysis of the development process is interwoven through the microeconomic section. The formal competitive model of the development process is set out in Chapter 2, the developer response to occupier demand signals in Chapter 3 and behavioural and institutional analysis of the supply of buildings considered in Chapter 5. This reflects the authors' views concerning the importance of the interactions between development, user, financial asset and land markets. To treat the development process in isolation is to ignore these critical connections. The role of development in the macroeconomy and cyclical processes in the supply of buildings are examined further in Part 2 of the book, while investment and financial aspects of development are considered in Part 3.

Chapter 6 opens Part 2 of the text by examining *macroeconomic* themes of relevance to the study of property markets. The linkage between property development and theories of *fixed investment* is explored. The chapter discusses the impact of the property development process on the macroeconomy, financial aspects of property booms and the impact of monetary policy on commercial property. The *short-run* perspective adopted in Chapter 6 is complemented by the *long-run* analysis contained in Chapter 7. This chapter, drawing on the themes of *growth theory*, examines the behaviour of property as a long-term investment good and discusses whether there is an efficient long-run allocation of resources and capital to commercial property or whether overinvestment and overbuilding occurs on a systematic or cyclical basis.

Chapter 8 develops the theme of *property cycles*. The property market and the economy as a whole are prone to irregular fluctuations of output and prices. Property markets, in particular, are characterised by boom periods with high levels of investment and rental growth followed by sharp downward adjustments. Explanations for property market cycles may be *exogenous* (in that the stimulus for growth or decline lies outside the property market) or *endogenous* (where the characteristics of property market behaviour generate the cycle). Both are discussed.

Chapter 9 focuses on *econometric modelling and forecasting* of property markets. The main principles of economic models are introduced and the different modelling approaches adopted are critically examined. The chapter highlights the many difficulties encountered in modelling property markets. These include the lack of reliable data, the heterogeneity of commercial property and the complexities of supply-side adjustment processes.

The final part of the book deals with financial economics and financial investment in commercial property. Chapter 10 considers the *investment characteristics* of commercial property, comparing these to those of bonds and shares in a discounted cash flow context. Property is seen to have specific characteristics that make direct comparison across asset classes difficult. One key feature of property markets is the absence of timely transaction price data. As a result, great reliance is placed on estimation of likely selling price – *valuation*. Traditional property valuation techniques are examined critically. The possibility of variations between valuations and selling prices has important consequences for the price mechanism in the adjustment processes analysed in Parts 1 and 2 of the book.

Chapter 11 considers the place of property in the *investment portfolio*. The chapter looks at the application of portfolio theory to the selection of assets and the allocation of funds for (financial) investment in property markets. This entails further examination of the returns to, and risks of, commercial property as an asset class. The chapter also examines measurement of *investment performance*. The reliance on valuations as the basis for the benchmark indices of property market behaviour makes direct comparison with other asset markets complex and may result in misleading comparisons.

Chapter 12 considers investment in paper assets that are related to commercial property – *indirect investment*. Indirect equity investments include property company shares, property unit trusts and Real Estate Investment Trusts. Indirect debt investments include bonds and loans secured on commercial property. The characteristics of the various investment vehicles are described. A critical question – whether these instruments truly are property investments – is addressed. Finally, Chapter 13 examines *international investment* in commercial property. The chapter explores the growth of overseas investment, the rationale for that investment and the practical difficulties facing investors as they seek to allocate funds to overseas markets.

Although each of the three parts of the book is relatively self-contained, they complement each other and develop common themes. The linkages between the microeconomic, macroeconomic and financial themes reflect the interactions between the user, developer, land and financial asset markets outlined at the start of the book. All three, thus, contribute to a full understanding of the economics of commercial property markets.

Part 1

MICROECONOMICS AND COMMERCIAL PROPERTY

INTRODUCTION AND COMMENTARY

Part 1 of the text examines the *microeconomics* of commercial property markets. Microeconomic analysis investigates production and consumption decision-making and their influence on the allocation of resources within an economy. The focus of this analysis is markets. Within markets, consumers and producers react to prices which act as signals to bring about a balance between supply and demand – equilibrium. Microeconomics has two broad approaches. The first is that of partial analysis: the examination of one market in isolation. This is accomplished by assuming that everything outside the subject market is held constant. In the second approach, general equilibrium, all markets are examined simultaneously. In the analysis of property markets, the partial approach is most fruitful and is adopted here.

Krugman (1991) has argued that there is no complete microeconomic model of urban land and property markets. The specific characteristics of commercial property, detailed in the four chapters in this part, allied to complex interactions across space and time make analysis highly complex. It is thus important that a micro-level analysis examines the nature of property markets and the role of individuals and firms – the actors – in these markets. Additionally, given that land and buildings are fixed spatially (unlike most commodities), it is important that a spatial component is introduced to the analysis.

Microeconomics uses models which are a simplified representation of reality. They can be tested empirically, using real world data. These models make a number of simplifying assumptions from which it is possible to deduce how individuals and firms are expected to behave. These may include the idea that all individuals behave in an economically rational manner, that information is widely and costlessly available and that prices adjust quickly (frictionlessly) to changes in supply and demand. The models then form a valuable framework for organising thinking about problems and for asking 'what if' questions about the changing economic environment or about the policy decisions of government or businesses. However, markets are complex and many of the simplifying assumptions may not apply. This is particularly true of urban land and property markets.

13

In commercial property markets, the demand for consumption might come from a firm deciding whether or not to lease new space for its business operations; a production decision might be a developer deciding whether or not to build a property for sale. Price, in the former case, is the rent payable under the lease contract; in the latter, it is the sale price achieved or anticipated for the completed scheme. The rent and the sale price are linked through activity in the investment market – a theme developed more fully in Part 3.

Chapter 2 introduces a model of commercial property markets. The model examines the role of rent as the price mechanism that balances supply and demand, achieving equilibrium in four interlinked markets: the *user market*, the *development market*, the *financial asset market*, and the *land market*. Rent may be viewed in different ways. On the one hand, rent may be considered as the amount a business is able and willing to pay to occupy a particular site and building. The property enables the firm to carry out profitable trading. Rent is an input cost which affects profitability. On the other hand, the owner of the property anticipates a return on capital invested that is competitive when compared to other possible investment assets and allowing for the risks of ownership. These two views of rent produce, respectively, the demand and supply curves for the property.

In the *user* market, firms seek to occupy a stock of buildings. The amount of space required will depend on output levels, profitability and asking rents. As output expands, firms seek more space and hence demand increases, raising rents in the absence of an increase in supply. However, if rents are high, firms may seek to occupy space more intensively – for example by reducing the floor space per worker – or may substitute another factor of production for land and buildings. Space available to occupiers depends on the existing stock and any new stock completed. Although it is subject to obsolescence and depreciation and must be replaced over time, the stock of buildings has a long economic life. New stock is generally small as a proportion of the existing stock and takes time to produce. As a result the short-run supply curve will tend to be *inelastic*.

Property is also an investment. In the *financial asset market*, owners seek a return on their capital comparable to the returns available in other asset markets allowing for differences in risk. The relationship between this return and the rent determines the price or capital value of the property. This capital value acts as a signal for construction firms and property companies in the *development market*. When capital values (prices) are higher than the cost of provision, new stock will be constructed, altering the supply available in the user and financial asset markets. Since it takes time to construct new property, decisions are made on the basis of expected prices. If new development is to take place, sites must be released in the *land market*. Competing land uses and sectors compete for land and space and so determine the price.

Changes in any one of these four markets lead to changes in the others. An increase in demand in the user market raises rents. Other things being equal, this increases the price of property in the investment market. Higher prices may encourage developers to increase the supply of buildings and persuade landowners to release land for that development. The resultant increase in the stock of buildings leads to downward pressure on rents in the user market, thus restoring equilibrium.

The interrelated markets have to adjust continuously to new demand and supply conditions and must accommodate shocks. The chapter, thus, considers the adjustment processes in those markets. Features of the property markets, including fixed locations, durability, high costs both to supply and demolish buildings and institutional constraints, result in adjustment processes that are slower than in most other markets. It may take three to four years for developers to complete a city centre office building. Failure to anticipate employment growth may, therefore, result in rising rents as occupiers compete for space in the existing stock. The possibility that such lags in adjustment processes contribute to property cycles is considered further in Part 2.

Chapter 3 examines user demand and its relationship with the land market. The demand for commercial space varies by sector of the economy and by geographical location. Sectoral activity levels provide an indicator of property demand. Thus, growth of business services employment is linked to increased demand for office space, increased consumer spending leads to greater demand for retail space and increases in manufacturing output are associated with demand for industrial space. However, the relationship between output and demand for space changes over time as production technologies change and as firms vary the proportions of capital, labour and land. Within an economy, the mix of service and industrial activity alters over time and is reflected in levels of demand for particular types of property.

Within urban markets, there are spatial variations in demand. In Chapter 3, broad explanations of these patterns are examined. The *export base* model suggests that demand in a city or region is induced by exports. The assumptions of this approach are subject to criticism. *Transport cost* models suggest that the attractiveness of urban locations, and hence spatial variation in demand for space, depends upon accessibility. Many of the traditional transport models assume that the city centre is the point of maximum accessibility. With technological change, urban diseconomies and decentralisation of population and firms, this assumption is questionable. Finally, *agglomeration economies* – the advantages of firms clustering together – are considered. Agglomeration economies may relate to a sector, for example, manufacturing firms in an industrial district benefiting from shared information and economies of scale in obtaining factor inputs. Alternatively, they may occur due to the scale and diversity of large cities.

The supply-side response to changing levels of demand depends on reaction in the land market. Demand is constrained by inelasticities in supply. This is addressed in the final section of Chapter 3. The responsiveness of landowners (and developers) to price signals is critical to market adjustment processes. The existence of externalities and the wider impacts of urban development have been used as justifications for intervention in the property market, for example through planning controls or differential taxation. The potential implications of such actions are considered.

Chapter 4 examines spatial variations in demand in more detail, focusing on the locational decisions of firms. It develops the themes of accessibility and agglomeration economies introduced in Chapter 3. Within the framework of the model developed in Chapter 2, rent should function as an allocation mechanism to ensure that each site is in its 'highest and best' use, the land-use that is most profitable at that location. Firms in the most profitable sectors are able to outbid firms in other sectors for use of a site. The rent bid is associated with the site and building attributes and with accessibility to other factors of production. Since these advantages will vary by type of activity, spatial separation of function should occur. Thus, location theory should help to explain the geographical patterns of land-use.

The chapter examines the classical models of location theory by sector. The traditional models of location, those of Alonso, Christaller, Lösch, Weber and others. These models, based on the transport costs of inputs, including labour, and the finished good, were developed when the central areas of cities were the most advantageous in terms of accessibility. The rise of private car ownership, decentralisation of population, congestion and environmental problems in cities, technological change and new working practices and consumption patterns have changed the balance of advantage. For many types of activity, an out-of-town location may be favoured. The locational decision is also influenced by, and influences, the price of land and buildings in different locations.

The model set out in Chapter 2 and developed in Chapters 3 and 4 is an abstract model that contains simplifying assumptions about individual behaviour. In translating the model to reality, it is necessary to relax many of those assumptions. Chapter 5 considers the role of actors and institutions in the property market in more depth, relaxing the assumptions of perfect competition, economically rational behaviour and the absence of scale effects. The chapter emphasises the importance of individual behaviour in the land, development and investment markets and hence its importance in the supply of space in the user market.

There is a wide variety of approaches to the analysis of individual and *institutional* behaviour in markets. Neo-classical economic approaches maintain many of the assumptions of the equilibrium models and explain actual behaviour in terms of *rational expectations, transaction costs* and *asymmetric information. Historical approaches* emphasise the role of individuals and the contingent nature of decisions. *Conflict theory* attempts to identify groups with interests in the development of a particular site and explains the development process as the outcome of a struggle between those interests. Finally, there are wider-scale social explanations of urban processes, the *structure and agency* approach and the concept of *structures of provision*, which seek to provide a framework for the analysis of local, regional and national outcomes. Chapter 5 considers these various institutional approaches and assesses their strengths and weaknesses in explaining development, land-supply and investment in property markets.

The market adjustment models outlined in Part 1 of the book provide an analytic context for subsequent sections. Part 2 outlines the macroeconomics of property markets and the interaction between property markets and macroeconomic variables. The impacts of macroeconomic changes are translated into local property outcomes through the mechanisms described in Part 1. Part 3 considers property as a financial asset – how the property investment market functions. The impact of investment decisions on prices affects land release and the development decision and, through these, the supply of space to the user market. The interlinkage of the user, development, investment and land markets thus forms a critical backdrop to the rest of the book.

2

A MODEL OF COMMERCIAL PROPERTY MARKETS

INTRODUCTION

This chapter considers supply and demand in property markets. First, a short-run model of supply and demand is presented diagrammatically in the four interlinked markets already described in Chapter 1 – the user, financial asset, developer and land markets. Then the long run is examined. Following this, the short-run model is developed to include expectations. This enables consideration of two theories of market adjustment: namely, the cobweb and building lag approaches. A final section summarises and draws some conclusions.

The purpose in presenting this model is that it forms the theoretical underpinning what follows in the subsequent chapters of this book. It presents the micro-foundations of economic behaviour in property markets. There are many different aspects of property market economics that are covered throughout this text, and the distinct languages of the social sciences, finance and the property world are used at various points to examine these issues. On occasions the form of the reasoning may seem a long way from this simple model, but little of the analysis contradicts its principles. The model makes strong simplifying assumptions but the greater complexity of later chapters should be regarded as additions to this approach, rather than alternatives to it.

There are many analyses of what can broadly be termed the 'economics' of property markets that do not adopt this form of analysis, relying instead on geographical, institutional, sociological or radical theories. There are some contexts in which these alternative views are clearly right. Behavioural supply and demand models cannot answer all the questions of relevance, including examination of the organisational structure of property markets and conflicts over land-use. Mainstream economics, nonetheless, still has many useful things to say on these matters, as later chapters will show. Moreover, the alternative perspectives would benefit from an understanding of how the property market 'works'. This requires investigation of the constrained behaviour of agencies demanding and supplying commercial accommodation.

RENT AND MARKET CLEARING

Supply and demand models examine the interaction of the factors determining the supply of a good or service, and those influencing the demand for it. The general outcomes are equilibrium prices and quantities, although it is the causal processes by which that equilibrium is reached that are of greatest interest. When setting up a model of commercial property markets, it is initially necessary to define the meaning of prices and quantities.

In the user market, the payments a firm makes in order to use a given amount of commercial property for a particular time period is called building rent here. So building rent is the full cost to users of hiring commercial space. Owner-occupied commercial property has costs of use that implicitly constitute rent – often known as 'imputed rent'. Building rent plays the role that price usually does. It acts as the key signal to agents active in the market, and, through its rises and falls, clears these markets by equating the quantity supplied with that demanded. (Some rent models do not assume market clearing, and these will be elaborated at various subsequent points in this book.)

In the financial asset market, the price of a commercial building is the current estimate of its value. Virtually all commercial properties are bought and sold on the basis of a professional valuer's estimate of their current worth, rather than simply on the basis of a direct trade between buyer and seller. Criticisms can be made of those valuations, as Chapter 10 notes, but for the purposes of the model, commercial property prices are assumed to reflect true market prices. Land costs are treated as a simple, quality/location adjusted, land price per hectare.

Quantity requires some simple, standard measure: assuming away, for ease of exposition, the complexity of real supply where commercial buildings come in many different forms, qualities and locations. A standard unit of offices is used as the quantity measurement. One way to consider this is that office buildings provide an annual service by providing a quantity of office space, so a unit of office services would be the time specific measure.

The level of analysis for which the model is relevant is variable. Its usefulness depends on the type of questions being asked, and the applicability of its assumptions to that issue. The model could refer to the national commercial property market as a whole or to a more spatially disaggregated level, such as a city or region; alternatively, it could focus on functional divisions in terms of the type of building use, the most obvious being a separation into office, industrial and retailing uses. The most important limiting factor on the applicability of the model is that it assumes competitive markets. It could be argued that the more localised the analysis, in either spatial or building use terms, the less likely is it that the competitive principle holds in practice. This is because a world of many consumers, developers and producers of commercial buildings should be sufficient to ensure the existence of competition, but this is less likely to exist the smaller is the market in question. To adopt such a stance, however, would be to deny the existence of competition at any level of analysis, because aggregation across monopolistic markets does not of itself make those markets competitive. What is required instead are behavioural processes generating the conditions for competition at all market levels. Few active players in a market, and bilateral negotiation rather than autonomous market signals, may be necessary conditions for monopolistic practices – but they are not sufficient.

Competitive principles will still hold if users can relatively easily substitute one location for another. In 'small town' cases, for example, most of the time, users would be able to relocate to another town if property owners tried to exercise their monopolistic powers too strongly. An assumption of competition would also still be valid, if new suppliers can easily enter the commercial markets of particular localities when returns in them rise above the norm. Local markets may, in other words, be contestable, even when competition seems limited.

As with standard price theory, it is important to note the principal causal role of rents and prices – quantities adjust to changes in prices. It is conceptually possible to envisage the direction of the causality the other way round from quantities to prices, or for the simultaneous determination of both. However, the point is that, in competitive markets, it is price that provides the key market information to the thousands, or even millions of, unrelated market players. Each agency then adjusts the quantities it wishes to buy or sell in relation to price, given its objective function – say, profit or utility maximisation. Quantities could not play this central role because it is impossible for everyone in an uncoordinated market to have a good knowledge of available quantities of supply and demand at any particular price level.

The following section explores simple, interrelated supply and demand models of user, financial asset, developer and land markets to reach an understanding of the market clearing roles of building rents, property and land prices and construction costs. Offices are used to illustrate the model.

Property markets as interlinked markets

Supply and demand analysis for property markets is rather more complicated than that given in standard introductory microeconomics texts, because the property market is best conceived as made up of several interlinked markets.

- In the *user market*, there exists a *stock* of offices, which house the activities of office users or are temporarily vacant. This stock may be owned directly by the users themselves, as owner occupiers, or rented from a property company or financial institution. The existing stock of offices is subject to wear-and-tear depreciation, requires regular maintenance, and becomes technologically obsolescent.

20

- A stock of offices is also a set of *financial assets* to those owning it. If owners are economically rational, they would compare the risks and rewards of property ownership with those of holding other financial assets. The behaviour of the markets where property is a financial asset consequently is driven by the opportunity cost of the capital invested in offices. (Part 3 of this book deals with property as a financial asset, including the risk pricing of property investments.)

- In locations where the demand for office accommodation is increasing, the stock of offices will need to be expanded or the floor space per worker allowed to fall. So development greater than that required to replace obsolete buildings in the locality will be required. Office building takes place in the *development market*. In this market, developers – in conjunction with construction companies – generate new office buildings to be owned by investors.

- Finally, both the user and the development markets are connected to the *urban land market*. Given the limited availability of land at any location, competition over land use generally exists. Existing offices have to compete with new office developments and other land uses for a plot of land. Opportunity cost is an important factor in determining land rent at any particular location.

Market clearing in the four property submarkets

For there to be full equilibrium in the overall property market, all four submarkets must simultaneously be in equilibrium. That this is not always rapidly achieved is hardly surprising, and raises interesting questions of dynamic adjustment. When property markets are out of equilibrium how do they get back to equilibrium? Demand and supply analysis is generally comparative static in method – that is beginning and end points are considered. With property markets, however, it is often the dynamics that are of most interest. The tools and information that exist are not, unfortunately, always adequate. Nevertheless, some interesting dynamic issues can still be explored. Some will be examined later in the chapter, when a simple interlinked market supply and demand model is developed. Others are taken up in later chapters, particularly those in Part 2 which covers macroeconomic issues.

Another feature of the four interlinked markets is that three of them are associated with stock relationships – the stock of office accommodation, the stock of property assets, and the stock of land; while the other market is concerned with product flows – the supply of new office buildings. This interlinked stock/flow set of relationships is one reason why it is conceptually better to consider the property market as the product of a set of interlinked markets.

Equilibrium modelling is an ideal construct, illustrating the adjustment pressures in a market rather than describing their normal states. This is because, in reality, markets are continuously having to adjust to new conditions of demand and supply, including unforeseen shocks and, thus, are unlikely to be in full equilibrium at any point in time. Processes of disequilibrium adjustment are likely to feature highly in property markets. In other markets, such as some financial ones, adjustment is very rapid. In many consumer goods markets, adjustment can also be fast. Excess stock, for example, can be disposed of through cut price sales in a matter of weeks. Offices, however, are fixed in location, expensive to demolish and long-lasting. Institutional arrangements and conventions such as long leases induce further lags. Adjustment processes in property markets are, therefore, inevitably slower than in many other markets. Rents also tend to be sticky – for a variety of reasons that are elaborated at various points in the rest of the book.[1] Rents consequently do not tend to fall rapidly to short-run market clearing levels, whenever there is a temporary glut. This mixture of quantity and price stickiness in commercial property markets makes adjustment in them far longer than in many other markets.

A SIMPLE MODEL OF PROPERTY MARKET CLEARING

The four submarkets that need to be simultaneously in equilibrium for the overall property market to clear were identified in the previous section as the user, financial asset, development and land markets. This section presents a relatively simple set of demand and supply relationships to indicate how these markets function and interrelate.[2]

The model is presented diagrammatically in Figures 2.1 to 2.4. Its main assumptions are laid out as the model is explained. The first, and crucial, assumption is that property markets are broadly competitive, so that a competitive market analysis can be applied to them.

The second important assumption is the time span covered by the analysis. The figures refer to the short run. The short run is defined in economics as the period when at least one factor of production is fixed. This analysis assumes that the available stock of offices is fixed in the particular time period in question, t. New office building undertaken during that period can then be added to the existing stock to create the available stock for the next period, t + 1. Long-run equilibrium will be considered later.

The user market

Figure 2.1 considers supply and demand in the user market. The solid lines give the initial equilibrium position. There is a fixed stock of offices, Q, at time, t. This stock is assumed to be well-maintained, and there is no technical obsolescence, so that depreciation can be ignored. As the stock is fixed,

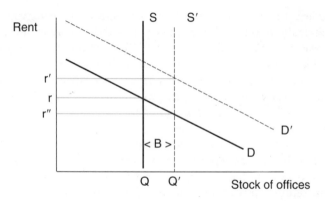

Figure 2.1 Supply and demand in the user market

supply is perfectly inelastic. It will exist, in that quantity, whatever price is paid for it. Over time, of course, some parts of the stock will be withdrawn and some added through new building. This will shift the vertical supply curve to the left or right respectively. The dotted supply line in Figure 2.1, for example, is a hypothetical example of the stock, Q', in year t + 1, when the stock has been increased by an amount, B.

The scale and the longevity of the stock of commercial buildings means that new supply is only a small proportion of total supply. For example, the total stock of offices in England and Wales increased by only 28 per cent between 1984 and 1994, despite the period being one of record new office building. If the growth rate had been even over that ten year period, this means that new supply would have expanded by 2.5 per cent a year. Of course, the period was marked by an extreme boom, but, even in the boom years, net stock additions were still a small proportion of the overall existing stock.

The demand for offices is shown as downward sloping in Figure 2.1. This reflects standard demand analysis, whereby a lower price stimulates extra demand. A simple demand model for offices would suggest that the quantity demanded is a function of rent, r, a firm's output, O, and the amount of office space it uses per worker, WS, in any period t, that is:

$$D_t = f(r_t, O_t, WS_t) \tag{2.1}$$

The time subscripts will be ignored from now on for simplicity. Notice that the function refers to a 'firm'. Again, for modelling simplicity, it is easiest to assume a demand function for offices with its augments based on typical firm behaviour. This makes it possible to aggregate across firms, allowing demand and supply analysis to move easily between the individual and the aggregate levels.

Demand curves represent the pure response of the demand for office space to changes in rents. They assume all other arguments in the demand function remain the same. (In the case shown in equation 2.1, firms' outputs and office space per worker ratios are held constant). Why does demand change when rents alter? The key lies in the ways in which firms chose to produce. When firms see a fall in rents, while the price of all other inputs remains the same, they will be encouraged to substitute away from other factors of production towards offices, *for a given level of output,* insofar as the technical conditions of production allow them to substitute. The lower the rent, the greater the likely substitution into extra accommodation and vice versa. (Formally, the demand curve for offices represents the marginal revenue product of office use as a factor of production for creating a good or service. This can be derived by setting up a production function, for a known range of technologies, input prices and final product price, and solving the constrained maximisation problem (see, for example, Gravelle and Rees, 1992).

In practice, short-run office demand curves are unlikely to be very sensitive to rent levels and, therefore, tend to be inelastic. This is one reason why rents are sticky in a downwards direction. As they face relatively inelastic demand schedules in the short run, landlords would have to reduce rents considerably in order to have much effect on the quantity of office accommodation demanded. The longer the time period, however, the easier it is for firms to change their production methods and the location of their activity; so, in the long run, office demand is likely to be the more elastic. The demand curve over the long run consequently is likely to be flatter than that shown in Figure 2.1.

So far movements along the office demand curve have been considered. Which conditions lead it to shift, either to the left or the right? The answer is whenever any of the other non-rent arguments in the demand function change. In equation 2.1, the other influences on firms' demand for office space, apart from rent, are their outputs and office space per worker ratios. When output changes, the demand curve will shift – to the right if output rises, and to the left if it falls; similar adjustments will occur with increases and decreases in office space per worker. The curve will also shift when any other factors in more complex demand functions change.

The dotted demand curve, D', represents an upwards shift caused by an increase in firms' turnovers. The rise in business, for example, may mean that more staff need to be recruited and that they all require desk space. More office accommodation is, therefore, required by firms to achieve their new higher outputs. With fixed supply, rent rises. If demand for office-using firms' outputs falls, conversely, lay-offs of staff will take place, and the office demand curve shifts to the left and rents fall.

The demand function for office accommodation is based on firms' production decisions. Offices confer no ultimate utility to their users, only the conditions for the production of particular goods and services. Office demand is consequently a *derived* demand; it is derived from the demand for the goods

24

and services produced using office accommodation. This argument even holds for the marble laden hallways or glamorous atriums often seen in prestige office developments. Such characteristics either help firms conduct their business, for example, by signalling probity or success to clients, or confer some implicit payment to managers and staff. Baum and Crosby (1995) refer to this latter aspect as 'psychic income'.

Putting the supply and demand functions together enables market equilibrium to be determined. The initial equilibrium position in Figure 2.1 is a rent r and a stock of offices Q. Here the market is cleared, with demand matched by the available supply, because at the rent r just as much office space is demanded as is supplied. At equilibrium, the office vacancy rate is either zero, or, more realistically because of market frictions, some finite number often called the 'natural rate of vacancy' (see Chapter 9). For simplicity, it is assumed that the vacancy rate is zero.

Property as a financial asset

The equilibrium rent, r, is one of the variables determining the value of a building. The annual net rental flow has to be multiplied by the inverse of a capitalisation factor, 1/k, to determine its value or market price, P. This is shown in Figure 2.2. The capitalisation factor, k, is determined in the two main ways described below.

- By *valuation rules*. The various approaches are surveyed in Chapter 10. Whether professional valuation is equivalent to an implicit economic evaluation is one of the criteria for judging the 'efficiency' of the property market, as that chapter discusses.
- By *economic evaluation*. Here the annual rental flow is capitalised into a net present value, taking into account depreciation and rental growth. The appropriate discount rate is the long-term bond rate, with any necessary additional premiums for risk and subtractions for expected rises in property rents/capital gains (see Chapters 6 and 10).

Here, again for simplicity, it will be assumed that valuations accurately reflect prevailing market prices, so that the two are synonymous.

There is an inverse relationship between the value of a building with a known future rental stream and the rate of interest. When interest rates rise, the present value of a flow of rents falls; conversely, when interest rates fall the present value rises. This relationship is shown in Figure 2.2. Each ray from the origin shows the value of a rental stream at a given capitalisation factor k. Higher interest rates shift the ray to the left, k^*, and lower ones to the right, k^+; leading to new values P^* and P^+ respectively.

For the purposes of this analysis, therefore, a simple formula is sufficient to identify the determinants of the price of an office building:

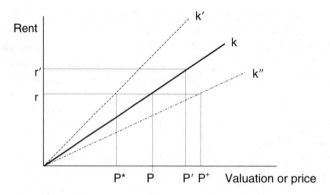

Figure 2.2 Property as a financial asset

$$P_t = \frac{I_t}{k_t} \qquad\qquad (2.2)$$

where P_t is the price of a standardised office unit at time t; I_t the prevailing net income derived from letting the property; and k_t the capitalisation factor.

Is a competitive capital market a realistic assumption?

The implicit economic model illustrated in Figure 2.2 argues that there is a perfectly elastic flow of capital into the holding of commercial property as a financial asset. This is based on the principle that investors are indifferent between the characteristics of financial assets, once the distinctive features of each have been priced into its market value, and that financial markets are competitive. It may be argued that these are unrealistic assumptions, because specific types of financial institution, such as pension funds and insurance companies (frequently called the Institutions), invest in property and, therefore, in some way 'control' the market. This, for example, has been suggested by Minns (1980) and Ingham (1984). Quite what control means, however, is unclear. The competitive principle, when used as an ideal construct, allows some clarification of what the implications may be.

1   The control proposition argues that there is an incompatibility between the existence of a specific set of large investing Institutions and a competitive market. This is not necessarily true. Some institutional forms may have lower (transaction) costs when dealing in property, and hence are more economically efficient than others (see Chapter 5). If specific institutional forms do generate economies within property markets, empirical observation that they are important actors in property investment, consequently, may be a sign of competition working rather than its negation.

26

2   A reason for the existence of particular types of institution may be that particular tax breaks are given for specific institutional structures (non-profit pension funds, for example) and for some investment vehicles. Governments for whatever policy reason are, in effect, subsidising particular financial institutions through these actions – allowing them to prosper over others. Whether this distorts the financial market for property assets depends on the conditions under which those benefits are conferred. The tax breaks are also likely to alter the relative post-tax prices of property assets, rather than be expressed in institutional market power. So, again, control may mean little that is different from competitive market practices.

3   Financial regulation may have restrictive effects on competition by allowing only certain types of financial institution to be active in a market. Traditionally, many countries' financial systems have been segmented, and foreign competition limited. If such traditional restrictions constrain the flow of capital into property investment, then those that are allowed to invest can command a higher return from their property investments than would be determined competitively. The market prices of buildings will be lower than in a free market, because, implicitly, property investors have raised the capitalisation rate above that in a free market. Lower prices will discourage new developments, and hence restrict office supply and raise rents. The effect of monopoly in property markets, therefore, is similar to that in other markets – prices are higher for users and quantities supplied lowered. If such constraints are imposed on property markets through financial regulation, the efficiency loss may be high.

    Financial regulation may however have the opposite effect in the property market, and cheapen funds, because regulation does not allow them to flow to their most remunerative activity. Traditional financial controls often included a requirement that specific types of institution can only enjoy tax and other regulatory privileges if they invested in specific assets. Pension funds and insurance companies in the UK, for example, had great difficulty in investing overseas prior to 1979, because of exchange rate controls. This would have encouraged them to invest in UK property, depressing returns from it, raising property valuations above their free market levels, and encouraging a greater than efficient supply of commercial property.

    In practice, most modern property markets have access to a wide range of sources of capital, apart from financial institutions, including capital from overseas, bank lending and share and bond issues. So, the impact of financial regulation in many countries is a characteristic of the past rather than the present day.

4   Another situation when property market 'control' by financial institutions might have real effects is when they explicitly or implicitly collude.

It is difficult for such agreements to work over the long term, however, especially when others can enter the market.

5   Financial liberalisation in world markets has weakened any previous adverse effects that may have existed in property markets as a result of the influence of privileged financial Institutions, although the scale of liberalisation has varied considerably between countries. When liberalisation occurs, competition forces risk-adjusted investor returns towards the long-run interest rate. In situations where they were previously higher than the long-run interest rate, the effect will be to raise valuations. The resultant temporary capital gains may then help trigger off a property boom. The extra stock supply of offices will then push down rents in the user market. The end result, after feedback adjustments, should be lower office rents and a wider spread of investors in property. Conversely, if returns had previously be lower than the long-run interest rate, then the reverse process would happen.

This discussion suggests that it is generally reasonable in modern property markets to assume that financial institutions have little market power, and that the competitive principle is likely to be a valid analytical tool. Ultimately, however, this is an empirical question and contexts may exist where this rule does not hold. These situations need empirically to be demonstrated, nonetheless, rather than assumed simply because big firms exist.

The development market

Figure 2.3 shows the development market, where new offices are created. Here it is assumed that there is a separate property development industry that conceives schemes, assembles land sites and builds offices. (Offices, it should be recalled, are being used for simplicity as an example of commercial property.) The completed projects are then sold on to investors, which hold the offices as financial assets. These simplifying assumptions do not precisely correspond to general practice in property markets because many real developers are also investors and retain some properties as investments – both to take advantage of their superior knowledge about them and for cash flow reasons.[3]

In the overall property market model, the development market is perhaps the most difficult to understand because it creates the flow of new offices into the stock. When new offices are not required, the flow ceases and development does not occur. No development to replace obsolescent buildings is assumed in this model. However, it is unlikely that replacement developments would have an independent effect on the market, but rather would respond to similar market forces to any need to accommodate increased user demand.

Two important conceptual ideas have to be explored. First, what triggers development? In terms of a diagrammatic analysis, this requires examination

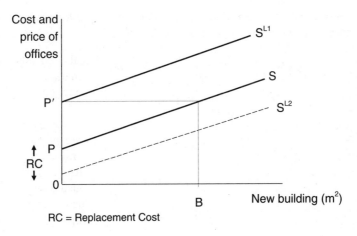

RC = Replacement Cost

Figure 2.3 The development market

of where the intercept of the new office supply curve cuts the vertical axis. Second, how does supply respond to changes in the selling price of offices? To answer this, the slope of the new office supply function has to be determined, and the factors that may cause the supply function to shift have to be identified.

The development market in this supply and demand model has no separate demand curve. Rational office users should be indifferent between new and existing buildings in the absence of technological improvements, so the same demand function is common to both the user and development markets. The influence of new building on rents and the available supply of offices takes place in the user market, where it is added to the existing stock in the following time period.

On the model's assumptions, new office building takes place only when overall office demand exceeds supply in the existing stock. Development then occurs until the excess demand for offices is satisfied, at which time office building will cease – unless there are further demand increases. Once again the price mechanism, through changes in rent and development costs, brings this about. There are essentially two versions in the literature of how this occurs: one is based on replacement costs; the other is also based on replacement costs but includes an 'option price' to reflect the benefits of delaying projects until better information is available. The replacement cost approach is considered here, while the option pricing method is examined later in Chapter 8.

Replacement costs and new building

The point at which no development occurs is where it becomes unprofitable for developers to build new office projects. This point is where property values just equal their replacement costs. Property values, P, are determined in the financial asset market by the interrelation of the prevailing level of rents and interest rates. The cost of replacing offices, RC, is their site clearance, construction, financing and land costs. That this is the case can be seen by imagining what would happen if property values were higher than replacement costs. If the price of office buildings is higher than replacement costs, then developers will be encouraged to build more offices, adding to the existing stock, which causes rents to fall. Assuming constant interest rates, lower rents will then be capitalised into lower office selling prices, and this process will continue until prices fall to replacement costs. Rent levels determined in the user market are consequently simultaneously stimulating or discouraging activity in the development market, through the subsequent stock changes in the user market caused by the addition of new developments. Development, in effect, is a disequilibrium phenomenon - equating stock supply in the user market with stock demand at the prevailing equilibrium rent level.

The process can be illustrated in the user market diagram in Figure 2.1. Equilibrium as was noted earlier occurs with the demand curve D and the stock supply S at rent r. Once capitalised, r is the selling price of offices and equal to their replacement cost, so it is the rent that generates equilibrium in all three markets: user, financial asset and development. At this rent there will be no development.

What happens if a surprise surge of additional development during the previous period leads to a rightwards shift of supply from S to S', in Figure 2.1, along the same demand curve D, so that Q' is the new stock supply of offices? At this stage, the effect is easiest to see by assuming all input costs to development are fixed and exogenously determined; the next section will relax this assumption. It can be seen from Figure 2.1 that rents fall below r as a result, pushing down the selling price of offices. Investors then do not receive the income they expected from investing in offices, and would wish to quit the sector; while developers find no takers for their current schemes at the equilibrium selling price of offices, and so find it unattractive to build any more offices. Development stops, but there is an overhang of empty office space. This leads either to a fall in rents, until sufficient offices are withdrawn from the market that the stock returns to Q, the stock of offices in the initial equilibrium, or alternatively, if rents are slow to fall, stock obsolescence has the task of reducing office supply back to Q. Meanwhile no development occurs. The surprise surge of development consequently only leads to excess supply and a depressed office market until that excess supply is removed.

Replacement cost, consequently, fixes the minimum price at which developers are prepared to build. This enables the position of the supply schedule to be determined in the development market. The supply schedule cuts the vertical axis at the value RC, which, if the property market is in equilibrium, is the same price as the current selling price of offices, P.

Fixing the slope of the supply curve

In Figure 2.3, the supply schedule S rises with a positive slope from the vertical axis at P. The slope is determined by the rising cost of providing new offices. As with usual supply schedules, the developer supply curve is based on fixed input prices – in this case financing and land costs. Any change in these input costs shifts the supply schedule – to the left, if the costs rise, and to the right, if they fall. The cause of the upward slope is an assumption that diminishing returns exist in construction – in other words, as more offices are built, marginal costs rise because of production conditions in office building. This assumption is based on empirical evidence from building cost data, which show costs rising and falling over time with the commercial building cycle, as seen in Chapter 7 for the UK. Rising construction supply costs in the short run seem plausible for most increases in construction workloads. For example, if the building industry has more work to do, project delays, and the cost of overcoming them, are likely to rise; while builders' margins are pushed up in the face of rising demand. In the long run, more resources will be drawn into construction by the higher prices there, so diminishing returns are likely to be less, but it takes time to switch resources to the sector and train them, especially in the complex processes associated with office building. Short-run construction costs consequently are assumed to be endogenous to the model, and a positive function of the level of new development, which is what gives the developers' supply schedule its positive slope. This positive slope to the developers supply schedule means that more offices are built as the price of offices rises above P.

Increases in input costs shift developers' supply schedules to the left, so they build less at any selling price because replacement costs have risen. The shifts in the developers' supply schedule in this model are caused either by changes in development financing costs (that is, short-run interest rates) or by rises in the price of development land.[4] In order to attract land supply from other uses, developers have to bid up the price of office land. As more development takes place, therefore, the developers supply schedule drifts to the left – reflecting the need to pay more for building inputs and land. The supply schedule S^{L1} in Figure 2.3 illustrates a leftwards shift in the supply schedule from S caused, for example, by an increase in the price of land. The schedule S^{L2}, conversely, shows the effect of a fall in the price of land.

How is development triggered in the model? This can be illustrated by reference to an increase in the demand for offices and its effect on the development market shown in Figure 2.3. The starting point is an equilibrium, where rent levels and the capitalisation rate lead to a price of offices P, which is equal to their replacement cost RC. Developers face a supply schedule, S. The selling price P is insufficient to induce any development, because development profit will be zero at this point. Now, suppose an increase in the demand for offices occurs. The effect of an increase in user demand was illustrated earlier, using Figure 2.1. The extra demand raises rents, increasing the selling price of offices to the new equilibrium value P′ in Figure 2.2. It is now profitable for developers to supply B units of office space. This space is then added to the current stock and the new supply of offices clears the user market at rent r′. Stickiness in rent levels, as was noted earlier, could make this process of adjustment drawn out.

If rents are set at r′ and the developers' supply schedule remains S, offices will continue to be supplied at the rate B per period. This would lead to over-building at the new equilibrium rent r′. If that occurred, the stock of offices would continue to increase and rents would have to fall below r′ to maintain equilibrium in the user market. Overbuilding is avoided, however, because of the role of the land market. The extra demand for land induced by new development increases its price, and that shifts the developers' supply schedule to the left. No further development will occur when land prices raise the development supply curve to S^{L1} in Figure 2.3, because here, once again, development is just unprofitable at the new property price P′. Explaining how this occurs requires reference to the land market.

The land market

The land market is the last of the four interrelated property markets. Here, offices have to compete with other uses for land. To increase the supply of land used for offices, the price of land has to be bid above its next best use. Similarly, office developers have to compete amongst each other to acquire their development sites. So the supply schedule has a positive slope – more land is supplied for office use as its price in that use rises.

The land market for offices has stock and flow characteristics. The stock dimension refers to the land already used for office space; while the flow aspect relates to the conversion of land from other uses or the redevelopment of land with existing offices on it. The stock and the flow demands for office land determine the total demand for land for office use at any time.

The demand curve for land is downward sloping for two reasons. First, a higher price of land raises office rents and this causes office users to economise on office use. Second, developers can intensify the scale of any structure built on more highly priced land. Here they are substituting capital for land because the relative price of land has risen. Because of this input substitution effect, which alters the intensity with which land is used, the demand curve for land cannot be immediately derived from the user demand curve for offices and, so, unlike in the development market, it is shown separately in Figure 2.4.

The land supply schedule is determined by the need to raise prices in order to attract land from other uses. Once more, the role of price is to equate the demand and supply of land. When demand is represented by D_1 in Figure 2.4 and supply by S, then the price of office land will be P_{L1}, and Q_{L1} of land will be supplied for office use. If there is a rightwards shift in the demand

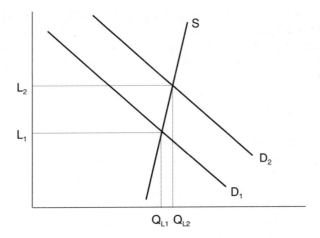

Figure 2.4 The land market

schedule for office land – say, because rents rise and more offices are supplied – then land prices rise from P_{L1} to P_{L2}.

Again, the land demand and supply schedules in Figure 2.4 simply reflect
the impact on quantities demanded and supplied as land prices change.
Every other influence is held constant, and, if they change, they alter the
position of the schedules. Two of these other factors are the planning regime
under which property developers operate and public expenditure on infrastructure. If planning regimes become less restrictive for property development, for example, this eases land supply and shifts the supply curve to the
right, because more land is available at every price. If the public sector
spends more on infrastructure, this has a similar effect because it opens up
new locations for office development. The supply schedule, in effect, has
also been shifted to the right – with more land available at every price.
Modern developer-led urban programmes can be thought of in this way.
They combine the characteristics of more lax planning regimes with extra
infrastructure expenditure (plus, possibly, tax breaks or subsidies for the
developer). The extent to which they actually increase office land supply, of
course, depends on the location and the quality of the sites created through
the programmes. Their impact, however, is not simply a local one – insofar
as they influence the overall land supply function.

Prevailing land prices are based on expected values. A rational landowner
will make forecasts of likely development possibilities in a locality over a
particular time period, given prevailing planning constraints and forecasts of
property cycles, macroeconomic variables and the state of the local economy.[5] Attached to a large number of potential (re)development sites is a
'hope' value, which expresses the probability that the site will be developed
rather than others. In a realistic scenario, there would be more potential sites

for development than development opportunities in any time period (i.e. the number of standardised available sites is n and potential developments, m; where n > m). If each site has an equal chance of being developed, *prior* to developers committing themselves, then the 'hope' value of a site, in a one period model, is:

$$H(L_p) = (m/n)(L_2 - L_1) \qquad (2.3)$$

where $H(L_p)$ is the hope value of a site; L_1 is the value per hectare in its current use; m/n is the probability of a site being developed (for example, 20 possible sites and 10 developments yields a probability of 0.5); and L_2 is the price of a hectare of land in its developed 'best' use. Prior to development, consequently, each plot of land will be valued at its current use value plus the hope value. The smaller the number of competing sites, the higher the hope value, and the closer the pre-development value of any site is to its developed value.

Hope value is sometimes referred to as floating value. The original report on the impact of land-use planning on land values that influenced the formation of the British planning system, the Uthwatt Report (1942), suggested that land-use planning would simply reduce the number of sites, n, over which hope value would float. Land values would consequently be shifted between sites, rather than affected in terms of the actual realised land values at development. Unfortunately, this reasoning is false, because land-use planning also alters the numerator associated with the hope value in equation 2.3 (that is, m, the number of final developments), and thus developed land prices as well, L_2 (Cullingworth, 1992). Quite how the m and n sites are altered, and the resultant effects on land availability and prices, are at the core of the debate over planning. In principle, planning should reduce the number of potential sites on which development can take place, but it may either decrease or increase the actual number of developments. Many commentators suggest that, in practice, the British system reduces development (see Chapter 3).

A final point to note is that both the effect of land prices and of the developers' supply schedule is to dampen the consequences of a shock increase in new development, considered previously in the section on the development market. This is because as developers start to assemble land and let contracts to build their projects, they find that their input costs have risen, discouraging some of the potential schemes from being built.

Simultaneous equilibrium in the four markets

It is now possible to close the system, and recapitulate, by tracing through the simultaneous inter-relations of the four markets. This is done by following through the effect of an increase in the demand for offices.

If, from an initial equilibrium position, the demand for offices rises, say because of an increase in office users' outputs, then the demand schedule shifts from D to D′ in the user market (Figure 2.1). This raises rents, and thereby increases the value of offices as a financial asset. In Figure 2.2, the rent rise with the same capitalisation rate increases the value of offices from P to P′. The higher price that investors pay for offices encourages developers to build them in quantity B, thereby adding to the stock of offices available to satisfy user demand (Q′ in Figure 2.1). The extra development increases the land required for offices (Figure 2.4), which shifts its demand schedule to the right. The four markets are again in equilibrium when land prices rise to P_{L2}, with Q_{L2} of land devoted to office use. Development ceases because the extra demand has been satisfied – partly through the additional office space supplied and partly because some demand would have been discouraged by the new higher rents. Office rents are now r′, with Q′ units supplied. The stock is valued at P′ per standard unit.

Supply and demand in the long run

The short-run period-by-period adjustment model examined above enables predictions of user market supply and demand relationships in the long run.

The demand function is downward sloping for the same reasons as the short-run model. The slope of the demand curve is likely to be more elastic, however, because, in the long run, firms have greater opportunities to adjust their production activities to prevailing property market conditions (for example, by moving to cheaper locations). The supply function is also likely to be more elastic because stock can be added when rents rise. In the long run, moreover, construction cost changes are likely to be less steep as input supply constraints are overcome. More land presumably can be converted from other uses, and so land supply is improved. However, higher prices are needed to induce land into office use, so that the long-run office supply function is positively sloped to reflect this fact.

Such a long-run model is logically elegant as it enables temporal completeness of the system. Most of the interesting questions about property markets, however, lie in their short-run behaviour. This is shown in the vast array of studies that implicitly or explicitly look at short-run property market dynamics (see the surveys in Chapters 8 and 9). The long run is essentially a heuristic device. It generates the sensible rule that short-run dynamics should not come into contradiction with potential long-run equilibrium solutions; but this is as a matter of logic rather than of any realistic expectation that the long-run solution will eventually occur.

Introducing expectations

This property market model, like others, has one over-riding aim: to predict future outcomes on the basis of today's information and theories about how property markets work. However, academic theorists are not the only ones interested in making predictions. All of the agents portrayed in the property market model have a keen interest in predicting the future, because their profitability and success depends on making reasonable estimates of key variables. For example, users moving into new accommodation may be concerned about whether their businesses really need extra office space. For them, there is a downside risk that, say, the rising sales figures – which led to the hiring of more labour and the search for new offices – may turn out only to be a temporary surge. If sales are less than forecast, then the new offices may become a liability. Similarly, in the development market, property firms have to forecast market conditions at future times when projects are completed, or ready for sale, perhaps several years hence, and so need to form views about highly uncertain futures.

Expectations, in other words, pervade economic decision-making in property markets, because decisions made now generally affect future outcomes. Expectations formation, consequently, is influential in determining economic behaviour and models have to incorporate behavioural theories of expectations formation. If agents operating in property markets simply made their decisions on the basis of the current values of important variables affecting their decisions, they would behave as though they thought key variables, such as price, were going to remain constant in the future. Such a view of the future is termed *naïve expectations*, because those who hold to the belief naïvely think that the future will be the same as the present. This is an unrealistic treatment of most agents' expectations, particularly in property markets where experience of sharp changes is common and players are aware of the existence of cycles, even if they cannot predict them very well.

Instead of using constant expectations, rational agents base their views about the future on what they see as the best available current information: *rational expectations*. (Economic theories of expectations formation are considered in more detail in Chapter 5.) In doing this, they use their knowledge of the property market, the wider economy and the best available theories of how the two function and interrelate. This would include taking account of the behaviour of others.

Introducing expectations is particularly important in the investor and development markets. Investors are concerned to make forecasts both of rents and of interest rates before they are prepared to agree to purchase a project for a particular price from a developer. Developers, similarly, will have to make forecasts of construction costs and the likely prices they can obtain for their completed schemes. In the model above, therefore, property prices should more accurately be put in expectational terms.

Adjustment processes

The theory of expectations formation chosen influences explanations of market behaviour in fundamental ways. The argument so far, for example, has been based on rational developer behaviour; whereas it is commonplace to believe that they are irrational – overly optimistic especially. Such a position is an extreme one, however, and those who hold it must justify why developers are particularly afflicted, when producers in other markets do not seem to be. It seems far better to rely on the implications of models of rational behaviour, and to examine their effects, before invoking irrationality as an explanation.

The cobweb theory

The dynamics of market adjustment are affected by the theory of expectations adopted. This can be illustrated by considering one potential explanation of the dynamic behaviour of property markets – the *cobweb theory* of market adjustment. This was first formulated for the hog (pig) market, so it is often called the hog-cycle.

Figure 2.5 illustrates a cobweb type of market adjustment. The solid line is the adjustment process, through one period temporary equilibrium points, after the market has received an unexpected shock that pushes prices down to their level at A. Demanders and suppliers, it is assumed, behave according to naïve expectations. This means that they react only to the current price when fixing the quantities they wish to demand and supply in the following period respectively. Market price then rises or falls in each period in response to which side of the market is short. Because agents are assumed to have naïve expectations, they then behave as if these new prices will remain steady in the future and, once again, set their demands and supplies according to that price. As long as the supply curve is steeper than the demand curve, the

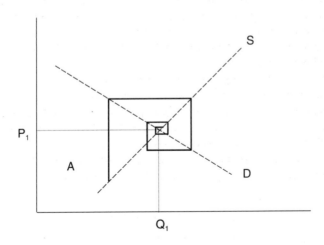

Figure 2.5 A cobweb market adjustment process

period-by-period adjustment will gradually settle down at the initial equilibrium again (Needham *et al.*, 1994).

Property users, investors and developers are likely to have different expectations of the process of adjustment from the myopic ones assumed in the
cobweb process. If rents rise fast, for example, users might delay moving
when they believe rents will shortly come down again. Similarly, at cycle
peaks in property values, rational investors and developers are likely to have
expectations of subsequent decline, which they price into their schemes. This
is not to say that any of these agencies correctly predict the adjustment
process of the market, but the dynamics are likely to be different from those
suggested by a cobweb process.

The effect of a supply lag

Figures 2.1 to 2.4 have already been used to illustrate the effect of an increase
in user demand caused by a shift of the demand curve for office space from
D to D'. In the illustration, developers conveniently built B amount of new
office space in one time period to clear the market at the new equilibrium
rent r'. What would happen if they had built less?

One reason for building less is the time required to complete commercial
developments caused by the need to search out land, design, fund and build
them. If less than the market clearing amount of new offices were built in a
particular time period, then there is a positive demand shock: there would be
excess demand that would push up rents beyond their final equilibrium point.
Does the higher rent induce extra office building?

The answer again depends on the theory of developer behaviour and how
developers form their expectations. When developers are rational it should
not. If they make the correct forecast, they will recognise the overshooting of
the rent rise, because they know more new supply is shortly to come on
stream. Consequently, they will not increase their building plans in response
to the temporary rent overshooting. The time it takes to build presumably is
fairly well known and predictable. Its existence puts an effective limit on
supply for a given future period, determined by the number of projects started
in a locality and the duration of their development period. So developers in a
particular local market should be able to make a good prediction of available
supply for a period ahead.[6] Added to this prediction, they will have to make
one about future demand. The building lag means they will have to make a
demand forecast over a longer time than if buildings were produced instan-
taneously. The longer time might increase the error of the forecast, but as the
error should be random, the consequence is as likely to be an under-forecast
of demand at the final equilibrium point as its over-estimation.

A building lag, in other words, should increase the statistical noise in time
series of office building rates but not alter the cyclical pattern of new building.
The latter would occur if developers made calculations of the profitability of

projects on the basis of current rents only, and built according to that unrealistic profit calculation, which would represent the short-sightedness of naïve price expectations. The theory of building cycles based on building lags is, thus, a theory of developer expectations rather than of the time it takes to build. Building lags models of short-run property cycles are examined in Chapter 8 below.

This section has only considered a single shift in demand, but its conclusions can easily be altered without changing the broad conclusions to account for continuous, but variable, growth in office demand.

SUMMARY AND CONCLUSIONS

This chapter has outlined a four part model of the property market, using simple supply and demand analysis. It has then introduced the notion of expectations and their importance for understanding property markets. Although the model is relatively simple, it incorporates many of the features of property markets that subsequent chapters explore.

There are four inter-related markets in the model: the user, financial asset, developer and land markets.

- In the *user market*, it is assumed that demand is determined by property users' levels of output, office space per worker ratios and the level of office rents. The stock supply of space is fixed in any given period. The interaction of demand and supply then determines the rent level.
- In the *financial asset* market, rents are capitalised into property values using a capitalisation factor. Changes in the value of commercial properties are inversely related to changes in the interest rate.
- In the *development market*, new development (assuming no replacement demand) only occurs when the price of commercial property rises above its replacement cost. Rising construction and land costs raise the cost of replacement and, so, the price of commercial property. New developments are added to the stock of buildings in the user market in the following period, altering the balance between demand and supply.
- In the *land market*, the price of commercial land is determined by the existing stock of land used for commercial purposes and the additional land that has to be drawn into the sector to facilitate new development.
- The four markets are brought into simultaneous equilibrium through the role of rent in each of them.
- In the long run, the slopes of property market demand and supply schedules are likely to be more elastic than in the short run.

The model's simple behavioural characteristics can be improved by introducing expectations into the demand and supply relations. User demand, for example, is likely to be affected by forecasts of future output and employment rather than their current levels. Cobweb and building lag adjustment models of property development assume the existence of naïve expectations, which limit their theoretical usefulness.

3

USER DEMAND AND THE
LAND MARKET

INTRODUCTION

The previous chapter set out a model of adjustments in the commercial property market. This chapter focuses on user demand for commercial space and the response from the supply side, in particular in the land market. Demand for space by occupiers is a derived demand resulting from the property needs of business. Occupier demand for space varies in terms of amount, type and location. These requirements vary across time and by type of industry. All three aspects are considered in this chapter, although a detailed discussion of the location of business activity is reserved for Chapter 4.

Changes in the nature of business activity are likely to result in shifts in the demand curve and, hence, have impacts initially on rents and then on the investment, development and land markets. However, demand for space is not simply a function of output or employment. Changes in the way that firms organise their business activities affect both the quantity and the quality of space required. For example, the trend for firms to 'downsize' and 'outsource' functions previously contained within the firm reduces individual firms' space needs but may create a greater demand for smaller sized buildings. Similarly, 'hot desking' and 'office hotelling' reduce the amount of floor space needed per worker by making more intensive use of space.

It is also necessary to examine sources of demand carefully. In some cases greater activity levels in an industrial sector result in induced additional demand for property from suppliers of goods and services to that sector as the impact of the expansion creates multiplier effects in the local economy. Other forms of demand do not have these multiplier effects. If these types of demand are not distinguished, then it is possible that the supply response to a change in demand will be too large, resulting in overbuilding, or too small, creating upward pressure on rents.

It has long been observed that different types of industrial activity cluster together. Historically, this might have resulted from a particular location's natural resource endowment. However, functional specialisation of particular cities and regions is more generally attributed to agglomeration economies

– economic efficiency gains that result from spatial proximity and the scale of activity in an area. The existence and importance of agglomeration economies has been disputed, but the competitive position of a region or city is an important component sustaining demand for space.

Demand for property leads to distinct patterns of land-use as different occupiers compete for a limited supply of land. The patterns that emerge result from the differential ability of users to generate profit from particular sites (and hence pay rent) and from the reaction of developers and land owners. Developers assemble sites and build new structures or refurbish existing structures. The price they are prepared to pay for land depends upon their assessment of future levels of demand for the space they are creating. Landowners, similarly, react to demand signals in releasing land for development. The responsiveness of these two sets of actors is critical in determining adjustment processes in the urban land market. The planning system also plays an important role in the spatial distribution of land uses.

Krugman (1991) has argued that there is no adequate microeconomic explanation of urban property markets. Traditional views and models do not seem adequate to deal with the complexities of market interactions and, hence, are not sufficient to explain patterns of demand for space or deal with changes in industrial structure. The chapter sets out some of the models that seek to provide insights into supply and demand relationships in property markets and explores their strengths and weaknesses.

In the next section the nature of demand for commercial property is examined. The links between industrial sectors and types of property are considered, as is change in the importance of different sectors over time. In particular, the increasing importance of service industries in developed economies has been instrumental in the growth in demand for office space.

Next, spatial variations in demand are discussed. Three aspects are examined: the link between industrial structure and growth in the 'export base' model; the role of accessibility and transportation networks; and the impact of agglomeration economies on the clustering of economic activity. It is suggested that these models do not provide complete or powerful explanations for the variation in demand for space.

One weakness of the models discussed in relation to demand is their implicit assumption that land and buildings will be made available for any increase in activity. A proper explanation, however, must consider the interaction between the user market, the development market, the investment market and the land market.

The fourth section considers the impact of land supply. Users compete for scarce land which, in general, is allocated to those uses able to bid the highest rent. The reaction of developers and landowners to the resultant price signals and the adjustment processes in the land market are discussed. Finally, the role of public sector intervention and planning controls is briefly examined.

THE NATURE OF DEMAND FOR COMMERCIAL SPACE

Analysis of demand for commercial property in the UK has traditionally focused on three broad sectors – industrial, office and retail space.[1] These sectors correspond approximately to types of industry and economic activity. Industrial space is used by the manufacturing sector, office space by the business, financial and professional services sector and shops by retailers supplying consumer products. Demand for commercial space is thus a derived demand relating to economic activity and output. This means that both the amount and type of space demanded vary as patterns of economic activity change in a city or region.

Historically, the growth of cities was linked closely to industrialisation and to manufacturing employment. During the second half of the twentieth century, however, developed economies have seen a move away from manufacturing employment and towards service employment. This trend has been most pronounced in larger cities which have lost much of their manufacturing employment as a result of mechanisation, suburbanisation of industry and the 'global shift' of production to the developing economies (Dicken, 1992).

The process of change in employment structure has been referred to as tertiarisation (the move to a service economy) or deindustrialisation. The trends within the UK are shown clearly in Figure 3.1. There was a sharp fall in primary and manufacturing employment between 1961 and 1991 and a compensating growth in the service sectors which accounted for 71 per cent of employment in 1991. The fastest growth has been in banking, financial services and insurance which have grown nearly five-fold over the period, from

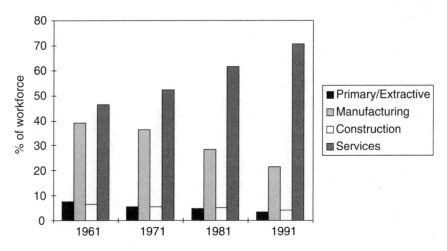

Figure 3.1 UK employment by sector, 1961–91
Source: *Social Trends* (various)

43

2.5 per cent to 12.1 per cent of the workforce. Such figures should be treated with some caution. Definitional changes may distort the year on year comparisons, while out-sourcing of specialised jobs may lead to reclassification. For example, an accountant within a manufacturing firm may have been classified to that sector; once accountancy services are externally sourced, they are classified as a business service.

These national level employment trends result in shifts in total employment within regions (such that regions once dominated by manufacturing may experience high levels of structural unemployment). However, changing employment structure is manifest at metropolitan level as well. Table 3.1 shows employment change in Greater London during the 1980s. In a city already dominated by service industry, the decade saw further concentration both into services and, within services, into banking, finance and insurance and away from transport and communications trades.[2]

Estimates of output by Graham and Spence (1995) suggest that there is no direct link between output and employment. They argue that manufacturing, notwithstanding its apparent contraction, experienced the fastest growth in per capita output of any sector. This suggests that output may be inappropriate for forecasting demand for space. Changes in the nature of production (discussed further in Chapter 4) may result in more or less intensive use of space for a given level of output. Increased technological inputs (for example, a rapid increase in the use of information technology) may result in an increasing demand for space even as jobs are shed: there is a substitution of capital equipment for labour. As discussed in Chapter 2, there may be shifts in relative prices leading to changes in the desired mix of factor inputs. If the relative price of capital equipment or labour compared to land and buildings

Table 3.1 Employment change, Greater London, 1981–91 (percentages)

Sector	Employment		Output		
	1981	1991	Change	1984	1991
Primary/Extractive	1.6	1.3	−27.8	2.7	2.2
Manufacturing	19.2	11.0	−47.5	17.9	13.7
Construction	4.5	3.6	−26.7	5.5	5.4
Services:	74.6	84.1	+3.0	74.0	78.6
Distribution, Hotels	*19.3*	*19.8*	*−5.9*	*15.2*	*14.2*
Transport and					
Communications	*10.3*	*9.5*	*−16.5*	*11.8*	*11.5*
Banking and Finance	*15.9*	*22.5*	*+29.6*	*21.9*	*29.3*
Other services	*29.1*	*32.2*	*+1.4*	*25.1*	*23.4*
Total employment	3.56m	3.25m	−8.6%		

Source: Graham and Spence (1995)

falls, firms substitute these for property. Thus demand for commercial floor space might fall despite an increase in output.

This will also be true of retail sales. A change in consumption patterns towards purchase of higher value products may result in an increase in sales volume with no increase in retail floor space. Nor does business service employment translate directly into demand for office space: it is mediated through the space per worker ratio. Firms that are expanding their activities may use their existing space more intensively, decreasing the space available to each employee. This decision is affected by conditions in the property market: the real rent level and the amount of available space. Similarly, in a recession a firm may be unable to reduce its operational property due to institutional constraints, for example, because of lease contracts. Thus a manufacturing company will still shed staff, leading to an increase in floor space per worker; a shop may lose sales leading to a decrease in sales per unit of retail floor space.

Despite these notes of caution, the move away from manufacturing and towards services and office based employment is reflected in the stock of commercial floor space. Figure 3.2 shows the floor space of the four types of commercial property – industrial, commercial offices, shops and warehouses – for 1974, 1984 and 1994, derived from government censuses (data on the value of commercial investment property in 1996 can be found in Table 10.1).

The most common form of commercial floor space in the 1970s and 1980s was industrial (55 per cent of the total in 1974). This share fell dramatically

millions sq ft

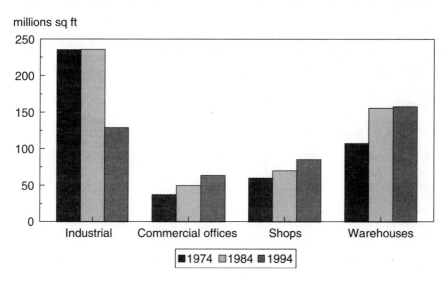

Figure 3.2 Floor stock in England and Wales, 1974–94

between 1984 and 1994, by over 45 per cent of the initial stock. This indicates the scale of deindustrialisation in the UK. Abandoned industrial sites form the source of most vacant land in urban areas. The absolute scale of the decline in industrial floor space is clearly unrepeatable, so vacant urban land will not be so plentiful in the future.

By the 1990s, warehousing had overtaken industrial space as the most significant commercial land-use (36 per cent in 1994). All non-industrial types of commercial property have grown. Commercial offices are still the smallest category in terms of floor space (only 15 per cent in 1994); although, when measured in value, the rank order is reversed (see Table 10.1).

Table 3.2 shows available floor space by type of commercial property for the regions of England and Wales. Regional variations broadly correspond to differences in employment structures, and, for retailing, the proportion of the population living in each of the regions. The overwhelming importance of the South East of England, and of London in particular, can be clearly seen. Fifty-five per cent of offices are located in the South East, and 22 per cent in London alone. In value terms, the concentration of office accommodation in London is even higher (Table 10.1).

Historically, institutions also held significant amounts of agricultural property as an investment. New sectors arise in response to changes in economic activity. There has been increasing interest in commercial leisure-related property including multiplex cinema complexes, sports facilities and entertainment facilities. Nor are sector boundaries clear cut. Many shopping centres have a significant leisure content. An out of town building in use as a distribution warehouse might equally well function as a retail warehouse, a leisure 'box' or even as a call centre.[3] This flexibility of usage was recognised

Table 3.2 Percentage of commercial buildings by type and region, December 1994

Region	Industrial	Commercial offices	Shops	Warehouses	All building types
Northern	7	3	6	5	6
Yorks and Humber	13	7	11	11	11
North West	16	10	12	15	14
East Midlands	12	5	7	9	9
West Midlands	16	8	10	13	12
East Anglia	3	3	4	5	4
Greater London	5	33	16	11	13
Rest of South East	14	22	19	18	17
South East	18	55	35	30	31
South West	7	7	10	8	8
Wales	7	3	6	5	5
England and Wales	100	100	100	100	100

Note: Figures show percentage of total floorspace. Data available for England and Wales only.

in the 1987 General Use Class Order in England and Wales which allowed the transfer from high technology industrial to office usage for 'B1' space without planning permission.[4] Thus it is the *use* of the building that determines the sector, not the building itself. This emphasises the derived nature of demand for commercial property.

Demand for commercial property is, thus, a complex mixture of the space needs of different sectors. Demand for different types of property reflects the business and employment structure in the economy. In the UK economy, the shift towards services has led to an increase in the demand for office and retail space and a decline in demand for traditional industrial space. Changes in the nature of production and consumption lead to changes in the type of space required and may result in demands for new types of space in new locations.

SPATIAL VARIATION IN USER DEMAND

Demand for commercial property always has a spatial component. Particular locations are more profitable than others for particular firms; certain regions and cities grow while others contract, leading to changes in the demand curve for space. Some cities specialise in certain types of activity, increasing the demand for appropriate buildings. In Chapter 4, individual locational decisions of firms are considered. This section provides a framework for understanding spatial variations in demand. First, the idea that change in regional output depends on export of goods and services – *export base theory* – is considered. Next, the advantages of particular locations in terms of *accessibility* are discussed. Finally, explanations of economic clustering in terms of *agglomeration economies* are examined. It is suggested that none of these models alone gives a full explanation of spatial variations in demand.

Export base theory

Growth in the demand for commercial property must be related to growth in economic activity. Growth in one business sector may induce growth in other, associated industries. An expanding firm may purchase goods and services from other firms who themselves begin to expand. Higher wages lead to consumer spending on local goods and services leading to growth in the retail and leisure sectors. However, the impacts of one-off growth in a sector dissipate over time. Export Base Theory (also known as economic base theory) attempts to provide a theoretical model for analysis of the impact of growth on a region. The analysis here links to a more detailed consideration of the macroeconomy in Part 3.

The income (Y) of a region is equal to the sum of consumption (C), taxation (T) and savings (S) – equation 3.1. It must also equal the sum of wages

(W), government transfers (G) and profits or interest earned outside the region (p) – equation 3.2. However, the model is deficient in ignoring private sector transfers which can have significant regional impacts.

$$Y = C + T + S \tag{3.1}$$

$$Y = W + G + p \tag{3.2}$$

Output of the region (Q) consists of consumption, the trade balance (exports (X) less imports (M)) and regional investment (I) – equation 3.3. It must also equal wages (W) and local profits (π) – equation 3.4. Profits here include rents.

$$Q = C + X - M + I \tag{3.3}$$

$$Q = W + \pi \tag{3.4}$$

Trade balances must equal investment flows. Where M > X, there must be a net contribution in the form of savings (S > I), taxation (T > G) or net profits (π > p) – equation 3.5 summarises these relationships.

$$(X - M) = (S - I) + (T - G) + (p - \pi) \tag{3.5}$$

External demand for a region's products, new investment and transfers are translated into regional income. Each pound entering the region goes to pay local factors of production (wages or rents in the export sector) and the income is spent either on imports (in which case it leaks out of the region) or on local goods and services (in which case it produces income for local factor owners). It follows that the strength of the export sector (*'basic'* industries) relative to other (*'non-basic'*) sectors is critical to the performance of the economy. The relationship between exports and the resulting impact on local incomes and output is the basis of the *regional (or local) multiplier* (see also Chapter 6).

Some proportion of income is consumed, the balance is saved: $C = bY$ where b is the fraction of income consumed (hence $1 - b$ is saved). Imports are a function of consumption $M = mC$ where m is the proportion of consumption going on imported goods and services and $(1 - m)$ is local consumption.

Applying these ratios to the identity equations (3.1) to (3.5) an equation (3.6) for regional income can be derived:

$$Y = \frac{X + I + G + p - \pi}{1 - b(1 - m)} \tag{3.6}$$

where $1/[1 - b(1 - m)]$ is the *regional multiplier*. If the proportion of income consumed were 0.9, the import share 0.4 and the domestic share (1 − 0.4) = 0.6, then the multiplier would be

$$1/[1 - 0.9\,(0.6)] \;=\; 2.174$$

This implies that £1 of growth in the export sector generates £2.17 of local income or production. In open economies, a regional import share of just 40 per cent is unrealistically low. If the share is 80 per cent, then £1 of growth in the export sector generates just £1.22 local income. Removal of trade barriers, economic liberalisation and improvements in transport technology have thus reduced the significance and predictive value of the export base model.

The effect of an export 'shock' takes time to work its way through the system.[5] Furthermore, the impact of a one-off exogenously induced increase in output declines over time. This is important in the analysis of demand for property. An increase in output as a result of an exogenous shock leads (other things being equal) to an increase in demand for space. The increase in output has multiplier effects leading to further demand for space. However, this will slacken unless there is further exogenous growth. It is, thus, important for developers and investors to distinguish between permanent and temporary sources of demand in framing their expectations of future levels of demand and hence future rental growth. In terms of the model advanced in Chapter 2, a one-off export shock induces a short-term shift in the demand curve with return to the previous equilibrium level after an adjustment period.

The export base model has been subject to much criticism. At its crudest, it implies that the bulk of demand for services and retail consumption (and hence office and retail space) comes from manufacturing exports. This is not sustainable in developed economies and may produce counter-intuitive results. The major difficulties associated with the model are identification of the 'base', the lack of a supply-side element, inadequate consideration of the causal nature of relationships and the probability of multipliers close to unity. Of these, the base identification problem may be the most critical. A further definitional problem relates to the geographical unit of analysis. It is not clear why analysis should be confined to a city and its hinterland or to a region within a nation when activity by firms crosses any such boundaries. This calls into question the existence of regionally-confined multiplier effects.

The identification problem relates to the need to divide economic activity into basic and non-basic sectors. Ideally this would be carried out following detailed survey work concerning the final destination of firms' output. Since the costs of such an approach are prohibitive, researchers tend either to use indirect measures (for example location quotients) or, more usually, classify industries by assumption – classifying as basic those sectors considered likely to export a high proportion of their output.[6] In the 'traditional' model, manufacturing industry has been assumed to be basic and service industries to be non-basic. Yet financial, business and professional services are exported and, in certain locations, the service sector may be the main exporter with manufacturing playing a secondary, domestic role. In London, New York and, to a lesser extent, Tokyo, much of the output of financial services is consumed outside the city-region (often outside the nation-state as evidenced by the contribution of invisible earnings to the balance of payments). In those cities, a considerable proportion of retail and leisure spending comes from outside the region. Thus, an export base model that failed to identify the destination of service outputs would be misspecified.

Given such theoretical and practical weaknesses of the export base model, its main value may be as a check to over-optimistic forecasts of demand growth. As McNulty (1995) notes, construction depends upon market participants' perceptions of the strength of the local economy. If there is a lag in the transmission of cyclical changes in the basic sector to the non-basic sector (such that the non-basic sector continues to expand when the basic sector is in decline) then this may send misleading signals to real estate decision makers.

Moscovitch (1990) cites an example from New England in the 1980s. Strong economic growth in the first half of the decade (associated with high technology manufacturing and increased industrial productivity) led to a growth in construction activity and consumption in the second half. However, this derived economic activity disguised the fact that the economic base was in decline, particularly in durable goods manufacture. Speculative construction activity based on the economic growth in the second half of the decade contributed to overbuilding as demand for space declined in the late 1980s and early 1990s.

Construction of commercial property can be seen as an important transmission mechanism between basic and non-basic activity. Within the theory, an increase in basic income leads both to an increase in non-basic (service) income and an increase in planned investment (in buildings for example). The construction of the planned investment produces further increases in non-basic income generating another round of demand. The additional lag between start and completion of a construction project adds to the time taken for a change in basic income to work through the system. McNulty (1995) provides empirical evidence of the existence of long-run multipliers for US metropolitan areas and of the importance of construction in sustaining multiplier effects. Much of the multiplier effects seems to relate to construction activity. Treating construction as a basic activity results in multipliers close to unity. McNulty's results show considerable temporal instability in the multiplier coefficients which must cast doubt on the general applicability of the model.

Given cyclicality in economic activity (see Chapter 7 for a detailed discussion), the lag between starts and completions in the development process may generate greater cyclicality and overbuilding in commercial property markets (see Chapter 8). Within the export base model, this is explained as part of the lag in transmission between basic and non-basic income. Given the conceptual weaknesses of the export base model, this may be an inadequate explanation. Nonetheless, it does emphasise that simply examining current aggregate demand and extrapolating trends may result in a misleading picture of the strength of a local property market. This implies that property developers, investors and lenders should look more carefully at the nature of demand for space.

Accessibility and transport networks

The value that an occupier places on a property (and, hence, the price that the occupier is prepared to pay) depends on the bundle of attributes that relate to the building, the site characteristics and the location of the parcel of land within the urban area. Much research in urban economics has sought to analyse the impact of location upon land values. This emphasises the importance of accessibility in determining the demand for space.

Two forms of accessibility are commonly identified: *special* and *general* accessibility. Special accessibility advantages cover the operation of the firm and the relationship of the firm to other organisations. These advantages are *agglomeration economies* and are discussed more fully in the next section. They relate to complementarity of activity, access to common services, reduction in information costs, the development of pools of skilled labour and scale economies both within and across industrial groupings. Certain types of activities are more strongly influenced by special accessibility than others – notably headquarters office buildings, banks and financial institutions, law and accounting firms. These firms are 'complementary in providing high-level business services that require daily contact between firms' (Heilbrun, 1987). As a result, such firms desire a central (or, at least, a common) location.

General accessibility results from minimisation of movement costs (in terms of physical distance and journey time) as a result of a particular location (possibly, but not necessarily, a central location). An occupier will bid more (or less) for a site depending on the impact on profitability of moving to that site. If labour (specifically skilled labour) is distributed evenly throughout the city-region, then a city centre location would maximise access to that labour. Any non-central location increases the average distance that the labour force must travel (resulting either in a welfare loss or higher wages to compensate). Similarly, for retailers, a central location historically maximised access to consumers as a result of public transport and consumer travel distance.

These advantages of general accessibility may be preserved by the inertial effect of existing structures. For example, transportation networks (particularly mass public transit networks) tend to be radial in nature, emphasising

51

the locational advantages of the central business district. The London office market provides an illustration. The labour force for London office-based services is drawn from a travel to work area that consists of the whole South East region and beyond. Commuter rail services typically run from suburban and commuter settlements into central London where they link with the underground (subway) network There are few cross-radial routes. As a result, any firm that needs to draw on the whole London labour market (firms with specific skill requirements needing to maximise labour market size) seeks a central London location. One of the difficulties confronting the early development of London Docklands as an office market was poor accessibility from the London hinterland.

Transport networks, accordingly, affect rental values. In an urban context, commercial rents might increase with proximity to major radial roads. With mass public transit systems, increases in accessibility occur close to stations and interchanges so a pattern of clusters of land-uses and higher rents and land values is expected. However, the evidence is mixed. In the United States, Department of Transportation studies show that prices and land-uses around a newly constructed rapid transit line in the Philadelphia region did alter to account for changing accessibility (Knight and Trygg, 1977). In contrast, studies of the Bay Area Rapid Transit (BART) system around San Francisco concluded that BART's impact on land-use in the first five years of operation was insignificant (Giuliano, 1986).[7] Most studies conclude that improved transportation (reduced transport time cost) results in greater pressure for residential decentralisation (since there has been a change in the relative price of space versus transport costs) but also encourages employment *centralisation* (since general accessibility in the centre has been enhanced).

However, technological and social change may erode the central city's advantage of general accessibility. Changing production technologies and the rise of service industries have reduced the significance of the costs of transporting factor inputs. For many service industries, the main input is information, transported through communications networks. Products are increasingly moved to final destinations by road rather than rail, making access to motorway and trunk road networks crucial. Labour markets are more dispersed with residential moves to the suburbs and to towns and villages beyond the urban fringe. This, in turn, leads to dispersal of retail markets. Increasing mass car-ownership (and usage) allied to the density of activity in the Central Business District (CBD) creates congestion costs and environmental diseconomies which erode the advantages of city centres.

These trends result in the development of suburban and ex-urban industrial, retail and office clusters. Where these clusters exist, there are local rental peaks. In certain areas, suburban locations may attract higher rents. This is the case in Reading, for example, where business parks around the edge of the built up area typically attract higher rents than town centre locations. Many of the firms occupying these business parks need good access to motorway networks, and central congestion and parking difficulties reinforce the advantages of a suburban location. Decentralisation is discussed in more detail in the next chapter.

Agglomeration economies

The tendency for individual firms in an industry to cluster together has been noted since the writings of Alfred Marshall (1893). Marshall suggested three principal reasons for clustering (Krugman, 1991):

1 clustering creates a pooled market for workers with specialised skills with associated benefits for workers (who can move between firms) and the firm (which can draw on the labour pool to expand operations);
2 a greater variety of inputs exist at lower cost as subsidiary trades grow up to supply inputs and services, while economies of scale mean that the suppliers can invest capital, even though each firm consuming the inputs provides only a small share of that investment, due to greater turnover and reduction in risk; and
3 information flows between firms create technology spillovers to the benefit of each firm.

Such agglomeration economies have been termed *localisation economies*. They derive from externalities created by proximity to other firms in an industry.[8]

The idea of Marshallian external economies in an industrial district is embedded in the literature on industrial localities and 'flexible specialism' following the work of Piore and Sabel (1984) and others. In the industrial localities literature, skilled labour pools, shared technical information and supportive institutional structures have enabled particular industries in certain local areas to develop competitive advantages and weather recessionary periods more successfully than other firms in that industry. This is discussed in more detail in Chapter 4.

Another potential set of agglomeration economies, *urbanisation economies*, are not specific to the firm or sector but are general to all firms within a city or region. As a result, factor inputs would be more productive in larger cities than smaller. Reasons for these economies might include greater variety and quality of business services, the opportunities available for firms to specialise, improvements in the general infrastructure (for example, education, transportation and communication networks, utilities), cultural facilities and the existence of a larger pool of suppliers, buyers and skilled labour (including managerial and professional staff). Jacobs (1969) argues that such economies result from general diversity and the scale of operation in cities. Diversification may serve to reduce risk in the city as the timing of business cycles and fluctuations differs across sectors and industries.

Helsley and Strange (1991) have extended the idea of risk diversification in large cities in a model based on credit allocation by banks and investors. Due to scale of operation and diversity, when a project fails, its next best use is more valuable when the density of possible uses is higher. As a result, risk is reduced since the bank can recoup a higher proportion of the loan following default. In larger cities, therefore, banks fare better in 'bad states of the world'. Since projects that are unattractive in small cities are funded in large cities, diversity of activity increases further. Helsley and Strange call this *urban scope*. The greater productivity of resources should mean that large cities receive more capital in equilibrium and perform more economic functions.

The mechanisms by which one location develops agglomeration economies while another does not are not clear. For traditional manufacturing industries, clustering may have resulted from the fixed location of natural resources used in production (see Chapter 4 for a further discussion of industrial location). However, that is an insufficient explanation for more recent clustering of economic activity, such as the concentrations of financial services activity in particular urban locations away from major metropolitan centres or of high technology manufacturing in 'silicon valleys' such as the M4 corridor in the UK or in California in the US. An adequate theory of agglomeration would also need to explain both the inertia that preserves the advantage of a particular location *and* the forces that lead to shifts in industrial activity both within a country and globally.

Krugman (1991) argues that models of agglomeration economies may generate multiple equilibria – that is more than one location could be the most profitable for a firm. As a result, he suggests that it is a matter of historical accident which site grows. Henderson (1985), by contrast, denies any role to history. Entrepreneurs exploit profit opportunities at the most efficient site. Thus, historic chance only matters when sites have identical endowments. Rauch (1993) presents a model in which history does matter and inertia has an effect. The old site has sunk costs that result from the operation of many firms.[9] These costs mainly relate to information transfer – 'learning by watching'. A firm moving to a new area would incur additional learning costs with the highest costs falling on the first mover. As a result, each firm would adopt a strategy of 'wait and see'. In order to induce movement, a developer or an urban government would need to provide incentives to the early movers. Rauch cites the example of differential (discriminatory) pricing of land on industrial parks as an example of the attempt to overcome inertia.

There is some common ground, then, that agglomeration economies are greater in some locations than others, and that this leads to lower production costs in those areas. The precise mechanisms that create and maintain these agglomeration economies are, however, disputed. The existence of agglomeration economies in a region or city encourages firms to locate there and permits a higher proportion of firms to survive and profit in a competitive environment. This, in turn, creates and sustains demand for commercial property with consequent impacts on rents and land values. However, the absence of an adequate dynamic theory of agglomeration makes it difficult to assess the long-run impacts of agglomeration economies on demand for commercial space.

Commercial property produces or causes externalities in a variety of ways. Some of these (for example, traffic impacts) are partly addressed through the planning system (see below). Perhaps one of the major positive externalities is the agglomeration economies generated by having a large amount of economic activity clustered together. Sometimes potential agglomeration benefits become internalised into particular property developments: this is a rationale for science parks, some major office developments and for shopping malls. Yet, most of the benefits of agglomeration just happen through the general development process and may not be achieved optimally. In so far as externalities are not incorporated into resource allocation decisions there will be a misallocation of resources; although how far this actually occurs is difficult to quantify.

The models examined in this section help to explain spatial variations in demand. However, they do not offer strong or complete explanations. In particular, they are insensitive to changes across time or to geographical patterns of economic activity. A further weakness is the absence of supply-side considerations. The models implicitly assume that land and buildings will be supplied in response to a demand shift. A full explanation, however, must consider the interaction between the user market and the land and development markets.

THE LAND MARKET

The location decision

Previous sections of this chapter have examined demand for commercial space, highlighting the importance of users' locational requirements. These are generated by the effects of particular locations on potential profits and, consequently, on production decisions. Particular locations may not only have good access to key markets but also provide a mix of external benefits and costs to users. For example, central city locations generate agglomeration economies, considered above, of benefit to financial users and particular types of retailing; but they impose external diseconomies, such as congestion costs, too.

Each commercial property user has to optimise its production decisions in a spatial context. Its spatial demand function shows willingness to pay for

55

commercial space at particular locations. The content of these demand functions varies between users and activities. One way of conceiving of spatial
demand functions is the idea of 'bid-rent' functions. These show the willingness-to-pay of particular users for property at specific locations in a defined
spatial area, say a city and its suburbs, for a *fixed* level of profit – in the case
of commercial users – or utility – in the case of households. Each user, therefore, has an implicit family of bid-rent curves: one for each level of net prof-
itability/utility. Higher bid-rent curves are associated with *lower* land user
profitability. This is because more has to be spent on rent, leaving less revenue as profit. Similarly, higher bid-rent curves in the residential market
imply lower consumer utility.

Figure 3.3 shows bid-rent curves for two uses, finance and retailing in a
simplified city. The curves represent willingness to pay rent, or bid-rents,
along a radius drawn from the city centre to the edge of the city. The financial company, user A, has a much greater pull towards the city centre than the
retailer, user B, and so has much steeper bid-rent curves. This is because it is
assumed that the agglomeration benefits of the city centre are strong for the
financial company; whereas the retailer is relatively indifferent between particular urban locations – the bond dealer versus the corner shop would be a
marked contrast of this sort. Other types of retailer and financial enterprise,
of course, are likely to have differently shaped bid-rent curves.

The traditional 'Alonso model' formulation of bid-rent curves focuses on
the intra-urban residential location decision. It assumes a uniform city in
which all jobs are located in the city centre. Workers face travel costs to and
from work, and so are less willing to pay for housing built on land at more

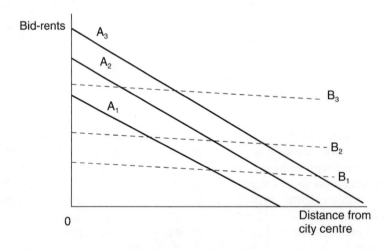

Figure 3.3 Bid-rent curves for two land users in finance and retailing
Note: Each curve represents willingness to pay at given levels of user net profitability/
utility.

distant locations from the city centre. The result is that bid-rent curves slope downwards from the city centre to the suburbs. As distance from the city centre increases, households are trading off extra transport costs against lower land prices. Competition between households, and between them and other land uses, then determines where each household actually locates. The resultant pattern of residential location is associated with a decline in house prices per standardised unit of housing as distance from the city centre increases, and a similar decline in the value of the land on which they are built. Households with a greater consumption of housing are suggested to be more likely to benefit from the cheaper land in the suburbs than others. As higher income groups consume more housing, they would locate in the suburbs and residential incomes would be progressively lower, the closer the distance to the city centre.

This version of the Alonso model is highly abstract. It ignores a city's social and physical geography; the possibility of employment opportunities outside the city centre and the existing spatial pattern of built structures. Households are also constrained in their choices as they can rent or buy only the current flow of dwellings in the market place. The latter excludes most of the existing stock and its location is biased by the location of new supply. In addition, the optimisation process at the basis of the model may also be unrealistic. It assumes that households minutely trade off differences in transportation costs and land rents. This is unlikely in practice because of information limitations and transaction cost barriers. Furthermore, it assumes a two-stage process by which the location of employment is first determined and then workers decide where they should live; whereas a simultaneous location decision-making process by firms and the workforces they employ may be both more realistic and theoretically satisfactory. In real cities, moreover, market rigidities may lead to the formation of residential submarkets that limit trade-off opportunities. Across submarkets, there may be significant price 'steps', rather than a common determination of the relative implicit prices of particular, homogeneous, housing 'characteristics' – such as living space, amenities, environment and distance from the city centre.

The Alonso model can be made more complex to take account of these factors (Evans, 1983), though some would argue that the fixity and heterogeneity of city neighbourhoods defeats any attempt to model residential location by focusing primarily on transportation cost differences. Within commercial property, a stronger case can be made for the differential pull of agglomeration economies, for example, than for explanations based on transportation cost differences alone. It should be noted, however, that agglomeration economies largely exist because of transport and communications costs. Nonetheless, a choice based on agglomeration effects might be more discrete (say, city centre versus a suburb or another centre elsewhere) than the continuous variations across a city implied by the bid-rent approach.

The Alonso model illustrates the central point that the urban land market is the place where the demand for property leads to specific patterns of land use as users compete with each other for a limited supply of land. The agency that makes this possible is the developer, as new built structures, or the refashioning of existing ones, gradually transform urban land uses and expand the urban fringe. The ways in which developers formulate their bids for land is, therefore, an important component in the role of the price mechanism in the provision of commercial property. The reaction of landowners to demand signals and the response of the planning system, are also central.

The workings of the land market

In the model of the property market outlined in Chapter 2, the land market had a key role in determining the equilibrium quantities of commercial property supplied and demanded. However, the section on the land market there presented only a simple demand and supply model. Its relationship to the discussion of locational influences in the land market, considered above, may seem distant. Yet, similar processes are at work as can be seen by examining the role of rent in modern economic theory.

The property market model also presented the process of land use change as unproblematic. In practice, the land market only slowly adjusts and is prone to inefficiencies. Some market reality, therefore, has to be added to the ideal land market construct of Chapter 2. It is argued here that such realism does not negate the earlier methodology; that approach enables a better understanding of the functioning of real land markets and of the problems they may face. This leads on to discussion of the ways in which developers formulate their land bids, and the role of the residual valuation method in this process. After this, two problems of land supply are examined: the issue of vacant urban land; and the propensity of different types of landowner to release land. The final section of the chapter then examines the impact of land use planning.

Land markets and rent theory

The theory of land rent has a long pedigree. In the classic political economy of Smith and Ricardo, the fact that land rent involved payments to landowners for the use of a particular piece of land had key theoretical importance in determining their understanding of the functioning of economies. The theme of the economic uniqueness of land rent processes was later followed up by Marx and the American Radical Ricardian, Henry George. Marx advocated the necessity of an economic revolution, and suggested that landowners might have different economic interests from productive capitalists; while George argued that land rent created nothing of value and so could become the source of all taxation (his Single Tax). Radicalism was revived in the

1970s with the development of a lively 'alternative' rent literature, in which land rent became the source of many urban ills (see the survey in Ball, 1985). Radical rent theory lost most of its impetus in the 1980s and is not examined in detail here.

With the development of neo-classical economics in the last decades of the nineteenth century, mainstream economic theory abandoned the idea that land rent needed a separate set of theories. Land became another factor of production, rather than the payment to a particular social grouping with subsequent economic consequences. Determination of rent needed no additional explanation beyond that applied to the other factor inputs, labour and capital. In doing so, Ricardo's rent theory, which is based on the marginal productivity of particular pieces of land, was generalised to the other factors of production.

Figure 3.4 illustrates the application of modern economic principles to the commercial land market. The demand for land is based on the marginal revenue product of commercial property (that is, the extra net revenue a firm gets from utilising more land), modified by the ability of developers to alter the configurations of the structures built on the basis of the relative cost of plots, as shown in Chapter 2. The demand curve is downward sloping on the principle of diminishing returns. The supply curve is upward sloping on the assumption that high prices induce more land to be converted to commercial property. The diagram also assumes a *competitive* market. This is a key assumption because it implies that there are many similar sites in competition with each other. The number of them released into commercial use depends only on the prevailing market price. As usual, equilibrium exists at the land rent that equates the quantity of land demanded with that supplied:

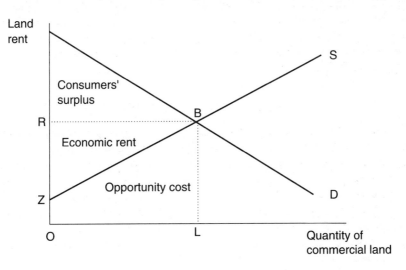

Figure 3.4 The components of commercial land rent in a competitive market

in this case, rent R and land quantity L. Total land value in Figure 3.4 is the rectangle RBLO.

There are three concepts of relevance to the understanding of the determination of land rent and total land value. The first is *opportunity cost*: the cost of inducing the supply into its current use. Only for the marginal piece of land – the last unit of land encouraged into commercial use at the prevailing land rent – does land rent equal opportunity cost. All other units of land could have been induced into commercial use at lower prices, as described by the position of the supply schedule. The total opportunity cost of the land in commercial use is consequently the area ZBLO. Intra-marginal land plots also accrue *economic rent*: the payment to a factor of production over and above that necessary to induce it into its use. This is the area above the supply schedule and below the market determined rent – in other words, the area ZRB in Figure 3.4. Each plot of land earns a different amount of economic rent depending on where it is on the supply schedule.

Note that use of the term, economic rent, is not limited to land alone but, instead, is applicable to all factors of production. Economic rent exists because the supply schedule is upward sloping. In the long run, the supply schedule of many factors of production is highly elastic, so that little or no economic rent arises with them. There may still be temporary *quasi* rents for such inputs, arising from short-run restrictions on their supply. With land, conversely, rising supply schedules generally prevail even in the long run, so economic rents are far more likely to exist.

The final area of interest in Figure 3.4 is the difference between land consumers' willingness to pay, as indicated by the demand schedule, and the actual market price they had to pay, R. This is *consumers' surplus*. The total amount of consumers' surplus is the area under the demand curve and above the market price, ARB. Commercial 'consumers' in this context are developers, existing property owners and commercial property users.

What happens if the land market is not competitive? An extreme case helps to illustrate the effect. Pure monopoly in the land market occurs when every site is so unique that near substitutes do not exist. In this context, there is no longer a supply function in the form shown in Figure 3.4, because higher rents cannot induce more supply. The situation is akin to that of price discrimination. Under price discrimination, suppliers are able to capture potential consumers' surplus through charging differential prices in particular market segments. Air and rail fares are good examples: lower prices are associated with onerous conditions, such as booking in advance or staying over a Saturday night. In this way, the potentially higher consumers' surplus of peak travel time passengers can be captured in higher fares by suppliers. In the case of pure price discrimination, the price of every unit is set to that of the willingness to pay of consumers as indicated by the demand schedule. Rather than one price, there consequently are a multitude.

Price discrimination is generated by creating market barriers. Similar services are bundled into different packages on the basis of characteristics such as time and quality. *Product differentiation* is created, and prices charged on the basis of different willingness to pay. Landowner behaviour can be treated in a similar way. If they can convince demanders of the uniqueness of their sites, they are also able to price discriminate.

The most obvious discriminatory attribute landowners can utilise is the locational uniqueness of their land. This is the basis of Ricardo's mechanism for rent. Agricultural lands are assumed to have known differences in productivity. Thus farmers are prepared to pay the resultant extra marginal revenue products as rent in order to use the better land, as long as they earn at least the normal rate of profit. They compete amongst each other until the whole area under the market demand curve for agricultural land is paid as rent. Differences in transportation costs to market for agricultural produce generate similar effects in producing distinct marginal revenue products net of transportation costs. The landowner can set rents on the basis of those known differences.[10] A simplified example of perfect price discrimination for urban land use is given in Figure 3.5. Opportunity cost has to be paid in this model to shift land from agriculture to the single urban use. Above that price, urban landowners price discriminate on the basis of distance from the city centre, and economic rent is paid accordingly.

Urban land is generally far more complicated. There is a great mix of land uses, making opportunity cost an important component of the price any user has to pay. The competitive model would seem to hold when there are many similar pieces of land, which may often be the case – especially in the suburban fringes of large cities. The greater the degree of monopoly, the greater the ability to price discriminate. Landowners can use other standard practices

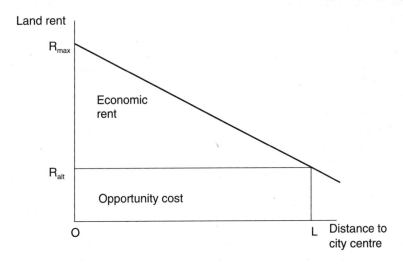

Figure 3.5 Land rent with perfect price discrimination in the commercial market

of monopolistic competition, including marketing, to improve the rental value of their land; and thereby lowering potential consumers' surplus from its use. Developers can adopt the same strategy. One innovation of recent decades has been the marketing of corporate images and styles amongst property developers. These strategies hope to signal the 'success' of a scheme and differentiate its characteristics from those of competitor developers. By doing so, building rents can be higher, and, by implication, consumers' surplus lower. The economic relationship between landowners and developers is considered in greater detail below.

The two approaches to the land market – one based on competition between landowners and the other on price discrimination by them – are not necessarily contradictory. The Alonso model, for example, assumes that each piece of land could be product differentiated on the basis of its location. Within such a framework, land supply is expanded in a city by shifting the final land price gradient from the city centre to the suburban fringe upwards, so that part of the non-urban fringe is drawn into urban use. This upwards shift in the rent gradient raises all urban land values. The quantity of land supplied in the city, therefore, is an increasing function of the *average* price of land there. A general demand and supply diagram could be constructed for the city based on such average prices. However, in contrast to the competitive model, the consumers' surplus has been appropriated as economic rent.

Efficiency in the land market

Figure 3.6 shows some potential supply and demand relationships in the land market. These will be used to illustrate the issues associated with the land market covered in this section. To recapitulate: the demand curve for land is

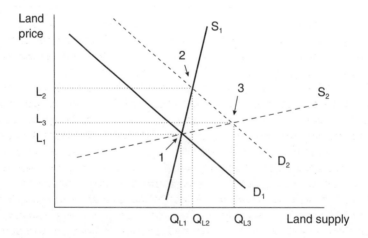

Figure 3.6 Efficiency in the land market

determined by the overall demand for commercial buildings and the amount of land used to produce a square metre of commercial space, given that developers can substitute greater building density for land when designing a project, say, by raising its height. The demand curve is downward sloping, because lower land prices filter through to lower building rents and more land intensive projects, increasing the quantity of land demanded as its price falls. The supply function is upward sloping because a progressively higher price is necessary to induce land away from competing uses. The initial equilibrium point is identified as 1 in the Figure, with a land price of L_1 (per hectare) and a quantity supplied of Q_{L1}.

Economic efficiency has a specific technical meaning. It refers to situations where resources are allocated optimally, so that the goods desired in the market place are produced in the cheapest possible way, given current technical knowledge. Consequently, efficiency in this sense is about making the best use of inputs to produce the maximum amount of output. If one market in an economy is inefficient, improving it releases resources to produce more of the same good, or means that excess inputs can be transferred to another market to produce more output there. Such an efficiency improvement makes someone better off, without making anyone else worse off. So full market efficiency occurs when no rearrangement of resources will make anyone better off without making someone else worse off. Efficiency in this sense is usually referred to as *Pareto efficiency*. Perfectly competitive markets, under restrictive assumptions, can be shown to be Pareto efficient.

The Pareto criterion, however, is an extremely harsh definition of efficiency which may come into conflict with moral beliefs. An economy can be efficient in the economic sense, for instance, while mass starvation prevails in the country in question. Economic efficiency alone, consequently, should not be a full guide to public policy. Most policy-making from road-building to welfare payments is not Pareto efficient, because it generally involves making some people worse off for the benefit of others. This does not stop an efficiency analysis from being worthwhile in policy formation; rather it helps with the selection and evaluation of policy options. The political process then has to deal with the inevitable conflicts of interest which result.

When looking at property markets, economic efficiency is a useful device, because it enables the right questions to be asked. For example, are property markets competitive? Do property users pay the fair market price for their accommodation? Are resources optimally allocated to the sector over time?

With regard to the efficiency of the land market, two issues are of concern. The first is the *feasibility of equilibrium*. For this to occur, buyers and sellers must be able to use the full available information when making their decisions, and are able to operate according to the arguments of their demand and supply schedules. This may not fully occur, for example, if planning regulation freezes land supply or restrictive long leases severely distort demand. The second issue is the *stability* of the equilibrium. If the land market receives an external shock, for whatever reason, and that shock temporarily knocks it from its equilibrium point, the equilibrium is stable when the market returns to point 1.

Equilibrium in land markets is empirically likely to exist; stability of equilibrium is more difficult to justify. If actors respond to temporary shocks, because they misforecast their nature (as suggested in the section on export base theory), then this might lead to users moving from their existing buildings and, more importantly, to developers altering their building plans. The effect is likely to be asymmetrical, because a temporary negative shock is likely to delay development plans and not much else; whereas a positive shock may actually increase the amount of new building. In most markets, mistakes are quickly written off through inventory sales or bankruptcy, but, once built, a commercial property project alters the available stock supply in the market, because it is too expensive to demolish. Temporary shocks, in other words, may have important *persistence effects* in commercial property markets, and alter the equilibrium position away from its initial point.

The next concern about the operation of the land market is a dynamic one, concerning the response of land markets to an increase in commercial demand. There are two issues here. The first one is how *responsive* are land markets to changes in demand. That is, what is the elasticity of supply? The second issue is the *speed* of that response – do land markets adjust quickly or slowly to demand changes? Both of these issues are highly dependent on the existing institutional structure of the land market, so it is not surprising that most of the literature on the development process has a strongly institutional perspective (see Chapter 5).

In land markets with highly inelastic supply curves, any demand increase raises land prices substantially for little extra supply; whereas the increase will mainly be on the quantity side with an elastic land supply. These two cases are illustrated in Figure 3.6 as new equilibrium points 2 and 3 respectively, that arise in response to a shift in the demand schedule from D_1 to D_2. In addition to institutional factors, the inherent scarcity of land at specific locations can have a major impact on the elasticity of supply. Obvious examples of land markets with inherently inelastic land supply are city business districts like those in London and Manhattan. Many suburban locations, conversely, have a more elastic land supply.

The speed of adjustment of land markets is important because it influences the path of adjustment from one long-run equilibrium position to another. As noted in Chapter 2, disequilibrium adjustment paths are difficult to model in economics, because they can take so many forms and, hence, are highly sensitive to the assumptions of any adjustment model. A number of general observations can still be made about the land market. Again, they can be illustrated with reference to Figure 3.6. Assume in this case that the inelastic land supply curve S_1, is the short-run, one period, land supply function, and the more elastic S_2 is the long-run one. With a shift in demand from D_1 to

D_2, constraints on the supply side lead to an initial *temporary* equilibrium at 2, with land prices increasing proportionately more than land supply. Eventually, as the land market adjusts, the long-run equilibrium will be at point 3. Here land prices are lower than the temporary equilibrium and extra supply is far greater.

Land markets that respond rapidly might exhibit little difference between their short- and long-run supply functions, and, hence, the adjustment path is a quick one from 1 to 3. Conversely, ones that adjust slowly might see a difference between the short- and long-run supply functions that lasts for years. A series of temporary equilibria, for example, would then be traced between points 2 and 3 in Figure 3.6 – the precise time path of which would depend on the market's speed of adaptation.

Tardy adjustment presents difficulties for two reasons. First, user efficiencies (which underlie the demand schedule) are frustrated by the slow adjustment of the land market. Second, the higher price of land, and of existing commercial buildings, during the adjustment process may encourage developments that are infeasible at the final land market equilibrium 3. A slow speed of adjustment, in other words, is likely to increase market-distorting persistence effects. An example might be the building of commercial projects in less preferred locations because of temporary restrictions on land supply, and hence new development, at preferred locations. Once bottlenecks in the preferred location are overcome, the peripherally located buildings then fall vacant.

How much to pay for land?

The most common way that developers value land is the *residual valuation* method. This is illustrated in Table 3.3. The price a developer is willing to pay for land on this method is the selling price of the completed structure minus the construction and financing costs associated with it. The willingness to pay for land is a residual because it is what remains of the selling price once all other costs and profits associated with the development have been subtracted from the building's price.

Does this method make economic sense? As an accounting method, it makes sense, as long as expectations of market conditions at the time of completion and sale in the face of considerable uncertainties are properly priced into the estimates. A frequent misconception arises over the residual approach, however, in that it seems to imply that land rent itself is in some sense a residual. This, then, apparently conforms to the radical Ricardian view that the returns to land are simply an unearned increment – a passive sum that can be taxed or redirected towards benefiting the poor or local communities without altering much else (as expounded by Henry George in the nineteenth century and urban radicals in the twentieth). Land rent determination is, unfortunately, not like that.

Table 3.3 The residual valuation of development land

	£
Gross development value	14,500,000
Less purchaser's costs @ 2.76%, say	400,000
Net development value (i.e. sale price)	14,100,000
Costs	
Construction	4,500,000
Professional fees: Design, Engineering, Project management, Legal, Financial advice, Valuation etc. (say 14% of Construction costs)	630,000
Site investigation, Planning and Building fees etc.	36,500
Interest charges on capital employed, say @ 15% over the three years[1] say	1,400,000
Total non-land costs	6,566,500
Less developer's profit on non-land costs, 20%	1,313,300
Residual from net development value	6,220,200
Divide by 1.87 to account for acquisition fees, interest charges on land and profit on land to yield	
Residual site valuation	3,325,065

Note:

[1] The calculation is based upon fees and site investigation for three years @ 15%, construction costs for half the development period at 15% – the conventional rule of thumb calculation. A full development appraisal would account for the timing of all cashflows.

As explained in Chapter 2, land rent is the opportunity cost needed to shift land into commercial use. In this sense, rather than being a passive force, land rents actively allocate land uses. Moreover, the residual approach to an extent is a fiction, because within the calculation variables are artificially fixed whose values in reality are influenced by land prices.

One implicit variable is the size and shape of the building conceived and constructed on a site. This is influenced by the land's cost, so that construction costs are not known prior to land costs, rather they are simultaneously determined. Another variable is the developer's return. While a normal, competitively determined profit rate for the developer may be priced into the residual estimate of a developer's willingness to pay for land, in practice developers will seek to maximise their returns rather than hand over all the residual to the original landowner. Furthermore, willingness to pay for land depends on the success of a particular project – and the returns are not guaranteed but depend on the characteristics of the scheme devised. Scheme conception is an entrepreneurial activity rather than one predetermined by the nature of the site and its price. In this sense, all commercial schemes are unique and innovatory, so that the value of the 'residual' available to pay for the land is an uncertain prospect. It is also difficult, in practice, for landowners to be able to estimate the residuals of individual projects accurately, and hence they are unlikely to capture them all. The ability of landowners to price discriminate between potential bidders for land consequently is limited. The price of land, in other words, is a product of bidding between competing uses rather than the simple extraction by landowners of some notional residual development value.

Whilst it is reasonable to assume competition as a guiding principle when looking at general development processes, it is less realistic when examining the actual negotiations between developers and landowners for new commercial sites. Bilateral negotiations of this sort are better dealt with in game-theoretic contexts. Developers, for example, frequently use the device of nominee purchasers when a proposed development site is fragmented to avoid owners holding out for higher land prices.

In summary, the residual approach to valuation may be a reasonable working hypothesis for evaluating the viability of a development in a way that is easy to understand. It is far less satisfactory as a theory of land price determination.

Landowners and supply responsiveness

The simple land supply model implicitly assumes that landowners are rational and have similar preference functions. When land prices rise, consequently, they uniformly release land for commercial development. Yet, empirical evidence for the UK suggests that the preferences of landowners, their strategies and the contexts in which they operate are highly varied.

Goodchild and Munton (1985) outline a behavioural model interlinking landowner and site characteristics and contextual factors (based on earlier work by Weiss and associates – see Kaiser and Weiss, 1970). They conclude that landowners do not respond uniformly to development opportunities. Adams and May (1991) found that landowners are frequently active in encouraging development on their land and also try to alter contextual factors, such as local planning policies. In contrast, some firms, public sector bodies and privatised industries have held on to derelict land for no ostensible reason; while others have held out for unrealistic sales prices (Adams *et al.*, 1985; 1988). Adams (1994) cites several case studies to support his view that landownership characteristics are important in explaining the development process.

What are the implications of varied landowner supply responses for the land market model presented here? Some would suggest that the approach is threatened by the reality of varied landowner characteristics (Adams, *ibid.*; Wiltshaw, 1985). It need not necessarily be so. In principle, preference differences are not limited to land markets and as such do not invalidate a market analysis. In specific land markets variations in landowner behaviour would alter land supply elasticity, and so the slope of the supply function. If many landowners are reluctant to sell, despite the clear economic gains, that reluctance reduces supply elasticity. This is one reason why the long-run land supply function should be expected to be more elastic, because, over the long run, more landowners are tempted to sell for development.

The other factors affected by varied landowner characteristics are the speed of adjustment of the land market and the location of land supply. Variations in landowner behaviour may slow down market responsiveness, for example, or may affect the spatial pattern of development.

Vacant land

Economic change has generated swathes of vacant land, previously occupied by urban uses, in the world's advanced economies. In the US, housing as well as commercial land has been abandoned. In Europe, social housing institutions tend to function in ways that lead to little abandonment of housing land, but many commercial sites have been vacated, often leaving contaminated land behind. The issue of vacant land became particularly important from the mid-1970s onwards, because deindustrialisation led to the abandonment of factories and other industrial uses, on the one hand, and because environmental concerns aimed at limiting the spread of cities has encouraged greater emphasis on development on brownfield sites, particularly in Europe.

Vacant land arises for a number of reasons. Cameron *et al.* (1988) usefully apply concepts developed for the analysis of unemployment to understand them. Three causes of land vacancy can be identified within this framework. The first is *frictional* - land is temporarily vacant and will be developed soon as part of the process of land-use change. The second is *structural*. Here, technical changes, the difficulty of rendering a site fit for use or the new locational preferences of property users make the land permanently redundant. The third is *demand-deficiency*. This arises from the cyclical characteristics of property development. When the development market is currently in a depressed state, a growing, but temporary supply of vacant land exists, which is drawn down again when the market is in the upswing phase of the property cycle.

Any public policy towards bringing vacant land back into use might usefully focus on the structural component of vacant land. Even there governments may be able to do little without the uneconomic expenditure of vast sums of money. In some countries, notably the US, polluters have been forced by legislation to clean up vacant land blighted many years previously. In Europe, governments are more willing to pay, although in the long term this helps to create a moral hazard of lax environmental treatment of land by users (see Chapter 5). Attempts to close down this element of moral hazard are implicitly embodied in modern strict controls over hazardous waste disposal. This is considered further below.

PLANNING AND INFRASTRUCTURE PROVISION

Land-use planning has considerable effects on the structure of the land market in two senses: it alters the conditions of land supply, and it may change locational benefits, shifting the demand function. A detailed description of planning systems and planning processes is beyond the scope of this text. This section is intended to set out the main arguments regarding the impact of planning and urban policy on property markets. Forms of public intervention are considered, then economic impacts of planning controls are discussed.

Forms of public intervention

Public intervention in the land and property markets takes many forms. These include:

- provision of public and collective goods and services, servicing of land and infrastructure;
- regional and urban policy;
- environmental policy;
- central and local taxation policies; and
- planning policy, planning controls and building regulations.

The significance of these different forms of intervention varies across space and time. Some nation-states adopt *laissez-faire* policies towards property markets and development, others have strict controls on what is built where. A country's planning environment may change considerably over short periods of time (for example the UK's switch away from direct state development activity in declining inner city areas to an emphasis on economic regeneration through private sector activity).

One key role played by the public sector is the provision of public and collective goods. Here the role of the state is as coordinator of activity that might not otherwise take place or that might occur in an imbalanced fashion. This includes provision and maintenance of basic infrastructure (the road and rail network) and provision of educational services. Infrastructure provision alters the accessibility of different sites thus having an impact on the price of land and buildings. Educational services contribute to the skill base of the labour force, affecting the comparative advantage of particular locations. An example is the Republic of Ireland's attempts to reskill its population in order to attract inward investment and boost the competitive position of its industries. This strategy is intended to produce greater relative economic growth which would be expected to result in rental growth in the commercial property sector.

The UK's privatisation policies of the 1980s make analysis of infrastructure provision more problematic. The public sector is no longer the dominant provider of infrastructure in the UK; private firms are now responsible for provision of, for example, gas, electricity and rail networks. The private utilities are regulated but the remit of regulators over new connections is unclear. The splitting of coordination and provision makes the negotiation process for planners and developers more complex and arbitrary (Marvin and Guy, 1997).

Within a nation-state, there may be regions of the country or particular towns and cities that are under-performing relative to others as a consequence of resource or factor endowment, locational disadvantages or frictional adjustment problems – for example, the consequences of the decline of a major industrial sector. Regional and urban policy may be enacted that is intended to counter the economic or social disadvantages of those areas. Examples include attempts to induce industrial development in 'backward' rural areas (in developing economies this may be to counter rural depopulation and over-rapid growth of urban centres); attempts to encourage decentralisation of manufacturing or service industries from core growth areas to peripheral areas or regions that experienced rapid deindustrialisation and high levels of unemployment; and urban policies that aim to deal with the decline of inner cities.

Policy measures may include restrictions on development in growth areas, incentives to locate in the target areas (tax breaks, employment subsidies, grants for site upgrading and development) and direct spending on infrastructure, environment or provision of public facilities. Within the UK an emphasis on direct public intervention and expenditure on social projects (for example, comprehensive redevelopment of city centres in the immediate postwar period, slum clearance and the provision of social housing, regional employment subsidies) has been superseded by an emphasis on economic regeneration through public–private partnerships and an emphasis on supply-side measures (see Lloyd and Black, 1993; Imrie and Thomas, 1993). Examples of policy initiatives include the declaration of Enterprise Zones in 'areas of economic and physical decay where conventional economic policies have not succeeded' (Department of the Environment, 1980) and Urban Development Corporations as in London's Docklands.[11]

Property-led regeneration has been an important tool in these area-based economic initiatives (Turok, 1992). Direct and indirect stimulation of construction activity is seen as a means to stimulate economic growth and inward investment by provision of industrial and commercial floor space and improvement of the physical environment. How successful such strategies have been is debatable. The property-market recession of the early 1990s cast doubt on the effectiveness of property-led regeneration. Brownhill (1990), pointing to the financial problems and (then) high vacancy rates of the Canary Wharf project in London's Docklands questions the value of the 'hidden' £470 million subsidy in capital allowances. Even prior to the property recession, Department of the Environment (DoE, 1987) research suggested that the majority of company relocations into enterprise zones were displacement moves, often over relatively short distances as firms benefited from tax incentives (some of which were captured in rents). This implies that the intervention has led to micro-changes in locational advantage without necessarily changing the quantum of demand for space.[12]

Environmental issues

Concern over the environment has led to the growth of legislation and regulation that has an impact upon the property market. In the UK, measures include the requirement that major development proposals must be subject to an environmental impact assessment, legislation concerning permissible levels of pollution, contamination and waste disposal, and changes to tax regimes on fossil fuels.[13] The underlying principle behind much environmental legislation is to ensure that the 'polluter pays' for any environmental consequence, that is, externalities are borne by the developer or owner. In practice, as Lizieri and Palmer (1997) suggest, environmental legislation has a much wider impact on actors in the property market. For example, the US 'Superfund' legislation has imposed major unexpected costs on landowners, occupiers and, in some instances, lenders. This serves to increase the risk of investing in certain types of property. The increase in the user cost of capital (through an increase in the risk premium) results in a fall in the investment value of the property and, hence, in terms of the model presented in Chapter 2, a reduction in supply.

Central and local taxation

Taxation affects the property market to the extent that there is a differential impact. If different local authorities levy different rates of property tax (or indeed other taxes such as sales taxes), this affects business costs and influences locational decisions. Local government spending of that tax income on the provision of amenities and services also alters the advantages and disadvantages of particular locations. In theory, the Tiebout effect (Tiebout, 1956) results in firms (and individuals) moving until they achieve their desired mix of local taxes and services. In practice, inertia and frictions to movement such as sunk costs in plant and machinery restrict locational flexibility (see Chapter 4 for a further discussion).

If taxes on property are at a higher rate than on other factors, there will be a substitution effect away from property and land.[14] Since some firms and sectors are better able to make this substitution than others, there are sectoral shifts in the distribution of productive capital. The impact of a general property tax also depends upon the final effective incidence of that tax – the extent to which the tax may be passed forward to final consumers in the form of increased prices, passed backwards from the occupier to the landowner or offset through tax relief.

71

A further form of property tax is a specific tax on vacant land and buildings. Such taxes are aimed at countering speculation and land hoarding, where it is considered that landowners are withholding sites from the market in the hope of future gains (perhaps from changes in permitted development) thus creating a supply-side shortage.

The Economic and social impacts of planning

Planning and zoning regulations control the type of development that can occur in particular locations while building regulations impose particular standards on the physical construction of properties and on the permitted density of development. Other controls include conservation policy – areas and buildings may be declared to be of particular architectural or historical interest and strict constraints placed on development. The nature and style of planning controls vary by country from detailed plot-based control, to zoning and land-use plans, to more broad-brush strategic planning. The economic impacts of planning controls are considered below.

Policies may result from a mix of objectives. For example, the controls imposed upon major out-of-town retail development in England (for example with the revised planning policy guideline PPG6) result from environmental concerns (out-of-town retailing uses greenfield sites and necessitates longer shopping trips), from concerns about the future of the town centre (the need to maintain 'vitality and viability' – emphasised by the adverse effects attributed to the impact of regional shopping centres such as Meadowhall and Merry Hill on the adjacent town centres of Sheffield and Dudley) and social concerns about the relative impact on poorer households in the inner city with restricted access to cars. Planning constraints may raise the investment value of existing out-of-town retail centres.

There are a number of justifications made for planning controls. It is sometimes argued that planning is necessary to secure a better or more sustainable environment. The validity of such a claim is dependent upon the planners' ability to define what is meant by a better environment (for whom?) and to determine what measures are necessary to deliver that environment. The planner must be mindful of the opportunity costs of planning action. Harvey (1987) cites the example of the green belt, the area of controlled development at the city fringe. At that margin, agriculture may not be the 'highest and best use' and the imposition of development costs increase commuters' travel time and distance. This must be set against the benefits of environmental protection and easier infrastructure provision.

A second line of argument justifying planning is that the planning system acts to ensure that there is an appropriate mix of land-use for current and future needs and to reconcile competing claims for land. A similar argument could be made for the price mechanism. However, it is likely that a pure price system (in a complex society) would fail to incorporate fully externalities imposed by development and change of use. Figure 3.7 shows the marginal price, marginal private cost and marginal social cost of supplying different quantities of land for a particular use. In an unfettered price-based system, the supplier (the land owner) is faced just with marginal private costs and, faced with a marginal price MP, supplies Q_1 units of land. However, the supply of land creates social costs (additional congestion costs and environmental costs with increasing density of activity). Accordingly, the marginal social cost curve rises more sharply and the appropriate social level of provision is Q_2. It is argued that the planning system may act to prevent the oversupply $Q_1 - Q_2$.

Planning controls generally serve to constrain supply. This generally leads to higher rents and prices, as Figure 3.8 demonstrates. The equilibrium supply of sites for a particular land use is Q_e giving a market clearing price of P_e. Planning controls constrain supply such that only Q_p units are supplied increasing the price to P_p. That higher price benefits the owner and developer of sites with planning permission. Higher prices will lead to substitution effects. Moreover, planning controls reduce uncertainty for developers while relaxation of planning controls increases risk (an argument made by Evans, 1990). It has been argued that municipal control of the supply of land for building in the Netherlands has contributed to the less volatile pattern of Dutch commercial rents.[15]

In addition to price effects, the planning system imposes private costs on the developer. These represent the balance between deferral of the receipt of the sale price and the additional land holding costs (such as interest charges) less the deferral of construction costs and any income received from the existing use of the site (Keogh and Evans, 1992). There may be social costs, too, where delays impose costs and externalities on other sites and users. These costs need to be set against the benefits of coordination, prevention of

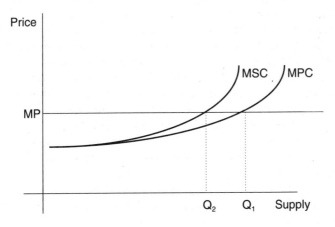

Figure 3.7 Externalities and the optimum supply of land

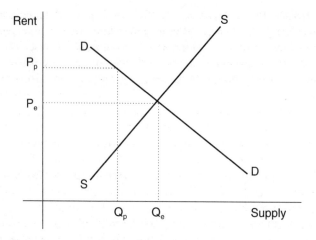

Figure 3.8 The impact of planning control on rents

undesirable development and the protection of the interests of potential losers in the development process. Keogh and Evans suggest that there may be an optimal balance of planning between restrictive and non-restrictive systems.[16]

SUMMARY AND CONCLUSIONS

Demand for commercial property is derived from the economic activity of firms. Land and buildings act as factor inputs in the productive process. As a result, there are variations in demand for commercial property across time as production technologies change and across space as different locations have advantages for particular types of land use.

In most developed economies, there has been a decline in the importance of manufacturing and an increase in the significance of service industries. This is reflected in increased demand for office and retail space and decreased demand for industrial property. However, output and employment do not directly translate into demand for commercial space. Increases in productivity and substitution of capital equipment or labour for land and buildings can result in output increases with no concomitant increase in demand for property. Similarly, changes in the organisation of production and the nature of consumption may result in increased demand for property with no change in activity levels.

Demand for commercial property has a spatial component. Individual firms or industrial sectors may make greater profits at one location rather than another, while some cities and regions exhibit greater than average growth (or decline) in economic activity. However, no single theory offers an

74

adequate explanation for spatial variations in demand. Theoretical models of the competitive advantage of particular locations assist in the understanding of geographical patterns of demand for commercial space. These models, however, fail to incorporate a supply-side adjustment mechanism.

Commercial users attempt to optimise their production decisions in a spatial context. As a result they are prepared to pay particular rent levels to use particular locations. They compete with other users to occupy those sites. However, the land market is not fully competitive in that the number of sites is finite and no one site is a perfect substitute for another. As a result price discrimination and monopoly may arise. Thus the role of developers and land owners is critical to understanding adjustment processes in the urban land market. Traditional demand-side urban economic models tend to neglect this dimension.

Equilibrium in land markets may not be stable. This results from persistence effects; when developers and land owners react to a temporary shock, the resultant increase to the stock of property is semi-permanent. If demand falls away, this may result in vacant land and buildings. There is evidence that land markets are not responsive to changes in demand, partly due to institutional factors. The speed of land market adjustment influences the adjustment path from one long-run equilibrium to another. It seems likely that the short-run supply curve is inelastic (partly due to landowner behaviour) but the long-run land supply function is more elastic, subject to physical constraints.

Land-use planning and public intervention have considerable effects on the structure of the land market. Planning alters the supply of land for particular uses and changes the locational benefits of particular locations, for example through infrastructure provision. Planning systems may act to ensure an appropriate mix of land-uses for both current and future needs and to reconcile competing claims for land, taking into account social costs and externalities. However, public intervention alters pricing relationships and hence affects the price allocation mechanism.

This chapter has attempted to provide a framework for the understanding of spatial and temporal variations in demand for commercial property and the responses to those variations that occur in the land-market. This analysis is developed in the remaining chapters in Part 1. The next chapter focuses upon the locational decisions of individual firms in the three main property sectors. Chapter 5 then examines behavioural and institutional explanations of decision-making in land and property markets.

4

THE LOCATION OF
COMMERCIAL PROPERTY

INTRODUCTION

The commercial property markets consist of thousands of parcels of land and buildings. Individual properties have distinct attributes, so product-differentiation exists, with no property a perfect substitute for another. The property industry's mantra of 'location, location, location' indicates the importance of geography on rents and values. Property market dynamics are also influenced by the changing attractiveness of particular locations.

The price payable for a commercial location reflects the present value of the benefit which the highest bidding producer derives from operating at that location. The location chosen and the price a firm is willing to pay depends on the site's relative benefits and others' bids to use it in a process of constrained optimisation. The degree of competition for a site influences the amount of the producer's locational benefit that is captured as land rent.

As discussed in Chapter 3, the relative attractiveness of particular locations changes over time because of alterations in demand patterns or through shifts in cost structures. Locational costs may change because of transportation factors, the provision of new infrastructure, adjustments in the location of factor inputs or their relative prices, or through developments in production technologies. Models of spatial change in property markets consequently can be complex or have to make strongly restrictive assumptions in order to focus on specific influences.

Producers in different industries have specific locational requirements, and, hence, willingness to pay to occupy space in a particular area, leading to a pattern of separation of land-use by function. In a competitive market each land parcel should go to the activity able to profit the most from locating there; land should therefore be allocated to its 'highest and best use' – the spatial equivalent of Pareto optimality (see Chapter 3).

Locational models, like all economic models, are both deductive and normative. They are deductive in that they proceed from a set of basic propositions, or assumptions, about the objectives and behaviour of firms. They are normative in that they specify an optimal outcome, *given* the simplifying

76

conditions and assumptions imposed. This has to be remembered when reviewing the location theory literature. Spatial behaviour that does not conform to a model's expectations may indicate a suboptimal distribution of activity, or it may imply that some of the model's underlying assumptions and simplifications are invalid. Institutional and policy factors may also have to be added to any model's conclusions. Land ownership and the role of planning and development control in influencing spatial patterns of land-use need to be considered, for example, as does the inertia of relocation costs.

In terms of the model outlined in Chapter 2, the slope and position of the demand curve in any user market are determined by the net sum of the competing demands for specific locations, so location is a key underlying element of the model's composition and explanatory power. Changes in site locational advantages lead to demand shifts, which alter the pattern of rents. The adjustment process is generally asymmetrical because a downward shift in a property market demand curve (caused, say, by a decline in locational advantage) generally leads to longer periods of disequilibrium than upward shifts, since it is harder to reduce a stock of existing buildings than to increase it.

To property practitioners, location theory may not seem to have much relevance to general valuation methods. The contents of this chapter suggest that this is not the case. Crucially, the valuation and appraisal (pricing) models used in practice (see Chapter 10) require valuers to use evidence from 'comparables' – transactions relating to similar properties in a vicinity. In doing so, they implicitly contain, or neglect, locational theories and theories relating to the process of adjustment to changing spatial advantage. An ability to use 'comparables' implies that the urban land market is in continuous and competitive spatial equilibrium. With this assumption, there is limited need to consider whether those equivalent transactions are actually equivalent, correctly priced or currently subject to changing forces which make them less equivalent. 'Comparables' in economic terms are near perfect substitutes, so valuation practice implicitly attempts to define the degree of spatially influenced product-differentiation in property markets. To do this, views on the determinants of locational advantage have to be formed – with a theory of some sort, no matter how trivial, brought into the process of forming those views. 'Comparables' may also be weighted by pricing the differential spatial attributes of particular properties, which again implies the existence of a locational theory.

Despite the importance of location to the functioning of commercial property markets, the property industry has undertaken little rigorous analysis of the spatial differentiation of demand. Most locational research, instead, has come out of economic geography, regional economics or, in the case of retail activity, marketing. Nonetheless, the range of models utilised to explain location of commercial activity has a long history. Modern industrial location models originate in the work of Alfred Weber and Marshall in the early twentieth century; explanations of retail activity and service location can be found in the writings of Christaller, Hotelling and Reilly in the late 1920s and early 1930s. Any reference to location consequently has to start with these early theories, and then move on to the more recent theories added on to them.

The object of this chapter is to examine theories that help explain the geographic distribution of commercial property activities and, hence, the demand for commercial space. Some of the models examined address the locational decisions of individual firms. Others seek to explain the competitive advantage of particular locations over other sites. The chapter's content is arranged by property sector.

The next section examines the location of industrial property by considering theories of manufacturing location. Much of the research on industrial location has developed from Alfred Weber's analysis of the *least cost* location. Least cost location theory needs to be adapted to deal with competition and to emphasise the importance of agglomeration economies. This has led to a new industrial geography which both suggests a shift in the late twentieth century away from mass production to more small-scale flexible production methods and, at the same time, looks back to Marshall's concept of the *industrial district*.

Then retail location theory is considered. This combines an analysis of consumer spatial behaviour (much of which is based on Christaller's *central place theory*) with a consideration of the location of shops (derived from Hotelling's *spatial competition* work and Reilly's *gravity model*).

This is followed by an investigation of theories of office location and the formation and persistence of central business districts in cities, expanding on the discussion on rent and location in Chapter 3. The key roles played by *agglomeration economies* and the shift in locational pulls resulting from the *internationalisation of services* are discussed.

The final section summarises the principles found and considers the impact of social, economic and technological change on spatial patterns.

INDUSTRIAL LOCATION

As noted in Chapter 3, in terms of floor space, the amount of industrial and warehouse property greatly exceeds that of office and retail sectors. Demand for that space depends on the locational decisions of individual manufacturing firms and the legacy of the historical development of industrialisation. Traditional industrial location models sought to identify the best location for a factory, focusing on transport costs and factor inputs. More recently, attention has shifted to analysis of the regional location decision, examining growth, decline and revival of manufacturing towns and districts. In part, this reflects changes in the organisation of manufacturing and in the relative importance of inputs. This section initially considers traditional, micro-locational models then examines the industrial organisation literature.

Weber and least cost location

Many models of industrial location are based on the work of Alfred Weber (1909; 1929). Weberian location theory, reflecting the prevailing industrial technology in the early years of the twentieth century, focuses on the costs of transportation in assembling material inputs and transporting them to single point markets. The underlying principle is that of the least cost location. Material inputs may be ubiquitous or localised. If they are localised, a material intensive industry is pulled towards the resource location. Ubiquitous resources tend to lead towards a market location. In similar fashion, if the manufacturing process reduces product weight then a resource location is favoured. Given that a cost–distance function can be defined from the resource points and the market, the least-cost location can be defined. It is the point that minimises transportation costs (see Figure 4.1a).

Weber recognised the role of labour costs and the possibility of agglomeration economies. As Figure 4.1b shows, an industry may locate at a point of low cost labour if the saving exceeds the additional transport costs. The model is adaptable to account for non-linearity in transport costs (longer journeys tend to have lower costs per distance than short journeys), insurance costs and the impact of additional trans-shipment costs when a journey is broken (for example, transfer from ship to rail or road at a port). However, the model is static in that it does not allow for the impact of competitor firms. It makes the assumption that demand is held constant, and that all output can be sold. As Lösch (1954) argued, the least cost location is not necessarily the same as the site of maximum profit, since profitability depends upon the relationship between input costs, output levels and sales.

Theoretically, location should affect price. As transport costs increase, so prices should rise, in turn reducing demand. In practice, firms tend to adopt

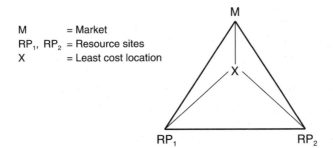

M   = Market
RP_1, RP_2 = Resource sites
X   = Least cost location

Figure 4.1a Weberian location triangle

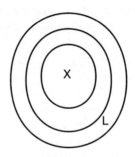

X = Minimum cost location
L = Point of low cost labour

Figure 4.1b Weberian location with a low cost labour point
Note: The concentric rings are isodopanes – lines of equal cost – which increase with distance
from the minimum cost location X. Firms will locate at L rather than X if labour at L
exceeds the value of the critical isodopane that runs through L. The same applies for
agglomeration economies.

spatially uniform pricing within a region. Isard (1956) attempted to synthe-
sise the cost approach and a demand-based profit-maximising approach, but
models based on demand are more prevalent in retail analysis than in manufacturing.

When manufacturing industry was heavily dependent on raw material
inputs (both for fuel and for the basic inputs of production), resource-based
location dominated industrial patterns. This resulted in the development of
manufacturing towns and districts based on coal fields or near to iron ore
reserves. As raw material inputs declined in significance compared to the
pull of a market location or labour, so these traditional manufacturing districts declined. The fall in demand for manufacturing space created high levels of vacancy in the industrial stock, vacant land and dereliction.

Hoover (1926), noting that industry was clustered rather than dispersed,
suggested that more weight should be given to agglomeration economies, as
discussed in Chapter 3. For manufacturing, these apply at three levels. First,
there are *scale economies* at the plant level. These derive from organisational
efficiency and technical/engineering savings. Second, there may exist *localisation economies* where independent businesses within a sector can gain by
locating in close proximity. This allows the development of specialisation
through separation of parts of the production process, permits the development of specialist producer services (that must otherwise be internalised by
the producer) and assists in the development of a skilled labour pool. Third,
urbanisation economies occur which are not specific to the firm or sector but
are general to all firms. These might include greater variety and quality of
business services, improvements in the general infrastructure (education,
transportation networks, for example) and the existence of a larger pool of
suppliers, buyers and skilled labour.

Webber (1972) argues that agglomeration occurs in response to uncertainty.
Within production, plant and firm size is restricted because uncertainties

increase the cost of capital and, so, restrict the scale of capital investment. With smaller size, firms cannot internalise specialist services and must locate near those services. The service providers, conversely, must also locate near their market, reinforcing concentration. Similarly, demand uncertainties necessitate locating near to the largest market to ensure that the firm can react to information on sales, customer demand, product innovation and financial markets. Whatever the strength of these particular hypotheses, they highlight the informational benefits of agglomeration. Earlier, Marshall (1919) explained the existence of specialised industrial districts through special labour force factors, producing agglomeration and a larger scale of production. These arguments reappear in the new industrial literature, discussed below.

Another strand of the industrial literature recognises that suboptimal behaviour may occur. Smith (1981) has developed the idea of a spatial margin of profitability. This suggests that there exist geographical areas around the optimal location where a firm may make sufficient profit to continue in operation (see Figure 4.2). Firms may not seek the best location, but be content to survive. This links to the work of March and Simon (1958) on economic behaviour and to Pred's (1967; 1969) research on location, information and the ability (and willingness) to use that information. Institutional and behavioural approaches are discussed in more length in Chapter 5, in relation to the supply of land and buildings. With firms having a choice of feasible locations, the ability of developers to market and promote particular sites and buildings assumes a greater importance (see Chapter 3).

The regional location of industry

It is generally argued that technological progress has reduced the significance of resource-input location and transport costs in the developed

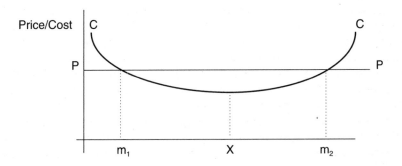

Figure 4.2 Spatial margins of profitability
Notes: A firm is in profit when the cost curve CC falls below the price curve PP. The optimal location is X, but the firm is profitable between m_1 and m_2.

economies. This results, among other things, from changes in power source and usage (the dominance of electricity over fossil fuels, greater efficiency in machinery), from reduction in the unit cost of transport and from increases in the ratio of unit price to unit material and power costs. Thus, the regional location decision depends on:

- market potential (size of market, competitive factors);
- agglomeration economies (at industry and city level);
- labour factors (wages, skill-base, level of unionisation);
- resource costs, energy costs and other factor inputs;
- communications infrastructure and transport networks;
- tax structure and governmental incentives;
- globalisation of ownership and markets; and
- environment and amenities.

These factors vary in importance across industrial sectors and across time. For example, the impact of labour inputs as a location factor depends on the skill level required. If the labour skills are ubiquitous, then an industry is likely to seek a low labour cost location, probably non-unionised and away from metropolitan areas. Globalisation has meant that this may be in a different country, or a different continent from the parent firm's head office. However, an industry requiring high skill levels needs to maximise its access to large labour markets, with cost-reductions being less critical. The production of computer hardware illustrates this. Much of the basic production takes place in cheap labour areas in, for example, Asia or using low wage labour in peripheral areas of developed economies. However, research and development activity and skilled production tend to be clustered in locations within developed economies such as Silicon Valley in California. A further factor is inertia: an existing firm faces considerable search and removal costs. These costs act as a friction to movement to a profit-maximising location and may explain the apparent suboptimal distribution of industry.

Evidence for the changing importance of locational factors may be drawn from shifts in the pattern of industry. In developed economies, there has been a shift in activity away from traditional heavy manufacturing industry areas and away from metropolitan areas. This can be seen in the UK with the 'deindustrialisation' of peripheral regions such as the North, the North West and Wales, and in the United States with the shift away from the traditional industrial heartland of the North East – the 'Rustbelt' – towards the South and West of the USA (Martin and Rowthorn, 1986; Dicken, 1992).

Ó hUallacháin (1990) analysed inter-metropolitan shifts in US manufacturing between 1977 and 1984 in an attempt to test whether agglomeration economies, labour factors, climate or amenities explain the change in distribution. He modelled employment change for 264 metropolitan statistical areas (MSAs) – the total areas of major cities, incorporating suburbs that may fall outside the city's administrative boundary. As a proxy for urbanisation economies, the total size of the labour force was used. Localisation economies were measured in terms of the relative share of industry in a particular location. Other variables captured climate, unionisation (argued to act as a proxy for wage rates), average establishment size, the proximity of a research park, the presence of a defence industry, racial mix and tax factors. Regressions were estimated for growing and declining urban areas separately, and the results broadly conform to the general predictions of the causes of urban locational change.

1   In *growing* employment MSAs, urbanisation economies have a positive influence on employment. Employment growth is also higher in larger MSAs and in MSAs in milder regions (although this latter effect may be capturing the shift to the Pacific South West from the North East rather than signifying a causal relationship). High levels of unionisation conversely have a negative impact on growth (although this, again, could be because the variable is correlated with the employment shift in the US from the old, unionised, industrial districts to traditionally low wage, non-union locations).

2   When *declining* MSAs, with both falling employment and population, are considered, urbanisation has a negative impact on employment change, as does average establishment size. These results probably highlight the decline of traditional manufacturing plants and the cities in which they are located.

Industrial organisation and flexible specialism

Another strand of industrial literature argues that developed economies have shifted away from 'mass-production' to 'flexible-specialism' or from 'Fordist' to 'Post-Fordist' production technologies.[1] Piore and Sabel (1984) provide a historical analysis of industrial organisation, stressing the importance of technological innovation on working practices and organisational structures. They suggest that, in the late nineteenth and early twentieth centuries, there was a switch away from craft methods, undertaken predominantly in workshops, to the factory-based manufacturing of standardised products. The dominance of the modern factory system was sealed by the application of scientific methods to production techniques ('Taylorism') and the adoption of mass-production, through assembly-line techniques and vertical integration of production to maximise economies of scale ('Fordism').

If their argument is interpreted in a property perspective, a 'Fordist' industrial structure requires large-scale factory space, often purpose-built for the individual firm. Smaller manufacturing outlets, however, could still utilise standardised smaller scale, manufacturing 'sheds', such as those provided on traditional industrial estates.

The essence of the flexible specialism thesis is that, by the early 1970s, the return on investment in the older mass-production industries fell as product and market saturation set in, and because inefficiencies began to be increasingly experienced within rigid mass production methods. Subsequent manufacturing collapse and restructuring meant that many of the world's traditional industrial regions experienced severe recessions in the years following the mid-1970s. Some regions declined significantly, with high levels of unemployment, urban decay and deprivation. They now rely on a new, but much narrower, manufacturing base – with employment profiles that are different from their traditional ones.

Good examples in Britain are the old mining districts, traditional single industry towns, shipbuilding districts and the major ports. Market processes, often aided by strong government intervention, have transformed a few of them into new industrial or service districts – for example, Telford a new town in the old coal and iron smelting district of Shropshire and London's Docklands. Most have gone through a long, slow process of adjustment that is still incomplete – twenty years or more after the initial shock of industrial decline. As so much of traditional manufacturing was located in old urban districts, the loss of manufacturing jobs has been associated with inner city decay.

Although most manufacturing industries remain within traditional urban areas, there have been marked trends towards the suburbanisation of employment. Most of this literature examining this phenomenon comes from the USA. It emphasises shifting agglomeration benefits and the peculiarly US characteristic of white suburban flight (Garreau, 1991; Henderson, 1988; Mieszkowski and Mills, 1993; Mills and Lubuele, 1997).

In addition, new industries and industrial processes have encouraged the growth of new industrial regions and urban areas. Piore and Sabel (1984) identify a particular group of them, claiming that these industries and regions have outperformed their competitors. In Europe, they include the various 'silicon valleys', based on information technology industries, such as the 'Third Italy', stretching from Veneto to the Adriatic Marshes. Here small-scale engineering, textiles and metal manufacture have prospered through networks of inter-connected specialist producers. Other areas have different mixes of characteristics – like those associated with the area around Salzburg in Austria or Baden-Württemberg in Germany. Successful industries in these two areas include textiles, ceramics, 'mini-mills' in steel production, industrial instrumentation, and speciality chemicals.

There are several features of these industries and localities, which are identified as important by Piore and Sabel:

• considerable use is made of high technology equipment – in particular the use of IT, computer aided design (CAD), computer integrated manufacture (CIM) and computer numerically controlled (CNC) machine tools that allow rapid changes;

- 'craft-based' labour structures are common – that is a skilled workforce, flexible in the tasks performed, with flat organisational hierarchies;
- most plant is small-scale;
- product lines are characterised by fast product innovation, rather than long-term growth and decline cycles of individual products;
- production is often organised in districts and networks permitting inter-firm transfer of research and development, a creation of a locationally specific, trained workforce and the establishment of cooperative structures; and
- locally organised production is linked into the world economy to maximise the market for speciality products, using new communications technology for coordination.

The major locational implication of the flexible specialisation model is thus, once again, the significance of agglomeration economies, although they are spread throughout a region rather than being specific to one city. In this vein, Scott (1986) and Cooke (1988) argue that *economies of scope* have become more important than economies of scale. Economies of scope arise when the unit cost of producing two or more goods simultaneously is less than when they are produced separately. They may arise within the firm, as Chandler (1990) has explored – through savings in overheads, marketing and the like. Or they may arise because of the external benefits conferred on a firm when they locate in a particular district – producing a variety of products or components in locally based producer networks. The benefits they derive are said to include the local pooling of research and development initiatives, the presence of specialised business and producer services, knowledge transfer and labour sharing (or, at least, the mutual development of labour skills in an area). Such externally generated 'scope' economies are similar to traditional explanations of agglomeration economies.

However they are classified, these benefits point to the advantages of local networks of producers. Such modern, geographically specific, advantages serve to offset some of the spatial freedoms provided in recent decades by developments in information and communications technologies.

Of course, flexible specialisation is not the only theory available to explain such industrial change. There is considerable debate in the literature over the precise nature and causes of industrial change and its spatial implications. The debate has considerable implications for predicting the future of the industrial property market. Piore and Sabel (1984) predicted that successful countries would be ones that adopted non-hierarchical craft-based, cooperative industrial structures; a prediction that has largely proved to be wrong. A more traditional, neo-classical, approach to industrial change would forecast similar broad processes of location change, given the scale of technical transformations, altered factor input prices, improved transportation and freer world trade. It would, however, put far less emphasis on the production process characteristics highlighted by Piore and Sabel, or on some unique regions of Europe. Porter (1990) also emphasises the importance of 'clustering', in which related groups of successful firms and industries emerge in one nation to gain leading international positions. However, his justifications for these clusterings are on more traditional agglomeration economy lines, focusing on the specifics of particular industries, rather than some conception of flexible specialisation in general.

The modern debate over locational advantages finds an echo in the writings of Alfred Marshall (1919) and his concept of the industrial district. In the Marshallian industrial district, special labour factors (local traditions of specialist skills, for example) produce agglomerations of industries and permit larger scale production. Examples, cited by Marshall, included skilled engineering districts, such as small arms manufacture in the West Midlands, and jewellery quarters (see, for example, Wise, 1949). Clusters of specialist activity encourage and permit the supply of appropriate industrial space.

Other aspects of changing production technology may similarly lead to new types of industrial clustering. One feature of modern production is the breakdown of vertical integration. Core business is the new emphasis with the removal of previous vertical linkages. Much cited is the automobile industry's adoption of just-in-time components delivery in place of either making the part themselves or holding large stocks of standardised components from a limited number of suppliers (Imai, 1986; Schoenberger, 1987). In place of production agreements and guaranteed sales, the component supplier must, at short-notice, meet the requirements of the producer/assembler while carrying the inventory and variable capacity costs. This has spatial property impacts in that the components suppliers need close access to the production plant. This can be seen in the development of industrial parks to serve Nissan in the North East of England. Vertical disintegration and outsourcing change the nature of industrial property required: the large integrated factory may give way to smaller units of productive space, clustered geographically.

One further aspect of contemporary industrial location should be noted: a tendency towards greater geographical separation of firms' activities. Rather than being concentrated on a single site, as was common up to the 1970s, the head office may be in one location, research and development in another and productive plant in totally separate locations. Massey (1984) has called this a restructured *spatial division of labour*. The separate functional aspects of production, once they are freed from the need to be located together, can adopt the preferred locations for their particular spheres of activity. For example, the head office and research functions require access to skilled labour markets and gain from urbanisation economies, while the production plants may be located in areas of lower cost labour.

Improvements in information technology and communications have allowed greater potential for assembly plants to be based in different countries. Thus, firms operating internationally seek low-cost labour sites in the newly-industrialising countries, or on the periphery of developed regions. Senior and general managerial functions concentrate elsewhere, particularly in the multi-national firm's home country; while specialised business and producer services are sourced predominantly from the world's major metropolitan areas. From a commercial property perspective, the spatial division of labour implies a sectoral separation of industrial and office property.

The extent to which these changes have empirically changed the configuration of industrial location across the world is difficult to assess. Some writers have suggested that 'globalisation' is overstressed; that industrial production is still overwhelmingly based in the advanced industrial nations and perhaps that large-scale regional trade blocks are emerging, instead of true globalisation – for example, the three regions of the Americas, Europe and SE Asia (Hirst and Thompson, 1996). Precise trends in industrial property markets are, therefore, difficult to predict. There is strong evidence of change, but disagreement over its nature and future trajectories. Nonetheless, the spatial implications of the different views affect the volume, type and location of the industrial property required. Each of them suggests that the domestic economy is no longer the prime focus of large-scale industrial concerns, and this trend, if nothing else, has encouraged a greater international dimension in industrial property markets.

The space needed for new working practices is often distinct from that available in traditional industrial buildings, increasing their functional obsolescence. Operations are smaller scale due to the small-batch nature of production and increased use of out-sourcing. Space must be more flexible. Institutional market structures – such as lease lengths – need to be more flexible in response to a more volatile business environment and shorter product cycles. Thus the process of industrial change has a major impact upon local property markets.

Deindustrialisation has led to much redundant industrial property in, for example, the North of England and the 'rustbelt' of the North-East United States. A lack of industrial property demand in such areas produces high vacancy levels, and may have a blighting effect on the surrounding area. The consequences may persist for years – not least where old industrial processes have resulted in contamination and pollution.

RETAIL LOCATION

Theories of retail location cover two interrelated areas: the consumer's store choice decision and the retailer's store location decision. In both these areas, the classical models do not completely explain changing patterns of retail behaviour. For store choice, Christaller's (1933) central place theory is predicated on consumers making single purpose shopping trips. It copes less well with multi-purpose shopping trips. For store location, most models of competitive behaviour (derived from Hotelling's (1929) pioneering work) predict a dispersed pattern of retail outlets rather than the retail clustering observed. Thus, although the models provide a basic framework for considering consumer and retailer behaviour, they need to be adapted to account for observed spatial patterns.

Consumer behaviour and the store choice decision lead to geographical variations in sales potential and, hence, profitability for retailers. As a result, willingness to pay rent to occupy land and buildings varies by location. Retailers' locational decisions depend on their assessment of sales potential, the location of competitors *and* the availability of space in the form of existing shops or land for development. Supply of space depends on landowner and developer behaviour and on planning rules and regulations. Supply-side constraints have been neglected in the retail location literature.

Store choice models

Central place theory, developed by Christaller and adapted by Lösch (1954), is based on the concepts of *range* and *threshold*.

The *range* of a good is the maximum distance that a consumer will travel to buy it. This is a function of its utility to the consumer, its price and the cost of the journey to purchase it. The range is the geographic point where price and transport costs equal utility. Low price, convenience and perishable goods all have a short range. For low value goods, a long journey would add too much to the total price while, in Christaller's time, perishable goods might be impaired by a long journey time. In contrast, higher value goods have a larger range. Goods with a short range tend to be purchased more frequently, while those with a large range have a lower frequency of purchase.

The *threshold* defines the minimum demand needed for a store to be profitable. It varies according to the nature of the goods sold. If the population is distributed evenly across space, and has identical preferences, the most efficient location for a store offering a particular good is at the centre of the trade area defined by the range – the central place. If transport costs are uniform, the range defines a circular trade area. A network of central places with circular hinterlands, however, would leave some of the population unserved. The nearest mosaic pattern to a circle that ensures that the whole geographic area is supplied with shopping facilities is that based on a hexagon Thus central place theory proposes a hexagonal net of trade areas.

It was shown above that articles required less frequently have the greatest range. There are, consequently, fewer central places supplying them. Higher-order central places also have hexagonal trade areas. Lower-order goods consequently have hexagonal trade areas nested inside the wider trade areas of the higher order central places

Empirical tests of the Christaller model are, at best, mixed.[2] There is evidence for an urban service hierarchy, but consumer behaviour fails to conform to the predictions of the model, except in predominantly rural areas. Theoretical problems arise with the assumptions that consumers make a single trip to purchase specific goods and patronise the nearest store supplying them. A shopper purchasing a higher order good from a more distant centre may, at the same time, purchase a convenience good, thereby reducing total shopping transport costs.

Consumer shopping behaviour has also altered considerably since Christaller's time, weakening the theory's applicability. Initially, mass transit favoured city centre shopping; then rising car ownership and growing congestion reduced the appeal of the CBD. Higher living standards have led to new shopping mixes. In addition, changes in domestic storage technologies, through the advent of fridges and freezers, have reduced the need for frequent shopping trips to ensure fresh produce. As a result of these changes, the dominance of the town centre as a favoured retail location has been eroded and new types of retail property – notably the out-of-town grocery superstore and the large floor area retail warehouse – have arisen in response to these changes in consumer behaviour. These are discussed further below.

Gravity models and market potential

A second family of models dealing with store choice and consumer behaviour derive from Reilly's (1929) *law of retail gravitation*.[3] Reilly argued that a city attracts trade from a town in its hinterland in proportion to the size of the city and inversely to the square of distance between a city i and a town j:

$$T_i = P_i/d_{ij}^2 \qquad (4.1)$$

where T_i is the trade pull of the city; P_i is the city's population; and d_{ij} is the distance between the town and the city. The break-point, the trade boundary between two cities i and k be given by:

$$d_{ix} = d_{ik}/(1 + \sqrt{(P_i/P_k)}) \qquad (4.2)$$

Thus, if the population of city i is 250,000, the population of city k is 500,000 and the distance between them is 120km, then the break-point will be $(120/(1 + \sqrt{(500/250)})$, or around 50km from city i.

The Reilly model defines a break-point between two cities or shopping centres and assumes that all the consumers resident in a particular settlement go to just one of the cities. In more complex settings, with many competing centres, there may be overlapping catchment areas. Retail analysts seek to estimate what proportion of consumers in a town or village goes to particular stores; or, equivalently, estimate the probability of shoppers patronising

89

specific ones. Huff (1963; 1964) generalised the Reilly model to estimate the probability of a consumer from place i visiting a store or shopping centre located at j. The probability of patronising each shopping centre or city is a function of its own attributes and those of competitor locations. In the Reilly model, a city's attraction is based on population size. However, other factors might be retail floor space, the mix of retail outlets or other non-retail factors. The probability of a consumer visiting a particular centre is given by:

$$C_{ij} = (A_j/d_{ij}^{\lambda}) / \Sigma \, A_j/d_{ij}^{\lambda} \qquad\qquad (4.3)$$

where:

C_{ij} = the probability of a consumer from i patronising centre j
A_j = the attractiveness of centre j (population, retail floor space or other factors)
d_{ij} = the distance between i and j
λ = a coefficient measuring consumer sensitivity to distance (not necessarily = 2)
$\Sigma \, A_j/d_{ij}^{\lambda}$ = a summation over all competitor stores

Application of Huff's model can be demonstrated with the following simple example. Assume three shopping centres with distances from a residential area and floor sizes as shown below. Let the distance sensitivity coefficient, $\lambda = 2$ (the Reilly gravity model assumption), and a centre's attractiveness be a consequence of relative floor size of the centre:

Centre	Distance (km)	Floor size (m^2,000s)				
A	5	60	$P_A = 60/5^2 / (60/5^2 + 80/7^2 + 50/4^2)$	= 0.335
B	7	80	$P_B = 80/7^2 / (60/5^2 + 80/7^2 + 50/4^2)$	= 0.228
C	4	50	$P_C = 50/4^2 / (60/5^2 + 80/7^2 + 50/4^2)$	= 0.437

The coefficients of the Huff model can be estimated empirically using survey data on the behaviour of individual shoppers at rival centres. Such a model may be used empirically to determine how much trade a new store might be expected to attract from competitors. The model may be adapted to include a more complex measure of shopping centre attraction.

In measuring the retail attractiveness of a city for consumers, population is only a crude proxy for the attributes that draw consumers. It is based on the assumption that the size of a centre is proportional to the number and range of retail outlets present, as in the Christaller model. Property-specific variables might include the number and mix of outlets, price competitiveness, and the total retail floor space in a centre. The attractiveness of a centre may also be a function of local accessibility, such as public transport routes and available car parking, environment and other non-retail attractions such as leisure or cultural facilities. Survey data may be used to assess the significance of these variables. Alternatively, where sales turnover figures or rents are known, statistical analysis may be used.[4]

The expected market potential of competing locations is the critical factor in store location decisions. Turnover determines profitability – and hence shops' ability to pay rent. Once a retail development is completed, its rental information can assist in decisions to expand and build another development nearby. Rising rents may act as a signal for developers and investors to produce more retail space, or change non-retail space into shops, provided that planning controls permit the development or change of use.

As more stores locate in an area, so the attraction of that area for consumers increases, leading to greater sales potential. For the retailer, however, diminished returns may set in. Retailers thus seek to identify market saturation. One method is to calculate an index of market potential based on population, income levels, consumer spending patterns and the number and size of stores. Empirical results point to market saturation following an S-shaped curve, with sales per unit initially increasing as new stores open then flattening (or even declining) as saturation sets in.

Retail clustering

Analysis of retail competition was initially based on Hotelling's (1929) model of monopolistic competition. This implied that two retailers offering minimal product or service differentials would cluster together. Subsequent work in this framework, however, argues for a dispersed equilibrium (Eppli and Benjamin, 1994). Empirical evidence, highlights a clustering of retailers. There is both heterogeneous clustering – where different types of retail outlets are in close proximity – and homogeneous clustering – where similar types of outlets are found at the same location. Traditional retail competition theory and fact seem to be at variance with each other.

With heterogeneous clustering, the theoretical difficulty can be resolved by recourse to scope economies in shopping and the external benefits clustering provides to individual retailers. When heterogeneous stores cluster together, consumers may make multiple purpose shopping trips, and so benefit from economies of scope by reducing transport costs. Lower-order goods retailers gain external benefits from the drawing power of larger, higher-order stores. In planned shopping centres, there are usually one or more 'anchor' stores – department stores or prestige retailers – to draw in consumers. The extra shopping traffic results in a higher probability of sales for the lower-order retailers. The anchor stores are normally able to capture a share of those external economies through negotiated lower rents or incentive packages.

The impact of the loss of an anchor store can be seen in studies of US shopping centres, where rents are normally linked to sales turnover. For example, Gatzlaff *et al.* (1994) report a 25 per cent decline in rental rates for tenants after the loss of anchor stores in malls in Florida and Georgia.

Explanations of homogeneous clustering, for example, jewellery or clothing quarters, generally rest on consumer uncertainty. For comparison goods, product-differentiated goods bought less frequently, the consumer is uncertain whether individual outlets have the desired product. Clustering reduces the consumer's search costs and makes a purchase more likely. The consumer may also gain from price competition between adjacent outlets.

The problem of complexity

Vandell and Carter (1993) suggest that the increasing complexity of shopping models may undermine the apparent usefulness of retail location theory. Models of retail location based on single purpose shopping trips have had to be adapted to deal with the complexities of consumer and retailer behaviour. In doing so, it has become more difficult to translate theoretical models into practical contexts because of the increasing number of variables and the interactions between them. Furthermore, trading areas overlap and there is greater competition between shopping centres. The statistical problems in handling such complexity may be intractable.

Ideally, following Bacon (1984), the objective should be to develop an equilibrium model. In it, store location is the supply side and consumer's store choice is demand. Equilibrium is reached when the distribution of outlets is such that no store can improve its sales by moving. Given the complexities of consumer behaviour and the changing nature of retailing, this may be unrealisable. Furthermore, such an equilibrium framework needs to consider the supply of retail space: Bacon's model treats retail property as given, elastically responding to shifts in retailer demand.

Traditional models of the location of retail property have emphasised the retail hierarchy and the importance of the town centre as a focus for shopping activity. They may need to be adapted to deal with changes in technology and consumer life-styles.

Technical change and new shopping patterns

The locational advantages of city centres have been eroded by two factors.

- The outmigration of city populations, particularly of wealthier households. This has tended to encourage the decentralisation of retail activity, with the development of out-of-town neighbourhood shopping centres.
- Technical developments in transport. The decline of public forms of transit and the growth of car ownership have both had a major impact. Households take longer trips and carry more shopping on a single

journey, breaking the hierarchical shopping centre pattern envisaged by Christaller. At the same time, congestion and the difficulty and cost of finding car parking in city centres is a major disadvantage. Retailers are unable to provide car parking in city centres because of high land values and so seek out-of-town locations where land costs are lower and accessibility better.

These changes have created waves of out-of-town retail development (Schiller, 1986). Following the development of neighbourhood shopping centres, many 'large ticket' stores selling consumer durables moved away from the traditional high street to out-of-town locations with ample parking and sufficiently low land costs to permit the more extensive display of goods. These sites were initially individual, stand-alone developments but increasingly clustered together into retail parks.

North America and parts of Europe also saw an expansion of retail 'strips' alongside major roads on the edges of cities. Retail parks and retail warehouses were a major growth sector in property development and investment in the 1980s and 1990s. A further phase of decentralisation came with the movement of grocery superstores away from the high street. As these sold an increasing range of products, and were able to price competitively due to economies of scale, many high street retailers (butchers, bakers, for example) were unable to compete and survive.

Verdict (1991) suggests that floor space for out-of-town retail superstores increased from 1.7 million m^2 to 8.5 million m^2 between 1980 and 1990. Their share of overall retail space increased from less than 5 per cent in 1980 to around 17 per cent in 1990. The share of retail sales mirrors that of floor space, with superstores capturing 17 per cent of all retail sales in 1990. The major retail sectors occupying superstores are do-it-yourself outlets (40 per cent of space) and grocers (31 per cent). The grocery chains dominate sales, with a 68 per cent share in 1990.

The growth of out-of-town superstores was followed by the development of regional shopping centres, large covered shopping malls offering a large number of outlets and mix of shops.[5] In the UK, the first centre opened was Brent Cross in North London (approved in 1968), followed by Milton Keynes. In the late 1980s and early 1990s, the Metro Centre near Newcastle, Merry Hill in the Midlands, Meadowhall outside Sheffield and Lakeside near Thurrock opened. Regional shopping centres can have a devastating impact upon the retail property markets in neighbouring town centres – for example, Merry Hill's effect on Dudley and Meadowhall's impact on Sheffield. Sales diversion, business failure and out-migration of multiple retailers leads to high vacancy rates and falling High Street rents and values. A vicious circle may set in where boarded-up shops, graffiti, vandalism and fringe uses create an unfavourable environment leading to further loss of sales.[6]

While the impact of major centres is easy to recognise, the other forms of decentralisation have a similar, if less dramatic impact on the traditional high street, with shrinkage of the most favourable area (the 'prime pitch') and a decline in the investment activity needed to refurbish and modernise the retail stock. Planning action may be taken to address the decline of the town centre. In the UK, planning guidance has attempted to restrict out-of-town development to preserve the 'vitality and viability' of town centres. Town centre management schemes aim to upgrade the environment, encourage pedestrianisation, increase accessibility, improve security and create events that draw in shoppers. The difficulty with such schemes is their funding: any tax on local retailers worsens their financial position in the short run and voluntary contributions from retailers lead to coordination problems and difficulties associated with non-participation.

Technological developments have other impacts on the demand for retail space. Information technology tends to reduce the overall requirement for retail space as automated stock control, electronic fund transfer and similar innovations reduce the need for inventory and administrative space. This has created redundant areas in the upper floors of shops on the high street. This can be seen most starkly in the reduction in space requirements of retail banks with the rapid growth of automatic teller machines, increasing use of telephone banking services, and the out-of-town computer and administration centres. More profound impacts may result from the growth of home shopping by catalogue, by telephone and, increasingly, through the Internet.[7] Shops may thus become merely showrooms, with customer delivery a separate process. This creates a new property demand – for retail distribution warehouses. These need to be near major population centres but, due to high space demands, require low land costs. However, good access to the road network may be the key locational variable.

OFFICE LOCATION AND THE CENTRAL BUSINESS DISTRICT

The general influences affecting the location of offices are similar to those of manufacturing industry, although the weightings differ. They include factor input costs (such as labour and rent), transport and communication costs, agglomeration economies and the quality of life in specific urban areas. The locational decision is a two-stage process. A firm must decide on its 'regional' location. The scale of the region considered has grown over time. This dimension for many firms is increasingly an international decision about which continent and country provide the best options. Then, for most enterprises, urban areas offer advantages, so the firm has to think about the best urban location – taking into account supply constraints as well as the net benefits of specific urban districts.

International and regional location

Dunning and Norman (1983; 1987) conducted survey research on the factors underlying international office location. They found seven factors dominated the decision:

- ease and quality of communications;
- housing and healthcare for senior executives;
- availability of suitable office space;
- language and cultural factors;
- the overall cost of living;
- availability and quality of executive and professional staff; and
- government attitude to new firms.

These factors are dominated by labour force and market considerations, if communications are regarded as a proxy for market access. Moore *et al.* (1991) obtain similar findings from a survey of 1,400 European firms. Twenty-seven per cent of firms stated that customer access was the most important factor in office location – followed by regional assistance (emphasising the important role played by government); conditions for future expansion; the quality and size of the available workforce; and, finally, wage costs.

Regional location also depends on the nature of the service provided. The headquarters of firms with national and international markets tend to cluster in major cities – the upper level of the 'urban hierarchy'. More localised firms have a more dispersed office pattern. International financial and business service firms are concentrated in a small number of what are often termed 'global' or 'world' cities – where agglomeration economies are greatest. These cities are argued by some to be the modern command centres of an increasingly global economy (Friedmann, 1986; LPAC, 1991; Sassen, 1991; Llewellyn-Davis, 1996). Cultural factors (arts, theatres and other facilities) add to their attractions. Some cities have a regional function while others serve a more restricted hinterland. Figure 4.3 sets out the Noyelle and Stanback (1984) description of the US urban hierarchy – a model much used in subsequent US office research.

There is some US evidence of a dispersal of corporate headquarters away from major cities, in contrast to the centralising tendencies considered above. Several factors may be encouraging this trend. Some arise from the greater attractiveness of non-central locations, and others from structural changes in firm size and economic activity. Physical relocation might result from the greater locational flexibility caused by improvements in communications technology. This has cut the need for the physical movement of both goods and people, reducing the impact of transport costs on location. Pressures to locate in major cities for proximity to high-order business

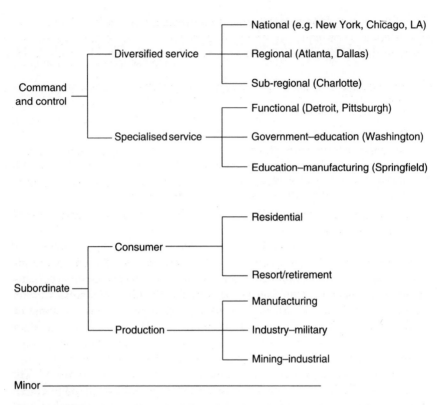

Figure 4.3 The urban hierarchy in the USA
Source: Adapted from Noyelle and Stanback (1984)

services have also been weakened for similar reasons, enabling relocation to avoid urban diseconomies. Both O'Brien (1992) and Peet (1991) argue that the general role of geography in business activity has been eroded by developments in information technology. The greater size of many modern large corporations has also reduced the number of locations at which major headquarters are sited. Mergers and acquisition activity has been part of this process. Holloway and Wheeler (1991), for example, suggest that 20 per cent of corporate headquarters losses in US cities in the period 1980–7 were the result of merger and acquisition activity. Finally, suburbanisation stems from *in situ* growth and decline and from broad economic shifts, such as that away from manufacturing towards services. All these factors have weakened the role of the central place of most US cities as the necessary location for at least one or more corporate headquarters.

Metropolitan diseconomies may have encouraged a drift away from the CBD. Traffic congestion has grown. Higher incomes have encouraged more journeys, and the mode of travel has shifted towards greater reliance on car usage. It reduces the accessibility advantages of the CBD and contributes to air pollution and poor neighbourhood environments. Greater relative costs have become a consequence of the earlier success of the central city. In four key areas, the relative cost disadvantage of the central city has become worse:

- rent on land and buildings, which is of particular importance to firms seeking to expand their operations, and so needing more space;
- labour costs are higher to compensate the workforce for high commuting or residential costs;
- taxes may be higher in major cities as a result of out-migration of skilled labour to suburban and small town locations, leaving a population with higher levels of social deprivation and dependency and a lower tax base to make transfer payments; and
- out-migration of skilled labour lowers the labour market advantage of large metropolitan areas.

Evidence on the relative importance of these effects can be found in the literature. Lyons (1994) examined change in the top 250 corporate headquarters in the US between 1974 and 1989, using the Noyelle and Stanback urban hierarchy model, noted earlier, as a framework. Table 4.1 sets out some of Lyons's results. He found that the proportion of headquarters in 'command and control' cities had remained very high, at 95 per cent. Although the proportion of headquarters in major cities had fallen from 60 per cent to 49 per cent, this was almost entirely explained by the decline of New York – still home to nearly a third of the largest American corporations. He suggests that relocation is a minor factor in explaining shifts; instead *in situ* growth and decline of firms was the main explanation. These results cast doubt on the idea of a movement away from major cities to those lower in the urban hierarchy. Lyon's also notes that significant growth of regional centres was limited, perhaps indicating the emergence of new national centres rather than evidence of dispersal.

Evidence of decentralisation of office activity in London from 1964 to 1992 is shown in Figure 4.4. During that period, nearly 200,000 jobs were lost from central London as a result of office relocation (JLW, 1990). In the

Table 4.1 Change in corporate headquarters location, USA, 1974–89 (percentages)

Type of centre	1974	1989	Change
New York	44	32	−12
Other national centres	16	17	+1
Regional diversified	18	24	+6
Subregional diversified	1	3	+2
Specialised command centres	17	19	+2
Subordinate and minor	4	5	+1

Source: Lyons (1994)

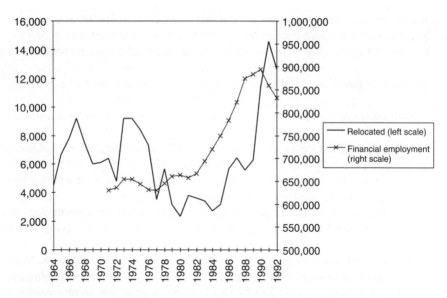

Figure 4.4 Central London office relocation and financial services employment, 1964–92
Source: JLW (1990); Hendershott *et al.* (1997)

early years of the period, decentralisation was encouraged by government as part of regional policy, through agencies such as the Location of Offices Bureau. However, office relocation was not associated with a decline in office-based employment in central London. Financial services employment in the area grew over the same period. It may be that certain types of office uses moved out of London (particularly lower-order administrative functions) but were replaced by high-order, international firms requiring a central location.[8] A number of pension funds and life insurance companies moved their retail and administrative functions out of London in the 1980s, but at the same time a large number of overseas banks and securities houses established a presence in central London.

Intraurban location and the CBD

Many of the advantages of particular urban locations have already implicitly been considered in the previous section. The best way to approach the issue explicitly is to consider the benefits of the CBD, and then to compare them to the locational advantages of other urban locations.

The benefits of the CBD are surveyed in Daniels (1991). He suggests that centralisation allows service firms to reduce uncertainty: through optimal access to a diverse labour market; communications technology infrastructure; and client and market information. CBD concentrations reflect both inertial forces and agglomeration economies. Inertia results from the embedded infrastructure and institutions in historic cities that facilitate communication and investment. Agglomeration economies follow from these initial advantages. One key reason why firms continue to seek central locations is that face-to-face contacts are important in preserving competitive advantage. This emerged from the empirical work of Goddard (1973) on functional linkages between firms in London and in the US studies of Archer (1981) and Clapp (1980). Goddard (1975) and Daniels and Holly (1983) suggest that more routine office jobs have shown dispersal patterns similar to manufacturing plants.

Rapid advances in information technology have reduced some of the information advantages of a central location. A non-CBD located firm can trade electronically, pass information via electronic mail, access information on the Internet, use video conferencing – enjoying many of the benefits of a central location without bearing the associated urban diseconomies.

A two-fold intra-urban division is implied by the arguments above. Non-routine, decision-making and research jobs, relying upon direct information transfer and contacts, are pulled towards large, diversified, service oriented CBDs at the top of the urban hierarchy (Malecki, 1991; Hepworth, 1989). Firms using less specialised labour inputs, conversely, seek a suburban location. As early as 1977, Daniels observed that administrative and clerical functions were moving to the suburbs at a faster rate than professional and managerial tasks. Applying Massey's (1984) concept of spatial divisions of labour, a firm may separate out functions within its own organisation and decentralise 'back-office' functions – administration, routine clerical and data-processing tasks – to lower labour cost and building rent locations, leaving higher-level information-intensive decision-making tasks in the CBD. In terms of the spatial models analysed in Chapter 3, higher order office users will have a steeper bid-rent curve than more routine office functions and hence outbid such uses for central locations (see Figure 4.5).

The office space required at the centre is high specification; while ancillary office activity, located further out, has lower requirements. However, firms supplying business services at the offices of clients distributed throughout an urban region (business software companies, for example) may locate outside a metropolitan area but close to good road links. The office space in this case will be higher specification, such as that found in office parks in the Thames Valley area.

The final aspect of intra-urban location is that of suburban centres. Arguments similar to those used to explain the benefits of the CBD can be used to explain their existence, although the scale of the agglomeration effects will obviously be lower in a subcentre. A simple model has also been used to explain the development of office subcentres (Helsley and Sullivan, 1991). A firm enters a market and selects a location. The costs at that location are sunk costs, acting as an inertia to movement. Other firms entering

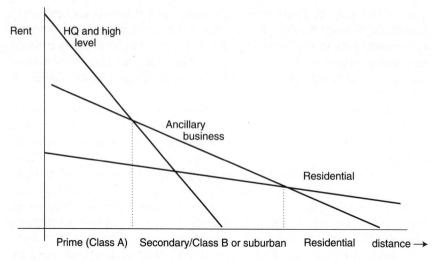

Figure 4.5 Office space and functional specialisation
Source: Adapted from Clapp (1993)

benefit from agglomeration economies but, as the centre increases in size, total costs rise until it becomes profitable for a new subcentre to form. Shifts in the nature of business organisation that reduce agglomeration economies encourage new centre formation and decentralisation.

New working practices

A number of recent trends in business organisation suggest that there are some new influences on the locational dynamics of the office sector. The new developments include home working and 'telecommuting' – whereby work-ers spend some, or all, of their time away from a formal office but remain connected to it via computer modems, telephones and faxes. Both imply changes in the relationship between a firm's number of employees and its requirements for office space. Another change in the desired office space per worker ratio arises from intensification of office usage through 'hot desking' and 'office hotelling'.[9] Workers no longer need to have their own office or desk, but can share space in a central office.

To date, radical predictions of the decline of the office as a result of such developments seem overstated. It may be that some office demand has been displaced elsewhere to dispersed meeting places or into the home. Further-more, most of the well-publicised cases relate only to IT firms and manage-ment consultancies, where staff spend a great deal of their time with clients. Other types of office activity may be less suited to these developments. Nonetheless, better technology still facilitates the more intensive use of office

100

space. This alters both the quantitative relationship between employment growth and demand for business space, and the geographic relation between employment growth and office demand. In the latter context, for example, a firm with a central location may take on more staff but those staff may be accommodated in out-of-town satellite offices, in serviced offices or have no formal office space at all.

Business practice has also changed in the 1990s with the greater use of team working, growth in outsourcing of services, noted above in relation to industrial property, and 'delayering' – flattening the corporate hierarchy. Such practices lead to smaller firms, with a peripheral workforce of part-time and contract staff. 'Core focused' businesses may also rely on ancillary firms to meet cyclical increases in demand. Out-sourcing creates a network of linkages between firms and their suppliers reinforcing agglomeration economies. These trends are increasing the number of enterprises that require smaller, more flexible property. This may be unavailable in traditional central business districts, encouraging location on the fringe of city centres. The new office accommodation may be based in converted industrial or warehousing space – vacated through the decline and dispersal of manufacturing. Traditional office buildings in city centres may be inappropriate for firms making extensive use of team working. Newer, out-of-town space may, therefore, be favoured, unless planning rules permit city centre redevelopment or major refurbishment.[10]

Trends in business practice, consequently, have a considerable impact on the nature and location of office demand. Some of the changes in business methods reflect technological developments; others are a product of changing input and marketing requirements; while contemporary management fashions have considerable impact on organisational structures and interfirm relationships. The combination of these influences makes prediction of future office requirements difficult. There is some evidence in the late 1990s that the break-up of old corporate structures may be going into reverse. Market pressures and the need to hold on to scarce highly skilled labour, for example, are leading to greater concentration of several 'high-order' activities – notably in giant mergers taking place in investment banking and accountancy. In the late 1980s, the demise of the large-scale office was widely predicted, and developers were criticised for building too many of them. That prediction proved to be wrong. A decade later, the most acute shortage of office accommodation in major centres, like London, was precisely of such large-scale, high quality accommodation. This example illustrates that property development is not simply risky because of the existence of property cycles but also, and more fundamentally, because of the substantial uncertainty associated with predicting future demand.

In summary, the geographic demand for office space is influenced by the type of service activity in question. The higher the level of activity, the more agglomeration economies encourage spatial concentration. Major metropolitan centres are capturing an increasing share of high-order business service sector growth; face-to-face contacts and knowledge transfer and processing can make a city centre location critical. Routine administrative, clerical and data processing activities are more cost-sensitive and are moving away from city centres to reduce labour, property and congestion costs. There are opposing tendencies, consequently, in the impact of technical change on office location. Some technical change is increasing the attractiveness of agglomerations, while others are reducing its benefits. Yet, even for the latter, the inertia deriving from sunk, search and moving costs acts as a friction to movement. In the UK, the contractual nature of leases further discourages relocation (Lizieri *et al.,* 1997). There is little evidence of the end of the office, though new work practices are changing office requirements in some types of economic activity. Predicting future office demand is, and will remain, a highly uncertain activity.

SUMMARY AND CONCLUSION

As noted in Chapter 3, the rent paid for a property reflects its utility to the user. This utility is a function both of land and building characteristics and locational advantages. Rents will thus vary spatially. Firms will make locational decisions based on the profit they can make at different locations. Competitive pricing should ensure that, in equilibrium, land is allocated to its 'highest and best use' – that is the use that can make the most profit from occupying that site. Inertia and the effects of the planning system have an impact on spatial distributions.

Standard location models were developed in the early years of the twentieth century. Changes in the nature of transport and communications, in the organisation of business activity and the behaviour of consumers require that they be amended considerably if they are to provide good approximations of observed behaviour or form the basis of locational decision-making.

Industrial location models that follow Weber's framework suggest that firms seek the lowest cost location taking into account transportation costs for input and shipment to market, labour costs and agglomeration economies. Technological change has led to increased mobility for manufacturing firms. This has emphasised the importance of agglomeration economies, both localisation economies (specific to the sector) and urbanisation economies (benefits for business in general). It has also led to considerable regional restructuring of industry. Deindustrialisation may lead to rapid falls in property and land values, with many vacant and derelict sites.

A number of authors have proposed that a shift in industrial organisation is occurring, moving from mass-production (Fordism) to craft-based smaller scale production (flexible specialism). Flexible specialism should lead to specialised industrial localities (similar to Marshallian industrial linkages)

102

benefiting from linkages, specialist labour skills and knowledge transfer. Empirical evidence for this shift is mixed.

Massey has noted that improved communications technology and changes in business structure have enabled firms to separate different aspects of their operation geographically – generating a new 'spatial division of labour'. The locational requirements of the separated elements (for example, assembly or research and development) may be quite distinct and cross international boundaries. Whereas, previously, a manufacturing firm might have had its office headquarters located at its main production site, now the office and industrial property may be far apart.

Retail location models cover both the store choice decision (where the consumers chose to shop) and the store location decision (where a retailer should site a store to maximise profit). These choices affect demand for space and, hence, shop rents.

Christaller's central place theory, based on single purpose shopping trips, suggests that retail activity should be organised in a hierarchy. Frequently bought low-order goods should be bought locally, while consumers make longer journeys to buy high-order comparison goods. The prevalence of multi-purpose shopping trips cast doubt on some of central place theory's basic assumptions.

Gravity models, developed from Reilly's original formulation, attempt to measure the attraction of particular stores or retail locations. They enable retailers to estimate market potential and the likely sales impact of new stores Favoured locations experience demand pressure, higher rents and, subject to planning constraints, more retail development.

Retail outlets cluster together. Dissimilar stores cluster together since consumers make multi-purpose shopping trips to minimise costs. This enables stores to gain external economies due to the drawing power of other retailers. Stores selling similar and comparison goods cluster since this reduces consumer uncertainty and search costs.

Technological change and congestion and environmental diseconomies in city centres have led to a tendency for retail activity to move to out-of-town locations. Grocery superstores, retail parks, retail warehouses and regional shopping centres have all resulted in loss of sales in traditional high street locations. New property forms have been created to meet the demand for out-of-town retailing, in particular the large floor space retail warehouse. Planning intervention has attempted to check the tendency towards decentralisation and greenfield site development.

For office location, urban agglomeration economies play a major role. This would be expected to produce an intensively-used central business district. The dominance of office-based services in city centres has been increased by decentralising tendencies for manufacturing, warehousing and some elements of retail. However, in city centre locations, there are diseconomies (congestion costs, higher labour costs, high property costs). These act as a decentralising force and have resulted in the growth of suburban and non-urban office clusters. Developers have provided office parks to meet the needs of decentralising office users. Routine administrative, clerical and data-processing tasks are more likely to migrate out from the central city than higher-order information processing and decision-making tasks, due to the importance of face-to-face contacts and access to specialised business services for the latter functions.

Technological change and changing business practices are altering both the locational requirements of firms and the relationship between employment and office space needs. Examples include telecommuting, homeworking, office hotelling and hot-desking. These tend to reduce office space per worker ratios, such that an increase in employment results in a smaller increase in demand for commercial space than previously. The evidence suggests that the impact of such changes is more muted than is sometimes argued.

While the discussion of location has been structured around the 'traditional' property sectors of industrial, retail and office property, it should be noted that technological and business change has blurred the sectoral boundaries. The property and locational requirements of high technology manufacturing firms, out-of-town retailers and business service firms seeking space for back office operations are very similar. All require good transport linkages and access to labour (consumer) markets. The specification of a high technology factory with a high research and development component, a call centre and a retail warehouse are similar and accommodated in the 'big box' structures found on retail and business parks. This specification is similar to that required by leisure operators – for example, for multiplex cinemas. Higher order office users may require higher specification (or prestige) buildings in city centre locations, while the property needs of comparison goods retailers for town centre shops or units in shopping centres remain distinct. This will have implications for property investment decisions, explored in Part 3.

A major weakness of many of the traditional models of location is their neglect of the supply side. They implicitly assume that land is available and appropriate buildings are supplied in response to changes in demand. Chapter 3 examined the theoretical response of the land market to changes in demand. Chapter 5 now discusses the behavioural and institutional aspects of property market adjustment.

5

PROPERTY SUPPLY AND
INSTITUTIONAL ANALYSIS

INTRODUCTION

The supply of commercial property has been examined in two contexts in earlier chapters: in the development supply process in Chapter 2, and in the workings of the land market in Chapter 3. Those analyses for many economists are sufficient specification of the supply side. This chapter, nonetheless, explores the broader institutional context of property development; so it is necessary to give greater than usual justification for its existence.

Formal completeness of the earlier supply analysis can be seen from a brief recap of its propositions. The competitive property market model in Chapter 2 has separate developer and land markets, which, when combined, generate the supply function for new commercial property. New building only takes place if property prices rise above replacement costs. Above that trigger point, extra supply is subject to a rising supply price because of diminishing returns in the construction industry. The level at which replacement cost is currently set depends on land prices, as well as on construction and other development costs. Land prices are determined by supply and demand in the land market. Commercial property owners compete amongst each other, and against other land uses, for desired land sites. All the inputs to the supply process are covered in the model and equilibrium conditions are assumed to be met.

Chapter 3 then introduced more detail on the land market. There the determination of land rent for any particular location and commercial use was examined, the dynamics of land supply considered and the role of land use planning investigated. Externalities and public goods, such as agglomeration economies and public transportation infrastructure, enhance the usefulness of any land site to its potential users and the prices bid for the land. Some of the benefits of the existence of those externalities accrue to the landowner as rent.

The models of new supply surveyed in Chapter 9, for example, are based on the supply variables cited in Chapter 2, or a subset of them. For a large number of other analyses of property supply, the characteristics described above are sufficient. The reasons centre on the approach adopted by most mainstream economic analyses: an assumption that property markets are competitive. To define an industry as perfectly competitive means that there are many firms, each of which is too small to affect the market price of the homogeneous good they all produce. Firms use similar technologies, face identical input and output prices, and any differences in the preferences and practices of individuals in any of them have no tangible effect on the market. The firm, in the famous phrase, can be 'treated as a black box' with no need to look at what is inside. How firms function, and the institutional contexts in which they exist, have no consequence for market outcomes, by assumption. The competitive model also abstracts from any contextual factors in the supply process, such as acceptable lease lengths and conditions.

If the competitive assumption is dropped, the possibility arises that firms can adopt 'strategic behaviour' with respect to their supply decisions. Strategic behaviour means that firms can adopt strategies in attempts to affect market outcomes for themselves, with a reasonable prospect of those strategies having some positive effect. In this way, firms can hope to earn long-run above normal profit (or economic rent in the terminology of Chapter 3). Many strategic options are open to firms in the appropriate contexts: they can alter the internal organisation of the enterprise, according to prevailing managerial criteria; try to differentiate their product from others on the basis of some advertised characteristic such as 'quality' or 'service'; decide on which markets to supply; try to beat competitors to technical innovations; become a market leader or accept that generally they will follow the pricing behaviour of a larger competitor; undertake acquisitions; and so on.[1] In this way, individuals within firms – either individually or as part of joint decision-making processes - can exercise to some degree their own preferences and beliefs. Individuals may also be partly able to follow their own preferences at times when they are in conflict with the stated objectives of the firm, in what is known as 'opportunistic' behaviour. Making a career move against the interests of the firm or practice, or simply having a quiet life in the office would be two examples of such opportunistic behaviour.

Once strategic behaviour is admitted as a possibility, the context in which it is implemented becomes important – because a strategic move is likely to be successful if it takes account of the circumstances into which it is introduced. The context of history, geography, culture and institutions, therefore, becomes important. Another way of saying this is that the competitive model assumes only certain constraints on maximising behaviour, such as costs and existing technologies. Once outside the world of perfect competition, other constraints become significant: particularly, the likely behaviour of others and the institutional context in which decisions are made and acted on.

The maximisation assumption of the competitive model has also been criticised. It is impossible for humans to maximise across everything, even if they have such objectives in some contexts. This is because of uncertainties, the vast array of necessary information, its costs of acquisition and analysis, and limitations on the processing ability of the human brain. Knowledge and reactions to it are, in the terminology, 'bounded'. Instead, responses to many situations that individuals have to deal with in their daily lives and work-places vary from standardised, unthinking ones through uninformed guesses and calculations based on limited information. North (1990) argues that, at best, only a limited number of decisions made by individuals can ever possibly be based on maximising criteria. The rest are based on bounded information. Such decisions are formed through routinised and other behaviours which seem non-rational when every decision is examined individually, but rational when placed in the context of information and decision-making overload. Institutional practices are one routinised means of making and channelling such decisions. Institutional analysis consequently enables non-maximising behaviour to be investigated without having to assume that individuals replace one goal 'maximising' with another, possibly less credible, one – such as 'satisficing' (that is, a 'quiet life' strategy of doing what is regarded as enough) or a firm maximising sales rather than profits.

The above omissions of the competitive approach to property markets seem good grounds to consider the relevance of a broader range of theories to property supply. Most of the suggested omissions in the competitive model, moreover, have something to do with institutional contexts; so focusing on its domain is useful. However, it is easier to criticise the supposed inadequacies of a particular, well-used theory than to construct good alternatives. So, the other potential approaches must be investigated for their own limitations as well as their benefits.

AN INSTITUTIONAL APPROACH

The previous section suggested that most of the alternatives to the competitive approach of neo-classical economics can be classified in one form or another as institutional approaches to property analysis. It could be said that institutions exist in the model outlined in Chapter 2. It examines property markets in terms of broad generalisations about the behaviour of users, investors, developers and landowners. Yet, beyond this fourfold classification, market agents are undifferentiated. This chapter, conversely, looks at the real life actors, and how they operate in property development – that is, 'organisations and institutions' in the broadest sense. These include not only the financial concerns that invest in commercial property, frequently called 'The Institutions' in the property world, but also other firms and the range of institutional structures through which property markets work. Taking examples from the UK, the chapter considers the complexity of the relationships involved in the development process.

The common practice in institutional research of distinguishing between 'organisations' and 'institutions' is adopted. Organisations are the corporate bodies directly or indirectly involved in commercial property; institutions are the practices and networks that influence the ways in which those organisations operate and interrelate (Rowlinson, 1997). Using North's (1990) analogy, organisations are the players and institutions are the rules of the game. Individuals working within organisations may determine the actions of organisations, depending on the institutional approach adopted, and may indirectly alter institutional practices over time.

Putting emphasis on organisations and institutions when studying a social phenomenon like property supply is called *institutionalism*. Rather than endlessly repeating the phrase 'organisations and institutions', this chapter adopts the standard practice of shortening the phrase to 'institutions' alone; when either institutions or organisations are specifically referred to the context should be clear.

While it is tempting to think that institutional analysis is simply an exercise in realism, putting some descriptive flesh on a previously arid, analytical model, three key theoretical issues are raised in the exercise.

1   *Relevance* If the earlier model is robust and convincing, the additional complexity of real life institutions could simply be descriptive flab – adding nothing of real importance. So the issue of whether institutions matter in understanding property markets has to be considered.

   A simple word count of the current UK literature on property markets would suggest that institutions are enormously important, given the sheer scale of the number of books and articles devoted to analysing them and their effects. What is missing from the earlier model that leads to this response? Reviewing the literature on property development institutions can help to answer this question.

   Even a cursory review of these writings would reveal that each of those analyses has an explicit or implicit understanding, or 'theory', of the role of institutions in property markets. These theories, like the earlier economic model, involve the making of simplifying assumptions and deductions on the basis of them. The discussion of institutional approaches, therefore, has to involve theory when evaluating any of their empirical findings.

2   *Theories of property markets* What theoretical tools are available when considering property institutions? A classification and elaboration of the different approaches to institutions is required to answer this, with the strengths and weaknesses of each considered. This chapter does this by dividing the institutional approaches into six perspectives: neo-classical economics, historical, conflict, behavioural, structure–agency and structures of provision. The relevance of these divisions will become apparent later. It is important to note that few of them represent holistic

theories of institutions, rather they attempt to draw an institutional perspective into wider theoretical approaches to property analysis. To avoid unnecessary digressions, only the institutional component of their analyses are considered, with the broader theoretical stance ignored.

3   *Competing or complementary?* The third, and final, issue is the extent to which the different approaches to property institutions complement or contradict each other and mainstream economic analysis in general. Frequent concern over the abstract nature of economic models suggests that institutional approaches are a real alternative to them – but is the divide, in practice, so great? Conversely, some institutional theories are at variance with mainstream economic approaches; but they might still provide insights that should be added to that standard analysis where relevant.

These three issues about institutions are closely interlinked because, if institutions are important, theories are needed to understand them, and those theories either complement, or conflict with, the early economic model. Each one needs to be kept in mind when approaching this potentially vast topic.

The subsequent two sections briefly describe the institutional structure of commercial property in the UK. The first looks at the institutions that have a direct role in property, as users, developers and owners; while the second examines a wider range of bodies that potentially influence the nature of property development in the context of the 'development pipeline'. Most of the rest of the chapter is then concerned with surveying the approaches adopted to property organisations and institutions in the development process.

The tone of this chapter is more one of critical commentary than other chapters in this book for two reasons. First, institutionalism is often seen as an alternative, although seeing it and the more usual economic approach as complements is the conclusion argued for here. Second, distinctive approaches to institutionalism do not exist in isolation. To an extent, developments in one arise because of problems with others; so, in order to understand the differences and the difficulties in institutionalism, it is necessary to examine each one critically.

Organisations with direct relationships to property development

There are several types of organisation that own and develop commercial property in the UK, so the simple question 'who does what' unfortunately has a complex answer. There is no clear-cut, easy, functional distinction between particular types of organisation and what they do in the property world.

There are three types of relationship to property – lessees (or renters), developers and owners. Three organisational types can also be distinguished, defined by the functional characteristics of the enterprise – users, property developers and financial investors in property.

There is no one-to-one correspondence between the potential relationship to property and type of organisation. Users may own the commercial property they use, having built it in the first place, and so also have investor and developer roles. Alternatively, they may just rent. Even when they are lessees, they might still play a key role in the development process; for example, in sale-and-lease-back operations or as influential tenants in new shopping centres.

Property developers and companies may develop or own – with a feasible continuum ranging from pure developer to pure owner. The financial institutions that invest in property may be shell companies or trusts, used as vehicles to hold property assets, or they may be major companies, employing thousands in their non-property spheres of activity. In the latter case, the institution is a considerable user of office space as well as a property investor. Property investors may develop themselves or purchase speculatively built property. More commonly, a developer tries to gain the interest of a financial institution, as the final investor/purchaser, at the conceptual stage of their project. This means that final investors are often involved in independent developer's development processes as well as their own.

There are several feasible economic explanations for these different combinations, some of which are considered later in the chapter. There may also be non-economic or historical reasons for their existence, which a specifically institutionalist approach may identify. Finally, some institutional arrangements arise for specific tax reasons, such as the traditional tax breaks of the Institutions, which are not considered here.

Empirical evidence of the complexity of organisational arrangements highlights the need for institutionalist perspectives to simplify in order to undertake analysis. As a method, consequently, it cannot be regarded as more 'realistic' than a supply-and-demand oriented economics model *prior* to analysis. Both, unsurprisingly, have to make particular simplifying assumptions when addressing specific questions.

Already this chapter has added a note of caution about the earlier supply-and-demand model. The fact that organisations can simultaneously operate in all four property markets (user, investor, developer and land) and on both the demand and supply sides, suggests that it is certainly possible for at least some of them to use strategic behaviour. The nature of Institutional property investment strategies, for example, is examined in Chapter 10. Such strategic behaviour is bound to have an effect on property prices, although the degree to which prices are altered is empirically unclear.

Organisations with indirect relationships to property development

The institutions with indirect relationships to property are much wider than the array described in the previous section. This is particularly true of development. The additional ones there fall into several categories. Among them are landowners, the utilities, land-use planners, property agents, banks and other financial institutions, legal and financial advisors and, in construction specifically, there are more specialist professionals, project managers and firms. They include: architects; a range of engineers, such as those advising on structural, value, mechanical, heating and ventilation, and lift matters; particular types of surveyor, such as quantity and building surveyors; materials producers, who often supply and fix their products; and several types of construction firm in the guise of project managers, specialist contractors or organisers of labour gangs.

The overall number of specialist types of firm and separate professions is extremely high. Their complexity makes the interest in institutions in property development explicable. The subdivision of specialisms is particularly large in the UK. In construction, for example, there is a long-lasting, historical division between building, undertaken by construction firms, and the costing and cost monitoring of building projects, undertaken on large schemes by parallel teams of quantity surveyors working for the client and builder respectively. Such a division is unheard of in most other Western European countries and the USA.

THEORIES OF PROPERTY INSTITUTIONS AND ORGANISATIONS

Diagrammatic Approaches to Institutions

To smooth the cross over from theory to practice, it is perhaps best to start with the ways in which most people experience institutional analysis in property markets – flow diagrams of organisational interrelationships. They might relate to a specific project, identifying the sequence of functions and which type of enterprise does them. Alternatively, they might be more general in order to comprehend the complexity of the interrelationships in property development. A number of flow diagrams have been devised by researchers to describe the 'development process' – that is, the conversion of land from one use to commercial structures. Figure 5.1 reproduces the sequential flow diagram for a hypothetical project suggested by Punter, which is self-explanatory in content.[2] In their survey of these diagrammatic models, Gore and Nicholson (1991) identify five main approaches to flow-diagram models of the land development process. They follow quite closely the different institutional theories elaborated below.

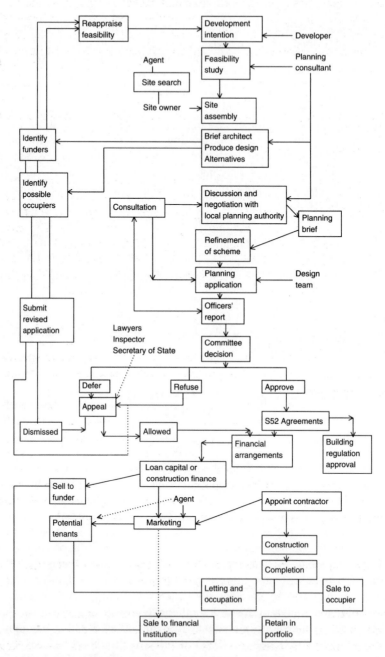

Figure 5.1 The development process for speculative offices
Source: Adapted from Gore and Nicholson (1991) after Punter (1985)

Functionally, the process of property development seems straightforward. A development has to be devised, financial backers found, planning permission obtained, design and construction commenced, and a purchaser of the completed property identified. Short-term finance is needed for the development and construction phase, and long-term finance for the finished building. These functions are *sequential, linear*, project-based models, which Gore and Nicholson suggest presume the current structure of the development industry, rather than help to explain its existence. These two authors argue that these models may be useful in explaining who does what in particular projects, but not why projects take place in the ways they do, nor why specific outcomes result - such as project delays or cost overruns.

A more sophisticated variant is the *development pipeline* model of Barrett *et al.* (1978), which approaches development as a cyclical process with three stages – development pressures and prospects, development feasibility and implementation. The pipeline is then envisaged as a dynamic spiral with a new pattern of land-use emerging at the end of every cycle. The problem with this model, Gore and Nicholson suggest, is the unrefined nature of the way in which many influences on development are classified as unknown (black-box) constraints. The development pipeline model is often used in the context of the *structure–agency* approach to institutionalism.

Two final uses of flow diagrams can be identified. *Behavioural* approaches stress the decision-making processes of different actors in the development process when specifying their flow models. Finally, there is the *structures of provision* approach, which may use a flow diagram to specify the key organisations involved in property development and their schematic interrelationships.

The theories used in these sorts of study are the focus of the rest of this chapter. Most investigators of property institutions have adopted a broadly sociological approach.[3] As a result, the discussion is divided into two parts. The first considers economic theories of institutions, which are associated with a lack of information. This leads to theories of transaction costs, moral hazard, adverse selection and signalling. The second surveys the broader literature on property institutions, dividing them into historical, behavioural, conflict, structure–agency and structures of provision approaches.

MAINSTREAM ECONOMIC THEORY AND PROPERTY INSTITUTIONS

It is sometimes argued in property research that mainstream economics has no theory of institutions beyond the simple perfect competition, oligopoly or monopoly market structure divisions of the structure–conduct–performance model (for example, Healey, 1992). Although many urban economics texts do not have an institutional dimension to their analyses (Mills, 1987;

DiPasquale and Wheaton, 1996), this view is incorrect as there are a number of specific institutionally related theories. These fall into four broad categories, though few of them have actually been applied extensively to property markets. They are production characteristics, transaction cost minimising, game theory and information theory perspectives.

Technical production characteristics

Classic examples here are studies of economies of scale. If large firms in an industry can gain substantial economies it is to be expected that the industry would be populated by a handful of large firms. No studies of these characteristics have been undertaken for property development apart from the recognition of the benefits of pooling risks.

Transaction cost minimising

This approach argues that institutions and organisational structures evolve to minimise the transaction costs associated with market exchange (Williamson, 1985; Martin, 1993; North, 1990). Transaction costs are those costs associated with the processes of exchange. They are incurred in enforcing property rights, identifying potential trading partners and carrying out transactions (Jacobson and Andreosso-O'Callaghan, 1996). The supply-and-demand model of Chapter 2 assumes there are no transaction costs. In practice, they are often high in property markets; so agents need to include them when optimising. The benefits of moving for a user, for example, have to be higher than the threshold of the transaction cost of doing so. An absence of transaction costs would lead to far more moves by commercial tenants than occur in real life.

Firms, according to transaction cost theory, exist only because it is frequently difficult or expensive to organise activities through market exchange. Internal firm governance rules might undertake certain coordination tasks more cheaply than the market. So, rather than economies having only individuals trading with each other through the market place, firms emerge to take over some of the roles. Firms can also reap the benefits of economies of scale and scope. Yet, firm internal governance has limits, because of factors such as bounded rationality, so situations equally exist where use of market exchange is cheaper than internal firm hierarchies. Firm size in any particular activity, consequently, depends on the net benefits of internal firm governance over market exchange.

Transaction cost minimising may help to explain the array of organisations and institutional and professional practices existing in commercial property. The use of specialist professional advice, the roles that particular organisations undertake, and the context of custom, practice and professionalism all have explanatory hypotheses based on transaction costs. If all the elements of the property development process, for example, were done by one large enterprise, it would lose the considerable benefits of specialisation. Senior management would suffer from information overload, and have great difficulty in monitoring employee behaviour. The latter would consequently be able to indulge in opportunism – acting in their own interests rather than that of the firm, say, by working less hard than they claim, or cutting corners.

Use of the market may resolve some of these internal firm governance problems because market contracts are in many circumstances more transparent and enforceable than job descriptions and promises of meeting deadlines. Competition between market suppliers reduces the incentives for any of them to be opportunistic because each firm knows it will not receive another contract if it is caught abusing the current one. There are, however, limits to the contracts that can be written for market transactions. They cannot specify every contingency in detail, especially for complex, uncertain situations like property development. A construction contract for a large commercial property project, for instance, cannot take account of all the uncertainties that may arise or ensure that subcontractors do the specified work without detailed monitoring. Building up relations of trust and mutual obligation is one requirement of transaction cost minimising market relations in such contexts.

As highlighted above, the central hypothesis of transaction cost minimisation is that activities are undertaken within firm hierarchies, or through the specification of market contracts, depending on which form minimises the transaction costs of undertaking a particular task or activity. The theory argues that actual use of markets or internal exchanges with firms depends on the moment in history and the characteristics of the activity. Hence, a range of firm/market structures exists across industries depending on the characteristics of the activity in question. Large integrated firms may emerge or, conversely, a network of specialist enterprises may trade with each other. There are many other possible mixes of markets and enterprises. Each depends on the nature of the transaction costs. Asset specificity in the form of large research and development costs or an expensive dedicated piece of equipment, for example, encourage the emergence of integrated firms. Industries without such technical constraints and a need for flexibility in face of variable demand would evolve a more dispersed range of enterprises and a greater use of market transactions. Property development has more of the characteristics of the latter type of industry, and so transaction cost minimising predicts the broad institutional spread within it.

Transaction cost analysis assumes an impure world in which people may not keep their word or tend to interpret ambiguities to their own advantage. Avoidance of such opportunistic practices may be a reason for using either market relations or internal firm governance depending on the circumstances. The threat of such opportunism, however, is difficult to quantify or to interpret in monetary terms.

Transaction cost minimising is generally posed as a theory of the evolution of industry structures (Williamson, 1985). Evolution means that what currently exists is superior to its predecessors in terms of succeeding in the contemporary business environment. This gives history a specific role. Evolving patterns of transaction cost minimisation fix optimal firm/market structures; historically existing firms and markets then undergo the required changes or fail. Not even all supporters of the transactions approach are satisfied with this strong, dynamic efficiency assumption. North (1990), an economic historian, proposes an explanation of the historical development of societies in transaction cost terms, but is acutely aware that societies can economically regress – and so he finds the evolutionary stance unsatisfactory.

Transaction cost theory has drawbacks. Its predictions cannot be directly tested because of a lack of hard data on transaction costs and their internal firm governance equivalents. Costs are difficult to measure in the broad way that the approach requires, so empirical analysis usually involves looking at organisational forms and deriving hypotheses about how to minimise transaction costs, without actually being able to verify or compare those implied costs. This weakens the conclusions derived, because hypotheses derived from other theories may also account for the observed organisational structures. Transaction cost and competing explanations, in fact, can be thought up for virtually any firm/market structure in existence. Standard hypothesis testing would fail to discriminate between them and, so, the empirical validity of transaction cost minimising theory remains uncertain.

Transaction cost theory runs the risk of being circular. Any explanation not based on the production side of the production–exchange dichotomy becomes a transaction cost theory even though the explanations might have varied, and possibly have had conflicting, theoretical origins. Transaction costs as explanations of firms' existence also ignore the innovative role of firms. Rather than adapting to markets, firms could be argued to create and mould them through their market power and innovatory practices (Lazonick, 1991).

These comments do not invalidate the general thrust of transaction cost minimising theory. There is a widely accepted, intuitive appeal to the idea that there are costs and benefits in using either market relations or internal firm governance and to the view that the organisation of markets and firms adapts to such trade-offs. Without greater empirical grounding, however, the theory is more useful as a signpost to explanations that the explanation in itself.

Notwithstanding this conclusion, transaction cost economising does provide a plausible hypothesis for a number of institutional structures in property development and ownership. The existence of property companies – firms developing and holding stocks of commercial buildings as investments with publicly quoted equity – has a transaction cost explanation. If investors wish to invest a moderate sum in property and do so on an individual basis, they are faced with three problems. Buildings are a lumpy investment, they are illiquid, and it is difficult to spread risk across a range of properties. Market contracts could emerge to take account of these characteristics (Chapters 10 and 12), but they are often difficult to monitor or expensive to set up. Property companies, by holding a portfolio of properties, to an extent overcome these three problems because investors can buy their shares.[4] The lumpiness and liquidity problems are resolved because the investor can now buy and sell the property company's shares at will. The property company also has sufficient assets to hold a risk reducing pool of commercial property. They can select on the basis of superior insider information, which of their developments they wish to hold or sell. A drawback is that the investor has to rely on the management skill of the company and accept the stock of properties and development schemes that the firm undertakes, which may not be optimal. Property companies are an example, in transaction cost terms, of where the characteristics of the asset encourage the formation of firms rather than the use of market transactions. Note that property companies themselves frequently use market transactions within their activities: for example, when they hire the services of lawyers, surveyors and accountants. In transactions cost terms, they specialise at what they are good at – partly overcoming the problems of small investors in property.

The benefits of buying shares in property companies rather than owning property directly are not positive for all investors. Large investors in commercial property, for instance, can achieve the same pooling benefits by owning a stock of buildings themselves; the scale of their holdings reduces lumpiness effects, and liquidity constraints may be less pressing. There are advantages of self-ownership for them as well because, by holding property directly, the monitoring of the asset base may be made easier and they can use their own judgement about property market trends and the best portfolio to hold (Chapter 11). Even so, large institutions may wish to use independent developers to generate new property in order to avoid the risks of development, and to benefit from skills which they could not fully employ. The varied relationship between the Institutions and property developers consequently also has a transaction cost explanation.

Information theory

Information is necessary for any economic activity but it is also bounded. No one can process more than a simple set of information nor expect to have more than a limited range of expertise. So every individual has to rely on the effects of habit or accept the consequences of ignorance in key features of their activities. The future is similarly unknown. Information about the future may be encompassed in current assessments of the risk and uncertainty made in current investment projects.

Different attitudes to specific types of risk can influence the structure of an industry. Users of buildings, for example, are generally concerned to limit the risks of acquiring new premises and so generally purchase ready made buildings; or they arrange for others to build and then sell or lease back to them. Property developers conversely thrive on those risks – because they can be a source of super-normal profits. This differential relation to property market risk helps to explain why specific property industry structures have evolved.

Often information is asymmetrical between the parties to a transaction, and this enables the holder of the superior knowledge to use it opportunistically (Macho-Stadler and Perez-Castrillo, 1997). This leads to three issues – moral hazard, adverse selection and signalling.

- *Moral hazard* occurs where an agent's behaviour is not observable or verifiable; for example, being less careful when insured. Not all people are less careful with valuables simply because they have insured them, but they do have the possibility of being so because an insurance company will recompense them for any loss. The moral hazard is in that possibility, and the problem is the fact it may not be priced into the insurance contract.

  Property developers could be said to exhibit moral hazard characteristics when they are allowed to be highly geared financially, because this encourages them to take far larger risks than their creditors think they are taking. It may also be difficult to price this risk into the cost of a loan. If the risk of failure for the highly geared developer is high, most of the downside costs are borne by the lenders to the developers rather than by the developers themselves. Yet, if the gamble comes off, the developer reaps virtually all the gain. Lenders consequently have a strong incentive to avoid developer moral hazard, through monitoring.[5] Such moral hazard risks may encourage them to call in loans more rapidly than otherwise, at times when the property-market falls. Fundamentally sound developers may, consequently, be sent into liquidation because of the threat, rather than the reality, of moral hazard behaviour.

- *Adverse selection* arises when one party has more information about key features of a transaction than others. The seller of a property, for example, knows more about its condition than a buyer and, when there are repair and maintenance problems, has an incentive not to reveal them. Adverse selection theory suggests that the risk of opportunism is highest when only infrequent, expensive transactions are conducted, such as buying a second-hand car or house. Car dealers and residential estate agents in such situations have strong incentives to maximise their returns at the expense of either purchasers and sellers. Even if the car or property dealers are honest, sellers and purchasers have no way of knowing because only repeated experience will provide them with the appropriate information. This information gap tends to drive quality out of the market, because sellers of quality second-hand cars have to accept the low-quality price because purchasers have no effective means of discriminating (Akerloff, 1970). This problem may be avoided if sellers can 'signal' their good's quality to the market place.

- With *signalling*, someone wants to indicate a characteristic in the market place, and so they signal it through some understood form of behaviour. An example is when someone acquires a qualification in order to enter a profession, even though most of the learnt knowledge will never be used. The person has 'signalled' to employers and customers a particular type of professionalism by doing so.

These different aspects of information asymmetry often interact, and they can provide explanations for institutions and organisations within commercial property. Asymmetrical information theory may help to account for the structure of the commercial property agency industry in Britain. The need for reputation, and the concomitant signalling of probity, may help to explain the importance of leading London based commercial agents in the national and international market, when ostensibly there are few scale economies and local agents should have an edge in understanding local contexts. They also frequently undertake research and information collection, when transaction cost economising would probably suggest that out-sourcing to specialists would be a better option. This again may be done to signal superior knowledge and skill. Leyshon *et al.* (1990) describe the spread of the main London agents throughout the UK but, in the absence of any theory, ascribe it to unspecified benefits of scale economies alone. The emphasis that commercial agents put on regular contacts with likely clients also fits within the theory. It is good business sense, because it may help to build up trust through continuous mutual interaction.

Game theory

Game theory is concerned with strategic behaviour in the context of pre-defined situations and rules of behaviour (games). Classic instances of the approach are the behaviour of two firms in particular market contexts, and the Prisoners' Dilemma whereby a lack of trust leads to less than ideal outcomes (Axelrod, 1990; Binmore, 1992; McMillan, 1992).

The Prisoners' Dilemma tackles the common situation where one person has less than full information about another's behaviour. When faced with high costs if an agreement is broken, he or she is likely to operate on the 'worst case' basis: that it will be broken. Information again is asymmetrical, because the individuals know more about their own actions. So two prisoners, who could get away with a severe crime by not confessing, are worried that during interrogation each will implicate the other in order to win a lighter sentence. Both consequently end up confessing, if they are rational. The outcome is that both are worse off than if they could be assured of each other's trust. The outcome of this game depends on the precise rules by which it is played. In repeat games, each player has potential sanctions against the other, and so the result is less clear cut. The game can also be extended to many players.

A construction project, such as a large commercial development, has all the makings of a classic multi-person Prisoners' Dilemma, and the approach may explain some of the organisational frameworks and difficulties of construction projects (Ball, forthcoming). The game theory approach unfortunately has hardly been used in the commercial property literature, but there is clearly scope for innovatory work in this field.

OTHER INSTITUTIONAL THEORIES

Few of the theories of property institutions outlined in this section claim that their analyses provide a comprehensive explanation of property markets and development. Rather each would suggest that they are either focusing on a particular aspect of relevance to policy or are proposing a means of incorporating institutionalism within wider theoretical discourses. The broader theoretical frameworks are not examined here, as was noted earlier.

Historical explanations

In its weakest form, the institutional approach dominates general property histories, analyses of redevelopment areas and studies of the role of financial institutions. There is no clear theory of institutions and organisations and how to study them; rather, varied elements are drawn together in explanations that relate a history of property development in a particular country, of a specific scheme or of a firm.

Classics are the histories of British property developers by Marriot (1967) and Scott (1996), and also the history of London's landowners by Jenkins (1975). Such studies provide useful information but, by the nature of their methodology, emphasise the actions of individuals over markets. The reasons given for individual success implicitly identify personal characteristics rather than treating those individuals as the embodiments of market outcomes. The emphasis is on the players rather than the process. This emphasis on behaviour is weakened by a lack of any clearly articulate theory through which it is being examined. Very little of this literature consequently is reproducible into generalisations about property markets. It has, therefore, had limited impact on wider research.

Conflict institutionalism

A change of land-use is an exclusionary process, as well as a market driven one, in that competing uses no longer have access to the land. Negative externality effects may also spill over from the project to affect the local neighbourhood. Such are the potential distributional effects associated with land-use change. Local residents and small businesses may, for example, have to move, with little or no compensation, when a major office or shopping scheme is developed. This could lead to a loss of lower income housing and employment opportunities; a charge, for example, made against the policies of the London Docklands Development Corporation (Brownhill, 1993). Such distributional issues may spill into overt conflict in the political arena, particularly at the local level, with developers or their opponents attempting to mobilise local political support for or against projects. Local planning authorities, which have local economic development and redistributional briefs, may also be lobbied for support.

There is a large literature on conflict within the development process that draws on the community action tradition of supporting low income/working class/ethnic minority protest over neighbourhood issues (Ambrose and Colenutt, 1975). On the one side is the institution of the 'local community' and, on the other, property developers. Planning authorities and other public bodies are the mediators of these conflicts. A number of studies have been stimulated by disputes in London over Coin Street on the South Bank (Thornley, 1991), Kings Cross railway land (Edwards, 1992), Spitalfields (Foreman, 1989) and Docklands (Church, 1988, Brownhill, 1993). International comparisons have also been made in this framework (Fainstein, 1992). The theoretical stance is generally radical or eclectic, with a bias in support of low income local communities' demands. Often the authors have been involved in local protests, so this is not surprising.

The community action approach to land-use conflict requires identification of the groups in conflict, and each has to have clearly articulated, opposing interests.[6] Yet, identifying groups and their interests is an extremely difficult exercise, as the vast number of attempts at social class analysis have demonstrated. People do not easily fit into homogeneous, single interest, social groupings, either at the local or the national levels. The 'local community' as a result may be a myth, in which case it is highly unlikely that community groups will actually speak for all of the local population. Unanimity in politics is rarely achieved. Fainstein (1992) points out, for example, that community protests in the US are severely demarcated on racial lines; whereas class or local interests are the only prescribed criteria in UK studies, with little analysis of potential local social conflict. The described local group unity, the coherence of the 'local community', and the democratic practices by which demands are supposed to be formulated, may be based more on the hopes of community activists than the true social reality.

Other conflict approaches have attempted to investigate the conditions under which group objectives can be brought together into formulated common urban regeneration aims. Here, the emphasis is on the positive externalities of property development. Local employers, developers, politicians and low-income groups may find common ground, for example, in specific urban regeneration schemes. Studies of such 'growth coalitions' have been undertaken in the US by Logan and Molotch (1987) and in the UK by Bassett (1996). The existence of local growth coalitions has strongly influenced urban regeneration policy in the 1990s. They provide a rationale for governments' policies of encouraging local public–private partnership and broad-based programmes encompassing housing, employment and training.

As Lawless (1994) has pointed out, the rhetoric of urban regeneration policy can disguise poor policy effectiveness. It is unclear whether many urban regeneration schemes have been worthwhile in terms of their high cost and frequently lower than expected achievements. Policy effectiveness apart, the approach could also suffer from the implicit theory of presuming pluralist style interest groups and the ability to find feasible compromises between them, within the context of a specific ideology – in this case a specific view of the 'market' and 'regeneration'. The problems of group identification and representativeness apply equally here as to the previously cited examples. Predictions of market conditions tend not to be based on hard headed evaluations, but on wish lists of desirable outcomes – classified as regeneration.

The fundamental difference between improving particular social problems – such as long-term, unskilled, male unemployment – and physically improving a neighbourhood is frequently confused. In fact, the two may be in conflict; for example, when regeneration leads to the uncompensated displacement from the neighbourhood of the disadvantaged groups that previously lived there. Moreover, such policies may divert the process of urban change, through infrastructure and other public good provision, away from more efficient, long-term, land use patterns.

Conflict approaches, nevertheless, help to identify the existence of potentially important social divisions over land-use and highlight the significance of major developments in altering the trajectory of urban growth. They have also strongly influenced the policy views of local politicians and key personnel in planning authorities. Policy makers' interest has been stimulated by the widespread practice of extracting a local return in the form of 'planning gains' such as community facilities, new roads, training schemes, or housing as the price for permitting development. Planning gain is partly about limiting the public expenditure implications of development by requiring the developer to cover the burden of knock-on infrastructure costs. It may also be treated as a means of redistributing the benefits of development, with local 'losers' compensated by the 'winners' – property developers. Planning gain is generally supported in the literature, as offering a local and flexible means of betterment taxation, in contrast to earlier attempts at general land development taxation. However, by being a negotiable 'land tax', it faces efficiency and distributional problems. Planning gain increases the uncertainty and potential delay surrounding any development; biases the tax outcome in favour of physical structures and greenspace over other local services, general taxation goals and cash compensation to affected individuals; and may give an incentive for spurious local group opposition because there is a high prospect of some form of planning gain compensation for protests made.

Behavioural institutionalism

This approach identifies particular types of agency – landowner, developer or financier – and suggests that they have behavioural characteristics, usually preferences, that are distinct from those implied by rational profit-maximising calculation. Preference differences are not random, according to this view, but influenced by institutional frameworks. The objectives of research of this type, consequently, are to identify the distinctive behaviour of key groups in property markets and to explain it in terms of the culture and traditional practices.

Landowners have been the group to receive the widest treatment of this type. Massey and Catalano (1978) define landed property to include the ownership of existing buildings as well as land, and group landowners into several categories and subcategories. The groupings are, first, 'former landed property' (which, perhaps, is better described as traditional landowners). This group is subdivided into the Church of England, the aristocracy and the Crown Estate. Second is 'industrial landownership', subdivided into farming, manufacturing and construction. Finally, there is 'financial landownership', subdivided into financial institutions and property companies. Kivell (1993) in his review added home owners and the public sector.

Massey and Catalano's interest specifically was to try to identify the power of these subgroups – 'the coherence of that power, its distinctiveness, and its relation to an economic basis in land ownership' (Massey and Catalano, 1978; 30). Their study suggests there are major differences in behaviour between these sub-groups. The differences exist because of variations in preferences – how sub-groups of landowners saw their roles and responsibilities and behaved according to them. Goodchild and Munton (1985) and Kivell (1993) similarly support the importance of identifying the behaviour of landowner sub-groups.[7] Adams et al. (1988) have highlighted the fact that public sector landowners, with their apparent preferences, have slowed down the release of vacant urban land. The implications of such behavioural differences on land markets were considered earlier in Chapter 3.

Other cases of behavioural institutionalism exist elsewhere in the property literature. The behaviour of financial institutions, for instance, has been argued to be a distorting influence on the spatial location of new offices.

They have an excessive preference for prime central London properties, which helps to explain the disproportionate role of London in office development and hinders the development of a speculative office building industry outside the South East.

There are several limitations to behavioural institutionalism. The first issue concerns data collection, in that sub-group behaviour is usually identified for the respective populations from small, non-random samples. This approach is made necessary for researchers by the secrecy surrounding landownership patterns and transactions behaviour in the UK. There is always a danger that respondents emphasise their distinctiveness and downplay what they fear might be seen as financial self-interest. Data quality control problems must arise, because there is no other way of checking the validity of the stated preferences.

Moreover, even if accurate answers are attained, the methodological status of the results may be uncertain. Generally, researchers examine case studies. If a behavioural trait is found amongst those interviewed, the question then arises of how easy it is to generalise from the finding.

Another difficulty arises in quantifying the impact of the identified behaviour, because differences in preferences do not necessarily lead to distinct outcomes. To take a trivial example, the supporters of rival teams clearly have different preferences, yet they still turn up to the same game when their teams are playing. Preference differences, in other words, have to be shown to matter as well as exist. In property markets, in contrast to the claims of behavioural institutionalists, a reasonable empirical generalisation might be that behavioural differences matter when looking at specific sites or development projects, but not at the aggregate city or national level. Justification for this is the hypothesis that preference differences are likely to be randomly distributed around some common behavioural norm: that norm being rational economic calculation. There may be specific cases when a particular type of landowner, say, has distinct preferences and has a significant market share. This seems to have been the case, for example, with vacant land in Britain in the 1980s held by public utilities, as noted in Chapter 3.

Finally, problems of causality may arise. This can be illustrated by examining the logic behind the claim that financial institutions prefer investing in prime London offices. This conclusion could be the product of an irrational preference for London on the part of those institutions – a historically generated institutional practice. However, the behaviour, if true, might also occur for entirely rational reasons, or, at least, correspond to them. The rationale may derive from differences in degrees of liquidity and risk associated with prime London and other UK markets. The former explanation is behavioural institutionalist; while the latter is not. The institutions' preference actually might be to maximise profits, say, and the risk-weighted outcomes identify London as the preferred location to achieve this.

Behavioural institutionalism is an important stimulus to remembering that the world cannot be reduced to a few simple abstract generalisations; though the general epistemological rule that less complex theories are preferable to more complex ones still applies. The benefits of recognising behavioural differences must be clearly demonstrated, and the costs in terms of lost generality shown to have been outweighed. This is more likely to be achieved in local or context-specific studies rather than at more aggregate levels. As such, behavioural institutionalism does not necessarily represent an alternative to mainstream economic theory, but may rather act as a complement.

Structure–agency institutionalism

In a series of articles, Healey (for example, in Healey (1992) and Healey and Barrett (1990)) has called for the use of a structure–agency institutional model in order to generalise about the nexus of the roles and relationships involved in the property development process. She argues that an institutional approach is necessary because of the complexity of development processes and the need to avoid missing out on key links in understanding how and why a particular project took place. As Hooper (1992) in his critical commentary notes, the intellectual origins on which the theory is based are diverse, coming from a variety of sociological and urban sources. For brevity, the model will be called the ASH (Agency–Structure Healey) model from now on.

Structures are said to be the material resources, institutional rules and organising ideas which agencies acknowledge (Healey, 1992: 34–8). *Material resources* refer to the 'primary ingredients of the production process' – land rights, labour, finance, information and expertise. *Rules* then govern the way these are used – set by organisations or the political process. *Ideas* influence the dynamic of resource use and rule formulation, because they 'inform the interests and strategies of actors as they define projects'. These structures specifically relate to property development itself, but exist in a broader context. For modern Britain, they are underpinned by the characteristics of that society – a medium-sized, advanced, market-based economy with all its general institutions, customs and problems. The importance of structures, consequently, is that they influence and constrain the behaviour of agents – that is, individuals operating within property markets. Structures, however, are given a strong causal role because they have a determining role in the property market.

In terms of the distinction between institutions and organisations, the ASH approach clearly ascribes institutions to be part of the structure. The place of organisations is less clear. They generally seem to act as a backdrop – the location where agents work. The emphasis, moreover, is on the agencies, as real people, rather than on either institutions or organisations. In this sense, the ASH approach could be argued as giving a theoretical framework to what were earlier termed historical studies. The objectives of the framework are to suggest a means by which to undertake case studies; to make a general state-ment that agencies as well as structures matter; and to make generalisations about the development process and the role of planners and policy makers within it.

The previous institutional studies surveyed here are partial in nature; investigating distinctive components rather than attempting to present a com-prehensive understanding of property markets. In contrast, the ASH approach aims to provide an all-embracing explanation. Its emphasis on structural causality is an apparent strength of the method, because it should enable application of clear structural characteristics of property market behaviour when investigating any particular development. It also seems to offer a genuine alternative to the competitive model. Many of its structural characteristics are at variance with the hypotheses of the standard economic model, because the components of the ASH structure include many factors not regarded as relevant in economics.[8] The structural route is unfortunately a weakness as well, because great weight has to be put on structural deter-minants *if* the approach is to be a genuine alternative to mainstream eco-nomic approaches. Yet, it is difficult in the literature arguing for the ASH approach to see precisely what structurally causes property market change, as Gore and Nicholson (1991) note – a problem that arises for both practical and theoretical reasons.

In practice, research attention is directed to the agency part of the dualism. The focus is not on defining what an agency is – it is either organisations or, particularly, individuals within organisations. Rather, it is the interplay between agencies and structures that is of interest. Healey (1992: 34) recog-nises that 'the range of actors which could be involved is potentially vast'. Limiting them requires some criterion by which to select, but that is implicit rather than explicit within the approach. As both structures and agents can cause property market change, the question arises of which does what?

The objective of this type of structure–agency analysis is to relate the *agencies'* roles, strategies and interests to the underlying *structural* resources, rules and ideas. A four level framework is proposed. First, a map-ping exercise has to be undertaken describing what happens in the develop-ment process. Second, a relational analysis is made: identifying who does what, when and to whom. Third, the strategies and interests of significant actors are analysed and related to the structural resources, rules and ideas. The fourth level takes the approach beyond empirical sifting by connecting it to underlying social theories. Healey cites as an illustrative example of this level, a corporatist style comparison of 1980s Britain and Germany and its explanation of differences in property development processes in the two countries.

This particular institutional model has been used in case study analysis on a number of occasions in the UK (Healey *et al.*, 1992) and the Netherlands (van der Krabben, 1996; van der Krabben and Lambooy, 1993; van der

Krabben and Boekma, 1994). These studies have highlighted potential fruit-fulness in examining agencies in property development. In terms of the discussion at the beginning of this chapter, they highlight the significance of strategic behaviour in the property market, and hence question universal application of the competitive model to it. This could also be said of the other institutional approaches surveyed here. Commentary has to be focused on the distinctive contribution of ASH. It has several problems but, to an extent, the difficulties depend on what is attempted with the model.

At a local level, ASH-type research is not that different from the partial approaches to institutionalism described earlier. The main difference is that ASH models have a normative content: prior objectives are set up against which to compare agency behaviour and outcomes. Useful analyses of local property development processes are likely to result. It may be difficult to generalise from them, however, because of the difficulties within the approach of distinguishing between general and development specific factors. The lack of generalisable conclusions highlights the absence of clear theoretical reasons for the form that ASH empirical studies take or the conclusions that they come to.

Other problems exist, such as the focus put on strategy. Outcomes may be attributed to it, which, in reality, are the product of external economic or other forces. A property developer's strategy, for example, is much more likely to come right in the upswing of a property cycle than in the downswing. The same is true of an urban regeneration project (Berry *et al.*, 1994). The outcomes are as likely to have been consequences of the stage of the property cycle as of the strategies themselves. These anonymous forces are part of the structure within the ASH framework, and illustrate the difficulty of attributing causality to the agency or to the structure. Because the focus of ASH-type research is most likely to be on agents, researchers may easily be biased towards attributing events to their actions; with implications for what are the structural property market processes. Constraints on individual behaviour consequently become elastic.

A problem with the structure–agency dichotomy is precisely that it is a dichotomy. Rules to differentiate between the two aspects, to identify causality and to explain change are necessary within its ambit. Agencies need to have some exogenous determinants of their existence to justify their separation from the structure, otherwise explanation of them merely collapses back into structural issues. So, in the model's formulation, it is conceptually hard to have social and economic (that is, structural) explanations of agencies' roles and existence. Conversely, structural change cannot be greatly affected by agency behaviour, even if feedback effects of agency actions on structural dynamics are recognised. This problem of duality is extremely important when looking at institutions in a national, or an international comparative, policy context, because of the scale and the degree of the differences that have to be considered. It is possible to envisage feedback loops between agency and structure, so that change in one is influenced by the other. However, this only heightens the difficulty of attributing causality within the framework. This, it should be noted, is a problem of this type of sociological theory in general, not of the ASH approach alone.

Structure–agency could be argued to be an exercise in taxonomy – putting various causal features of property development in the domain of either the structure or the agency, and then adding some feedback loops. Yet, once the division is made, its usefulness is subsequently limited – because, even if correctly assigned, the results can neither be generalised nor used to under-stand change. The fundamental problem is that change is likely to alter the taxonomy, so structure–agency relationships at one point in time need bear no correspondence to those at other points in time. In the absence of some overriding theory of change (in which it is hard to see any real role for agency), the approach collapses back into the historical institutionalism discussed earlier.

Theoretically, the dichotomy of structure and agency in the ASH approach contrasts with the evolutionary approach of, say, transaction cost minimisa-tion. For the latter, there is no separate structure, but rather transaction eco-nomic forces impose themselves on firms and cause them to adapt new organisational forms over time or go into liquidation. Modern economic institutional analysis, therefore, tends to be functional in its reasoning, in that market forces create institutional structures generating the most efficient out-comes. Individual behaviour, at best, affects the timing of these changes. There is no need for a structure–agency division within its ambit.

Similarly, microeconomic market analysis, like the model in Chapter 2, is based on the constrained behaviour of maximising individuals. This could be interpreted as a focus on agency, but that would be erroneous. The con-straints those individuals face do not of themselves constitute a structure. Nor is there a correspondence between the idealised individuals that consti-tute agents for economists and agencies in ASH. Agents in economics are abstract generalisations (for example, firms, consumers and the labour force). The aim, as was noted earlier, is to identify general behavioural prac-tices beyond the randomness of individual behaviour. This is the antithesis of the agent specificity of the ASH approach. Other theories, in other words, manage to avoid problems of identification involved in the separation of structure and agency by not having the difference.

It is suggested that the structure–agency distinction can incorporate many different theoretical approaches within its ambit. However, the point just made about the fundamental difference between its methodology and that of mainstream economics suggests that this is not the case. The focus in ASH is on agency behavioural differences and in mainstream economics it is on behavioural regularities across different agents. Making the two compatible is problematic.

The last major difficulty is the dynamics of the ASH model. How does property development change and why? As has already been noted, the struc-ture–agency formulation makes it hard to avoid misleading explanations, because the causality of change is unclear. Is it the sum of agency actions, impinging, say, on the structure, or is it pure structural forces, or a mix of the two? What aspects of change should be focused on in the absence of a clear theory? Putting it in a UK property context, do Gateshead, Sheffield and the West Midlands have large shopping malls because of local entrepreneurial drive or because of 'structural' factors, such as deindustrialisation, technical change and higher personal disposable incomes? The answer is probably a mix of all of these, but then why do similar places not have them? Is it, in ASH terms, a lack of entrepreneurs (structure) or just unlucky ones (agency)?

Structures of building provision

A structure of building provision (SoP) refers to the contemporary network of relationships associated with providing particular types of building. Those relationships are embodied within institutions and organisations and may take market or non-market forms. 'Provision' encompasses the whole gamut of development, construction, ownership and use. This institutional approach does not have to be limited to the built environment. Health care, for exam-ple, is associated with a number of structures of provision, as are local authority services.[9]

Structure is being used in a different sense from that of ASH models. For them, the structure exists outside the property world as well as inside it, impinging on development. Structure consequently has a strong causal effect and is associated with theories delineating the characteristics of the structure. Structure, in structures of provision, has a more limited status, describing the main organisations in property provision and their relationships. It is used in the same way as in the phrase 'the industrial structure of a country'. The phrases 'system of provision' and 'form of provision' are its synonyms. Prior theories are needed to examine the working of a structure of provision; instead of being subsumed within it. Different types of theory could be used in conjunction with it – mainstream economic, radical or otherwise – to pro-vide hypotheses about the workings of the property market. Those theories in various ways could be used to explain the existence of an SoP, the factors generating its dynamics, and the importance of this institution in determining the actual characteristics of specific property markets. It has been suggested, for example, that the characteristics and problems of homeownership in the UK are strongly affected by its unique SoP.[10] SoP can be said to constitute a methodology for examining institutions, rather than representing a theory of property markets in itself.

A structure of provision can be seen as a property market *institution* – the rules, practices and relationships that influence particular types of property development and use. It, therefore, is one among an array of institutional forces that affect the property world; a theoretical device for trying to incorporate institutions into economic analysis. So, rather than a means by which to relate organisational evolution to transactions costs; or agency behaviour to underlying structures, as in ASH models; or partial analyses of institutional characteristics; it is an attempt to provide criteria through which institutions can be drawn into a broader analysis of property development, when relevant.

Several more aspects distinguish it from the other institutional approaches outlined here, which for brevity are dealt with as a series of points.

1   As a network of organisations, institutional practices and markets involved in a particular form of building provision, there is no dichotomy between agency and structure. Agents are part of the structure of provision. They are constrained in what they do, but, nonetheless, it is still possible for agent behaviour to alter an SoP. The extent to which it is accepted that agencies do have independent influence depends on theories used with SoP and empirical circumstances.

The decision, for example, of many UK building societies to abandon their mutual status in the 1990s was couched in terms of the pressure of external forces, but was undoubtedly the outcome of individual decision-making within these bodies. These events were particularly important, because they altered a structure of building provision by changing the mortgage market. As was noted above, mainstream economic theories are able to avoid the structure–agency dichotomy through functionalism. SoPs can be dysfunctional, in the sense of producing non-optimal outcomes. At any one time, SoPs will have a past and be subject to pressures for change. Explanations of those dynamics depend on the empirical analysis undertaken and the theories used in that analysis.

2   Institutions, organisations and markets may all be part of structures of provision, because of the mutual influence of each on the others. Institutions are the conduits of market relations and so help to determine the nature of markets; while markets affect the nature of organisations with competition forcing them to change over time. Finally, institutions can affect both organisations and markets by influencing their dynamics. The argument is analogous to that used in transaction cost economics, though the causality is somewhat different.

3   Each type of building provision (such as houses or offices) is associated with historically specific organisations and institutions, and hence a unique SoP. Countries, moreover, are likely to have distinct SoPs. Several SoPs might also exist for a particular type of built structure at one point in time – for instance, in housing or infrastructure provision. There can consequently be no universal explanation of the development

process, although it may still be possible to draw out many useful generalisations about development without recourse to SoP. The approach
suggests that institutions matter, yet they have no overriding causal status. How they matter depends on empirical analysis. Hence, the SoP
approach is not in conflict with the competitive model of Chapter 2,
rather it suggests limits to its applicability.

4   SoPs are subject to continual change, arising from factors like market
pressures, changes in technologies, tastes and policies and the strategies
of the institutions involved. There is no prior weighting of the importance of these potential influences – the answers can only come from
specific investigation. This contrasts with the strongly determinist evolutionary position of transaction cost economics, which argues that institutions are forced along particular paths as a result of transaction cost
minimisation. SoPs are weakly evolutionary, in that actions can alter the
path of development of an SoP in ways that may not lead to efficiency
improvements. At any point in time, there may be no contemporary
rationale for the existence of a particular structure of institutions and
markets – it just happens to be there (although it has a history and
future).

5   SoP is a conceptual device for incorporating institutions into analyses of
the development process. It does not constitute a complete theory in
itself, rather it is a methodological theory – a series of statements about
how to examine institutions and their roles rather than an explanation in
itself. Other theories are needed to understand particular research questions formulated within its framework. Take the case of housing supply
within owner-occupied housing provision in Britain. A series of theories
are needed to understand the causes of housing market fluctuations, poor
supply responses and limited technical change (Ball, 1996). The use of
this approach to institutional analysis does not prescribe the theories
used in any research.

6   The relative importance of institutions is contingent, depending on the
research questions being asked, and with it the significance of considering SoP at all. There will be many property development issues where
institutions do not matter. Similarly, only particular elements of an SoP
may be relevant to a specific issue. Whether an institutional focus is
required or not is a matter of researcher judgement (which itself can be
questioned by alternative analyses of the same issue).

7   Defining what an SoP is has to be treated in the same empirically specific way. Which institutions and relations should be included, and
which distinctions are unimportant and can be ignored, depend on the
questions being asked. They are again a matter of researcher judgement.

8   Within commercial property development in the UK, the number of structures of provision is limited. There are probably two that matter – the provision of speculative and non-speculative accommodation. And even then the difference is relatively small, so that for many issues the distinction is unnecessary. Where SoP distinctions are more important is in the context of international comparisons (Carbonaro and D'Arcy, 1994).

A problem with the SoP approach is the historically contingent nature of SoPs. This makes it difficult to define them before hand, and to say when and how they should be used. It could also be accused of relativism in that many different theoretical approaches could be applied with it. The difficulty, however, is the same for all theories. There is no ultimate proof that can discriminate between them and fix their empirical parameters. As with any of the above institutional theories, consequently, its usefulness depends on the credibility of the results that emanate from studies that use it.

SUMMARY AND CONCLUSIONS

This chapter has examined the role of institutions in property markets, focusing on property supply. A distinction is made between institutions – rules, practices and networks – and organisations – firms and other agents. The analysis has been almost wholly concerned with theory because the role assigned to institutions depends on the institutional theory adopted. Definitions of what constitutes an institution vary. Conflict theories, in practice, tend to have different interpretations of institutions (broad, local, social groupings classified as the community) than behaviourism (tightly defined practices), for example. The hallmark of all institutional approaches is that they wish to be realistic, which means that empirical contexts to an extent determine what are institutions rather than some prior theoretical blueprint. This is not necessarily bad social science, but rather theoretically informed, empirical, policy-oriented research.

Three questions were raised at the beginning of the chapter about institutions to which partial conclusions can now be given – namely, relevance, appropriateness of theories and separateness of the approaches. The question of relevance is essentially an empirical one. The array of institutional forms in the property world suggests that institutions do matter, and all of the approaches in more or less convincing ways highlight that institutions (or agents within them) can have real and important effects. Dispute is more over the scale of the effects than of their existence at all. Institutionalism, therefore, seems to be a useful branch of property market analysis. Finally, do institutional theories conflict with each other and with mainstream economics approaches? The answer here surely is that it depends.

Some institutionalists overambitiously believe that they can explain the world with their theories. Yet, at best, institutionalism is likely to provide only partial answers, or needs to be put in the context of more general social theories. Others feel the alternative perspectives are mutually exclusive. The conclusion here is that they need not be. Theoretical difficulties have been raised with each approach, not so much to dismiss them as to limit the range of questions and issues that can possibly fall within their remit. History matters and, with it, so do institutional structures that partly emerge for efficiency reasons, partly through historical accident and partly through wilful manipulation. Disentangling causality and predicting the future in property markets are as difficult as they are elsewhere. Institutionalism in the final analysis helps to enrich the discourses through which these endeavours are attempted.

The diversity of the models aiming to highlight institutional relationships involved in property development arises because they are all theory-influenced. Researchers are using prior theories to understand and examine empirical information about what they regard as important. These theories, in turn, close off other forms of analysis. Each of the institutional models, in other words, put emphasis on specific pieces of empirical information and analyses of it, while downplaying others.

The institutional approaches considered were, first, the ones emanating from modern economic theory.

- *Transaction cost minimisation* is argued to determine what is done within organisations and what is undertaken through market exchange. The standard competitive model ignores the costs of market exchange. Once they are taken account of, the contemporary array of organisations and their functions can be explained.
- *Information constraints* lead to theories of moral hazard, adverse selection, signalling and game theory. *Moral hazard* arises when behaviour cannot be effectively monitored, so that someone may break the implicit rules of behaviour. Asymmetrical information means that buyers are faced with uncertain product or service quality, and so *adverse selection* arises – leading to market failure as good quality is driven out by the bad. *Signalling* is a means of convincing the market that an organisation's or individual's behaviour is credible. *Game theory* sets up games to understand how parties react to each other in specific strategic contexts, with the Prisoners' Dilemma being one of the most useful.

Many other theories of institutions have also been suggested.

- *Historical approaches* focus on individuals, organisations or localities. Their method tends to be descriptive and atheoretical.
- *Conflict institutionalism* classifies individuals into groups and suggests

that they are in conflict – classically, local communities versus developers. These conflicts influence development and suggest redistributional policy responses. One reaction might be to encourage local growth coalitions.

- *Behavioural institutionalism* argues that particular types of social agency have characteristics that are distinctive from the rational, profit-maximising ones of mainstream economics. They arise for institutional reasons, and can be generalised across specific types of agency, such as particular categories of landowner.

- *Structure–agency models* more ambitiously aim to provide a theoretical framework through which property development should be analysed. Structures determine resource availability, allocation rules and prevailing ideologies. Agents undertake, or intervene in, property development on the basis of them, but have a degree of autonomy in how they behave. Agency behaviour is the practical focus of this perspective.

- *Structures of provision* methodology argues that organisational relationships constitute one of the institutions of property development and use, and that they need to be incorporated into understandings of the operation of property markets.

Institutional analysis of property markets is still evolving in its theoretical forms and empirical studies. Although often seen as an alternative to the competitive model approach, outlined in Chapter 2, it can also be seen as a complement - enabling, for example, the investigation of situations where information asymmetries, strategic behaviour and local or national contexts matter. None of these necessarily requires an institutional approach, but its varied proponents can cite some success in providing plausible hypotheses that explain certain aspects of real world commercial property market behaviour and outcomes.

Part 2

MACROECONOMICS AND THE PROPERTY MARKET

INTRODUCTION AND COMMENTARY

The objective of the next four chapters is to explore the interrelationships between property markets and the macroeconomy in the short and long run. Property market dynamics are strongly influenced by the broad behaviour of the economies in which they exist. The demand for commercial space, for example, is driven by the level of general economic activity. Interest rates influence the capitalisation rates through which properties are valued and the decision to build and invest in new developments. As important components of national economics, property markets also affect the behaviour of macroeconomic variables – in the short run and the long run. This is seen most noticeably in the aftermath of major property market booms when economies experience negative demand shocks arising from a sudden decline in property market activity and the effect on organisational solvency of falling property prices. The impact is greatest when a property market shock is associated with a general financial crisis, one that itself is exacerbated by defaults on property loans. This phenomenon affected virtually all the major advanced economies in the early 1990s and helped to generate the crisis in South East Asia in 1997–8.

The short-run macroeconomic effect of property markets, of course, is not simply that of inducing negative shocks to nations' economies. Periods of upswing are stimulated by the converse of the property market characteristics that intensify recessions. These positive macroeconomic effects are less immediately obvious to the lay observer and, often, to property market participants themselves.

In the following four chapters, no attempt is being made to develop a macroeconomic theory of property markets, because they are only components of an economy rather than the macroeconomy as a whole. The analysis of the functioning of property markets is still underpinned by the model outlined in Chapter 2. There, it was pointed out that the model had applicability at a number of spatial levels – from the city to the national economy as a whole. Rather than inventing a distinct property macrotheory, the object is to consider the consequences of macroeconomic change for property markets and vice versa.

Within this two way relationship, Chapter 6 emphasises the impact of property markets for the macroeconomy and policies towards it. The subsequent three chapters then focus on the reverse direction – the consequences of macroeconomic factors for property markets. Chapter 7 examines property supply in the long run, its volatility and whether there is an efficient allocation of resources to property. Chapter 8 investigates theories of property market cycles; while Chapter 9 looks at property market models.

Chapter 6 examines short-run economic behaviour, while Chapter 7 is more concerned with the long run. The short run in economics is the period when at least one factor of production is fixed. In the long run, all inputs can be varied to optimal levels, given relative prices. The short and long runs do not refer to any particular actual time period. The 'short run' in macroeconomics is an abstract device that keeps the capital stock at the same level throughout the period of the analysis.

The term 'investment' in this part of the book is used in a different context from that of the chapters examining the financial economics of property in Part 3. Investment in macroeconomic theory generally refers to investment in real goods, either as inventories or as fixed capital. In finance, conversely, investment means the purchase of the title to a property or to some financial instrument associated with it. This could be termed financial investment in property, which could be in existing, as well as new, structures. In the macroeconomic sense property investment refers only to the allocation of resources to the creation of new structures. For property in the macroeconomic sense, therefore, investment is the same as development – the creation of new commercial space. This new space cannot be used in the short run.

The business cycle is a common term for short-run macroeconomic fluctuations. The business cycle from peak to peak, or trough to trough, usually averages about four to five years. At the time of writing, the upswing of the first half of the 1990s, particularly in the US, has lasted far longer than is usual in the business cycle. This, however, has reflected unusually propitious conditions for investment and productivity improvement in the mid-1990s.

Modern macroeconomics tends to assume that economic responses are quite fast. Some key variables react extremely quickly, especially those in financial markets. Nonetheless, there may be structural problems that make, for example, unemployment persist for long periods at higher levels than would be expected simply from variations in the business cycle. One of the policy aims of macroeconomics is, therefore, to distinguish between cyclical and structural factors causing contemporary problems for an economy. Another is the extent to which structural problems in one economy are transmitted internationally to affect other countries. The 1997–8 economic crisis in South East Asia, for example, at the time of writing is seriously affecting those countries' financial systems. It is clear that their banking systems need major structural reform, but less clear is how to blend short-term adjustments with the necessary reforms, or how to avoid contagion to the world economy as a whole. The relationship between high risk property markets and financial systems is one of the areas where structural reforms can be important, as is highlighted in both Chapter 6 and Chapter 13.

Chapter 6 integrates key elements of macroeconomic theory with the behaviour of the property market. Some investment goods may take several years to enter production from the initial decision to invest, because of the time taken in detailed planning and production, so the size of the existing fixed capital stock can be a short-run constraint. Similar problems may arise with human capital – through the training times needed to increase particular types of labour supply or the time required for labour to switch from being unemployed in its old activities to new types of job. So, when investigating the causes and consequences of the business cycle, inflation, unemployment and exchange rates, it is assumed that the capital stock is fixed, so that only the amount of labour employed can be varied. As part of the capital stock, this means that the existing supply of built structures is fixed.

The standard theory of fixed investment is examined and, then, its relationship to the theory of property development, outlined earlier in Chapter 2, is drawn out. After this analysis of property development as a component of total fixed investment, the impact of an increase in property development on the macreconomy is investigated; followed by a briefer examination of the impact of the macroeconomy on property. This is followed by consideration of some of the financial aspects of the 1980s property boom. Finally, the effect on the property market of monetary policy is considered.

Chapter 7 examines the long-run aspects of macroeconomic analysis. As property does not feature explicitly in growth models, there is little point in reproducing growth theory directly. Rather, the chapter examines property in terms of some of the themes that come out of the growth literature and in terms of some widespread beliefs about the long-run behaviour of property markets. The chapter consequently contains a mix of long-run empirical and theoretical analysis. Modern growth theory is firmly embedded in microeconomic foundations; so a number of themes in this chapter pick up on those elaborated in Part 1.

The chapter deals centrally with two long-run issues. First, it examines the behaviour of property as a long-term investment good, using UK data as an illustration. Second, it considers whether there is an efficient long-run allocation of resources to commercial property or whether there is evidence either of peculiar long cycle behaviour or of overinvestment, as is sometimes claimed.

The first issue requires investigation of the long-run behaviour of new commercial development. It is widely believed that commercial property is one of the more volatile elements of the economy, whereas, in fact, the volume of property investment is one of the more stable parts of the economy, particularly when a long view is taken. The chapter shows that commercial building in the UK at a national level, although more volatile than national income fluctuations, is less volatile than housebuilding and little different from that of equipment investment. Rents and property values, of course, fluctuate more than output, as do the prices of all investment goods. These pricing aspects, however, are part of property finance and so are dealt with in Part 3.

The volume of property development is also subject to cyclical behaviour over the long and short term. The chapter identifies four cycles of varying lengths, two longer-term and two shorter-term, that have been suggested in the literature. The evidence on long cycles is less conclusive than for the short cycles. The short cycles are considered in Chapter 8. Chapter 7 briefly considers the long-term cycles and descriptively links them to the various theories of 'long wave' economic cycles. However, neither the available theories nor the data are robust enough to come to any conclusive relationships.

The second issue about long-run efficiency concerns both the overall allocation of real resources to property and the long-run effect of property market cycles. The focus is on the use of resources, rather than pricing. After defining what is meant by efficiency in this context, it is argued that, although efficiency cannot be conclusively demonstrated, the wilder claims about overinvestment in property to the detriment of the rest of the economy do not stand up to scrutiny. Part 3 highlights that property pricing shows signs of being inefficient over the short run.

The theme of short-run cycles is taken up in Chapter 8. Both the economy and property markets are subject to irregular fluctuations in prices and outputs, with cyclical upswings followed by periods of depressed activity, and the switch from one state to the other may be gradual or the product of a severe readjustment. Property markets, in particular, are prone to boom periods of intensive activity followed by a crash.

Two types of development cycle are considered: a four to five year fluctuation linked to business cycles; and a longer cycle of around ten years. Some property cycle theories rely on particular characteristics of the wider economy and their effect on property markets. These can be regarded as *exogenous* theories of property cycles, because the prime causality lies outside property markets themselves. Such models often use the accelerator theory of investment, outlined in Chapter 6, to explain property cycles. However, the timings of the business and development cycles are irregular and they do not move in synchrony.

Linked to this explanation is the hypothesis that conditions in the financial system influence the contemporary level of property development. Credit and capital streams may flow into property for a variety of reasons, stimulating price rises and a development boom; when the flow of credit dries up, a property market collapse ensues. Another approach would be a wider institutional one that emphasises not only changes in financial regimes, but also public policy frameworks and other institutional factors. This is also explored in Chapter 6.

An alternative approach to property cycles focuses on characteristics of property markets themselves. As such, it can be seen as the *endogenous* approach to theories of property cycles, because the prime causality lies within property markets themselves. These endogenous property market cycle theories are the central concern of Chapter 8. Two approaches are examined: one uses the lag between demand for property becoming apparent and the completion of development as a means of inducing specific patterns of cyclical behaviour; the other emphasises the role of vacancies, and oscillations around a 'nature rate of vacancy' – through which rents adjust to excess supplies or demand for commercial property.

Most of the theories of cycles include behavioural assumptions which require some degree of irrationality by key players, both exogenous and endogenous. Explanations which focus on valuers, developers and lenders are considered. Finally, there is a discussion of a relatively new theoretical innovation that uses financial option theory to explain the decisions of developers to build and property owners to let.

Chapter 9 explicitly focuses on property market econometric modelling. It surveys mathematical modelling approaches and the econometric estimation of them. The purpose of these models is both to explain property market behaviour and, more importantly, to forecast property market activity. As some readers may be unfamiliar with the approach, an early section introduces the principal modelling issues – and readers familiar with the material may wish to omit it. The models are broken down into multi- and single-equation approaches. The broad theoretical frameworks are set in the context of the model developed in Chapter 2. Models of demand and rent in the user market, and of development are the most common. In contrast, there is little on the investment market and there are no quantitative models of the land market. Key theoretical themes from earlier chapters are apparent, including endogenous versus exogenous influences, investment theory approaches using a flexible accelerator, vacancy adjustment and development profitability.

Property market forecasting is made more complex by broader economic influences, and the dynamic, cyclical, contexts in which they must be understood. Property forecasting models, like theories of property cycles, vary in the stress which they put on property market factors, such as contemporary vacancy levels, or on broader economic factors, such as expected output and employment in the economy as a whole or in specific user markets.

Property market modelling is also made difficult by a frequent lack of good data. Vacancy explanations of property market behaviour are extensive in the US, for example, partly because of a lack of reliable data on rents. As with so many other aspects of the economy, the content of property models is driven partly by theoretical considerations and partly by what data are actually available.

As with many aspects of macroeconomics, when reading the topics covered in this part of the book, it is useful to bear in mind the, often implicit, microeconomic foundations of the theories being examined. As was already noted, the microeconomic arguments of Part 1 are not in conflict with macro concerns; nor are theories of finance and property markets, the theme of Part 3.

6

PROPERTY MARKETS AND THE MACROECONOMY

INTRODUCTION

The spectacular world-wide boom and bust property cycle of the late 1980s and early 1990s considerably raised the awareness of the important links between commercial property development and the macroeconomy. Generally, in the property literature they are only tangentially incorporated; so this chapter aims to explore some significant relationships between commercial property markets and the macroeconomy, rather than to summarise pre-existing work. After explaining what is meant by the macroeconomy, particular issues are examined. First there is an examination of the investment function, and its relationship to the theory of property investment which was outlined in Chapter 2. Second, an overview of the consequences of an increase in property investment for the economy is presented. Third, the impact on property of the macroeconomy is discussed. Fourth, as a means of introducing financial behaviour into the discussion, the financial aspects of the late 1980s property boom are considered. Fifth, the effect on the property market of the workings of monetary policy is examined. Finally, some brief comments are made on the success of economic forecasting models.

INTRODUCING THE MACROECONOMY

What is the macroeconomy?

Macroeconomics is concerned with the behaviour of a whole economy – usually defined at the level of the nation state, although supra-national groupings, such as the European Union or the world economy, are important because international trade has significant affects on national well-being.[1] Macroeconomics investigates the causes and consequences of booms and recessions: rates of inflation, unemployment and growth; changes in the balance of payments and exchange rates; and the determinants of the level of total national output. Its fundamental approach is to look at the interactions between three simplified aggregate markets – *goods* markets, *labour* markets and *financial* asset markets – with limited distinction made between the types of goods, labour and assets. Commercial property features in two of those three market groupings: in the goods and financial asset markets.

Property features in the goods markets in two senses:

1 It is part of the capital stock used by firms to help them produce their current outputs of goods and services. As firms produce, they will use up some of their capital stock, so it is subject to depreciation, and will need replacing through new investment. More investment will be required if firms plan to increase their output. In the short-run time horizon of macroeconomics, it is assumed that none of the new investment is usuable in production; rather it adds to the future size of the capital stock.

2 The principal short-run effect of investment in real property is that it is adds to demand in the goods market: so part of what follows relates property to general theories of the demand for investment goods.

Note that property investment here is used in the real sense of a physical structure being erected, and the resource costs to the economy of doing so. It is not 'investment' in the sense used in property finance. Nevertheless, property is also a *financial asset*, competing with others. This aspect of property is primarily dealt with in Part 3 of this book. The financial elements that are of important here are their roles in the transmission of macroeconomic fluctuations. The nature of these will be explained as the model of the macroeconomy is elaborated.

Macroeconomics in terms of its methods is essentially no different from any other aspect of economic analysis. The interaction of supply and demand within markets is investigated. The difference is that total economic activity is being considered. Overall demand in an economy is called *aggregate demand* and overall supply, *aggregate supply*. The interaction between the two fixes the level of output, known as *national income,* and the *price level.* These are the quantity and price variables of concern to short-run macroeconomics. Not all market activity is included within aggregate demand or supply, because much of it is associated with intermediate goods, whose value is then incorporated into final goods within the same time period. To avoid the double-counting, therefore, only value added within a specific time period is included within aggregate demand and supply. If, say, the tyres, engine and electronics of a car are produced within the same year as the car itself, to include the value of those inputs, as well as the final value of the car would be to count them twice – once, by themselves and once as components of the final value of the car. Adopting a value-added approach avoids this problem.

There is a circular flow of income in an economy in the sense that all new output is produced by factors of production (labour, capital and land) whose owners are paid incomes for their services in the form of wages, profits and rent. These incomes in turn are directly or indirectly spent. National income can consequently be alternatively seen as expressing either total *output* in the economy, total *income* or total *expenditure*. All three are equivalent in theory; although, in practice, national income statisticians find it difficult to account for all economic activity in the three ways and have to reconcile them in the final published estimates.

Aggregate supply at a point in time is the output produced in the economy. Aggregate demand can be measured by adding up the different types of expenditure. Total expenditure, Y, can be divided into four parts: consumption, C (by far the largest component), government expenditure, G, investment, I, and the trade balance, NX (where net exports, NX, are exports minus imports).

$$Y = C + I + G + NX \qquad (6.1)$$

At any point in time, effective demand is met by supply. This follows from the definition of national income, where the output, income and expenditure are equivalent by definition. The accounting identities may be true by definition, but a theory of the workings of the national economy can be developed from the identities by considering what determines the levels of the components of expenditure and aggregate supply, and how they will change when out of equilibrium.

The definition of national income discussed here is that of gross domestic product (GDP). This excludes net factor income earned abroad, which, when summed with GDP, is called gross national product (GNP). Finally, taking account of capital depreciation leads to net national product (NNP). By convention, most countries' national incomes are usually expressed as GDP, although in the USA the GNP measure is preferred.

Short-run macroeconomics

The analysis of macroeconomic fluctuations is a short-run analysis. The short run is defined as the period when at least one of the factors of production cannot be increased. Prevailing technologies will similarly be fixed. This means that production has to use the existing stocks of labour, capital and land. When all inputs can be varied, the long run is entered. Long-run concerns of macroeconomics centre on the determinants of growth. In modern growth theory, emphasis is put on how the stocks of labour, capital and land are increased and improved, and the broad social and political conditions under which they are able to operate. The World Bank (1997) *World Development Report*, for example, focuses on the importance of reliable states and governance procedures in the growth processes of contemporary developing countries.

The business cycle

Macroeconomic fluctuations are often termed the *business cycle*. Although the business cycle is a recurring event, fluctuations in market economies are generally quite small, outside of catastrophes such as the 1930s depression. The trough of the early 1990s recession, which occurred in the second quarter of 1992 in the UK, for example, was 3.4 per cent below the previous peak in the cycle in the first quarter of 1990; yet it was one of the most severe downturns since 1945.

Another way of looking at the business cycle is in terms of fluctuations of the economy around the trend of potential economic growth, which in the UK post-1945 has, according to the Treasury, averaged around 2 per cent a year in real terms.[2] Booms would then see the economy above its potential growth and recessions below it.

Cycles for some imply the idea of a periodic re-occurrence of events with causal mechanisms determining an underlying regularity. The experience of the business cycle in the postwar era has not conformed to such iron laws. Most economists see the business cycle as influenced by random as well as predictable events. Hence, short-run macroeconomic theory looks at what happens to macroeconomies when they are subject to 'shocks' – that is sudden, sharp exogenous events. Change, in other words, does not come from any of the variables specified within the model.

The macroeconomy can be modelled in its main constituents, and the parameters of the models are assumed to be stable and well-behaved. The metaphor, thus, is not one of a regular cycle but rather of a well-behaved model being periodically bombarded by random, equilibrium disturbing events. These shocks may come from various sources – for example, mistaken government fiscal or monetary policy, rising raw material prices – as seen most clearly in the OPEC-induced oil price rises of the 1970s – or in the turbulence of foreign exchange markets. Unification of East and West into the new united Germany was a shock for both the German and European economy in the early 1990s. And war, the least savoury of all shocks.

Some economists put emphasis on particular types of shock. 'Real' business cycle theorists, for instance, place central emphasis on the pattern of technological change as the motor of economic fluctuations. Most economists, however, regard shocks as coming from a wide variety of sources because economies are complex systems existing in an unpredictable world. The heuristic device of a 'shock' thus avoids the probably fruitless search for underlying regularities to the short-run business cycle. Business cycles in this respect are like sports teams – they are known to exist, some broad understanding of their behaviour and changes in them can be gained, but predicting when and how big the winning and losing years are is beyond even the most enthusiastic interpreter. The same could be said of property market fluctuations themselves. Forecasts can be made, which give some indication of likely future events, but the future is still fundamentally uncertain.

Macroeconomics, of course, is not simply about forecasting: it is also about understanding the workings of the economy – giving insights that can be used within government macroeconomic policies. Macroeconomics has an added advantage for property market economics in that a number of theories developed for the macroeconomy are applicable, with the appropriate adjustments, to understanding its workings. This, for example, was seen earlier in Chapter 3, in the section on vacant land, where macroeconomic terms originally applied to the labour market proved useful to policy formulation.

Full employment

One of the principal concerns of macroeconomics is devising policies to ensure that resources are fully employed. Full employment in common parlance is when every economically active person who wants one has a job. Full, in this sense, means zero unemployment. This is not the way the term is used in economics. Rather it refers to the optimal use of resources, as defined by equilibrium in markets. *Aggregate market equilibrium* is the point of *full employment*, not when every input is fully employed. When, for some reason, not all markets clear and resources are under-used, unemployment arises, or markets may work at above their optimal rates at the cost of growing inefficiencies and inflation.

Under this definition of employment, some labour will still be unemployed even though the economy is defined as being at full employment. This occurs either because of a mismatch between the skills and abilities of the unemployed and the demand for labour in the economy (known as structural unemployment), or because of the general process of job change (frictional unemployment). Associated with full employment equilibrium, therefore, is an amount of unemployment – generally referred to as the natural rate of unemployment. The natural rate will vary depending on the closeness of the skills and regional location match of jobs and workers. Big shifts in the structure of the economy, as occurred in the UK in the 1970s and early 1980s, are generally associated with substantial increases in the natural rate. For the UK, in the 1990s, there is evidence that the natural rate has declined from its 1980s peak. Flexible labour markets, in which workers have skills that can easily be transferred from one activity to another lead to a lower natural rate than more rigid labour markets – hence the frequent policy emphasis on labour market flexibility, educational standards and skills training. Reduced labour market discrimination lowers the natural rate; as do any improvements in job search and transfer, which reduce frictional unemployment.

Conceptually, other inputs can be treated in a similar way to labour. So parts of the capital stock, including offices, can be under- or unused at full employment. They can be outmoded, because of technological change, shifts in demand or because of their location. Empty offices by themselves are consequently not necessarily indicators of a depressed office market. A literature has grown around the natural rate of office vacancy – see Chapter 9.

One of the major controversies of macroeconomics is the extent to which evidence of under-used resources suggests a lack of demand in the economy or, alternatively, indicates supply problems caused by unrealistic selling prices or poor adaptation to modern productive techniques. Dispute also exists over the extent to which the economy automatically and quickly reverts to full employment after a shock, and whether the process can be speeded up by appropriate government intervention.

THEORIES OF INVESTMENT AND PROPERTY

This section considers the relationship of property investment, as a physical rather than a financial asset, to the more general theory of investment. Property investment is part of aggregate investment in the economy. The majority of investment is in *fixed capital* on equipment used in production, new built structures and any refurbishment of the existing structures. Added to this is investment in inventories, although this latter type of investment will not be considered here.

Real investment in property is encountered in several ways in macro-economic models. One aspect that is not directly treated as an investment good is public sector investment in property. Expenditure on structures, including offices, in the public sector is treated as part of general government expenditure on goods and services – on the grounds that expenditure decisions are arrived at on different criteria from those of the private sector. However, this component generally is rather small. Government expenditure on goods and services is only a part of total government expenditure, the rest of which consists of transfer payments, such as pensions, income support and debt repayments.

Most property investment takes place in the private sector, where it can broadly be divided into residential and commercial. Residential investment in the textbooks is usually treated differently from other investment goods because so much of it depends on the individual actions of consumers. Housing market models are, therefore, well-developed. Commercial property, conversely, is not analysed in such a distinctive way in the textbooks, but rather as a component of private sector investment. Sophisticated macro-economic forecasting models do break down investment into a series of submodels, including those for property markets.

General theories of fixed investment are applied to property as much as to plant and machinery. It may be objected that property is different, because it lasts longer and is built and owned in part by an independent development industry rather than for the ultimate user. Yet, it could be argued that such issues are complications rather than fundamental differences. Much equipment, after all, is now leased by firms rather than directly owned, so there is as much of an institutional disjuncture there as in the world of property.

During the 1990s, investment has typically constituted about 16 per cent of total UK expenditure, with consumption taking about 64 per cent and government expenditure consuming about 21 per cent. Investment is more important than its size suggests, however, because it tends to fluctuate much more than consumption and government expenditure and so has a disproportionate effect on the business cycle.[3]

The optimal capital stock

Investment theory builds up from the *production function*, the relationship between outputs (Y) and the capital (K) and labour (L) used to produce those inputs (land, for simplicity, is ignored), which can be expressed using the following notation:

$$Y = f(K,L) \tag{6.2}$$

What combination of inputs is optimal to produce a given output will depend on prevailing technologies and the relative prices of those inputs. The cost of labour is the wage rate that has to be paid (ignoring payroll taxes and employer pension payments). The price of capital is more complex and is defined as the *user cost of capital* – the cost of using an extra unit of capital. Inputs will be used up to the point where the revenue gained from employing one extra unit is the same as the cost of employing it. So capital is used up to the point where its marginal revenue product equals its user cost.

The interplay of technology and relative prices gives a desired (or optimal) capital stock, K^*, for any level of output. If it is assumed that there is a positive relation between output and inputs, when output rises, the amount of capital used has to increase. In addition, individual inputs are subject to diminishing returns, whereby any increase in capital with the same amount of labour leads to a fall in the marginal productivity of capital.

In terms of offices, these relationships imply, first, that there is an optimal amount of office space at current levels of national output, given the prevailing rental cost of offices, and, second, that the benefits of extra office accommodation decline as more is provided. An implication is that users will be less willing to pay for more office space as its amount increases, other things being equal, because offices are subject to declining marginal productivity as much as any other type of capital.

Investment and the optimal capital stock

Assume for simplicity that investments cannot be used for production in the same time period. This means that investment does not add to productive capacity during the time horizon under consideration when looking at fluctuations in the macroeconomy. There are two types of investment – *replacement investment* that makes up for the wear and tear of production depreciating the existing capital stock and *net investment* which adds to the existing stock.

If the relative price issue is left to one side for a moment, a very simple theory of investment can be provided – the *accelerator* theory. This simply states that investment occurs when output rises because, as output rises, more capital is needed to produce it. So investment is the difference between the desired capital stock required to produce today's output and that required to produce the previous period's output. With a fixed technology, the desired capital–output ratio, K^*/Y, is a constant, v, so that investment is simply the difference between the two periods' actual outputs multiplied by this capital–output ratio.

$$I_t = v(Y_t - Y_{t-1}) \tag{6.3}$$

The capital stock is typically 3 to 4 times national output. So this model implies huge increases in the level of investment as output rises, as each extra unit of output requires three to four times as much extra capital to produce it – hence the term accelerator. By implication, massive disinvestment (scrapping of the existing capital stock) should occur as output falls.

A more realistic variant, called the flexible accelerator, assumes that only a proportion of the adjustment takes place each year, because firms face installation costs and uncertainty about future requirements, so that there is a gradual shift from the existing capital stock to the desired one rather than an immediate period-by-period shift. Expressed in terms of the capital stock:

$$I_t = z(K_t^* - K_{t-1}) \tag{6.4}$$

where z is the proportion of the difference between the desired and existing capital stocks met in the period; and K^* is the desired capital stock for the current level of output. This relationship states that increases in output induce extra investment over a number of periods as the capital stock is gradually brought up to its desired level. Yet, although the adjustment is gradual, the fact that three or four times as much extra capital is required to produce an extra unit of output still implies that investment will fluctuate far more than output. This model may still produce unrealistically high levels of investment because it does not include the dampening effects on investment of factors such as higher interest rates, which are considered below.

Greater fluctuations in investment than output are typically observed in real economies, and the model helps to explain why investment is so volatile. This capital stock adjustment investment model has been used in the literature to examine building and office cycles as Chapter 8 shows.

Producers would be unwise, however, simply to invest in response to short-term changes in output. Several factors are likely to temper their reaction to such changes. The first to consider is the cost of employing more capital in production.

The user cost of capital

The cost of a unit of investment can be estimated by considering the costs involved in using it, known as the user cost of capital, *uc*. This concept was briefly introduced in Chapter 2 in relation to commercial property markets, here the analysis will be generalised and deepened.

There are four principal components to user cost. The first is *the real rate of interest*. To purchase the desired capital, a firm has to borrow or use internal funds that have an opportunity cost. For simplicity, assume there is only one real interest rate, r, and that the firm wishes to use the extra capital stock for only one period (to avoid the complications of present values).

The real interest rate cannot be observed, only the nominal one, i, so the real interest rate for the firm will be the nominal rate minus the firm's *expectation* about inflation for the year, p^e. So the expected real interest rate is:

$$r = i - p^e \tag{6.5}$$

Index-linked gilts, however, provide a measure of the *risk-free*, long-run, real interest rate. (It should be noted that the notation here is standard for macroeconomics texts, but that it differs from that in financial economics, and from that used in Part 3.)

Next, the extra capital stock will wear out during the course of the year as it is used, so a *depreciation rate*, δ, has also to be included. It may also appreciate or depreciate in price over the year, so that any *real change in its value* should also be included, $\Delta V/V$. Again, if the user cost capital is to influence investment decisions, it is the expected change in real value over the year which is relevant, $\Delta V^e/V$.

Finally, *operating costs* and *tax effects* have to be added. Obvious tax effects with respect to property are the uniform business rate, tax relief on company borrowings and the rate of tax deduction permissible for depreciation. Both of these components of user cost, in practice, are extremely important in property, but, for simplicity of exposition, they will be ignored here.

Drawing these factors together, apart from tax and operating costs, the expression for the user cost (*uc*) of capital consequently is:

$$uc = r + \delta - \Delta V^e/V \qquad\qquad (6.6)$$

A rise in real interest rates, in other words, discourages investment and an expected rise in asset prices encourages investment. The formula can be adjusted to take account of longer time periods than a year, adding greater complexity without altering its broad economic meaning. It is analagous to equation 10.16 in Chapter 10, although the terminology there is different.

There have been many empirical studies of the user cost of capital for firms since Jorgenson's initial work in the late 1960s/early 1970s (Jorgenson, 1971). The approach has also been used in the housing market in the USA (Poterba, 1984 and Smith *et al.*, 1988) and in the UK (Miles, 1994). Studies of commercial property sometimes start from the notion of building rent as a user cost of capital (see, for example, the discussion of Hendershott *et al.* (1997) in Chapter 9).

Expectations and output

So far it has been assumed that producers' investment response arises from a shift in actual output. Yet the change may only be temporary and followed by a decline. As investment typically lasts for several years, or longer, firms are more likely to invest in reaction to changes in their expectations of future output streams than simply by responding to today's output alone.

As was noted in Chapter 2, expectations are particularly important for investment in new commercial property for two reasons. First, they are one of the longest lasting forms of private investment, and, second, many developments are undertaken speculatively without a known user in mind. Commercial developers have to guess demand patterns a long time into the future and, when building speculatively, have to second guess the future outputs of the firms likely to rent or buy their projects in order to assess expected future user demand. They also have to form expectations about the future patterns of the other variables relevant to the investment decision considered above.

Such considerations about the importance of output expectations suggest that property investment should be relatively insensitive to short-run variations in output over the business cycle. If a long-run view of output is necessary when coming to a property investment decision, it is unclear why the course of a short-run business cycle should alter that longer-term view. Empirical evidence supporting this 'long-term' view, however, is weak. There is not a perfect correlation between property cycles and the business cycle (see Chapter 7 for the UK evidence), which could be cited as evidence of the long view. Yet, many empirical models suggest that recent changes in national output are the most important influence on the current levels of property investment (see Chapters 8 and 9). 'Short-termism', for whatever reason, may consequently limit the applicability of this hypothesis to the commercial property market.

Keynes, in particular, put great emphasis on uncertainty in the investment process, suggesting that the long time horizons required for investment calculations make any decision highly uncertain. The optimism or pessimism of investors (their 'animal spirits') would predominate as a result. This has led certain modern post-Keynesians to argue that investment is so uncertain that it cannot be predicted at all (Gordon, 1993). Alternatively, Keynes' views have been used to justify the argument that investors merely go with the herd – a belief commonly seen in journalistic accounts of property investment. Weak versions of the 'animal spirits' viewpoint suggest a reason why property investment might vary with the business cycle. During upswings property developers are more optimistic and, therefore, bring on stream more projects.

An alternative approach to such pessimism about the rationality of investment decisions is to formulate a theory of how expectations are formed. There are three basic variants: naïve, adaptive and rational expectations. People holding *naïve* expectations expect tomorrow to be the same as today; in other words, they have a constant view of the world. *Adaptive* expectations argues that people gradually adjust their views to new experience based on past changes. In this case it will be several years, for example, after a burst of price inflation and a subsequent fall in the inflation rate, before people believe that inflation is going to stay low again, even if, in reality, the inflationary surge is soon over. The other theory is *rational* expectations, whereby people use the best currently available information to come to decisions about the future.

All three theories of expectations are used in property market models. Adaptative expectations predominate in most as the theory of behaviour (see Gardiner and Henneberry, 1991 and Chapters 8 and 9 below). Valuation methods can also be regarded as being founded on adaptive expectations. Evidence presented in Chapter 10 indicates that there is serial correlation in the appraisal process. By implication, this means that valuers are using adaptive expectations when making their valuations, because they seem to be taking account of past values, as well as present-day fundamentals, when assessing current property values. Rational expectations can be seen in the greater use of forecasting models in property development in recent years. It is an attempt to use the best available information before coming to a decision about investment. This, of course, does not make forecasting models infallible – if for no other reason than that they can only use the best available information and the best currently available theories – neither of which may be perfect.

Finance constraints

External finance constraints may arise because of different risk perceptions between borrowers and lenders. A developer may calculate that the expected return from a project makes it worthwhile at prevailing borrowing costs, yet find that no one will lend on the security of the project. This probably reflects a different, and more conservative, assessment of the project risks by lenders. The developer may be a risk taker, while lending institutions are risk averse. What is of concern when looking at property investment and macro cycles is that lenders may alter their risk assessments or their attitudes to risk. In either case, financial constraints on the level of property investment will change. If lenders become more optimistic, they will sanction more property loans. Most accounts of the late 1980s property boom have, for instance, suggested that lenders optimistically altered both their risk assessments and their risk preferences, and then later, when events turned sour, switched to greater realism and conservatism (see Chapters 8 and 12).

Individual property market lenders, moreover, do not have to change their preferences or rules over the property cycle for this phenomenon to occur. This happens when their lending strategy is based upon tracking market performance or the performance of competitors (see Chapter 11).

Rising supply price of capital goods

Further factors limiting increases in investment are capacity constraints in investment good industries, which cause investment good supply prices to rise as they are encountered. Many investment goods are internationally traded, which limits capacity constraint effects. Commercial property, however, is a non-traded good, so supply constraints are often seen in property development booms. Their effects were considered in the initial property market model in Chapter 2.

In general, the state of investment theory as a predictor of actual investment over the business cycle is mixed (Chirinko, 1993; Berndt, 1991). This is perhaps unsurprising given the importance of long time horizons and expectations in the investment decision.

PROPERTY INVESTMENT AND THE MACROECONOMY

This section considers the impact on the economy of an autonomous increase in property investment. An autonomous increase means that it is not induced by other variables in the macroeconomy, such as higher national income or lower interest rates. Put less technically, the question being asked is what are the macroeconomic implications of a property boom?

As property investment contributes to overall investment, any stimulus to the economy is first seen in the investment goods market. The stimulus to demand however does not end there because of the circular flow of income in the economy – someone's expenditure represents someone else's output and, hence, income. This leads to the idea of a demand multiplier (see also

Chapter 3). The money spent on new commercial building is paid to those working on the new projects. A second round spending impact is caused as a result when part of that first round income is itself spent. That spending again constitutes income for its recipients. They too spend part of their new income, and so on. So the initial stimulus to income caused by the new investment in commercial building has a multiple stimulus to expenditure. The size of this multiplier is determined by how much of any extra income is spent.

This multiplier effect is weakened by the existence of taxes, which draw money out of the circular expenditure flow, and by expenditure on imports. Commercial building uses a large amount of imported equipment and materials, so that the dampening effect of imports will be experienced immediately in the first round of expenditure. Initially, nonetheless, it is useful to assume that the economy is closed with no recourse to foreign markets.

The stimulus to demand is only the first impact of the increase in property investment. It will also raise interest rates. The increase in transactions in the economy arising from the new property investment will raise the demand for money. With a fixed supply of money, interest rates will have to rise. The higher interest rates will then depress investment demand.

This can examined in more detail when expressed in terms of the IS/LM framework, as shown in Figure 6.1. The IS curve identifies equilibrium combinations of the interest rate, r, and national income, Y. It moves to the right as a result of the autonomous increase in property investment and the subsequent multiplier effects. In the absence of an accommodating increase in the money supply, which would shift the LM curve to the left, equilibrium combinations of r and Y in the money market remain the same. So interest rates rise, choking off some of the increase in aggregate demand. Without the rise in interest rates, aggregate demand would have grown from Y' to Y^p in Figure 6.1, but the rise in interest rates limits the increase to Y''.

So far only the effect on aggregate demand has been considered. The question now to be asked is what is the effect of property investment on aggregate supply? Are there enough productive resources around to build the newly demanded offices or will the extra demand be dissipated in rising prices? Figures 6.2 and 6.3 show the aggregate demand and supply schedules, equilibrium supply and demand relationships between the price level, p, and national income, Y. The aggregate demand schedule is derived by shifting the LM curve up and down to reflect changes in the price level for a given money supply; as a result it has a shape similar to the IS curve.

Figure 6.2 is drawn with a completely inelastic supply schedule; whereas, in Figure 6.3, the supply schedule is elastic. The distinction between Figures 6.2 and 6.3 obviously has important implications for the effects of the rise in property investment on the economy. In Figure 6.2, all resources are fully employed and no extra output can be squeezed out of them, so the rise in property investment leads only to higher inflation rather than higher national

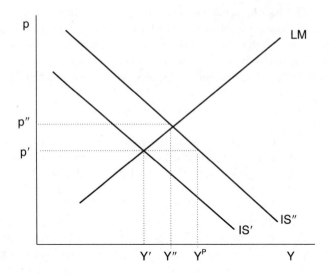

Figure 6.1 Impact of an autonomous rise in property investment in the IS/LM framework

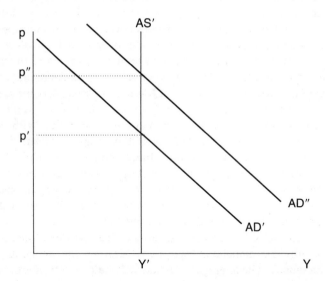

Figure 6.2 Impact of an increase in property investment with an inelastic supply schedule

income. The resources diverted to office building have to be withdrawn from other productive activities, and all the extra aggregate demand does is to push up the price level. In Figure 6.3 there is some possibility of getting extra output from the inputs used in the economy, although at the cost of a

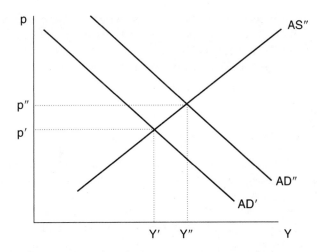

Figure 6.3 Impact of an increase in property investment with an elastic aggregate supply schedule

higher price level. In the latter case, the extra property investment does raise national income.

Which of the two scenarios in Figures 6.2 and 6.3 is more likely depends on one's view of the speed at which the economy adjusts. Another possibility is that, for some reason, aggregate demand is below the full employment level. In such a situation of *Keynesian unemployment*, the stimulus to property investment then draws on idle resources without increasing the price level.

Before looking at the open economy, a number of policy conclusions can be drawn. Most important, it is clear why the monetary authorities and the Treasury become concerned about property booms in general. Booms put upward pressure on interest rates, are inflationary and draw resources away from other possibly more 'useful' economic activities. If, for example, the government were concerned about the low level of equipment investment in manufacturing industry, a property boom would be extremely bad news – the interest rate rise would discourage manufacturing investment and the rise in the price level would make domestic manufacturing less competitive.

A government concerned about the scale of a property boom could use depressionary fiscal policy to deflate demand in the goods market, shifting the IS curve to the left again; or monetary policy could be used to shift the LM curve to the right (through a squeeze in the money supply or a rise in interest rates). Either strategy is replacing, with policy instruments, the market induced rise in interest rates and the price level as the mechanism for limiting the shift of resources into commercial building. Again, whether policy or the market is more effective depends on views of the speed of adjustment of markets, and policy preferences over the final distribution of economic activity between sectors of the economy. A nudge from the Treasury or the central bank may accelerate what is otherwise a lengthy adjustment process. The government has few macroeconomic means of specifically targeting the property sector beyond exhortation; although it could use secondary measures by adjusting the regulatory framework for lending to the property sector to make it more difficult or costly.

An open economy

So far, the analysis has been based on a closed economy. Several different conclusions are reached when trade and the balance of payments are introduced. There are two components to the balance of payments: the *current* and *capital* accounts. The current account includes the balance of trade (that is, exports of good and services minus imports of them) and current flows of net income arising from investments abroad by UK firms and residents, and in the UK by foreign firms and residents, plus intergovernment transfers. The capital account identifies the net flow of financial assets plus movements in the currency reserves and a balancing item. The latter ensures that the balance of payments is zero overall. Deficits on the current account can be offset by surpluses on the capital and vice versa.

If capital mobility is assumed to exist between countries, the impact of an autonomous increase in property investment will depend on whether the economy is subject to a fixed or floating exchange rate policy regime. Under fixed exchange rates, governments try to maintain exchange rates at a parity with one or more other currencies. The most well-known fixed exchange rate regime in the 1990s is the European Exchange Rate Mechanism (ERM) to be followed by monetary union amongst members of the European Union. With floating exchange rates, governments allow the market to determine the value of currencies.

Until the 1970s, most governments in the advanced world adopted fixed exchange rate policies. Then, after a period of generally floating rates, some countries adopted exchange rate targets or returned to fixed ratios with partner countries. The UK, in the past twenty years, has had a number of exchange rate policies. In the mid-1980s, a flexible exchange rate policy was first replaced by a 'dirty float'– as the pound began to track currencies in the ERM. From 1990 to 1992, the UK joined the ERM, but, since 1992, when exchange markets forced the UK government to abandon its previous policy, the pound has floated on the foreign exchanges.

The most important policy instrument governments have to influence exchange rates is the rate of interest. With high or near perfect capital mobility, as is the norm in today's international financial markets, if real interest rates are higher than in other countries, the real value of the currency[4] will rise, other things being equal; whereas if real interest rates are lower, the currency will fall in value. It is obvious from this that, under a fixed exchange regime, interest rates are tied to maintaining the value of the currency, so that monetary policy has no independent existence; whereas under floating rates interest rate policy can be used independently.

Under fixed exchange rates, a large increase in property investment will lead to a substantial expansion of aggregate demand. Figure 6.1 shows that an increase in investment raises the interest rate. This will encourage capital to flow into the country, putting upward pressure on the exchange rate, and forcing the central bank to increase the supply of money in order to lower the interest rate again and maintain the fixed exchange rate. The 'crowding out' effect is thereby neutralised and the demand expansion is consequently larger. The demand expansion also has less of a supply constraint because imports can augment the output of tradable sectors of the economy. Non-tradable sectors, however, will still exert substantial inflationary pressures, and most non-tradables are in the service, utilities and construction sectors.

A further consequence of the extra investment is a deterioration in the current account as imports are sucked in to satisfy the new demand. A deterioration on the current account is a corollary of the expansion of demand. This may create a conflict between maintaining full employment and the trade balance, particularly if government is reluctant to use fiscal restraint.

With fixed exchange rates (or exchange rate targets), property booms are difficult to control because monetary policy has to be used to maintain the current exchange rate parity. Governments could still use fiscal policy to dampen down aggregate demand through raising taxes and/or reducing public expenditure – but they tend politically to resist such measures.

With flexible exchange rates, the central bank is not forced to adjust money supply to accommodate pressures on interest rates, instead the exchange rate varies according to supply and demand in the foreign exchanges. If property investment rises under floating exchange rates, the upward pressure on interest rates, caused by the rightward shift of the IS curve, again encourages capital to flow into the country. This time there is an upward movement in the exchange rate as well. It makes exports less competitive, causing aggregate demand to fall until the IS curve is pushed back to its previous point. In effect, the extra property investment has replaced (or crowded out) exports within aggregate demand.

THE EFFECT OF THE MACROECONOMY ON PROPERTY MARKETS

What are the most important implications of macroeconomics for property markets? The investment function provides several insights. The first is the link between output and investment demand. Upward pressure on rents occurs during the upswing of a business cycle as firms expand their outputs. Yet, how much this affects the demand for offices and property investment

159

depends on the time horizon of the actors involved. Rational firms and developers should be aware of the business cycle and so discount temporary upturns in demand given the high transactions costs of finding and moving to new offices and the cost of building them. Commitment to new office accommodation by both users and providers is consequently longer-term – it straddles one or more business cycles. Investment, consequently, should be fairly insensitive to short-run output changes, because they should have little effect on expected output over the course of several years. Yet empirical analysis of the property market in both Europe and North America, surveyed in Chapter 9, indicates that demand and new building are highly sensitive to short-term output changes. This could indicate irrationality, in the form of excessive short-termism in the property market, or conversely it may be the consequence of other unknown factors that correlate with those variables, such as a pro-cyclical availability of credit for property (see the section below) or 'options pricing' in developer investment decisions (see Chapter 8).

The second aspect of the general investment model is that it predicts an inverse relationship between interest rates and new property investment. So, when interest rates rise, the amount of property investment should fall. However, it is important to remember that expectations of future output, interest rates and capital values are the main drivers of the investment schedule rather than current levels. If property investments are funded at variable rates of interest, as they often are in the UK, short-term interest rate changes should have little direct effect on the level of investment, unless they alter expectations of future interest rates. The precise effect will depend on the expectations time horizon of the developer and, as already noted, this is often regarded in practice as being a short-term one. If expectations are heavily weighted to the near future under a regime of variable interest rates on property loans, changes in short-term rates will have a greater effect on investment. With fixed interest finance, the impact of a rise in interest rates should be more immediate than with variable rates, because a property developer is locking into a higher long-term nominal interest rate. Delaying a project until interest rates fall again in such circumstances will have considerable impact on the profitability of any scheme – hence, a greater interest rate sensitivity. A rise in interest rates will also have an indirect effect on expected output in the investment schedule, because it will lower aggregate demand by making borrowing for consumption more expensive, choke off investment, and lower exports through the resultant rise in the exchange rate.

Changes in interest rates also affect the capital values of commercial property. When interest rates rise, present values fall, and vice versa. Changes in interest rates consequently can have considerable effects on the net worth of property companies. A lower net worth may discourage such firms from investing in new property and banks from extending new loans to them. One author (McWilliams, 1992) has suggested that the value of commercial property has another important indirect effect on investment. He argues that banks use firms' asset values as solvency guidelines and collateral for loans to those firms, so that if a firm needs to borrow to invest and the value of its property assets is falling, profitable investment is constrained. Thus, as a high proportion of the assets of most UK firms are represented by their property holdings, all types of private sector fixed investment are influenced by the see-sawing of the property market. Under this argument, the early 1990s recession led to unnecessarily depressed levels of aggregate investment in the UK, arising from exceptionally low property prices. This argument, however, conflates two factors. First, firms in the main do not use short-term bank borrowings to fund long-term investments but rather retained earnings or bond and share issues (outside property). Second, an inability to obtain funds at the prevailing interest rate, even though its expected value is positive, implies the existence of a binding liquidity constraint and so the problem, if it exists, is one of credit constraints rather than the performance of property values over the course of the business cycle. The argument of credit constraints induced by falling property values does have greater credibility when applied to the high risk investments of highly geared property companies, but the point is probably over-stretched when it is generalised to all types of enterprise.

Investment fluctuations tend to be less than they were prior to the 1940s, as the evidence presented in the following chapter will show. The exceptions to this investment trend are speculative bubbles of which there have been several in property markets in recent decades. Part of the explanation for them have been changes taking place within the financial sector and the means through which monetary policy is transmitted. The property market bubble of the late 1980s and the role of this in financial markets are considered in the following section. Wider and more generalisable explanations of property cycles are the subject of Chapter 8.

FINANCIAL MARKETS AND PROPERTY BUBBLES: THE CASE OF THE 1980s

Several countries in the 1980s were subject to spectacular property booms, which affected both housing and commercial property. The US, the UK, the Nordic Countries, Japan, Australia and New Zealand all experienced substantial booms and severe adjustments in their aftermath. Other European countries also experienced booms in particular regions, such as in the Paris region (Schinasi and Hargraves, 1993). Although there were some underlying conditions encouraging buoyant conditions in 1980s office markets – particularly the growth of service industries and the diffusion of computer technology (Ball, 1994) – much explanatory emphasis has been put on financial excess. This view can be treated as suggesting that a 'shock' occurred to

161

the macroeconomy as a result of unexpected behaviour among financial institutions during a particular phase of financial liberalisation and internationalisation.

Particular features of the USA's boom were associated with problems in its partly liberalised Savings and Loans Institutions (S&Ls), which are the US's equivalent of UK building societies. S&Ls had traditionally lent solely residential mortgages at long-term fixed interest rates, using variable rate savings deposits to fund them. This arrangement brought severe difficulties when inflation rose in the 1970s, and the US housing market, as a result, was subject to periodic mortgage famines. From the early 1980s, both the setting of deposit and lending rates of the S&Ls were liberalised. They were also given extended powers, so that they could diversify away from mortgages by investing in commercial property and financial assets. At the same time, savings deposits with S&Ls were still insured under a Federal government scheme introduced in the 1930s. The S&Ls would pay an insurance premium into a fund at a flat rate for every dollar of funds deposited with them. This situation meant that savers did not have to worry whether the institution failed or not, as the insurance scheme would recompense them if this happened. The problem was the flat rate insurance bore no relation to the riskiness of the new areas in which the S&Ls could invest.

A classic problem of *moral hazard* arose. Moral hazard can arise when someone does not have to bear the full economic cost of their actions. Self-interest may encourage the breaking of the 'trust' implicit in hoped for behaviour. The moral hazard with the S&Ls was inherent in the insurance scheme because, if S&L managers invested in higher risk investments and drew in large sums of savings, by paying a higher than average deposit rate of interest, no higher premium had to be paid for the deposit insurance; yet depositors with the S&L were guaranteed to get their money back. The only loser would be the insurance scheme, if the downside of the high risk investments came to fruition, and the S&L defaulted because of the scale of bad loans. The higher the risk, the greater the chance of failed investments so moral hazard had the potential to make many S&Ls go under, which is precisely what happened.

The S&Ls went on spending sprees, lending to dubious property schemes and buying large quantities of high-risk 'junk' bonds. Some criminal activity was subsequently discovered. The principal cause of the mass collapse of S&Ls was excessively high risk lending. Earlier predictions (Kane, 1985) of the bankruptcy of the insurance scheme, because of the moral hazard element, came true in the years 1986–8. The Federal Government had to bail out the deposit insurance scheme and many S&Ls were closed. Billions of dollars of badly performing assets were taken over by a temporary federal agency and sold. The S&Ls' deposit insurance scheme was merged with that of the banks, along with their regulation (Ball, 1990; Hendershott and Kane, 1992; White, 1991). The mass closure and enforced merger of weak S&Ls,

and tightened regulation since the late 1980s, together seem to have abated the moral hazard problem, at least until the time of writing.

Other countries faced related problems with their financial institutions in the 1980s (Schinasi and Hargraves, 1993; Kennedy and Andersen, 1994). During this period, many countries liberalised their financial systems. This eroded previous formal or informal cartels and enabled investment in new areas. Many deposit-takers experienced marked declines in loan requests from traditional borrowers as the latter switched to direct use of new instruments in capital markets. Savers also reduced the proportion of funds they put on deposit, as they diversified their financial assets by investing more in securities and other investments. Furthermore, financial flows had become more internationalised; a trend exacerbated by huge Japanese trade surpluses, which were offset by an export of capital. Finally, new lenders entered markets with little experience of their operation. The combination of these factors led to considerable pressure on financial institutions to move into new markets with poor means to make detailed assessments of the riskiness of the loans they were making. While many traditional lenders were under structural pressure, monetary policy was relaxed after the world-wide stock market crashes in 1987. The operation of monetary policy had anyhow been weakened by the changes taking place in financial markets. So it is argued that a series of events led to a surge of credit looking for borrowers (Kennedy and Andersen, 1994).

It was argued earlier, in the section on the investment function, that investment may be constrained by a shortage of credit. In property investment, there are generally likely to be a range of projects of varying degrees of risk, and it is often difficult to assess precisely the riskiness of projects. Borrowers of property loans, in addition, have an incentive to underplay the riskiness of their schemes. Weaknesses in loan monitoring will be particularly high for those who have little experience of property investment, or of lending to property, because such institutions will not have the information already available to existing lenders (known as 'insiders') on degrees of risk. Because of a lack of full information on the viability of lending to specific projects, lending institutions might rely on the reputation of particular companies rather than detailed assessment of projects.

In summary, if lenders want to lend more to property, they may have only limited information on whether they are undertaking progressively higher risk investments. If there is pressure within financial institutions to lend more, as there was in the credit surge years of the 1980s, the temptation to underprice risk is large. The subsequent large-scale failure of property developers was virtually guaranteed. This was not foreseen by many at the time. The boom conditions, brought about by the credit surge, fooled many into believing that economic conditions had permanently improved, rather than recognising that the boom was a particularly strong upswing in the business cycle. The combination of events, consequently, gives the financial excess explanation for the late 1980s boom some credibility.

The long depression in property markets after the late 1980s, when many of them took five or more years to recover, also fits in with the financial excess explanation. There would have been a large overhang of empty or poorly performing property assets and bad loans associated with them. This kept down property prices and rent levels, discouraging new investment. Property firms, moreover, had poor balance sheets and high gearing (loan to asset) ratios. They would have taken several years to improve, during which time few new projects could be contemplated. Pessimistic expectations would also have prolonged property investor gloom. Finally, the credibility of the property sector with the financial institutions on which it relies for funds would have taken a long time to recover. That property markets were depressed for so long in the early 1990s consequently is unsurprising.

There are two ways of looking back at that period of financial excess. The first suggests that financial institutions and monetary authorities were on a learning curve during the 1980s, coping with new market contexts. On this viewpoint, which is the more common, the 1980s were a one-off event to be repeated only if financial markets go through such uncertain structural change again, and even then the experience of the 1980s will still be a useful antidote to further excess. The other view suggests that there are systemic characteristics of financial markets that generate such behaviour. So property booms and busts are an endemic feature of modern societies. This is the view of Kindleberger (1978), for example, who suggests that it is common for funds to flow into property after a stock market crash because investor sentiment sees it as safe, although those sentiments are rudely broken shortly afterwards. There is, however, no detailed empirical evidence for or against this proposition.

Another explanation for the observed close correlation between short-term changes in output and the amount of property investment, mentioned earlier, is the hypothesis of a positive relationship between property market credit availability and the business cycle. It has been argued that information asymmetry in financial markets, and shifts of lenders' trade-off between risk and return over the course of the business cycle, lead to pro-cyclical variations in the availability of credit (Stiglitz, 1992).

If credit availability does vary pro-cyclically over the course of the business cycle, and property investment is generally credit constrained, then property investment will be correlated with short-term output fluctuations. The behaviour of financial institutions, rather than the myopia of property investors, is the driving force in this theory. Again, there is little empirical evidence to judge whether this hypothesis is right or wrong, but the data presented in the following chapter show that property investment is only weakly correlated with changes in national income. This suggests that the credit constraint thesis has more purchase at particular times rather than others, for example, in relation to the 1980s.

PROPERTY MARKETS AND THE TRANSMISSION OF MONETARY POLICY

The impact of monetary policy on the economy and the property sector has probably changed over the past decades because of changes in financial markets. The effects outlined above were directly on investment and consumption through interest rate, wealth and exchange rate effects. High interest rates depress demand. But there is evidence from a number of countries that the financial system now reacts differently to monetary policy shifts (Economist, 1996; IMF, 1996). In most countries examined by the International Monetary Fund (IMF, 1996), bank lending rates did not rise as much as the increase in official short-term rates, when monetary policy was tightened – and the responsiveness has fallen in the 1990s. The impact on investment schedules of a rise in the monetary authority's interest rate may consequently have weakened over time. So if official interest rates are raised, for example, the impact in property markets will be dampened.

A converse situation arises whereby financial markets can reinforce a central bank's actions. Important here is the credibility of government policies towards key policy variables, such as inflation. Governments have considerable impact on expectations in international financial markets by the interpretation those markets have of their behaviour. The *credibility* of macroeconomic policy is determined as a result. In an open economy, the credibility of governments' policies has substantial implications for interest rates. Real interest rates in the UK, for example, have had to be higher than those in Germany for many years. This is because UK governments have not persuaded the financial markets that British policies towards inflation are as credible as those in Germany. Credibility itself is formed in the markets by analysis of real economic information and prejudice.

Experience has also shown that there is a ratchet effect in credibility formation. It takes a long time to be believed, but far less time to be disbelieved. So the relationship between long-term and short-term interest rates may be different across countries depending on how financial markets view the credibility of policy statements. In countries with high credibility at fighting inflation, a monetary authority induced rise in short-term interest rates may see long-term rates *fall*, because the markets believe that in the future inflation will be lower. By contrast, in countries with poor reputations at fighting inflation, a rise in short-term interest rates is more likely to signal that inflation is going to rise for some time to come, and hence long-term rates *rise* as well. This issue illustrates the difficulties of generalising about the relationship between property markets and the macroeconomy.

The final point about the transmission of monetary policy is also one that directly affects property markets. The argument here is that the central bank can alter banks' lending behaviour. The point is an asymmetrical information one – borrowers usually know better than lenders their ability to repay a loan. Banks as a result may put a maximum limit on their total lending; one which is below regulatory requirements and the apparent profit-maximising sum. When interest rates rise, furthermore, there is a higher risk of default from banks' existing borrowers. To avoid this, it is argued that banks vary the upper limit on their total lending in line with changes in interest rates. As interest rates rise, the upper lending limit is reduced, and with it the supply of credit in the economy. Borrowers consequently are doubly hurt by the higher interest payments and the threat that their loan will be called in as banks try to reduce their lending to the lower maxima. High risk sectors, like property, are likely to be hit badly by such a credit crunch.

THE LIMITS OF MACROECONOMIC FORECASTING

One of the outputs from robust macroeconomic models is the ability to apply them to real world economies in order to make forecasts of key macroeconomic variables. Macroeconomic models, unfortunately, have a weak track record, particularly in predicting major economic change. This is partly because of the way in which they are formulated – major changes in the forecasts are almost assumed out of existence by the tendency of such models to have rapid equilibrating mechanisms designed into them. The second problem is that models try to forecast the future based on past relationships. Behavioural characteristics implicit in the parameters of the models can only be discovered by estimating them from data that are drawn from the past. To obtain a reasonable time series, the past may be a decade or more. Yet the future may not be like the past.

One of the main difficulties of macro modelling in recent years is that there seems to have been a number of important changes in behavioural relationships. An often cited one, for example, is a change in consumption behaviour linked to financial liberalisation (Miles, 1994). Another characteristic of modern economies is that their underlying structures can shift quite rapidly, again making parameter estimation fraught. The stripping out of many layers of middle management common in the early 1990s recession, for instance, must have altered many firms' optimal office needs at particular levels of output. Finally, the forecast itself may become the problem. If many people believe forecasts this should change their behaviour, yet the models have been specified on the assumption that people's behaviour is constant. These criticisms do not entirely negate the use of forecasting tools, but rather qualify their role. There is no easy route to perfect knowledge in an uncertain world. Economic reasoning is perhaps better at ruling out impossible scenarios rather than providing exact prediction.

SUMMARY AND CONCLUSION

The relationship of property to the macroeconomy is complex as the wide ranging anlysis of this chapter indicates. A central relationship is the role of property as an investment good, and the consequential effects on aggregate demand. This issue was therefore covered in some depth. The added advantage of doing this is that it informs examination of current models of property development, which are considered later in Chapters 8 and 9. Property is also a key financial asset and plays a role in the transmission of monetary policy.

The impact of property booms on the economy as a whole is likely to be significant – raising interest rates and crowding out other economic activity, for example. What happens crucially depends on the degree of openness of the economy and whether a policy of fixed or floating exchange rates is being followed. Conversely, the property market cycle is influenced by macroeconomic changes, but there is no reason in theory to think that the links are simple or direct ones. Property markets have their own autonomy and dynamic, precisely because they are a specific and unique sector of the economy.

Expectations have been highlighted as central in understanding how the macroeconomy responds to shocks. Whether agents respond to economic stimuli in a rational way, or on the basis of some other formation of expectations, is another important factor determining the type and speed of economic responses and the same could be said of property markets themselves.

A variation on standard macroeconomics was introduced in the discussion of the potential for credit constraints, leading on to an examination of the thesis that property booms are sparked off by changes in the propensity of the financial sector to lend to developers. Finally, a health warning was put on macroeconomic forecasting. This is not to suggest that it is a fruitless exercise but rather that there are well-recognised limits.

7

LONG-RUN SUPPLY, STABILITY
AND EFFICIENCY

INTRODUCTION

The previous chapter looked at short-run macroeconomic behaviour, where it was assumed that at least one economic input was temporally fixed in supply. In the long run, all factors of production can be varied. These factors include, of course, fixed capital, such as commercial property. Over the long run, moreover, a number of interesting questions arise over the role of commercial property in the economy.

This chapter starts by providing and analysing some long-run data on UK commercial property development. The objective is two-fold: to highlight the need to examine data and its origins before undertaking causal modelling; and to see whether commonly held views about the extreme instability of commercial property markets are borne out in practice.

First, there is a methodological discussion of this type of exploratory data analysis. Conclusions made from data series depend on how the data are constructed and the techniques used to refine and present them in ways that are easy to interpret. The section then examines long-run data on the amount of new commercial building in the UK, and compares it to the growth of national income as a whole.

There is no modelling of the data in this chapter but, instead, a descriptive analysis of its characteristics. This is useful given the importance of certain widely believed 'stylised facts' about property supply. Some property characterisations are shown to be true from the UK. For example, building cycles longer than the business cycle can be seen in the volume of commercial development. Yet, several widely held beliefs about commercial property markets do not stand up to scrutiny. For instance, it is widely believed that commercial property is subject to marked short cycles; in other words, that it is a particularly volatile market. This is shown not to be the case for the volume of development over time. Reasons for this relatively low volatility are then examined. Furthermore, many believe that property takes too large a share of national fixed investment; yet the data show that new commercial building represents only around 1 per cent of annual national income on average. So, neither of these two views seems likely to be true on the basis of reasonable conjectures from the available data.

The sort of data analysis undertaken in this chapter is an important pre-requisite of all time series modelling, although it is frequently neglected. It highlights features and absences in data of which modelling strategies should take account. Apart from their own interest, consequently, the metho-dological discussion and empirical information presented both provide useful background material for the later discussion of cycles and models in Chapters 8 and 9.

Arguments for a long-term bias towards property investment are then con-sidered. It is sometimes claimed that commercial property is unproductive investment crowding out the real benefit to economic growth of investment in manufacturing equipment. This claim is subject to critical scrutiny. This is followed by an examination of potential inefficiencies within property mar-kets. This section draws together conclusions from other chapters and, in addition, examines the case for and against the efficiency of relative price determination in user markets.

There is no formal discussion here of the relationship of commercial prop-erty to economic growth theory because, within that theory, it is simply treated as part of the capital stock. Commercial property also has not fea-tured within modern endogenous growth theory. Rather than take the high theoretical route, consequently, it is more instructive to investigate how much new commercial property is provided and the long-term nature of the market contexts in which it is delivered.

THE BEHAVIOUR OF UK PROPERTY INVESTMENT OVER THE LONG RUN[1]

Examining long-run commercial building data

When examining data on commercial building, there are two procedures that need to be undertaken to make the best use of the information they provide. The first is *exploratory data analysis* (Tukey, 1977). This aspect looks at the characteristics of the data, the broad pattern of its variation over time, and whether particular extreme observations – or outliers – exist, which might influence the results of any subsequent statistical analysis. The second aspect is to use the data in *formal modelling techniques* to see whether any particu-lar hypotheses about the causes of the fluctuations in the data are more plau-sible than others. Models in the literature that utilise these data are examined in Chapters 8 and 9.

Mills notes that relatively few time series texts spend much time on exploratory data analysis. However, he highlights its importance:

it cannot be stressed too highly the importance of good preliminary data analysis: it will lead to better models, more efficient computing and a greater understanding of the relationships between the data at hand, the underlying economic theory, and the modelling techniques employed.

(Mills, 1991: 5)

When long-run data on commercial property are subject to EDA (Exploratory Data Analysis), some interesting features are revealed. This is the purpose of this section: to present time series information on commercial building from 1955, the earliest date for the present quarterly time series, until 1996, to comment on its characteristics and to suggest some avenues that subsequent modelling could explore. The following two chapters then take up the modelling theme by reporting, and commenting, on models from the literature in the UK and USA.

Several characteristics of the data are examined here. The first one is based on a decomposition of the series into trends and cycles. The second is its volatility – the magnitude of the fluctuations in the data. The ways in which these time series are formulated are likely to affect the volatility of the data, so they are then examined. The final one is the behaviour of the time series on commercial output in relation to that of other relevant variables, especially national income.

Investigating trends and cycles

Decomposing time series data into trend, cycle, seasonal and error components has a long history. A traditional way of doing it is to use the technique of moving averages. For example, Weber in his study of British housebuilding used a six period moving average (Weber, 1955). The problem with simple moving averages, however, is that they can lead to significantly biased estimates of underlying trends, because the technique gives undue weight to outlier observations. This can easily lead to the estimation of spurious cycles. This problem, known as the Slutsky-Yule effect, was noted as early as the 1920s (Harvey, 1989). As identification of long waves in building has been an important element of historical research, the use of a technique which is biased towards exaggerating cyclical movements is problematic.

Modern techniques have improved upon simple moving averages considerably. Each available detrending technique, however, does not give a definitive trend; rather trend decomposition is a researcher-influenced technique, strongly dependent upon individual judgement (Ball and Wood, 1996). As these aspects of detrending techniques are important when interpreting the estimates provided in the rest of the chapter, it is worthwhile summarising the consequences of them.

Trends are not inherent in data but rather are conceptual tools applied to them. In principle, there can be no firm rule for deriving an ideal trend, apart from avoiding statistical biases in its compilation. When choosing a trending technique, causal theories about the subject in question may be of use. For example, many economic time series exhibit log-linear behaviour over the long run, arising from economic growth, so a technique, such as regression, can be used on the log of the data to produce a linear trend.[2] It may, then, be of interest to investigate whether there are structural breaks in the series, to see if particular events have affected the trend rate of growth. Looking at the raw data on property development, however, makes it clear that a linear trend is inappropriate; hence a technique that permits the possibility of a non-linear trend is preferable.

For more adequate understandings of causality, prior theoretically informed models need to be formulated and their hypotheses evaluated in relation to the data. Detrending analysis is descriptive rather than causally prescriptive. However, there may be situations where causal models are unfeasible. This may be because of an absence of relevant information, breaks in the series, or because the time period is such that parameter stability within the model cannot reasonably be assumed. For example, a time series that stretches from the nineteenth century to today is unlikely to be explained by one causal model. Similarly, international comparisons may require distinctive and complex models for each country, the results of which may confuse rather than illuminate the issue in question.

Trends can be estimated that follow the data series quite closely, but they are likely to fluctuate considerably if the data series itself is volatile. With such data smoother trends, conversely, are likely to exhibit marked cycles around the estimated trends. When examining cyclical characteristics of the data, a prior emphasis on trend smoothness helps more clearly to identify cycles in the data. Property cycles, consequently, are best revealed by a trend that is smooth.

The length of the time series from which trends are estimated is likely to influence the decomposition of the data into trend and cycle. Over the very long period, even sharp variations in economic series, like recessions and booms in national income, may well reduce to variations around a log-linear trend. Yet, this log-linear trend may not be identifiable over shorter time periods. An example of this is the contrast between the trend of UK housing output since the middle of the nineteenth century to the 1990s, which is log-linear, and that for post-1948 which is definitely not (Ball and Wood, 1998). The difference, of course, is that the latter 'trend' more closely resembles one of the 'cycles' of the longer series. Both of these trends derived from the same data series are perfectly valid – they just happen to be for different lengths of time. The period of study may be fixed by the limited availability of data – good commercial development data in the UK, for example, do not exist prior to 1955. Alternatively, it may be determined by concern with a particular epoch, such as the post-1970 period. Whether relevant information is incorporated in the trend or the cycle, therefore, depends on the length of time period studied, the nature of the fluctuations in the data, and the questions being addressed.

The detrending method chosen for use in the analysis presented in this chapter is Structural Time Series Analysis, as developed by Harvey (1989), and available in the STAMP computer software package. There are many advantages to this technique, especially its ability to present the broad trend and cycle characteristics of a series in a clear and unambiguous form. Another advantage is that trends do not have to be linear (or, more strictly, deterministic), making it easier to identify major changes in the behaviour of the series. Moreover, the method avoids the creation of spurious cycles to which other detrending methods are prone, including the commonly used Hodrick-Prescott filter (Harvey and Jaeger, 1993; Canova, 1993).

The pattern of new UK commercial building, 1955–96

Figure 7.1 shows the quarterly, constant price, time series for the log of output of new commercial property (offices and retailing) from 1955 to 1996. Henceforth, this series will be called property development, in line with standard property analysis.[3] The solid line in the graph represents the actual data, and the dotted the estimated trend. There are several features of the data and their decomposition that are interesting.

1   *Variable growth* There is no steady growth in development over the time period. Unlike many other aspects of economic life, commercial

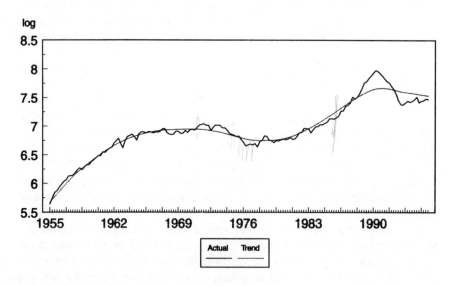

Figure 7.1 Commercial output, actual and trend, 1955–96

property development has not been subject to continuous trend growth, but to variations in the level of building activity. This long-run characteristic of property development is one reason why property researchers have directed attention to property cycles.

2   *Outliers and structural breaks* Cyclical fluctuations are generally small. Only the late 1980s boom and the subsequent 1990s bust stand out as exhibiting major deviations from the trend. The characteristics of the period from the late 1980s to the mid-1990s, therefore, seem distinctive from earlier years. In statistical terms, this may be because it is an outlier period, leading to observations that are untypical of the general behaviour of the series. An outlier characterisation is commensurate with underlying 'shock' behaviour in which a particular event, or combination of events, caused a unique surge in commercial building – leaving in its wake a large amount of overbuilding that left the market depressed for several years afterwards. Alternatively, the mid-1980s may represent a structural break in the series caused by underlying changes in market behaviour. A hypothesis perhaps justifying the existence of a structural break would be some long-term consequence of financial liberalisation on property investment. However, such is the nature of the properties of this time series that, even a decade or more later, it is not possible to distinguish satisfactorily between the outlier or the structural change hypotheses (although more complex modelling may shed some light). Whatever the underlying characteristics, the distinctive aspects of the 1980s boom make analysis of the series as a whole more difficult.

3   *Cycles and long waves* There have been several separate phases of property development since 1955. Due to the low variance of the data, additional historical information is necessary to make them clear. Between 1955 and the mid-1960s, there was rapid growth in commercial building; then expansion declined to be followed by several years of stagnant output in the late 1960s.

1955 was the year when British postwar building controls were removed following a period of severe rationing of commercial construction. The next decade can, consequently, be seen as one of catching up, since little commercial building had occurred since the onset of the Second World War in 1939. This was followed by a period of consolidation as the market absorbed the new building, in line with the characterisation of property cycles given in Chapter 8.

The next period, from the late-1960s to the mid-1970s was one of a slight increase in output, accompanied by a sharp rise in property asset values from 1973–4. For four or five years after this, output fell, then stagnated. From the early 1980s, property investment then grew rapidly, with a marked spike in output peaking in 1990, after which output fell rapidly and then stagnated.

173

By 1997, the market was again picking up. Associated with both the earlier 1970s and the late 1980s commercial development booms were marked increases in property lending by financial institutions, with much property debt written off in the ensuing slumps. These peaks, consequently, could have financial or property market explanations, as the following chapter examines.

Overall, this description of property development from the mid-1950s to the mid-1990s suggests the existence of a property cycle of roughly ten years duration. The small fluctuations in the property development data, however, suggest that the peak to trough change is usually rather limited. So, in general, the data highlight that cyclical behaviour in the volume of new development at the national level is less than is commonly believed.

The trend information suggests a broadly similar pattern of growth and stagnation but there are also signs of a long cycle in the data – running from the mid-1950s to a trough in the mid-1970s and then another trough to trough cycle running from the mid-1970s to the mid-1990s. The first cycle is 26 years long, running from the beginning of 1955 to the end of 1980, and the second is somewhat shorter, running from the end of 1980 to the beginning of 1996 (Table 7.1).

The previous data examined the absolute level of property investment, Figure 7.2 shows it as a share of national income.[4] The long commercial building cycle is dampened when commercial output as a share of national income is used. Yet the timing of the cycles is approximately the same. The two most spectacular British postwar property development booms in 1972–3 and 1988–90 stand out as marked surges above the trend in the share of property development in national income; whereas the volume data hardly indicated the early 1970s boom at all. This suggests a strong autonomous

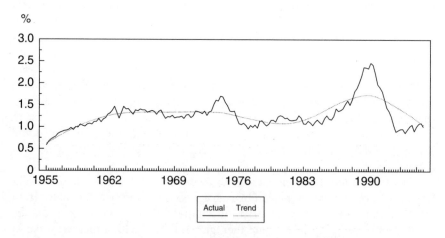

Figure 7.2 Share of commercial output in National Income, 1955–96

Table 7.1 Long cycles in commercial output, 1955–96

	Cycle	Change in output (%)
Trough to peak	1955 q1–1971 q2	+117
Peak to trough	1971 q2–1980 q4	−20
Trough to peak	1980 q4–1990 q1	+61
Peak to trough	1990 q1–1996 q1	−40

Note: Constant price quarterly data.

element to commercial property development that is independent of current changes in national income and the business cycle. The distinctiveness of the behaviour of national income (GDP) and commercial output can be seen in Figure 7.3 – where national income has a linear trend in the post-1955 era and commercial output does not.

In summary, there seem to be two types of cycle in the development data: around a ten year one and a twenty-five year one. Variations in the twenty-five year cycle are greater than in the ten year cycle. The ten year cycle has been commented on by others. Barras (1994) argues, from orders data, that the peaks are in 1964, 1972–3, 1981 and 1988–9, which fits in with his theory of a nine to ten year office building cycle (Barras and Ferguson, 1987a and b).[5] Key *et al.*'s (1994a) study reinforces Barras' analysis. It concludes that there is a recurrent cycle 'apparent in almost all indicators of market activity, though it has a highly irregular character'. For development, they found evidence of a four to five year cycle in detrended construction starts but caution against drawing firm conclusions from a relatively short time series.[6] They also suggest that two major cycles in development, peaking in the early 1970s and the late 1980s, stand out. A case could also be made for a much smaller intermediate peak. They conclude that there is a business

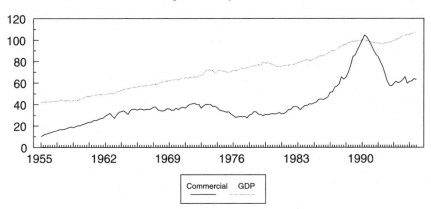

Figure 7.3 Real commercial output and National Income, 1955–96
Note: Indices of quarterly data (1990q1 = 100)
Sources: Commercial output (DoE); GDP (Office for National Statistics)

cycle influence and a ten year cycle effect in UK property development.

One reason for the differences between Ball and Grilli's (1997) periodisation, which identifies a ten year cycle and a longer one, and those of the other two cited British studies, is that the former uses output data for new commercial developments, while the other two sets of results are based on orders data. The output data are smoother than the orders data for reasons which are examined below. Statistical practices may also account for the differences. The detrending method used here is that of Structural Time Series Analysis; whereas the others used first difference and spectral techniques. These variations highlight the importance of being aware of the methodologies used when examining the literature on cycles.

CLASSIFYING ECONOMIC AND PROPERTY CYCLES

So far empirical evidence has been examined for UK property development in the post-1955 era. When examining the data and formulating hypotheses about its behaviour, it is important to bear in mind general findings and explanations regarding economic cycles. Four types of cycles of varying lengths have been suggested to exist in the literature. They may refer to general economic activity; to property or a subset of it, such as housing; or to interactions between property and the wider economy.[7]

- *Cycles of 4–5 years* These are driven by the business cycle. This affects economic activity in general and, through the impact on occupier demand, influences development, rents and prices in commercial property markets. Business cycles were considered in Chapter 6. They can be seen as a trigger for development cycles, as investigated in Chapter 8.

- *Cycles of 9–10 years* In addition to the analysis and discussion in the last section, several other authors have identified approximately ten year property development cycles. Wheaton (1987) identifies a 10 year cycle in US office market vacancies and a similar cycle in office development. Leitner (1994) also suggests a US office development cycle of 10–11 years. These cycles are argued to occur in property, rather than in the economy as a whole; although some claim, without extensive support, evidence for such an economic cycle in long-run historical data (termed a Juglar cycle, after its first proponent). Barras (1994) argues that there is a link between property cycles of this length and the 4–5 year business cycle, because of a tendency for property supply to outstrip demand every other business cycle (see Chapter 8 for details).

- *Cycles of 20–30 years* These are usually called Kuznets cycles, because of Kuznets pioneering work on the USA on nineteenth-century building waves (Kuznets, 1930). Building long waves, through their effects on

176

aggregate demand and the size of the fixed capital stock, then have demand and supply impacts on general economic growth. By the late 1960s, building long waves had gone out of fashion in the USA litera-ture, when they were argued to have ended in the USA in the interwar period with the introduction of immigration controls (Abramowitz, 1968; Hickman, 1973). More recent, internationally-oriented work highlights marked long fluctuations in the volume of house building and new built structures in general, and also long cycles in the proportion of national incomes devoted to creating them. These cycles seem to continue in most advanced economies through into the post-1945 era (Ball *et al.*, 1996; Ball and Wood, 1998). The length of postwar housebuilding cycles, how-ever, seems to be less than that suggested by Kuznets. Ball and Grilli (1997), for example, identify an approximately 12 year cycle in the vol-ume of housing investment in eleven European Union countries, which corresponds more to the UK commercial markets ten year cycle noted above. Lack of data makes a parallel exercise for commercial property in the European Union impossible.

• *Cycles of up to 50 years* These are the most controversial in terms of their existence and causes, and are suggested to be associated with waves of innovation and the widespread adoption of a new technology. They are termed Kondratiev waves and, although championed by some, they have been substantially criticised (see Maddison, 1991). No one has suggested any causality arising from the property market, but if Kondratiev waves do exist they would have considerable consequences for the demand for commercial property. During a Kondratiev upswing, commercial prop-erty demand would presumably be growing on average; whereas it would stagnate or decline in a downswing.

Explaining the Kuznets cycle

Of the four types of cycle, the first two associated with the business cycle and some period of around ten years seem to be clearly of relevance to the British property market, and probably to many other countries' markets as well. (These two cycles are referred to together as property cycles in the next chapter following standard practice.) The relevance of the twenty-five year Kuznets building cycle to the commercial market is less clear.

A variety of hypotheses have been suggested to account for Kuznets cycles. Such building long waves are generally ascribed to population change and movements (for example, Hickman, 1973), or to technological change, par-ticularly in transport (Isard, 1942). In both cases, subsequent long, but vari-able, lags in supply responses exacerbate the cyclical upswings and downswings the initial population or transport changes generate. Hickman (1973), among others, argues that the population change itself is an endo-genous part of the process of economic growth, rather than an independent

177

influence on it. He suggests this is because migration and household formation are encouraged by rising incomes in growing regions. When economic
growth tails off, or goes through a cyclical downswing, so will population
and household growth. Lags in property markets then have a feedback effect
on economic growth itself.

On the basis of the population change hypothesis, it could be argued that
the 1930s to the 1960s was a unique period of low US immigration, which
stimulated belief in the end of Kuznets cycle effects. Population movements
(associated with three migration phenomena: rural to urban; interregional;
and international) and a growing number of households have again become
significant factors affecting property markets in the developed, as well as the
underdeveloped world, in the post-1970 era. There is little modern research,
however, on their long-run property market effects.

Neither the transportation nor population explanation seems to have much
direct relevance to commercial property, but the hypotheses could be adapted
to them. This could, for example, occur through transforming the population
ideas to increases in service sector employment and changes in the location
of economic activity; while transport could be transformed into changing
agglomeration characteristics and to the impact of general technical change
on office use.

Other hypotheses could be added to these suggestions for Kuznets cycles.
Ball (1996) argues that institutional factors and shifts in policy regimes have
had important effects on post-1945 housing investment cycles. Although not
specifically within the building cycle context, Aschauer (1989), and others,
have controversially argued that public expenditure on infrastructure helped
to generate the economic boom in the postwar decades. The timing of the
claimed postwar infrastructure boom, however, has a Kuznets cycle style res-
onance. According to Aschauer, additional infrastructure provides external
economic benefits that private enterprises can take advantage of (such as
cheaper transport costs). Implicit within this argument is a key role for commercial property markets, as they are the conduits through which firms can
relocate, and expand, to maximise their benefits from the extra infrastructure
provision.

Barras (1994) generalises from population growth, transport technological
change, and new patterns of economic activity over the long run to suggest
that building long waves affect commercial property markets. They are man-
ifested in major commercial development booms associated with distinctive
phases of urban development. Such large amounts of building generate the
need for its replacement in a later 'cycle'. Chapters 3 and 4, for example,
examine changes in service sector employment and changes in the technology of production and the location of economic activity over the past three
decades. These could be cited as possible causes of contemporary long
cycles in the commercial property market.[8]

The causal status of cycles

There is a danger of seeing patterns when each 'cycle' may have distinct and unrelated causes. Cycles may be spurious artefacts of the data, a result of institutional and policy changes or a consequence of random technological shocks. They may also be endogenous to economic systems and property markets, with clear causal structures. Disentangling causality presents data problems as well as those of theory. Data, moreover, do not inherently have cycles within them but rather fluctuations. These may be interpreted as regular, or irregular, cycles but the classification is still theory influenced.

Identification of cycles, ideally, requires a long time series of data which is far longer than the cycle being considered, in order that several cycles can be recurrently identified in the data. The longer the proposed cycle in relation to the available data, the more acute is the problem. This is especially so because of major world events, such as wars, major slumps and changes in technology that either lead to breaks in the data or to major shifts in underlying behaviour. Given the general quality of property market data, and the very limited evidence prior to the 1950s, even the ten year cycle may be open to some doubt. The pattern of economic shocks in the post-1955 era – shocks which are inherently random – as much as underlying regularities might explain why they happened.

Ascribing causality to cycles remains a matter of considerable debate. For all but the shortest cycle, modelling strategies are hard because of the likelihood of parameter change and the absence of key data for hypothesis testing. Some authors merely note the cycles from observation, while others have undertaken formal statistical analysis. Barras (1994: 184) argues that cycles are not random events but rather 'they have explicable causes deriving from particular combinations of circumstances which tend to be self-replicating over varying timescales'. This is not to suggest a mechanistic pattern in the occurrence of cycles. He argues that economic shocks determine the timing and amplitude of business cycles and so affect the demand for property; conversely, changes in planning policy and building technology affect development and so the supply of property. Nonetheless, he claims that cyclical forces are 'powerful and pervasive' (Barras, 1994: 195).

To conclude, two types of cycle may have some relevance in explanations of the characteristics of property development. The first is termed here the *property cycle*, which encompasses the interlinked effects of the business cycle and, more controversially, a somewhat longer property specific variant of around ten years in length. The second is called here the *building cycle* of 20 to 25 years. Several problems arise when applying the building cycle to property analysis. Testing of hypotheses about it is made virtually impossible because considerable data problems exist. At best, only two full building cycles could have occurred over the 40 year period between the mid-1950s

and 1990s. This makes it extremely difficult to generalise about their existence, causes and effects. Pre-Second World War information is weak, and
anyway is of limited help because of the distinctive nature of property
markets then. The issue probably cannot be empirically resolved until sufficient time has passed to see whether more building cycles exist – and, even
in that distant future, structural shifts may be so great as to obscure any
cyclical causality. Not surprisingly, therefore, formal modelling interest
has been focused on explaining the characteristics of the property cycle
(see Chapter 8).

THE LONG-RUN VOLATILITY OF DEVELOPMENT ACTIVITY

One reason for general interest in the property cycle is that it is widely
believed that property is a particularly unstable market, prone to booms and
slumps in extreme ways that do not afflict many other lines of business. The
frequently believed consequence of this is that the volume of property development itself is highly unstable. As the next section shows, some commentators have taken this perception of property market instability, and generalised
it to become a characterisation of the impact of commercial development on
the economy as a whole. According to them, the instability of commercial
property markets generates periodic booms that draw real resources away
from other economic activities during periods of frenzied property boom.
This crowding out of other economic activity is deleterious to the economy
as a whole, and many of the resources devoted to commercial building during the boom are wasted in empty buildings. More severely, it is claimed that
commercial development as a whole is unproductive. Evidence for such
extreme instability could be cited using the series of major international
property crashes in recent decades, or highlighting the higher than average
risk of property development as a business activity. Such evidence does not
tell the whole story. The intellectual basis of the extreme instability argument
is considered in the next section; here the evidence from quarterly data on
British commercial development since the 1950s is examined. It does not
indicate particularly instability for commercial development activity. Other
countries' data would produce similar evidence.

Table 7.2 shows the volatility of commercial development activity from
1955 to 1996 compared with that of private housing output, national income,
the share of commercial building in national income and the orders series for
commercial output.[9] Comparisons are also made of subperiods to see
whether there have been significant changes in property market behaviour
over the period.[10]

Standard deviations are a common measure of volatility, and are used as
its measure in Table 7.2. *Short-run* volatility is calculated as the standard

deviations of the first differences of the actual quarterly data, and *medium-term* volatility is derived from the standard deviations of the trend free cycles estimated from the previous de-trending model.[11] Examination of a longer period measure of volatility than quarterly fluctuations is important because of the cyclical characteristics of property development, described in the previous section. There it was argued that property markets appear to exhibit cycles that are longer than the business cycle. The medium-term measure of volatility should pick up these variations more readily than the short-term one.

As Table 7.2 shows, medium-term volatilities are, in fact, consistently higher than the short-term ones, highlighting the importance of the longer cycle in property development. Even so, the differences across time periods for both types of volatility have the same broad pattern. Commercial output

Table 7.2 Volatilities of commercial output and orders, private housing, National Income and share of commercial output in National Income, 1955–96

(a) Output

Standard deviations of quarterly data:

Period	Short term				Medium term			
	COM	GDP	PH	COM/ GDP	COM	GDP	PH	COM/ GDP
1955–96	4.53	1.05	6.67	6.33	9.49	3.84	11.79	13.89
1955–72	4.38	0.97	6.21	5.09	4.99	3.82	8.42	5.69
1973–96	4.58	1.10	6.85	7.09	**11.85**	3.86	**13.86**	**17.81**
1973–81	3.81	1.53	6.80	6.32	6.43	3.69	14.02	12.96
1982–96	4.94	**0.70**	6.83	7.59	**14.30**	3.24	13.82	19.86

Note: COM = Commercial Output; GDP = Gross Domestic Product; PH = Private Housing Output; and COM/GDP = Share of Commercial Output in Gross Domestic Product.

(b) Commercial orders

Period	Short term	Medium term
1964–96	13.53	25.18
1964–72	18.07	24.36
1973–96	**11.48**	25.51
1973–81	10.69	19.00
1982–96	12.00	28.22

Note: Short-term refers to the first-differences of the actual data and medium-term to the first differences of the cycles around the trends estimated from a Structural Time Series Model.

is generally the second least volatile of the four variables, after GDP. Private housing has a higher volatility and, interestingly, so does the share of commercial output in national income. The greater volatility of the share rather than the level of commercial output again indicates that property output has a cycle distinct from that of national income, which implies that it partly acts as an autonomous influence on national income.

Most of the volatility changes between the subperiods were not statistically significant, suggesting that there has not been much change in market volatility over time. The late 1980s' boom, however, shows up strongly in the volatility of the medium-term cycles. For commercial property the years from 1973 to 1981 stand out as having exceptionally stable output in comparison to the residential market.

The difference in the cyclical behaviour of property output in comparison to national income is an important characteristic, because many accounts of the property cycle start off from a stimulus to demand caused by a short-run upturn in the business cycle. Yet, autonomous effects appear to be important as well, and modelling strategies need to take account of these (see the following two chapters).

The common view of market irrationality, with property investors turning new development off and on in a herd-like manner is not borne out by the difference between the volatilities of commercial output and the other spheres of economic activity in Table 7.2. Several statistical and theoretical reasons might account for the relatively low volatility of commercial development activity.

Why UK property output has low volatility

It is difficult to investigate empirically why the aggregate data on commercial property output are relatively smooth compared to housing and to many other goods. Several factors, however, can be identified, even if their actual impact is unclear.

Orders smoothing

The building period of offices is quite long. It depends on the size of projects but can extend over several years, and the statistics count work-in-progress as output as well as completed structures.[12] The quarterly output series are consequently distributed lags of previous and current commercial building starts, so that any surge in orders is smoothed out by the time it becomes an output. This is not true of housing data, for example, because most homes are built within a matter of months. Furthermore, housing data tend to exhibit the opposite of a smoothing effect in that reported orders and output may be bunched by builder respondents to minimise form filling, so that housebuilding may appear more volatile than actually is the case.

Some evidence of orders smoothing can be seen in the DOE data series for orders and output shown for the 1964–96 period in Figure 7.4. Yet what is more noticeable about the two series is the inconsistency between them. Orders data lead the output series, as they obviously should, but they rarely exceed output and the excess of output over orders from the late 1980s is extremely high.

There are three reasons why these observed divergences may exist.

1   *Poor quality data* the DOE series are of highly variable quality. There are transactions costs in collecting data, and the respondents of construction surveys from which the property development data are derived bear many of them and, consequently, adopt predictable strategies towards government statisticians' requests. Many firms ignore them, if they possibly can, or fill in forms at times and in ways that suit them.[13]

    The volume of development orders identified in a time period as a result is likely to be significantly under-recorded, especially when project management is used and for smaller schemes. For the amounts that are captured by the statisticians' surveys, there are probably marked differences between the actual timing of projects and the time at which they are recorded in the data, because completion of the data is at the discretion of the building firms undertaking the work. Some of the extra volatility of the orders in comparison to the output data, therefore, is probably spurious because it suits respondents to bunch their survey submissions.

2   Clients may ask for *revisions after making an order*, either to the specifications to the structure or to its internal layout or fittings, and those revisions tend to make buildings more expensive and so appear only in the output series.

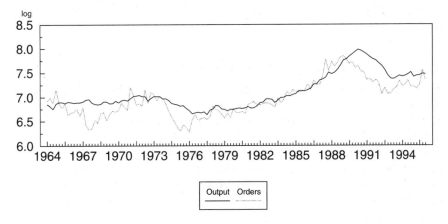

Figure 7.4 Real commercial output and orders, 1964–96

183

3   *Sub-contracting* affects both the output and the orders series. With the decline of main contracting, it is now rare to have a single contract signed for a project which can easily be identified as the value of the project. Orders surveys may fail to pick up all the subcontractors on a project, thereby underestimating the value of projects; whereas the procedures for output identify a wider – but probably still insufficient – range of project participants.

Unrecorded output may also be a cause of data smoothing. This happens when fluctuations in workloads are absorbed by sub-contractors, which fail to record the work done in workload surveys. The statisticians' estimates of that missing work are then likely to be smoother than the variations in the actual work done.

There are difficulties consequently with both the orders and the output series. Orders are most commonly used in property, but this is generally for the theoretical reason that it should signal the commitment to build projects (see, for example, Key *et al.*, 1994a). The greater inaccuracy of the orders series, which was suggested to exist above, may negate this apparent benefit. Output, though still subject to a wide range of error, in practice is likely to be a more accurate indicator of development activity, because of relative measurement errors. Conceptually, it represents investment coming on stream as new buildings, rather than commitments to providing new offices, the characteristic of orders. When adopting modelling strategies, however, researchers are faced with difficult choices because of the data problems discussed here.

Institutional and supply-side factors

Statistical problems apart, the institutional structure of commercial property provision may also help to smooth out the actual rate of new building. Property development requires land search and assembly, financial backing, conception and design, planning permission and identification of the building team. Each of these elements takes a variable amount of time, and some of the more risky decisions to proceed may be abandoned during the process, thereby smoothing output in relation to initial interest in new buildings. Building contractors, moreover, might dovetail projects and work at a pace that smoothes their own output and the output of commercial buildings in general. These long and variable lags in physical output mean that much of the short-run variance caused by property market shocks is likely to be seen in prices rather than quantities. They are examples of the low short-run supply elasticity that was suggested to exist earlier in Chapter 2. Lagged supply adjustment models are examined further in the next chapter.

Another supply-side element that potentially smooths off surges in output is the competition from housing and other construction for scarce inputs that commercial development faces during boom periods. This competition will be reflected both in rising input costs and in growing supply delays. Work reported in Ball (1996) shows that the detrended cycles of house and commercial building in Britain since the mid-1950s have moved in opposing phases – suggesting that such 'crowding out' effects may be strong. The crowding out most likely arises because of capacity constraints in the construction industry. As an alternative explanation to this pure supply-side effect, it could be argued that the housing and commercial property supply exhibit differential lags in response to the same macroeconomic demand stimuli, so that as building activity in the housing market is tailing off again it is only beginning to rise in the commercial sector. To have such coincidental and persistent long-lag structures, however, seems unlikely.

There are consequently several reasons why commercial output data are smoothed, which may partly account for the low volatility of the series. It is far from clear that the statistical inaccuracies, when taken together, alter the volatility considerably, because in part they contain random errors which partly offset each other. The 'pipeline' effects, noted above, are strong constraints slowing down surges in investor demand. National data, moreover, smooth out local variations, so development volatility might well be higher in individual regions or cities. This, however, is equally true for many other markets as well as commercial property. The national level smoothing effect is similar to the risk pooling effect of holding large stocks of property, mentioned in Chapter 5 and analysed in more detail in Part 3. It also shows the potential fallacies of extrapolating from the characteristics of individual developers to the market as a whole. Individual developers might face high risks because they are only undertaking a limited number of developments at one time and so are exposed to project risks, which may cause them to fail, that are diversified and lower at the level of the market as a whole. Hence, total commercial output is less volatile than that of any individual developer. It may also be that the underlying behaviours of property developers and investors are not as volatile, outside rare 'bubble' periods, as is sometimes suggested. Consequently variations in actual development plans, and hence measured output, are not as high as concern with 'the property cycle' would suggest. The extremes of property market activity seen during infrequent booms cannot reasonably be transposed as indicators of general property market behaviour.

One final point should be noted. The greater riskiness of individual projects than of the market as a whole, and the higher volatility of commercial property prices than of new development, highlight one of the important functions undertaken by financial markets in property development. They transfer, absorb and, to an extent, limit the risks of development, so that real behaviour in property markets is less affected by risk than it otherwise would be. The increasing sophistication of financial markets in the post-1950 era, and their growing internationalisation, may help to account for the much lower international volatility of structures building as a whole since the

Second World War (Ball *et al.,* 1996). Whilst recognising these positive benefits, nevertheless, some theories of property booms would still argue that financial markets may afflict major damage on property markets, albeit infrequently, through their role in generating unsustainable bubbles (see Chapter 6). The themes of cycles and property market instability are taken up again in Chapter 8.

HOW MUCH COMMERCIAL PROPERTY SHOULD EXIST?

Critics of property markets claim that much property expenditure is wasteful, diverting funds from productive investments. Property markets, in these contexts, usually get combined into criticisms of financial markets. Hence, Rubenstein, in his explanation of Britain's relative economic decline, says investment from the City

> into Britain's heavy industries has for decades been withheld at the expense of investment overseas or in highly profitable, but economically and socially useless areas, like property development, to Britain's long-term and severe economic detriment.
>
> (Rubenstein (1986: 135)).

The argument that the rising land values associated with commercial development represent a socially useless 'unearned increment' was examined earlier in Chapter 3.

These arguments have a long pedigree. The suggestion that property is a long-term drag on economic growth, however, is far fetched. It relies on some arbitrary classification of economic activities into 'productive' and 'unproductive' ones. In part, the claim is a familiar one that manufacturing is productive and services are not. Empirically, the claim has worn thin, because manufacturing in many advanced economies has been declining as a share of economic activity for thirty years or more, while these economies have continued to prosper and grow. In economic theory, all forms of economic activity that create added value contribute to national output, whether they are tangible products or service activities.

A subsidiary argument is that only manufacturing products can be internationally traded on a sustained basis, so that balance of trade problems arise within deindustrialisation. Many service activities, however, are internationally traded. Financial services are a major export industry, for example, with the City of London trading its output internationally and autonomously from UK manufacturing. Business and professional services are also major exporters, and prime users of office space. The argument also presupposes a relatively fixed relation between the level of national income and the proportion devoted to trade, which is not the case. The proportion of a country's economic activity devoted to trade depends on its initial resource endowments, the consumption preferences of its nationals, prevailing technologies, the comparative advantage gains that it can make from trade, and the scale of trade barriers, such as tariffs. None of these suggests a stable relationship of a necessary proportion of imports to national income; this ratio, in fact, varies considerably among nations. This proportion also changes substantially over time. In the 1930s, for example, almost half of Britain's imports were foodstuffs; now they are less than a tenth, with Britain now a net exporter of foodstuffs. Similarly, in the 1950s there was very little British trade with the countries of the current European Union; now these countries are the prime source of international trade and the share of international trade in the British economy has grown substantially as a result of the gains from trading with them.[14]

In light of these arguments, office using activities cannot be regarded as excessive simply by reference to some supposed superiority of factory production. Moreover, if office supply is as 'economically and socially useless' as Rubenstein suggests then low building rates, falling rents and property prices would be expected because no one would find much use for the existing office stock. There is no long-run evidence of these phenomena.

Commercial property and the growth of the service economy

The shift to a service economy should greatly increase the role of commercial property because offices and retailing have become relatively more important (see Chapter 3). In the UK, manufacturing declined from 36 per cent of national output in 1951 to only 18 per cent in 1996 (Ball *et al.,* 1989; NSO, 1997), with commensurate increases in service activity. A large increase might be expected in the share of national income devoted to creating the buildings in which those expanded activities operate. As can be seen in Figure 7.2, however, this has not actually happened. With the exception of the boom years of the early 1970s and the late 1980s, the share of national income being devoted to commercial building has remained within the range of 1 to 1.5 per cent since the early 1960s. Given the enormous increase in white collar work, this indicates substantial economising on the use of office space per unit of output, rather than wastefulness.

Some would cite planning constraints as a cause of this relative output stability. Evans has been a strong proponent of the view that the UK planning system has held back property development particularly in the suburbs (Evans, 1990). His arguments relate to housing but could easily be extended to offices and out-of-town shopping centres (see Chapter 3). If land supply for commercial development has actually been severely constrained, then the resultant shortage would have raised the price of the offices that were allowed to be built. There is some evidence for a constraint existing in the

187

UK, in that long-term real rental growth in the UK for shops is positive (see Table 7.3). Shops tend to be locationally sensitive, and, therefore, subject to planning constraints; whereas similar positive real rises cannot be seen in either offices or industrial buildings, both of which are less likely to be subject to overall planning constraint. In the USA, with its more open land markets, the rate of real rental growth for all commercial property is around zero.

Nevertheless, the price of commercial property relative to other types of fixed capital has still generally increased, because the world price of equipment investment goods has been falling rapidly since the 1960s (Ball, 1996). So one of the reasons why there has not been greater use of offices and other commercial property may be that the cost of using offices relative to capital equipment has increased. Firms have then acted as economic theory would predict, and substituted away from the more expensive input to the cheaper ones (see Chapter 2). Within the long-term demand for offices, in other words, two opposing forces have been at work. There has been a positive effect, caused by higher output levels with rising national income and the shift in the composition of that output towards office-using activities, and a negative effect of a rising price of office accommodation relative to other fixed capital.

A case could perhaps be made in relation to property in general for an economy like the UK's suggesting that periodic property booms destabilise the economy, through transmission effects via financial markets and through the trade balance, leading to a more extreme business cycle that discourages investment and innovation.[15] This argument, however, has greater credibility for residential property than for commercial property because of the impact of owner-occupied housing costs on household consumption and house prices on their wealth (Miles, 1994). The effect of commercial property is likely to be more limited. It is a smaller part of the economy and does not have direct effects on consumer wealth and consumption, prime transmission mechanisms between the housing market and the macroeconomy. Financial

Table 7.3 Real annual growth in commercial property returns, 1977–95

Type of property	JLW (%)	Hillier Parker (%)
Office	−3.2	−0.3
Shops	1.8	3.1
Industrial	−1.3	0.3
All	−1.6	n/a

Source: JLW and Hillier Parker (various)
Note: Returns are based on estimated open market rents and exclude capital appreciation. The JWL data include depreciation, whereas the Hillier Parker data are based on 'always new' estimates.

markets and the level of economic activity in specific regional economies are the direct recipients of commercial property stimuli. So commercial property is likely to have far less of a transmission effect to the macroeconomy as a whole than owner-occupied housing. On rare occasions, property lending may threaten to cause collapse in a country's financial system. The extent to which these are actually caused by commercial property markets is limited. It is likely to have been problems within the financial sector that led to the bad loans, and monetary policy failures would have to exist for the failure of a bank or other financial institution to lead to collapse of the financial system.

Institutional biases

Other reasons have been suggested for a long-term bias towards office development over manufacturing investment. Too many offices would be built, for example, if governments subsidised office development relative to other activities, or if private sector financiers for some reason offered lower than usual rates of interest to property developers. This process is implicit in the arguments of critics like Rubenstein. Lenders, he asserts, favour office development over manufacturing industry. The bias has two aspects: the irrational preferences of particular Institutions, and the generally favourable tax treatment given to them by the state. Two of the main purchasers of new office developments in the UK and elsewhere have been insurance companies and pension funds. Pension funds, in particular, have favourable tax treatments. They also are said to have a preference for long-term investments (see Chapter 10). This two pronged argument for the financial bias towards property was put forward strongly in the 1970s and 1980s (Minns, 1980; Massey and Catalano, 1978; Plender, 1984). It makes a number of strong claims about Institutional behaviour, however, which have not been borne out empirically.

Chapter 11 shows that insurance companies and pension funds have been steadily reducing their property portfolios since the late 1970s.[16] Several reasons account for this (see Chapter 11). Two are particularly pertinent. First, these Institutions can now invest in financial assets overseas, which government regulation had severely restricted prior to 1979. Second, the fall in property holdings corresponds to shifts in the relative returns of particular assets. So that bias, if it ever existed, is long gone, and it probably was never strong, as the Institutions have shown rationality in their long-term behaviour, even if not always in their short-term attitudes to property markets. Despite the partial withdrawal of these Institutions, the share of commercial investment in national income has not fallen commensurably – casting doubt on the validity of this double bias hypothesis. As Chapter 12 shows, Institutions may have substituted indirect exposure to property markets (for example through ownership of shares in property companies) for direct ownership.

HOW EFFICIENT ARE PROPERTY MARKETS IN THE LONG RUN?

Issues of market efficiency are themes running throughout this book. This chapter is concerned with long-run supply processes, so it is perhaps worth taking stock of the arguments over property market efficiency. If property markets do not function in reasonably efficient ways, it is highly unlikely that long-run supply will be optimally provided.

Economic theory argues that competitive markets are Pareto efficient, under a set of restrictive assumptions. By analogy, commercial property markets would also be, if they work in ways similar to those specified in the model of Chapter 2. The question then is how representative is that model of real property markets? Chapter 3 raised concerns about efficiency in relation to agglomeration economies, the dynamics of the land market and the role of the planning system, infrastructure provision and public policy. Chapter 5 noted that the competitive model avoided, by assumption, transactions costs, asymmetrical information, less than fully competitive markets, restrictive institutional frameworks and non-maximising behaviour; all of which could, in a variety of ways, weaken the efficiency conclusion. Chapter 6 examined theories of the impact of credit availability in generating property booms and slumps. If the pessimistic views considered there are accurate reflections of property market behaviour, they suggest further inefficiencies arising from the resultant property cycles. Other explanations of property cycles – which are examined in the following chapter – have different, and less pessimistic, efficiency implications. Part 3 considers the efficient pricing of property as a financial asset. There, it is suggested that pricing problems exist, because of the institutional framework of valuations (see Chapter 10).

The case for efficiency in commercial property, therefore, inevitably must be qualified. Yet, the degree to which commercial property markets exhibit these efficiencies is hard to measure or judge. This scale effect is important. It may be possible to identify the existence of some potential market failure but, by itself, that says little about its overall market impact. Most real world markets, moreover, contain inefficiencies. Whether they are better or worse in commercial property markets is a matter of conjecture.

Efficiency and adjustment

Economic damage may also be done by the impact of some medium-term adjustment processes that may operate within property markets. They take three forms, and can only be indicated because the scale of the consequences varies and is, in any case, difficult to quantify.

1   *Impact of booms and slumps on the rest of the economy* When the property market enters a severe cycle of boom and slump, as it did in the late

1980s through to the early 1990s in the UK, destabilising effects are transmitted to other sectors of the economy. That of itself, however, is insufficient to highlight a need to improve the efficient operation of property markets. It depends on what the causes of the boom/slump cycle were. If the causes are exogenous to property markets, then the problem lies elsewhere rather than with property itself.

2   *Temporary persistence effects* Office and retail buildings are tangible and expensive to remove or replace. The mistaken investments of a boom, consequently, remain to haunt future property market activity. Oversupply may freeze the location of the stock of offices in a locality for several subsequent years, as investors become excessively cautious until the supply overhang has passed. In the meanwhile technological and other change may alter the types and location of accommodation users require. The mismatch will only be resolved in the next upswing. This is an example of the persistence effects mentioned earlier, although the effect gradually fades away.

3   *Long-lasting persistence effects* The mistaken investments may also permanently alter the trajectory of a local property market, because of the reconfiguration of agglomeration economies that may result, through associated investment in infrastructure, or because of the new spatial configuration of economic activity. One of the best examples of this effect occurred with London's Docklands. The scale of commercial investment made there during the 1980s boom was, it is generally agreed, excessive. Yet its existence has tilted the direction of the expansion of the City of London and the pattern of new infrastructure investment in London. This type of persistence effect is long-lasting.

Overall, it is hard to judge the scale of these persistence effects, and whether they affect the national economy as a whole or predominantly only particular local or regional economies (for example, see Case, 1992 on the consequences of the 1980s property boom in Boston, MA).

The efficiency of relative price determination in user markets

Cross-sectional views on price formation in the literature come to differing conclusions on how efficient relative price determination is in property markets. In the commercial market, user costs are represented by rents; in the housing market, attention is paid to relative house prices. Two opposing views can be identified, as represented in the views of Evans, on the one hand, and DiPasquale and Wheaton, on the other.

Evans (1995) argues that inefficiencies creep in because all properties have some unique characteristics, so that they are poor substitutes for each other.

The prices of properties, he argues, are the sum of the prices of their characteristics – and these implicit prices are unknown to buyers and sellers. Because each property has a unique bundle of characteristics, the bargaining between buyer and seller ends up as a bilateral bargain with the price fixed somewhere between the seller's reservation price and the purchaser's maximum willingness-to-pay. Empirical predictions can be made of the prices of specific residential properties, by utilising estimates of the implicit prices of its characteristics derived from hedonic regression techniques; but those predictions, he argues, are only 90 per cent accurate (in practice, they are even less so). Valuers' estimates of the price of properties have a similar margin of error. So property markets are said by Evans to be '90 per cent efficient' – although that proportion should be thought of more as a didactic device than an accurate estimate of potential price inefficiency. He concedes that commercial markets are likely to be more efficient than housing markets, because it pays users there to get the best information (see Chapter 10 for comments on valuation accuracy).

DiPasquale and Wheaton (1996) suggest the opposite. They argue that properties of particular types, such as offices or housing, generally consist of close substitutes. There are two reasons for this. First, households and firms are highly mobile within metropolitan markets. This mobility quickly removes any over- or underpricing of properties relative to each other. Secondly, they argue that consumer preferences are constant over time (a standard neo-classical assumption) and so are the attributes of properties. This means that the relative prices of properties should be fairly stable. Relative prices may alter when demand changes because of variations in the cost of travel, job locations or demographic factors. Alternatively, supply may alter because changes in the attributes of properties, caused, for example, by the impact of new transit systems or changing neighbourhood effects (such as gentrification and other aspects of social composition and the crime rate). But these demand and supply changes are likely to be slow and so can clearly be priced into the value of affected property. Again, they present data to justify their claim, this time from the Boston, MA. housing market.

On the face of it, the second view of price formation makes more sense in situations of stable prices. Neighbourhoods vary but within them properties are often similar, so it is fairly easy to compare prices, after relatively limited search. Evans' point about bilateral bargaining, moreover, is not a criticism of price efficiency in the sense being used here because neither party should be able to gain, at the other's expense, from the relevant available public information. What each does not know is the other's price range. With substitutability, that range should be small. Where errors are more likely to occur is when the general price level for properties alters rapidly, because of boom or slump conditions. Over time, and over the course of a property cycle, the relative prices of particular attributes contained in buildings of specific types may alter because of changing demand and supply conditions for them. It may be hard consequently for consumers and valuers to be able to access their implicit prices by using comparisons with other equivalent properties. This argument leads back to temporal inefficiencies.

Commercial markets may conform more closely to the Evans view than the housing market. The reasons for this are their greater heterogeneity; the more limited number of sales; their greater locational specificity; and the fact that a large-scale office development is more likely to have an impact on the overall supply and demand balance in a city than a particular residential development. All of these factors limit the available comparable information.

It should be noted that these arguments about relative price formation in the user market are again essentially based on conjecture.

SUMMARY AND CONCLUSIONS

This chapter has examined the relationship between property investment and the economy in several ways. First, the long-term pattern of British property development was descriptively examined. It was shown that real investment in commercial property, excluding the industrial sector, has not continuously risen over time but, rather, has been subject to long cycles. The cycles could be interpreted either as four post-1955 phases of boom and bust, or as two long waves. How these cyclical phenomena are regarded depends on having robust causal theories that correspond to their existence; otherwise they could just be a spurious artefact of the data. It was suggested that it would be very difficult to explain the two long waves. Theories have, however, been suggested for the roughly decade long cycles, and they are reviewed in the following chapter. Empirical analyses of property development through time are dealing with time series that are strongly influenced by substantial spikes in the data, represented by sharp booms, which may be caused by external shocks to property markets as much as inherent property market behaviour.

Descriptive analysis of new commercial building over time showed that its level was imperfectly correlated with that of national income. Furthermore, the volatility of the commercial development is lower than that of residential building. The reasons for this lower volatility were suggested to be the fact that market instability is primarily transmitted through property prices and financial returns to property development and investment than through changes in the level of development itself. Supply lags, such as the nature of the commercial 'development pipeline', help to smooth out physical development. There also may be less pronounced herd-like behaviour among developers and investors than is sometimes suggested.

In addition to these smoothing factors, the data on development themselves are of variable quality. Partly, because of under-recording – a problem that particularly affects orders data. This questions their accuracy and applicability as measures of changes in the amount of development.

Commercial property investment takes up a relatively small and stable proportion of national income. In the UK, it is slightly more than 1 per cent on average annually – although the percentage exceptionally rose to 2.5 per cent in 1990 at the end of the 1980s property boom. The distinctive character of the 1980s boom, coupled with the generally low variance of the new commercial building series, creates problems for empirical modelling that attempts to explain the reasons for fluctuations in property investment – a fact that should be borne in mind when such models are reviewed in Chapters 8 and 9.

Turning to the questions of long-run economic efficiency, recurrent claims have been made that suggest that property investment in the UK has been excessive and to the detriment of manufacturing industry. Here it has been argued that these are much exaggerated.

The case for the property market being roughly economic efficient over the long term is mixed. The evidence does not point to a general overprovision of commercial property but there are several potential supply-side inefficiencies. Problems in the development pipeline are one set of causes because they generate varied lags in the effects and impact of decisions to undertake commercial projects.

Two opposing views exist in the literature with regard to relative price formation in property markets. One says that insufficient trades, based on limited information, restrict the ability of the price mechanism to match relative property prices with user preferences and the stock's attributes. The other argues that there are enough trades and information around to enable the market to do the job. Empirical evidence is not available to discriminate effectively between these views. The likelihood of the less than fully efficient view being right for large offices is perhaps higher because of the scale and lumpiness of property and moves by users to new accommodation.

8

PROPERTY CYCLES

INTRODUCTION

This chapter and Chapter 9 consider modelling of relationships between the property market and the economy. The focus of this chapter is property market cycles while Chapter 9 considers modelling and forecasting. However, the two chapters are closely linked and cover common ground.

Chapter 7 set out four types of cycle in economic activity. It focused on longer cycles in new output of commercial property. This was termed 'property investment' because it involves the application of real resources to the creation of new commercial buildings. This chapter considers the shorter property market cycles. In keeping with conventional usage in the literature, what was termed property investment in the last chapter is here called development.

In the last chapter, cycles were considered as fluctuations around a long-term trend. This is in contrast to the common usage of the term 'property cycle' which suggests a much stronger pattern of persistent rise and fall than is observed and, consequently, implies a predictability of the timing, amplitude and period of cycles which is far from the truth. There are recurrent fluctuations but these are irregular and do not follow a precisely predictable pattern.

Sharp rises in real commercial property rents, followed by rapid rises in the level of new development and then by sharp falls in rents are observable in many advanced economies. These occurred in the early 1970s and in the late 1980s, notably in the office markets of large cities. While the severity and timing differed, the incidence was remarkably widespread. There is, however, evidence to suggest that the timing of these 'cycles' is becoming more coincident (Lizieri and Finlay, 1995; Leitner, 1994). This can be attributed to increased integration in economies and in capital markets, although local economic and political circumstances still modify the patterns.

The four components of the *property market* were considered in Chapter 2. These are: the user market; the financial market; the development market; and the urban land market. They are strongly interlinked. In an upswing, for

195

example, economic activity generates demand for the occupation of property and, as user demand increases, rents rise and vacancy rates fall. Developers take these market signals and begin to develop, and lenders and investors are willing to fund the developments or to purchase the completed developments. Increases in development profitability lead to a rise in land values.

Fluctuations are found in all property market indicators which most observers believe reflect an underlying cyclical dynamic. There is a substantial literature on demand cycles in the user market, and on development cycles in the development market. Rental cycles (the user market) and capital value and return cycles (the financial market) receive attention in the specialist property literature (see, for example, Key *et al.*, 1994a; 1994c). Cycles in the land market have not received much attention, in part because of the difficulties of constructing a meaningful time series for such a heterogeneous market. This chapter is primarily concerned with development cycles and, to a lesser extent, rental, capital value and vacancy cycles, but other aspects are mentioned as appropriate. Chapter 9 then considers the modelling of some of the linkages within the property market.

The next section characterises the property cycle. Subsequent sections consider various exogenous and endogenous explanations of cycles. These include: the accelerator principle; the accelerator combined with a building lag; rental adjustments to the vacancy rate; the behaviour of key agents; and a model based on option pricing. Finally, there is a summary and conclusions.

AN IDEALISED CHARACTERISATION OF THE PROPERTY CYCLE

The pattern of an idealised property cycle, using an adaptive expectations framework, is summarised below (adapted from Barras, 1994; Key *et al.*, 1994a; LaSalle, 1996; and Witten, 1987). Much of the literature describes these broad patterns, perhaps with the exception of the fifth stage, but a variety of theories exist to explain them.

1 *Business upturn and development* An upturn in the business cycle, typically at a time of low real interest rates and high capital availability, generates a rise in economic activity and strong user demand. This occurs at a time of low levels of development, so available space is absorbed quickly. Vacancy rates fall and rents rise, so investor optimism increases. Capitalisation rates fall, as a result of lower interest rates, lower expected risk and higher expected rental growth (see Chapter 10). Capital values rise. This may be after a delay as valuations take time to adjust to new information.

The expected profitability of new development improves, new development begins and land values increase. As the boom continues, lending may be extended to more speculative development projects. Although a development boom has begun, there is a lag between construction starts and completed development. This means that limited new supply has reached the market, so rents and capital values continue to increase.

2   *Business downturn and overbuilding* Real interest rates rise in response to the boom and the business cycle turns downwards. Demand and absorption of new space level off and then fall. New development has reached the market. Vacancy rates begin to rise and rental growth begins to falter.

    Capitalisation rates rise with real interest rates and in anticipation of poorer growth prospects and greater perceived risk, and capital values fall. As in stage 1, this may be delayed because valuations are slow to respond. There is a fall in new project starts but much continues, in part, because it is already under way and there are substantial sunk costs.

3   *Adjustment* The fall in the demand for new space coincides with the peak in supply. Vacancy rates rise above their equilibrium level and rents fall, although the adjustment may be gradual.

    Developers are unable to generate income to cover the interest payments on their completed developments and lower capital values mean refinancing is not possible. There are bankruptcies and the poor returns lead to disinvestment from the property market.

4   *Slump* Demand and development are low and vacancy rates are above their equilibrium levels. Open market rents have fallen below equilibrium levels.[1]

5   *The next cycle* The effects may extend to the next upturn if the oversupply in the boom was so great that, when the next business upturn occurs, there is substantial vacant space left over from the previous upturn and so limited need for new development.

The following sections consider various explanations of these fluctuations. The focus is on the development, rental and vacancy cycles. The notation used by different authors has been standardised to enable easier comparison (see Table 8.1)

BUSINESS CYCLES AND DEVELOPMENT CYCLES

The simplest explanation of development cycles is that they are part of the general business cycle. Thus, if there are cyclical fluctuations in output, similar fluctuations would be expected in the demand for, and, therefore, in the

Table 8.1 Variable labels and descriptions: cycles

Variable label	Variable description
CD_t	new completed development
I_t	investment
K_t^*	desired capital stock
K_t	actual capital stock
M_{t-n}	the information set used to predict future output or employment in manufacturing
NC_t	nominal cost of capital (interest rate; sometimes taken net of tax)
ND_t^*	desired new development
ND_t	actual new development
OE_{rt}	operating expenses, usually as a rate
RR^n	real equilibrium rent
RR_t	real rent
S_{t-n}	the information set used to predict future levels of retail sales
T_t	the local tax rate
TD_t^*	total desired development
TD_t	total actual development
VR^n	natural vacancy rate
VR_t	vacancy rate
W_{t-n}	the information sets used to predict future output or employment in warehousing
Y_t	quantity of user output

production of, property. In essence, this explanation focuses on exogenous occupier demand for space as the primary mechanism driving development. A related explanation focuses on the pro-cyclical exogenous availability of finance. This is considered in Chapters 6 and 12. Some aspects are developed in the section below on behavioural explanations. These approaches have no role for other factors, such as rents, vacancy rates and yields (capitalisation rates).

The demand for property for occupation is a derived demand (see Chapter 2), that is, it is derived from the need to occupy property to undertake activities, such as the production of goods and services, for which demand exists. There is no direct measure of this demand so it has to be measured by proxy. The usual measures relate to output of, expenditure in, or employment in, sectors of the economy relevant to the type of property under consideration. These might, for example, be business services employment for offices, retail sales for retail and manufacturing output and warehousing activity for industrials. These are all measures of economic activity and fluctuations are evident in each of them.

Key *et al.* (1994b: 3) argue that the literature on business cycles suggests a persistent cycle, usually of three to five years, which is irregular in period and amplitude, and thus hard to predict, but which is systematic in most indicators of economic activity, although with various leads and lags. It is a universal phenomenon in modern economies (for example, Gordon, 1986 provides an exhaustive study of business cycles in the US).

Thus, if new property could be produced within a period, development would exhibit cyclical tendencies related to exogenous fluctuations in economic activity. This type of model has been proposed for the US industrial property market and is considered below. First, however, it is necessary to consider the concept of the accelerator.

The accelerator principle

The accelerator model was introduced in Chapter 6. The basic principle is that the *level* of net new investment in capital goods is proportional to the *change* in the level of the output of users of the capital goods. For a given level of technology, the capital to output ratio is constant. Thus:

$$K_t^* = vY_t \tag{8.1}$$

where K_t^* is the desired level of capital stock at time t; Y_t is the level of user output; and v is the desired capital–output ratio (K^*/Y) which, with fixed technology, is constant.

With fixed technology, if economic activity is constant, it is not necessary to increase the use of capital goods such as property. Investment is limited to the replacement of redundant stock and depends on the rate of depreciation of the stock. However, if output rises, it will be necessary to increase the amount of new property required and this will depend on the change in the level of activity. Thus:

$$I_t = v(Y_t - Y_{t-1}) \tag{8.2}$$

where I_t is investment.

In this model, property investment may exhibit large surges when output rises, resulting in intense development activity followed by periods of no development when output is static or falling. In practice, responses to increases in output are not so simple, as adjustment and relocation costs can be high and there is uncertainty about the future. Occupiers may first use 'slack' space and may then chose to 'overuse' space until they are sure that the increased demand will be sustained. Only then will commitments be made for additional or replacement space. This means that the market signals to developers in the form of changes in the rent and the vacancy rate may be delayed.

Developers may also delay initiating new development. There are a number of possible reasons: new building may already be in the pipeline from previous periods; there may be cautious expectations about future demand; and it may be impossible to reverse development decisions once work has started without incurring substantial costs. However, this suggests an insensitivity to variations in short-term demand which, empirically, does not seem to be the case in property development (see Chapter 6).

A more realistic version, the *flexible accelerator*, assumes that only a proportion of the adjustment takes place each period. Thus, there is a gradual shift from the existing level of capital stock to the desired level:

$$I_t = z(K_t^* - K_{t-1}) \tag{8.3}$$

where z is the proportion of the difference between the desired and existing capital stocks which is met during the period.

A US model of industrial development

An example of the use of the flexible accelerator to model development is found in Wheaton and Torto (1990). Other multi-equation US models of the property market, some of which contain an accelerator element, are considered in Chapter 9.

Wheaton and Torto (1990) consider the US industrial development market. They argue that, as most industrial buildings in the US are owner-occupied and a majority of rented properties have a single long-term tenant, the production of industrial property can be treated as an investment decision of a firm, and so the accelerator principle can be used to model it. They assert that there is little speculative industrial development and little evidence of a traditional property cycle in vacancy rates of industrial property. Some support for this view comes from Barras (1994) who argues that industrial development in the UK is more strongly influenced by the business cycle than by the development cycle. Grenadier (1995), however, suggests that industrial markets display cyclical behaviour.

The modelling starts from the assumption that the desired long term level of industrial plant depends on expected future output which, in turn, depends on current and past values of manufacturing and wholesale output or employment. The cost of capital is also a factor. Thus:

$$K_t^* = \alpha_0 + \alpha_1 M_{t-n} + \alpha_3 W_{t-n} + \alpha_4 NC_t \tag{8.4}$$

where K_t^* is the long run desired capital stock (industrial plant); M_{t-n} and W_{t-n} are the information sets used to predict future output or employment in manufacturing and warehousing, respectively; NC_t is the nominal interest rate (net of tax); α_i are constants; and $t-n$ indicates that a number of different lags may be important but these are not known until estimation.

However, because of the costs of adjustment and a dynamic outlook, firms phase the investment gradually. Thus, the flexible multiplier approach of equation (8.3) is adopted:

$$TD_t^* = \mu(K_t^* - K_{t-1}) \tag{8.5}$$

where TD_t^* is the total development desired in period t; K_{t-1} is the actual capital stock; and μ is a constant, analogous to z in equation (8.3).

Actual deliveries of new property are spread out after the desired investment with an adjustment factor β, so:

$$TD_t = \beta TD_t^* + (1 - \beta)TD_{t-1} \tag{8.6}$$

where TD_t is the actual total development (starts, but these are completed within the period); and β is the adjustment rate.

Finally, allowing for a depreciation rate of δ, the actual stock is:

$$K_t = K_{t-1}(1 - \delta) + TD_t \tag{8.7}$$

The above equations can be combined to give:

$$TD_t = \beta\mu(\alpha_0 + \alpha_1 M_{t-n} + \alpha_2 W_{t-n} + \alpha_3 NC_t) - \beta\mu K_{t-1} + (1 - \beta)TD_{t-1} \tag{8.8}$$

This equation is estimated for the US industrial market using twice-yearly data for the period 1967–89 and with a variety of lag structures.[2] The appropriate lag structure is derived from analysis of the data.

Unlike the Barras model considered below, this approach includes the cost of capital (NC). This is acknowledged by Barras to be a factor but he argues that output is the most important variable. Wheaton and Torto appear to use the nominal cost of capital, whereas it might be expected that the real rate would be more important. Interestingly, this variable is only significant with a five period (two and a half years) lag. This is much longer than the construction period for industrial property and it is difficult to offer a sensible economic interpretation. In general, nominal interest rates do not appear as significant models in the property market models considered in Chapter 9.

This approach has no endogenous cycle mechanism. Equation (8.6) is a way of dealing with the development lag. Although the authors do not do so, it can be expressed as:

$$TD_{t-1} = \beta TD_{t-1}^* + (1 - \beta)TD_{t-2} \tag{8.9}$$

and substituted in (8.6). If this is continually repeated, the new expression is:

$$TD_t = \Sigma\beta(1 - \beta)^n TD^*_{t-n} \qquad\qquad (8.10)$$

This shows that actual completions are a polynomial distributed lag of desired levels of new development from the current and previous periods. The amount of new development responds to a single period shock over a number of periods: the greater β is, the smaller the number of periods. If there are cycles in the level of desired development, there are cycles in completed developments, but these are dampened by β: the lower β is, the greater the dampening. Wheaton and Torto estimate a value for β of 0.5 which produces significant dampening of demand variations.

Thus, this approach gives a central role to business cycles in generating property development cycles. However, it is only for the industrial market, where Wheaton and Torto argue there is little speculative development and little evidence of a traditional property cycle in vacancies. Price and vacancy signals to developers are, therefore, unimportant.

Problems with the business cycle explanation

There is one important problem with this explanation. It does not explain the substantial difference between the pattern of fluctuations in development and that in user demand. There is evidence of a relationship between demand and development and of a coincidence between cycles of demand and construction *starts*. However, the patterns are more complex than those suggested by this explanation. Barras and Ferguson (1985) found that commercial and industrial property new orders are virtually coincident with the business cycle but that construction completions lag by three to four quarters. A similar conclusion is reached by Key *et al.* (1994a) who suggest that construction starts are coincident with the economic cycle and that construction completions lag it by one to two years. Chapter 7 also showed that property output has a different pattern from national income. The magnitudes of the cycles are very different. There may be an autonomous element in development and there are causal relationships from levels of development to levels of economic activity.

From the above, an upturn in business activity generally triggers an upturn in development. However, the differences in the patterns of fluctuations in demand and development suggest that the relationship is complex. The next section considers the theory that lags in building generate *endogenous* cycles in development.

BUILDING LAGS AND DEVELOPMENT CYCLES

A building lag model of UK office development

In the above version of the accelerator model, the production of capital goods responds during the period to provide for the investment demand. In reality, there is typically a delay which varies according to the good being considered. It has been argued that business cycles are the product of the delay in the production of inventories, and Evans (1969) shows that both the accelerator and a lag are necessary for generating cyclical fluctuations.[3] For property development, this delay is substantial. It plays a central role in the Barras model of the development cycle discussed below.

The most comprehensive study of the development cycle in the UK is to be found in the work of Barras (1983; 1994) and Barras and Ferguson (1985; 1987a; 1987b). Barras (1983), in common with most formal analyses of property cycles, focuses on the office market. His other work is more general, and that with Ferguson also covers housing. The basic modelling framework provided by the earlier work is outlined here. Much of the later work is beyond the scope of this book. The model gives central importance to demand both as the determinant of long run equilibrium level of development and, through the business cycle, as the main source of shocks to the property market.

Fundamental to this analysis is the notion that the lag between demand and supply, combined with the accelerator principle, produce an *endogenous* mechanism which generates the cyclical tendencies in property development. These cycles are independent of fluctuations in demand.

As in the model of Wheaton and Torto (1990), the flexible multiplier approach of equation (8.3) is used. Here, the time subscript, t, refers to periods equivalent to the construction lag.

$$ND_t = \mu(K_t^* - K_{t-1}) \tag{8.11}$$

where NDt is new development (starts); and μ is a constant, analogous to z in equation (8.3).

Barras (1983: 1384) explains that the stock adjustment equation (8.11) subsumes the link between changes in the demand for offices and the level of development induced. He suggests a transmission mechanism as follows: the greater the excess demand for floor space, the higher are rents and capital values, and so the higher the profitability of new development which determines the net level of new development starts. He notes that the proportionality of the stock adjustment equation requires the 'considerable simplifying assumption of direct proportionality relations at each stage of this transmission mechanism'. In the absence of speculative development, these assumptions are not required in Wheaton and Torto's (1990) model of the US industrial market.

One further term is added to the analysis.[4] This represents that part of new development which replaces depreciated stock:

$$TD_t = ND_t + \delta K_{t-1} \tag{8.12}$$

where TD_t is the actual total construction (starts); and δ is a constant depreciation rate.

Thus far, the basic approach is very like that of Wheaton and Torto (1990): the only difference is the treatment of depreciation. Whereas Wheaton and Torto subsume the replacement of depreciated stock into total development (replacement and additional space), Barras separates it out and models additional development.

A lag is now introduced. If it is assumed that new development takes a full time period (of unspecified length to simplify the formulation) to be produced, then:

$$CD_t = TD_{t-1} \tag{8.13}$$

where CD_t is new completed development; and TD_{t-1} is total development starts in the previous period.

The total amount of capital stock in any period is the stock last period, less the depreciated stock, plus the developments started in the previous period and completed this period, thus:

$$K_t = (1 - \delta)K_{t-1} + TD_{t-1} \tag{8.14}$$

From these relationships, the model for development starts is produced. There are two parts: the first represents the equilibrium path with respect to the exogenous path of user activity; and the second describes the deviation from the equilibrium path caused by a disturbance.[5]

The actual time pattern of TD_t depends on the values of three parameters: the length of the delay between development starts and completions; μ, the adjustment rate in equation (8.11); and δ, the rate of depreciation. Three aspects of the time pattern are of importance: the tendency to produce cyclical fluctuations; the period of these fluctuations; and the stability of the fluctuations. The relationship between these and the parameters is now explained.

1   *Cyclical fluctuations* These will occur if, with δ in the range 0.01 and 0.04, μ, the proportion of new demand for which developments are initiated, is greater than 0.25 to 0.27. As, according to Barras, μ is typically in excess of this in the UK office market, the model will generate cyclical fluctuations. This range for δ is consistent with values estimated in studies of depreciation, such as Salway (1986), Baum (1990), and Hendershott *et al.* (1997).

2   *Period of the cycle* With depreciation, δ, set at 0.03, values of μ in the range 0.5 to 1.0 generate a period in the range of eight to six unit time periods (not years). Thus, with δ = 0.03, μ close to 1.0 and a construction period of 1.5 years, a nine year development cycle will be generated. Note, however, that a value for μ close to unity means almost full adjustment to increases in demand and so undermines the need for the accelerator principle on which the model was built.

3   *Stability* If (μ − δ) < 1, the cycle will be dampened but if (μ − δ) > 1, the cycle will be explosive. With δ at 0.03 and μ close to 1.0, the cycle will have nearly constant amplitude. The nature of the development industry imposes dampening forces on any tendency towards explosive cycles: new development cannot exceed the short term capacity of the construction industry while a floor is imposed by the condition of no disinvestment, although, in practice, there may be some changes of use and demolition. The floor constraint means that slumps may be prolonged because vacancies may persist.

Thus, according to Barras, with realistic values of the parameters, the model produces the observed fluctuations in UK office development activity. Fluctuations in business activity trigger and sustain the development cycle: a business cycle of 4 to 5 years produces a development cycle of 8 to 10 years. The two are coincident every second business cycle and reinforce each other.

Problems with the building lag explanation

Despite the appeal of a relatively simple model which generates observed outcomes with plausible values of the input variables, the model suffers from a number of problems.

The accelerator principle allows no role for interest rates, prices and expectations (see Chapters 2 and 6). Development is generated by output and the model has no place for the inevitable adjustments to rents and capital values. Barras (1983) does identify other important variables affecting demand for office space: output prices, the user cost of capital and profitability. However, he goes on to state that the results of unreported analyses suggest that lagged output is the most important variable.

Grenadier (1995) suggests the lag explanation assumes myopic behaviour of developers. Developers can and do make errors in forecasting demand but a development lag is not a surprise to them. They should and do take into account the future state of the market. He also argues that there are cycles in the industrial market where lags are much shorter.

If the cycle generating mechanism is so important, it should be possible to exploit it, by investing counter-cyclically, to generate above normal investment returns (see Chapters 10 and 11) and, in doing so, remove the cycle's effect. If this does not happen, it suggests that developers neither learn from experience nor anticipate the future. Such a view is not without proponents (see the section below on behavioural explanations). On the other hand, if the mechanism is too difficult to identify to be able to act on, it must remain a proposition.

This section now considers a later model by Barras which introduces other variables but which maintains an endogenous development cycle mechanism.

A dynamic model of UK property development

In later work (Barras and Ferguson, 1987a; 1987b), a dynamic model of the development cycle is constructed and estimated from historical data. This is an altogether more complex framework than that set out above, but a brief description of its features and the conclusions of the estimations is of interest. Many of the basic features of the model discussed above are evident in this more complex framework.

The theoretical model comprises a long-run equilibrium solution combined with a short-run adjustment mechanism. The model comprises three equations for developer supply, user demand and investor demand and supply (this is the same basic framework established in Chapter 2 with the exception of a land market component). Developer supply is a function of capital value and costs; user demand is a function of rent and user activity; and investor demand and supply is a function of capital value, rent, the supply of investor finance and yields (capitalisation rates) on alternative investment markets. In equilibrium, a quantity of floor space is traded between developers and investors and is let by investors to users.

The main features of the model (Barras and Ferguson, 1987a) are shown below.

1   The commercial property market comprises two interrelated submarkets of users and investors. The supply of new buildings by developers and the demand for these buildings from users is mediated through the partly autonomous demand by financial institutions for property as a long-term investment.
2   The long run equilibrium level of development is assumed to be a function solely of the level of user activity which creates the demand.
3   An endogenous supply side mechanism is incorporated into the model by combining the accelerator principle of investment with a lagged response because of the production delay.
4   Exogenous demand fluctuations are generated by the effect of the business cycle on user activity. This affects the short-term demand for property.
5   Further short-term dynamics are included through changes in other exogenous variables which influence developer supply, investor demand

and user demand for new property. These include: property market prices, rents and yields (capitalisation rates); building costs; the supply of investor finance; and yields from alternative investments.[6]

The main results of the modelling (Barras and Ferguson, 1987b) are shown below.

1   The equilibrium level of new development in the industrial and commercial (defined as office and shop) property markets is most closely related to the level of user activity.
2   There is evidence of an *endogenous* cycle mechanism in development which operates through construction lags and which produces a major cycle of nearly nine years.
3   There is a shorter cycle of around 18 quarters which is produced by *exogenous* demand fluctuations from the business cycle. This cycle is weakest in the commercial sector which is dominated by its autonomous supply cycle (2 above).
4   In addition to the level of user activity, development is influenced by investment activity which may reinforce the short cycle effect (3 above). There appears to be an inverse relationship between the level of investment in property development and returns from alternative forms of investment.[7]
5   The weakest influences on the development cycle are development costs, such as construction costs and interest rates.

Problems with the dynamic model

One fundamental feature which distinguishes the above modelling framework from much other work is the explicit inclusion of an endogenous cycle mechanism caused by the lag in the development process and the application of the accelerator principle. It contrasts with the exogenous factors of user activity, construction costs, the cost and availability of credit and planning controls which reinforce or dampen the inherent cyclical tendencies. The endogenous mechanism suffers from the same problems discussed above in the context of the simpler model.

Another difficulty with this framework is the complete exogeneity of key property market variables such as rents, yields (capitalisation rates), building costs and the supply of finance. An argument might be made for rents as these are linked to profits, and thus to output, although they are also linked to the supply of space. The exogeneity of yields is rather less plausible as two components of the yields are expected income growth and expected risk (see Chapters 10 and 11) and both are causally linked to levels of development. Building costs are also linked to levels of building activity. The availability of finance, as discussed in Chapters 6 and 12, and below, is procyclical and, therefore, linked to levels of development activity.

The next section considers rental adjustment as an endogenous cycle mechanism. This approach is popular in the US.

RENT ADJUSTMENT AND RENT CYCLES

An alternative approach to property cycles focuses on cycles in rents and vacancies. It focuses on the slowness of rents to adjust to changes in the vacancy rate, and the consequent price signals vacancies give to developers (see, for example, Wheaton, 1987).[8] It sees the business cycle as being the most important influence. As economic activity slows, declining demand reduces the absorption of space and so increases the vacancy rate. However, rents are said to be sticky and to adjust slowly downwards to this, so returns are higher than demand should permit and construction continues. When the economy booms, rents are again slow to respond and, thus, construction is also slow to respond.

Central to this approach, which is found predominantly in the US literature, is the concept of a natural, or equilibrium, vacancy rate. This is analogous to the natural unemployment rate in labour economics and is determined by the optimal search procedures of the searchers (firms for space and landlords for tenants) and by tenant turnover and institutional and market characteristics specific to a city.

At the equilibrium vacancy rate, rent will be at its equilibrium level and capital value will equal development (replacement) costs. This has been developed by Grenadier (1995) to include the value of the option to postpone development (see below and Chapter 9).

According to Hendershott (1995), development will take place if, and only if, capital value exceeds development costs. When the effective rent (that is, taking into account rent-free periods and the like) exceeds the equilibrium rent and the vacancy rate is below the natural rate, development will take place until the vacancy rate and rents adjust to their equilibrium levels. However, if rent is below the equilibrium rent and the vacancy rate is above the natural rate, development will not take place. In this case, as demand rises, the vacancy rate will fall, rents will rise and development will become profitable. In either case, the market adjusts to equilibrium.

The rent adjustment model

The traditional rent adjustment model links the proportional change in rent to the difference between the actual and natural vacancy rates:

$$\Delta RR_t/RR_{t-1} = \lambda(VR^n - VR_{t-1}) \qquad (8.15)$$

where ΔRR_t is the change in real rent; RR_{t-1} is the real rent in time $t-1$; VR^n is the natural vacancy rate; VR_{t-1} is the vacancy rate in time $t-1$; and λ is the adjustment factor.

Wheaton and Torto (1988) estimate this model using data for the US office market and find a significant relationship. However, they argue that the natural vacancy rate has been rising in US cities because of the spatial expansion of office centres, the broader base of tenants, increases in tenant turnover and a shortening of the average length of lease. Accordingly, they adjust the natural rate from a constant to a linear time trend:

$$VR_n = \alpha + \beta\tau \qquad (8.16)$$

and so:

$$\Delta RR_t/RR_{t-1} = \lambda(\alpha + \beta t - VR_{t-1}) \qquad (8.17)$$

This formulation results in a better fit with a significant time trend. Clearly, such a time trend could not be a long-term feature of the relationship as it would suggest a consistently increasing natural vacancy rate.

There is no reason to suppose that the natural vacancy rate is constant across cities. (Nor is there any reason to suppose that it is temporally constant although this is a standard assumption.) Studies which aggregate data from different cities have been criticised for ignoring this issue. Shilling *et al.* (1987) use time series data for 17 city office markets, to estimate natural vacancy rates. Real operating expenses are also included.[9]

$$\Delta RR_t/RR_{t-1} = \beta_1\Delta OE_t/OE_{t-1} + \beta_2(VR^n - VR_t) \qquad (8.18)$$

where VR_t is the vacancy rate; VR^n is the natural vacancy rate; ΔOE_t is the change in real operating expenses; and β_1 and β_2 are constants.

In practice, this equation is estimated as:

$$\Delta RR_t/RR_{t-1} = \beta_0 + \beta_1\Delta OE/OE_{t-1} - \beta_2 VR_t \qquad (8.19)$$

where $\beta_0 = \beta_2 VR^n$.

The estimated natural vacancy rates range from 1 per cent in New York City to 21 per cent in Kansas City but are predominantly in the range 5–15 per cent. The operating expenses variable is rarely significant.

The analysis is then extended. The calculated natural vacancy rates are used as the dependent variable in a cross-section regression to identify the factors affecting the natural vacancy rate. Average annual change in the office stock, change in non-manufacturing employment, change in population, the annual property tax rate and average rent level are used as independent variables, but only the last is significant.

A more general adjustment model

A further development of the rental adjustment model to allow for a more general adjustment path is suggested by Hendershott (1995). In his model, there are two adjustments, based on both deviations from the equilibrium vacancy rate and from the equilibrium real rent:

$$\Delta RR_t/RR_{t-1} = \lambda(VR^n - VR_{t-1}) + \beta(RR_t^n - RR_{t-1}) \tag{8.20}$$

where RR_t^n is the equilibrium (natural) real rent. Note that it has a time sub-script as it includes the real risk free rate of return (time varying and linking the property market to the capital markets). It also includes the depreciation rate and the expenses rate.

Hendershott proposes this specification because of three problems which he identifies with the standard approach based only on the vacancy rate. First, it excludes the relationship between actual and equilibrium rent (based on the real interest rate, depreciation and operating expenses). Second, it requires the actual vacancy rate to overshoot substantially the natural rate in response to demand or supply shocks. Third, the equation cannot hold simul-taneously for leases of different periods.

These three are really aspects of the same problem: the inability of the standard approach to deal with the adjustment of rents for multi-period, as opposed to single period leases. He argues that the rent paid for a lease is a geometric average of expected future one-period rent rates. Therefore, if rents are below their equilibrium, it is rational to expect that they will rise towards it, and perhaps above it, as the market moves through a business cycle upturn. Accordingly, rents on multi-period leases, as opposed to single-period leases, should increase before the vacancy rate reaches its natural level. The inclusion of the equilibrium rent term thus overcomes the three problems identified by Hendershott and allows a rational expectations adjust-ment process for the rents of multi-period leases. Another advantage of the inclusion of the equilibrium rent term is that it provides an explicit link to the capital markets through the time varying interest rate in the equilibrium rent.

Although the model is an improvement on the basic specification, it is not without problems as it assumes a constant natural vacancy rate, a constant risk premium and constant lease length and terms. None of these assump-tions is likely to be true and the last two are likely to be functions of the vacancy rate. Given the possible advantages of the model, such criticisms might be considered harsh; and the extent to which they are of consequence empirically is impossible to assess.

Problems with rent adjustment models

In general, rent adjustment models suffer from the criticism that, if the process of slow rental adjustment is known, it should be exploitable by developers (see comments on the Barras model above). The models are largely a US preoccupation, driven as much by data availability as by theoretical urgency. They are considered again briefly in the next chapter in the context of multi-equation models of the property market. This chapter now turns to behavioural explanations of property cycles.

BEHAVIOURAL EXPLANATIONS

While conventional economics assumes rational economic behaviour, much of the explanation of cycles contained in the models discussed above appears to require varying degrees of irrationality in behaviour. These aspects are typically implicit or poorly developed. They have already been mentioned in passing in this chapter or are covered in other chapters but are drawn together here. There are two broad aspects of the irrationality: slowness to respond to clear market signals and failure to learn from experience. Three main groups of agents are covered: valuers, developers and lenders. The first two provide endogenous explanations of cycles, while the third is exogenous.

Valuers

Much has been written about the valuation process and the way in which valuers incorporate new market information. This is covered in detail in Chapter 10. In summary, a valuation is typically undertaken by comparing the capitalisation rate on similar properties which have been recently sold. It can, therefore, be viewed as a weighted average of current and past market information: a form of adaptive expectation (see Chapter 6). When the economic fundamentals move upwards or downwards quickly, valuations are slow to respond.

Following the 1974 UK property market crash, these traditional techniques were criticised by Greenwell and Co. (1976) for concealing the income growth assumptions. Baum and Crosby (1995: 23) suggest there was underpricing in 1986, prior to the boom, and overpricing in 1989, prior to the crash of the early 1990s. They argue that rational expectations, rather than perfect foresight, would have been sufficient to identify the mispricing. They criticise valuers for accepting rather than questioning market prices.

Valuations are a crucial part of development appraisals: so, if there is mispricing as suggested above in an upturn, development is slow to respond, and in a downturn the development boom is prolonged. In a downturn developers are encouraged to continue developing and lenders to continue lending. Plender (1984) suggests that valuers must accept some responsibility for the secondary banking collapse following the property market crash of 1974. Such concerns about valuations may have been a factor in the downward

211

trend, since the mid-1970s, of institutional portfolio allocations to property (see Chapters 10 and 11). Nonetheless, developers have been able to find finance from other sources.

There are sound institutional explanations for the slowness of valuations to respond to new market information, not least of which is case law requiring the use of the comparative method of valuation. This does not, however, explain why developers and lenders, in full knowledge of the limitations of the valuations, continue to use them in development appraisals or lending decisions.

Developers

Developers should initiate development on the basis of the expected profitability and risk of a project. Such calculations should combine current market signals with rational expectations of changes in key inputs such as rent, the capitalisation rate, vacancies and costs. There is, however, evidence to suggest that their focus is on current rather than expected values of key variables.

Key *et al.* (1994a: iv) build models of development activity and suggest that 'it is the rate of profit being achieved on developments currently being completed which is the dominant trigger for additional building'.

A similar conclusion is reached by Antwi and Henneberry (1995) who develop a model of the relationship between demand and development and argue that developers are 'habit persistent'. That is, they assume the continuation of current growth levels and incorporate these into their appraisals. The effect of such behaviour is stronger in rising markets. More development is started than would otherwise be the case, so peak construction and oversupply are increased, the speed and intensity of the downturn are greater and the time for adjustment to equilibrium is extended.

Why developers fail to learn from past experience is problematic. Such explanations are well-known and it might be expected that the lessons would modify behaviour and so remove the effect. It has been argued that, as few of the developers in one boom participate in the next, the information is less widely known among key players than might be expected. Those who survive may attribute their survival to superior entrepreneurial skills rather than to luck.

It is also argued that, in booms, people get caught up in 'the mania of speculation'. The phrase comes from Galbraith (1990) who shows that such 'irrational' behaviour is not the exclusive domain of property developers. Chapter 6 also discusses such behaviour and links it to Keynes' view that 'animal spirits' influence investment behaviour.

While inconsistent with conventional models of economic behaviour, such explanations have an appeal to those who, armed with the critiques of the 1970s boom, experienced the 1980s boom at first hand.

212

Lenders

The availability of finance is considered in Chapters 6 and 12; specific issues are developed here. When considering lenders, it is necessary to examine not only valuation and appraisal problems and 'the mania of speculation' discussed above, but also the issue of asymmetric information, considered in Chapter 5.

Demand for funds increases with the level of development activity and lending is pro-cyclical. Antwi and Henneberry (1995) suggest that, like developers, lenders may be prone to habit persistence behaviour. Thus, they are too optimistic in booms and too pessimistic in downturns and so exacerbate the boom and bust. Lenders use valuations and development appraisals in assessing loans. If there are problems with these, and these problems are known, lenders could be argued to be irrational in their loan making. When applied to lenders, this explanation has all the problems *and* the appeal suggested above.

While the insurance companies and pension funds contributed a relatively small amount to the flows of finance into UK property in the boom of the late 1980s, others displayed no such caution. Banks (both domestic and overseas), overseas investors (mainly from Japan and Sweden: see Chapter 13) and stock market issues by property companies provided the bulk of the funding (see DTZ, annual, for a detailed analysis). Many of these had limited knowledge of the UK property market.

The concept of asymmetric information (and related issues of moral hazard and signalling) between the parties to a transaction was introduced in Chapter 5.[10] If property development is highly geared, much lending is non-recourse and developers have a better appraisal of the risks than the lenders, the downside risks are borne by the lender and the upside risk benefits the developer. In part, the response of lenders to this *moral hazard* is to rely on *signals* from the valuation profession with its supposed expertise. However, given the problems with valuations and development appraisals, rational lenders should learn from past mistakes and ensure more thorough monitoring.

While injudicious non-recourse lending is a plausible explanation of overbuilding in some countries, it cannot be an important factor in countries, such as Canada, where it is uncommon but which, nonetheless, experience property cycles (Grenadier, 1995).

It has also been argued that banks, regardless of any understanding of the limitations with the appraisals, had to secure market share of lending against competition from other sources. This can be linked to financial deregulation in the UK in the 1980s (as discussed in Chapters 6 and 12) and Savings and Loans Institutions liberalisation in the US. In such a context high risk, if borne by all participants, is not a reason for inactivity. On the one hand, if the risks are rewarded and a lender has not made sufficient loans, its competitors will outperform it. On the other hand, if a lender does lend and loses, its competitors are all similarly affected. This is analogous to the concept of tracking error discussed in Chapter 11. There were also pressures on staff to make loans but the costs of the loans failing did not fall on them. Both are versions of the 'principal–agent' problem: the interests of the principal (the bank shareholders) were not coincident with those of the agents (the employees making the lending decisions). While again plausible, deregulation does not explain cycles in countries which did not experience it, nor does it explain previous cycles.

All of the above explanations have some appeal but all depend on assumptions of some sort of irrational behaviour. The next section considers the application of option pricing theory to development. This seeks to explain the observed behaviour of key agents using assumptions of rational economic behaviour.

OPTION PRICING AND PROPERTY CYCLES

A useful contribution to the modelling of development cycles is found in the work of Grenadier (1995). It has similarities with the flexible accelerator approach discussed above. He notes the existence of long periods of high or low vacancy and the failure of rents to adjust more quickly to restore the natural vacancy rate. The behaviour of owners and developers is considered under the combination of demand uncertainty, adjustment costs and construction lags. A theory is developed which explains two phenomena: the reluctance of owners to adjust occupancy levels, even in the face of large shifts in renter demand; and the addition of new developments in the face of already high vacancy rates.

The analysis involves the analogy of a financial option. An option is a financial instrument through which someone buys the right to trade at some specified future date on specified terms. A currency option, for example, allows an exporter to guarantee the exchange rate in the future when the firm will be paid in the importer's currency and this has to be converted into its domestic currency. In this way, exporters can insure against future adverse exchange rate movements at the cost of the price of the option.

In the rental market an owner may be able to let a property, but there is also an option to wait for a higher rent if the conditions become more promising. So, when a decision is made to let a property, not only are the direct costs of leasing (such as agents' fees, advertising and fitting out) paid, but the value of the wait option is lost. The consequence is that, even when demand increases, vacant space may remain vacant. A similar analysis applies to the occupier: even when demand falls substantially, occupied space may remain occupied. The greater the uncertainty about the future, the greater is the value of an option. Thus, an increase in uncertainty increases the 'stickiness' of existing vacancies. A further finding is that the greater are the adjustment costs, the greater is the stickiness.

A similar analysis applies to development. There are three findings:

1   the longer the construction period, the greater the probability of over-building;
2   the greater the adjustment costs, the greater the probability of overbuilding; and
3   the greater the uncertainty about future demand, the greater the probability of overbuilding.

The first of these is despite developers knowing that the longer the construction period, the greater the probability that the market will turn against them. The explanation involves the option value. If a developer proceeds with a project and demand is high on completion, the space will be let at a high rent. However, if demand is low, there is still the option to keep the space vacant for the market to turn. The consequence of this asymmetric impact is that a developer will err on the side of building rather than delaying.

In the second, although developers will wait for a higher demand before commencing development, this will not lower the probability of overbuilding. This is because, although the higher the adjustment costs the greater the probability of new space being vacant, these costs will only be paid when demand and rents are even higher. However, if demand is low the option not to let means the costs can be delayed.

The third is explained as follows. When volatility is high, the cost of overbuilding is lower, as it becomes more likely that the space will be valuable in the future. The excess space can be considered an option to let if demand increases and this will have a higher value, the greater the volatility.

Problems with the option pricing approach

While this analysis has some appeal in that it introduces rational economic explanation to the analysis of overbuilding and high vacancy rates, it is not without problems. First, the model is derived from finance theory. Specific assumptions about preferences are made which are less likely in the commercial property market. In financial markets, variable preferences do not matter and individual behaviour is unlikely to affect market outcomes because of the large number of investors. In commercial property markets, as there is a limited number of developers, differences in preferences do matter and are likely to affect outcomes. This reduces the predictive ability of the model.

Second, in a world of a limited number of developers, where individual actions matter, the model does not explain strategic behaviour. Individual developers are competing against each other and will not all be successful: strategies are determined by what others are doing (see Chapter 5).

Third, the analysis of development depends on the value of the option to wait with unlet buildings. While this may have some value to investors in the market for existing space, it has a less obvious value to a highly geared developer with creditors demanding interest payments which the developer had expected to pay from rents. In such circumstances, the option to hold unlet space may be the option to go bankrupt.

Finally, in a market with long leases, frequent upward-only rent reviews and where many of the adjustment costs are borne by the occupier, such as the UK, the value of a wait and see option for renting may be reduced. In such circumstances, the value of a tenant is high. In addition to rent, the tenant pays occupancy costs, such as rates, insurance, repairs and a substantial share of operating costs. Within five years rents could be reviewed upwards.

As with some of the other explanations, Grenadier's model may be context specific.

SUMMARY AND CONCLUSIONS

This chapter has considered explanations of short cycles in property markets. It was stressed that the normal use of 'cycle' which suggests regularity is far from the truth. There are recurrent fluctuations in the level of development activity, rents and vacancies, although the period and amplitude of these fluctuations vary. Two property cycles were considered. The first is a cycle of around four years linked to the business cycle. The second is a major cycle in development with a period of nine to ten years for which there is a variety of exogenous and endogenous explanations. As the period and amplitude of the business cycles vary, so do those of development cycles.

The chronology of an idealised cycle may be characterised as follows. There is an upturn in the business cycle and an increase in the level of economic activity. Demand for property increases but at a time of low levels of development so that space is absorbed quickly, vacancy rates fall and rents rise. Developers respond to these market signals and new development begins. Credit becomes more readily available and additional, more speculative development, begins. Rents continue to rise as it takes time for new development to become available. Rises in real interest rates and a downturn in the growth in economic activity leads to a fall in the demand for new space. This coincides with the completion of many of the new developments. Vacancy rates rise and rents fall as the market is oversupplied. Developers, unable to cover interest payments from rents, go bankrupt. The oversupply may last until the next upturn.

A simple model framework for development cycles includes the flexible accelerator principle. The basic principle of an accelerator model is that the *level* of net new investment in capital goods is proportional to the *change* in the level of the economic activity of users of the capital goods. In practice, the response is not so simple and is likely to be partial. From an occupiers' perspective, adjustment and relocation costs can be high. They may first use 'slack' space and may then chose to 'overuse' space until they are sure that the increased demand will be sustained. Only then will they wish to occupy additional space. For similar reasons, if the occupiers own their own space, they will phase the investment gradually.

Developers are affected in a similar way. There may be new development already in the pipeline from previous periods. Further, cautious expectations about demand when the property will be completed and the inability to reverse development decisions once development has started may mean the response is partial. Thus, only a proportion of the desired space will be built and occupied.

The problem with this explanation is that it produces a development cycle dependent only on the business cycle. A development of the basic model is to introduce a delay in the production of new developments. This delay can be substantial. The combination of the accelerator and a lag generates cyclical fluctuations and it is possible to model this process. These cycles are endogenous and independent of fluctuations in demand.

This model, while replicating observed patterns of development activity with reasonable inputs for the parameters, is not without problems. First, it has no place in it for rental and capital value adjustments which affect development activity. Second, the lag is hardly a surprise to developers and, while forecasts are never perfect, they should be able to take it into account and exploit it to their advantage. Not to do so would suggest irrational behaviour.

Another endogenous explanation of property market cycles is a model of rental adjustment based on the difference between vacancy rates and the natural vacancy rate. This explanation is based on the slowness of rents to respond to vacancies and to send appropriate signals to developers. This, it is argued generates a cycle which is longer than the business cycle. A refinement to the basic model involves the addition of the difference between market rent and equilibrium rent as an explanatory variable for rental change. Such explanations of cycles depend on the market being unable to learn from experience or to adjust behaviour to exploit or remove the phenomenon. This again suggests a degree of irrationality in the behaviour of key agents in the development process.

The slowness of key agents to respond to new information, or the failure to learn lessons, have been proposed as explanations of cycles. Irrational behaviour has been attributed to valuers, developers and lenders.

A valuation can be considered as a weighted average of current and past market information. Thus, when the economic fundamentals move upwards or downwards quickly, valuations are slow to respond. Valuations are used in development appraisals: so, in an upturn development is slow to respond; and in a downturn the development boom is prolonged. In a downturn, developers are encouraged to continue developing and lenders to continue lending.

There is evidence to suggest that developers use current market information in development appraisals rather than forecasts. The effect of such behaviour is stronger in rising markets. More development is started than would otherwise be the case: so peak construction and oversupply are increased; the speed and intensity of the downturn are greater; and the time for adjustment to equilibrium is extended.

Lenders, too, it is argued suffer from poor memories. They are too optimistic in booms and too pessimistic in downturns and so exacerbate the boom and bust.

The concept of asymmetric information has also been used to explain development cycles. If development is undertaken using non-recourse loans, the downside risks are borne by the lender and the upside risk benefits the developer. Deregulation and competition to ensure lending business have also been suggested as driving forces. These explanations do not help explain cycles in countries, or at times, where neither non-recourse lending nor deregulation featured.

The final explanation considered sought to explain observed behaviour using assumptions of rationality. This focuses on the existence of long periods of high or low vacancy and the failure of rents to adjust more quickly to restore the natural vacancy rate. The theory explains the reluctance of owners to adjust occupancy levels, even in the face of large shifts in renter demand; and the addition of new developments in the face of already high vacancy rates.

Central to the analysis is the analogy of a financial option. In the rental market, an owner may be able to let a property, but also has the option to wait for market conditions to improve. When a decision is made to let, the direct costs of adjustment paid and the value of the wait option are lost. Thus, even when demand increases, vacant space will remain vacant. The greater the adjustment costs and the greater the uncertainty about the future, the greater is the value of an option, so vacancy is more likely to persist.

A similar analysis applies to development and the conclusions are: the longer the construction period, the greater the probability of overbuilding; the greater the adjustment costs, the greater the probability of overbuilding; and the greater the uncertainty about future demand, the greater the probability of overbuilding.

This approach has some appeal but also has problems. Individual preferences and strategic behaviour are important in the property market, yet neither appears in the model. Also, the analysis of development depends on the value of the option to wait with unlet buildings. For developers with a need to generate rental income to pay interest charges, this value cannot be large.

While many of the above explanations have appeal, none is without criticism. Some depend on apparently irrational behaviour from key agents and the behavioural components of the models are not well-developed. Others provide a context-specific explanation rather than a general theory of cycles. None can be commended as the best explanation.

In the next chapter, multi-equation models and forecasting models are considered.

9

MARKET MODELLING AND FORECASTING

INTRODUCTION

The last chapter concentrated on models which were used to explain cycles in the commercial property market. The models considered in this chapter have a more general purpose of understanding the short-run dynamics of the links between the commercial property market and the wider economy. This is an evolving area of study, both academically and in practice where such models are used to produce short-term forecasts of key property variables. There is a range of detailed approaches for each variable so the chapter reviews and compares a number of models to draw general conclusions about the links between the property market and the economy. It does not suggest a definitive approach. This should assist interested readers to build their own models

Forecasts, whether implicit or explicit, are a central part of any investment decision. The expected return must equal or exceed the target (or required) return and the former can only be produced from a forecast of income. The target return comprises a risk free return, taken from the gilt market, and a risk premium. Both are time varying (see Chapter 10 for a detailed discussion).

This is not to suggest that all investment decisions involve an *explicit* forecast, but those which do not, nonetheless contain an *implicit* forecast. Recent years have seen a considerable expansion of commercial property market forecasting because more investors have been demanding explicit investment analysis and, also, because long-enough time series data are now available to enable better modelling (see Key *et al.*, 1994b for a general discussion of data availability).

Forecasts are required for a wide range of property investment decisions. First, forecasts of total return can be used for asset allocation in a multi-asset portfolio. Second, forecasts of individual sectors and regions of the property market can be used to construct and rebalance property portfolios. Third, forecasts for towns and individual buildings can be used for stock selection. The difficulties associated with forecasting increase with the level of disaggregation and, while good models can be constructed for the UK, the town level creates many problems. Forecasts are also of value for planning and public policy-making.

Chapter 2 set out a model of the commercial property market which considered four interlinked markets: the user market; the financial asset market; the development market; and the urban land market. In the literature, econometric modelling of the commercial property market has concentrated on the user and development markets. Financial markets aspects are not generally well-integrated into property models and land markets have not been the subject of a formal quantitative approach.

The following sections deal with both historical and forecasting models of the property market. First, a number of the practical issues involved in modelling are examined, then the theoretical bases of the models are discussed. This is followed by consideration of a number of multi-equation models covering US office markets and the London office market. Next, single equation models of rents, yields (capitalisation rates) and investment, and development in the office, retail and industrial markets are covered. Then, some of the difficulties of local market modelling are considered. Finally, there is a summary and conclusions.

ISSUES IN MODEL BUILDING

As readers may wish to construct their own models, this section sets out basic background issues. Readers with some experience of modelling should move to the next section. Particular aspects of data exploration are considered in Chapter 7; much more detailed treatments of the issues can be found in texts such as Maddala (1994) or Mills (1991).

Model building typically starts from hypotheses derived from theory which are then tested using actual data. It is normal practice to undertake analysis of economic variables in *real* rather than nominal terms, so variables may have to be deflated before the analysis can begin. A relationship (an equation) is estimated between the dependent variable (on the left hand side of the equation), such as development activity, and independent or explanatory variables (on the right hand side of the equation), such as demand for space, construction costs and interest rates.

There are two broad approaches which are considered in subsequent sections. These are multi-equation models and single equation (reduced form) models. In the former, dependent variables in one equation may appear as explanatory variables in other equations, that is, some of the explanatory variables may be determined endogenously. In the latter, there is a single dependent variable and all explanatory variables are exogenous. Multi-equation models are usually better in theory but a reduced form equation is easier to estimate.

A relationship is typically estimated using a regression procedure. Three types of equations can be estimated. A time series model considers observations through time from, for example, a single city; a cross section model considers observations at one time from, for example, a number of cities; and a panel model considers cross section data pooled for a number of periods. As dynamic relationships are typically the main interest, property market modelling generally uses a time series approach but there are also some cross section and panel analyses.

In the formulation of an equation, lagged (past) values of the dependent variable may appear on the right hand side of an equation as explanatory variables. These allow an adjustment process whereby changes in one variable take time to affect other variables. The appropriate lag structure of each explanatory variable is unlikely to be specified by theory (although long lags rarely have a plausible economic interpretation); so the preferred one is principally determined by the best statistical fit.

When a time series model is used to forecast, it is assumed that the relationship estimated from the historical data will hold in the future. Values of the independent variables are then used to produce forecasts of the dependent variable. If the independent variables are contemporaneous, simultaneous forecasts are required of all variables; if they are based on lagged values, forecasts can be made of the dependent variable without a forecast of the independent variable. Accordingly, in developing a forecasting model for several periods ahead, it may be important that the independent variables can be forecast and so a simple specification is preferred. Alternatively, the model can be used to forecast the dependent variable by assuming different scenarios for the independent variables (or in the case of multi-equation systems, the exogenous variables), rather than to produce a single point forecast.

When forecasting, a version of the model can be estimated on a restricted sample that leaves out several years of the data sample. It can then be used to forecast the dependent variable in the omitted years, and these forecasts compared with the actual data to test the 'goodness-to-fit'. This is known as 'in sample' forecasting.

In many of the models discussed in this chapter, the variables are in *levels* (that is, amounts) and not in first differences (that is, *change* or percentage change in the amount). While this was acceptable at the time many were published, econometrics now requires a different approach. A problem with using economic variables is that many move together over time in line with general economic growth, even when they are not directly causally related. If variables have a trend, the estimation of the effect of a particular explanatory may be biased. In order to remove spurious correlation, the variables used in a regression have to be made 'stationary' or have to be 'co-integrated' with each other. This requires prior testing. Converting non-stationary economic variables to first differences usually has the effect of ensuring stationarity. Detailed discussion of such issues is beyond the scope of this book.

Commonly, data are transformed into logarithms prior to estimating a relationship. This has several advantages: non-linear relationships can then be estimated by linear regression techniques; it may reduce the non-normality of the distributions; the coefficients may, where relevant, be interpreted as elasticities; and the difference between two log levels (for example, $CV_t - CV_{t-1}$) is approximately the growth rate.[1]

Prior to any statistical analysis, it is good practice to graph the data – deflated and in differences as appropriate (see Chapter 7 for an illustration). This helps to suggest relationships but is also a check on 'outliers', that is, observations which are unusually large or small. There are two main explanations for such outliers in the input data: a measurement error or an unusual event such as a strike. There may also be outliers when the model is estimated, that is observations which do not follow an otherwise strong relationship. This may result from the data or from the exclusion of an important variable from the model. If there is a plausible reason for the outlier, it can be removed from the analysis by including what is known as a dummy variable. This sets the error term in the regression to zero for that observation.

A variety of statistical tests are used to determine the appropriate specification and merits of a model. These include: measures of how much of the variation in the dependent variable is explained and how much is left unexplained; tests of the significance of individual explanatory variables and of the equation as a whole; tests of the assumptions required to undertake linear regression; tests of the time series characteristics of the model; and tests of 'in sample' forecasts.[2] These are not considered here but are available on any econometric package: a number of user friendly and cheap packages are widely available.

THE THEORETICAL BASES OF THE MODELS

As in Chapter 8, in the discussions below, the notation of the various authors has been standardised for easier comparison and is not that of the original authors (see Table 9.1).

Chapter 2 considered four inter-linked commercial property markets – the user market, the financial asset market, the development market and the urban land market – and set out the economics of the relationships in these markets. The relationships most relevant to the models considered below are now discussed. Two of the markets, the user and development markets, dominate most modelling.

The following paragraphs set out general formulations for models of four variables: demand in the user market; supply from the development market; rents in the user market; and yields (capitalisation rates) in the financial asset market. Only broad specifications are discussed, although, in practical model

Table 9.1 Variable labels and descriptions: modelling

Variable label	Variable description
A_t	net absorption
CC_t	real construction costs
CC^e	expected real construction costs
CD_t	completed development
CR_t	cost of replacement
CR^e	expected cost of replacement
CV_t	capital value
CV^e	expected capital value
D_t	demand for space
DV_t	development
d or δ	expected average depreciation rate in perpetuity
E_t	employment
ER_t	employment rate
EF_t	employment to floor space ratio
G	ratio of finance, insurance and real estate, service and government employment in 1980 to that in 1970
g_p	expected average income growth in perpetuity
GP_t	gross national product
GR_t	gap between equilibrium rent and the previous period's rent, if positive, otherwise zero
IN_t	inflation rate
k_P	the property capitalisation rate or initial yield
K_t	actual capital stock
K_t^*	desired capital stock
LC_t	land cost
LC^e	expected land cost
NC_t	nominal cost of capital
ND_t	net development starts
NR_t	nominal rent
O_t	output
OE_t	real operating expenses
OS_t	occupied stock
φ	the ratio of the value of the option to wait to the replacement cost
P_t	permits granted
RF_N	nominal risk free rate derived from the gilt market
RC_t	real cost of capital
RC^e	expected real cost of capital
RP	risk premium
RR_t	real rent
RR_t^e	expected real rent
RR^n	natural or equilibrium real rent

Table 9.1 Variable labels and descriptions: modelling (*cont.*)

Variable label	Variable description
RR_t^f	fitted real rent
T_t	tax laws
TD_t	total development starts
U_t	unemployment rate
VR_t	vacancy rate
VR^n	natural or average vacancy rate

building, the relationships can be estimated in levels or differences, and can include lagged values of the dependent or independent variables.

Demand in the user market

The demand function for new space is assumed to be the same as that for all space. Demand in the user market is generally hypothesised to be a function of the level of activity and the space used by each worker which is, itself, a function of the cost of the space (rent). Thus:

$$D = f(RR,O,EF) \tag{9.1}$$

where D is demand; RR is real rent; O is output; and EF is the employee to floor space ratio.

In essence, such a formulation assumes that an increase in output leads to an increase in profits and so to an ability to pay additional rent for additional space. The usual explanatory variables for estimations of the demand equation are measures of activity (either an output measure or an employment measure or both: see Chapter 3) and real rents. However, as suggested in Chapter 2, it might be expected that short-run demand is relatively insensitive to rental change. The dependent variable can be total demand or new demand measured by net absorption (new take-up less space vacated).

Elaborations of this basic approach include some version of the flexible accelerator principle discussed in Chapter 8, so that actual demand is a proportion of the difference between desired stock and actual stock. Such specifications appear in a number of the models discussed below. The models are discussed in detail because no particular formulation has consensus support. Readers may consider the possible formulations and develop their own preferred versions.

Development

The development market produces the new supply in the user market. The flexible accelerator models considered in Chapter 8 subsume the link between an increase in demand and the development induced. The obvious transmission mechanism is through an increase in profitability. Thus, the amount of development is based on the profitability of development, that is, the difference between new property values and the costs of replacing properties. As profitability rises, consequent land price rises should increase the cost of development (or the opportunity cost if the land is already owned by the developer) and so decrease the profitability of development. The absence of this relationship in all of the models considered below, while an empirical necessity resulting from lack of data, is a theoretical concern. Without the inclusion of land costs, development might appear to be more profitable than it is.

Development of a particular type of property will not occur unless the value is greater than or equal to replacement costs (which include the cost of site clearance and construction, land costs and the cost of finance). Thus, development occurs when:

$$CV/CR \geq 1 \tag{9.2}$$

where: CV is the current capital value; and CR is the current cost of replacement.

Hendershott *et al.* (1997), after Grenadier (1995), propose that this should be respecified to include the value of the option to wait for improved circumstances (and so achieve a higher capital value). However, there remains a problem with this specification: it is *expectations* of value on completion and costs that should be important. The risk of having to estimate future value and costs means that a risk premium should be added to the required return (see Chapter 10 for a detailed discussion). A more appropriate (expectations) specification is, therefore:

$$CV^e/CR^e \geq 1 + \varphi + RP \tag{9.3}$$

where CV^e is the expected capital value; CR^e is the expected cost of replacement; φ is the ratio of the value of the option to wait to replacement cost; and RP is the risk premium to cover the risk of estimating completed value and costs. Thus, a general specification for development supply might be:

$$DV = f(CV^e, CC^e, LC^e, RC^e, \varphi, RP) \tag{9.4}$$

where DV is development; CC^e is expected construction costs; LC^e is expected land costs; and RC^e is the expected real cost of capital.

The dependent variable can be one of several measures of development activity: new development permits, new construction orders, development starts or completed development. A modelling problem arises if CV/CR < 1 + φ + RP. In this case no new development will be started, although completions will occur if development has started in previous periods. One way to deal with this is to consider as an explanatory variable the *gap* between CV/CR and 1 + φ + RP, defined as its value, if positive, and as zero, if negative (see Hendershott *et al.*, 1997).

Problems arise in implementing these specifications as data rarely exist for land values, and φ and RP are theoretical constructs, the direct measurement of which is impossible, and proxy measurement extremely difficult. Market capital values are also hard to obtain and (for reasons considered in Chapter 10) valuations are unsatisfactory substitutes. In practice, therefore, development models tend to include rents (rather than capital values), construction costs and cost of capital as the explanatory variables.

Rent

Rent plays a central role in the model of the property market set out in Chapter 2. Before considering the bases of rent modelling, it is necessary to revisit the concept of the user cost of capital (see Chapters 2 and 6) as this can provide a link between the user market and the financial asset market. In equilibrium, rent is equivalent to the user cost of capital. It comprises several parts: the risk free interest rate, an appropriate risk premium, compensation for expected depreciation, the operating costs and expected capital gains or losses. (Note, however, that, if the market is in equilibrium and the capitalisation rate is constant, the rate of change in capital value is the same as the rate of change in rent.) Thus:

$$UC = RF + RP + \delta^e + OE - \Delta CV^e/CV \qquad (9.5)$$

where UC is the user cost of capital: the rental return; RF is the risk free rate; RP is the risk premium; δ^e is the expected rate of depreciation; OE is the operating expenses, either known or expected; and $\Delta CV^e/CV$ is the expected rate of change in value of the property.

This is a specification for the *equilibrium rent* (see Chapter 8 and below) and it is analogous to the initial yield (capitalisation rate) considered below and discussed in more detail in Chapter 10. Crucially it provides a direct link between the user market and the financial asset market and the capital markets through the risk free rate which is taken to be the gilt yield (see Chapter 10).

Rents tend to be 'sticky' in adjusting to changes in explanatory variables. There are two types of rental change models, both considering the interaction between supply and demand, one favoured in the US literature and the other in the UK literature. Rental adjustment models are used in the US, while reduced form equations, including separate supply and demand variables, are typically used in the UK.[3] The preference for one rather than the other is driven by data availability. The former relates rental change to the difference between the natural and actual vacancy rates; the latter uses a variety of demand proxies and supply variables as explanatory variables.

Empirically, it is *effective* rent which is of interest, that is, the rent paid when incentives such as rent free periods are taken into account. Caution is, therefore, often required when using published figures for rents.

Yields

The initial yield, or capitalisation rate, is the rate at which rent, derived in the user market, is capitalised in the financial asset market. It is analogous to the user cost of capital and can be approximated as the sum of a number of parts (see Chapter 10):

$$k_P = RF_N + RP - g_P + d \qquad (9.6)$$

where k_P is the initial yield, that is the ratio of current income to current value; RF_N is the nominal risk free rate derived from the conventional gilt market; RP is the risk premium; g_P is the expected average income growth in perpetuity of a hypothetical continually new building; and d is the expected average depreciation rate in perpetuity.

Movements in yields are, therefore, the result of changes in any of these variables and models of yields use measures of these components as the explanatory variables. One of these comes from the gilt market but the other three involve expectations. Accordingly, modelling yields is not easy.

Multi-equation models are examined in the next two sections. These typically include equations for demand, development and rents. Separate yield models are considered briefly in a later section.

MULTI-EQUATION MODELS OF US OFFICE MARKETS

This section outlines three multi-equation models of US office markets, by Rosen (1984), Hekman (1985) and Wheaton (1987). These models, particularly the first two, are considered here as an illustration of the development of modelling in the property market rather than as indicative of the current state of the art. None has an appropriate link to the financial asset market. The next section considers two contemporary models of the London office market, one of which does contain a direct link to the financial asset market.

In these studies, equations representing demand, supply and rent, link a number of exogenous and endogenous variables. The exogenous variables are typically an employment measure of demand (rather than output: see Chapter 3), construction costs, interest rates and tax rates. The endogenous variables are drawn from development, rent, absorption, vacancy, total floor space and occupied floor space. The models, therefore, cover the user and development markets and have some links with the property financial asset market through the capital markets.

An important part of these models is a rental adjustment equation. Thus, a positive/negative shock in demand leads to a fall/rise in the vacancy rate and then to a rise/fall in rents which generates/prevents development. This approach predominates in the US literature and has been influenced by data availability: supply and vacancy data are typically more available than in the UK.

Rosen (1984)

An early US office model is that of Rosen (1984) who estimated three equations for demand, rents and supply using San Francisco data for the period 1961–83. The logic is that a change in demand results in a change in the vacancy rate, which results in rental adjustment and then to new development.

The first equation is for total demand to occupy space. The explanatory variables are real rents and employment in finance, insurance and real estate (FIRE), the latter as a proxy for output. Space per worker is assumed constant.

$$OS_t = \gamma_0 + \gamma_1 RR_t + \gamma_2 E_t \qquad (9.7)$$

where OS_t is the occupied office space; RR_t is the real rent; E_t is employment (in finance, insurance and real estate); and γ_i are constants.

The equation is estimated in logs. All coefficients are significant and correctly signed and the adjusted R^2 is 0.98. As the specification is in levels, the high R^2 is not a surprise and may indicate spurious correlation.

The second estimated equation is a rent adjustment equation for change in nominal (not real as in the first equation) rent in the user market. Nominal rental change is taken to be a function of the inflation rate and the difference between the natural vacancy rate and the actual vacancy rate:

$$\Delta NR_t / NR_{t-1} = \beta_0 + \beta_1 (VR^n - VR_t) + \beta_2 IN_t \qquad (9.8)$$

where NR_t is the nominal rent; VR^n is the natural vacancy rate; VR_t is the actual vacancy rate; IN_t is the rate of price inflation; and β_i are constants.

The natural vacancy rate was discussed in Chapter 8. Here it is hypothesised as a function of interest rates and office suppliers' expectations of rent. It is suggested that suppliers attempt to maximise profit by holding more space vacant in anticipation of rent rises or less space in anticipation of rent falls.

Equation (9.8) is an unusual specification as, if $\beta_0 \neq 0$, there is an upward or downward drift in rental change regardless of changes in vacancy or inflation. A more standard equation would have omitted β_0 and used $\beta_1 VR^n$ as the constant, so avoiding having to input a value for VR^n. Instead, the natural rate was taken as 7 per cent, the actual average for the period 1961–83. The estimation produces significant coefficients, with the expected signs on both variables, and has an R^2 of 0.55.[4] The estimated coefficient on inflation of 1.82 is not significantly different from unity, thus allowing the possibility of a one-to-one relationship between nominal rental change and inflation. The equation might have been better specified with real rental change and no inflation variable.

The final equation is for the development market. New office completions are taken to be a function of the average of the vacancy rates for the last four periods, expected rent, construction costs, the interest rate and tax laws affecting commercial property.[5]

$$CD_t = \alpha_0 + \alpha_1(VR_t + VR_{t-1} + VR_{t-2} + VR_{t-3}) + \alpha_2 RR_t^e + \alpha_3 CC_t + \alpha_4 NCt + \alpha_5 T_t \qquad (9.9)$$

where CD_t is new completed office development; VR_t is the vacancy rate; RR_t^e is the expected rent (not explained in the paper, but perhaps from equation 9.8); CC_t is construction costs; NC_t is the interest rate (presumably nominal, but not specified); T_t is tax laws affecting commercial property (not explained); and α_i are constants.

This has the basic framework of a profits-driven model with variables representing value and costs. The results of the estimation are poor: the only significant coefficient is the vacancy rate and the adjusted R^2 is only 0.19. The finding that construction costs and interest rates are insignificant or relatively unimportant is common for models that exclude an equilibrium rent term and use nominal interest rates. One explanation of the poor fit of the supply equation may be that it does not include a demand measure, instead, demand acts through the vacancy rate and expected rent to generate supply. Rosen also points to the volatility of new development and the difficulties of explaining this volatility within an equilibrium model. Another possible explanation may be poor quality data or the use of data series covering different areas or different property types (see below).

Hekman (1985)

Hekman (1985) also focuses on the user and development markets, although he adopts a different approach from Rosen. Rather than a single city, he uses a panel approach with annual data for 14 cities for the period 1979 to 1983. He estimates equations for rents and development (but not occupied space as does Rosen) using a two-stage least squares procedure.

As supply in any year is determined by past investment decisions and does not respond to that year's market rent, rent is determined by the interaction of demand and a fixed short-run supply. Thus, the vacancy rate and demand variables are used to model rent:

$$RR_t = \beta_0 + \beta_1 VR_t + \beta_2 GP_t + \beta_3 E_t + \beta_4 U_t \qquad (9.10)$$

where RR_t is real rent (deflated using the GNP price deflator); VR_t is the vacancy rate in top class office buildings; GP_t is GNP at constant prices (a measure of national demand); E_t is total employment in the metropolitan area (a control for city size on rent); U_t is the metropolitan unemployment rate (a crude measure of local demand); and β_i are constants.

This is not the conventional rental adjustment model as it is in levels with the vacancy rate and three demand variables. It has some similarity to the UK models outlined below, except that the vacancy rate (a measure of the interaction between supply, demand and rent) rather than a supply measure is used. The natural vacancy rate is included implicitly in the constant (as in Chapter 8). In the estimation, the model has significant coefficients on all variables except unemployment, and the expected signs for all variables. However, its adjusted R^2 of 0.37 is poor. Part of the problem may lie in the implicit assumption that the natural vacancy rate is constant across cities (see Chapter 8). Moreover, cross-sectional variations in rent are modelled by two crude measures of local demand (total employment and the unemployment rate).

Development is modelled by the fitted values of rent from the first equation and demand and cost variables. Hekman argues that, as rent and the vacancy rate are related through the stock adjustment process which balances supply and demand, any model of office supply which includes both rent and vacancy is mis-specified.[6] This criticism assumes that rent and vacancy rates are closely related whereas, as discussed in Chapter 8, the relationship is complex. Equilibrium rent, derived in part from the capital markets, is quasi-autonomous from the natural vacancy rate.

The supply equation for the development market is:

$$P_t = \alpha_0 + \alpha_1 RR_t^f + \alpha_2 G + \alpha_3 CC_t + \alpha_4 NC_t \qquad (9.11)$$

where P_t is the amount of new office permits (a proxy for new development); RR_t^f is the fitted value of rent from equation (9.10); G is the ratio of finance, insurance and real estate, service and government employment in 1980 to that in 1970 (used as a proxy for expected growth); CC_t is real construction costs (deflated using the GNP price deflator); NC_t is the nominal interest rate on 10 year government bonds, less the three month T-bill rate (as a measure of credit availability); and α_i are constants.

Like Rosen, this has the basic form of a profits-driven model with value and cost variables. The development equation has significant coefficients with the expected signs for rent and growth, an insignificant coefficient with the expected sign for the interest rate and a significant, but incorrectly signed, coefficient for construction costs. The adjusted R^2 of 0.61 is unspectacular but is much better than Rosen's equivalent.

Hekman, like Rosen, clearly locates his analysis in the user and developer markets and ignores linkages to the financial market, except through nominal interest rates in the supply equation. In practice, investors in property seek a return that is related to capital market interest rates. This interaction between the user and financial markets makes the rental adjustment process more complex than the simple adjustments underlying these formulations. These points are considered below in the discussion of the Hendershott *et al.* (1997) model.

Wheaton (1987)

A more comprehensive approach is to be found in Wheaton (1987) who uses aggregate biannual data for 30 US markets for 1967–86. He argues that, as the turning points for these 30 markets are within one or two years of the average, there is evidence of a national office market which can be modelled. He estimates equations for stock demand (absorption) and supply. As with Rosen and Hekman, the analysis concentrates on the user and development markets.

He starts with three identities:

$$A_t = OS_t - OS_{t-1} \tag{9.12}$$

$$OS_t = K_t(1 - VR_t) \tag{9.13}$$

$$K_t = K_{t-1} + TD_{t-v} \tag{9.14}$$

where A_t is net absorption; OS_t is the occupied space; K_t is the stock; VR_t is the vacancy rate; TD_t is total development (starts); and v represents the lag between the time construction begins and the time at which the space is completed and ready for occupancy.

He then specifies behavioural equations for demand, supply and rents. The desired space is a function of office employment, the level of real rents and current employment growth as a proxy for future growth:

$$K_t^* = \gamma_0 + \gamma_1 E_t + \gamma_2 RR_t + \gamma_3(E_t/E_{t-1}) \tag{9.15}$$

where K_t^* is the desired space; E_t is the office employment in period t; RR_t is the real rent for new space; E_t/E_{t-1} represents current rates of growth as proxy for expected rates; and γ_i are constants.

Wheaton then allows a stock adjustment process, whereby the difference between desired stock this period and occupied stock in the last period is achieved over several periods. In any one period, actual absorption is a proportion of the desired absorption. Thus:

$$A_t = \mu(K^*_t - OS_{t-1}) \qquad (9.16)$$

where OS_t is the occupied space; and μ is an adjustment parameter for the fraction of desired demand which is realised each period.

This is similar to the formulations considered in Chapter 8 which use the accelerator principle. There are two differences: first, it is for absorption and not development; and second, it is for occupied space and not the actual capital stock, the difference being vacant space.

Combining equations (9.15) and (9.16) gives the equation for absorption:[8]

$$A_t = \mu[\gamma_0 + \gamma_1 E_t + \gamma_2 RR_t + \gamma_3(E_t/E_{t-1})] - \mu OS_{t-1} \qquad (9.17)$$

Thus, absorption is a function of office employment, real rents, employment change and the occupied stock.

The second behaviour equation is for supply, which is measured by the level of new permits. This is, again, a profits-driven model of development. Supply is taken to be a function of current market conditions (rents and vacancy rates) and expectations about them when the projects will be completed. These expectations are likely to be influenced by the current state of the economy (proxied by past employment growth). Supply also depends on the cost of development and the short-term cost of financing it. Finally, the absolute level of supply depends on the size of current stock. Thus:

$$P_t = \alpha_0 + \alpha_1 RR_t + \alpha_3 VR_t + \alpha_4 K_t + \alpha_5(E_t/E_{t-1}) + \alpha_6 CC_t + \alpha_7 NC_t \qquad (9.18)$$

where P_t is the level of new development permits; RR_t is the real rent; VR_t is the vacancy rate; K_t is the stock; CC_t is the cost of construction; NC_t is the interest rate (presumably nominal, but not specified); and α_i are constants.

The two preceding equations are for demand in the user market and supply in the development market. However, the traditional assumption of one-period market clearing – through rent fully adjusting each period to equate supply and demand – is unacceptable as it cannot explain the observed systematic cycles in the vacancy rate. Wheaton, therefore, proposes a rent adjustment model (see Chapter 8). This allows rents to adjust more slowly and so determines the vacancy rate endogenously. Thus:

$$\Delta RR_t/RR_{t-1} = \lambda[VR_{t-n} - VR^n] \qquad (9.19)$$

where VR_{t-n} is the vacancy rate with a variety of lags. (The suffix $t-n$ is simply a device to show the possible inclusion of an unspecified number of lags.)

Rent data were not available to Wheaton, but he argues that the relation-ship in equation (9.19) enables the lagged vacancy rate to be substituted in equations (9.17) and (9.18) to overcome the absence. The discussion in Chapter 8 on rental adjustment models suggests Wheaton's approach to rent is problematic, as a link to the capital markets creates an element in equilib-rium rent which is autonomous from the natural vacancy rate. Pollakowski *et al.* (1992) use the same basic framework but with rent data for a panel of 21 metropolitan areas for 1981–90.

The two equations are estimated with various lags on the vacancy rate in order to establish the best fit. For the absorption equation, a six period (three year) lag on the vacancy rate was best. All coefficients are significant and correctly signed. The R^2 is 0.82. For the new supply equation, a five period lag was best. Employment growth, the vacancy rate, and the stock of space are all significant and correctly signed but, as in many such studies, con-struction costs and the interest rate are insignificant. The R^2 is 0.91.

The results illustrate that practical estimation is a combination of theory and consideration of the statistical fits of a variety of lag formulations where theory does not strongly suggest which is most appropriate.

Wheaton uses the model framework to forecast under three economic scenarios, each containing forecasts for the three exogenous variables of employment, interest rates and construction costs.

Although an improvement in the modelling of office markets from the approaches of Rosen and Hekman, this approach also has weaknesses. The absence of rental data and the resultant reliance on vacancies as a proxy for them is unconvincing, particularly in light of the Hendershott (1995) critique of rental adjustment models (see Chapter 8). More fundamentally, this model, like the previous two, fails to link the user and development markets to the financial market, except through the nominal interest rate which is insignificant in the estimations.

A further development of this approach is outlined in the next section, before consideration of a model which makes explicit the link to the capital markets.

MULTI-EQUATION MODELS OF THE LONDON OFFICE MARKET

Wheaton, Torto and Evans (1997)

Wheaton *et al.* (1997) develop the model framework of Wheaton (1987) and apply it to the London office market using annual data for the period 1974–94. They again use three behavioural equations (for construction, net absorption and rent adjustment) but this time the rent equation is estimated. There are six endogenous variables (absorption, real rent, new construction

orders, vacancy, total floor space and occupied floor space) and three exogenous variables (nominal interest rates, office employment and real construction costs). The endogeneity of rent, as suggested above, is problematic as it
supposes no direct link to the capital markets.

There are three identities for the capital stock, the vacancy rate and the
occupied space:

$$K_t = K_{t-1} + TD_t(1-\delta) \tag{9.20}$$

$$VR_t = (K_t - OS_t)/K_t \tag{9.21}$$

$$OS_t = OS_{t-1} + A_t \tag{9.22}$$

where K_t is the total stock; TD_t is total development (starts); VR_t is the
vacancy rate; OS_t is the occupied space; A_t is the absorption; and δ is the rate
of depreciation (the fraction of new construction which goes to refurbish or
replace existing stock).

Equations (9.20) to (9.22) are the equivalent of equations (9.12) to (9.14)
in Wheaton's US office model. The difference is that a depreciation factor (δ)
has been included, but it is applied to the new construction starts (TD_t)
whereas, logically, depreciation is a function of the stock (K_{t-1}). There might
also be a concern with the assumption that all development started in one
period is completed within the period.

The first of the three behavioural equations considers absorption. The first
step is to consider the desired space for occupancy. This is a function of the
number of office workers and the rent:

$$K_t^* = \alpha_0 + E_t[\gamma_1 + \gamma_2 RR_{t-1}] \tag{9.23}$$

where K_t^* is the desired space for occupancy; E_t is the number of office
workers; RR_t is real rent; $[\gamma_1 + \gamma_2 RR_{t-1}]$ represents the space demanded per
worker; γ_1 is a base line square feet per worker; and γ_2 determines how much
the desired space varies with rent.

This is similar to equation (9.15) in the original Wheaton model. One concern is the use of 'headline' rent which, during the property slump of the
early 1980s was much higher than the 'effective' rent, that is taking into
account incentives, such as rent free periods (see Hendershott et al. (1997),
below).

Next, suppose that there is an adjustment process, whereby only a fraction
of the desired new space is occupied and that net absorption is a proportion
of desired absorption. Thus:

$$A_t = OS_t - OS_{t-1} = \tau_1[K_t^* - OS_{t-1}] \tag{9.24}$$

where A_t is the net absorption rate; OS_t is the occupied space; and τ_1 is an adjustment factor. This is identical to equation (9.16). Now substitute (9.23) in (9.24) to give:

$$A_t = \tau_1(\gamma_0 + E_t[\gamma_1 + \gamma_2 RR_{t-1}]) - \tau_1 OS_{t-1} \tag{9.25}$$

This final demand equation is similar to equation (9.17) in the original Wheaton model. In the estimation, all coefficients are correctly signed, and all but γ_0 are significant.[9] The R^2 is 0.71.

The second behavioural equation is for supply. It is again a model where profits, the difference between capital value and replacement costs, provide signals to developers. It includes variables measuring rent (but allowing for vacancy), a capitalisation rate and construction costs (as a proxy for total replacement costs). The capitalisation rate is proxied by a nominal interest rate as it is argued that the office yield (capitalisation rate) is endogenous. However, this ignores the link to the gilt yield in the capital market (see Chapter 10). The interest rate is also a measure of the cost of development finance. Thus:

$$TD_t = \alpha_0 + \alpha_1 RR_t + \alpha_2 VR_t + \alpha_3 NC_t + \alpha_4 CC_t \tag{9.26}$$

where TD_t is the level of construction; RR_t is the real rent; VR_t is the vacancy rate; NC_t is interest rate or yield, taken from 10 year gilts; CC_t is the real construction cost; and α_i are constants.

The basic formulation is similar to equation (9.18) except for the exclusion of employment growth and the size of the current stock. In this case, construction orders and not permits are being modelled.

In the estimation of equation (9.26), all coefficients are correctly signed and all except NC_t are significant. The lack of significance of the interest rate is a common feature of many development models. It might be expected that the correct rate to use is the real and not the nominal rate. Real rates and real rates net of tax were also tried, but nominal interest rates performed best, and the other coefficients were stable with different interest rates.

The R^2 is 0.88 but this achieved only by the omission of the period 1973–5, when high rents did not result in a construction boom. This is explained rather implausibly by 'restrictions on building activity' enacted by 'Labour Party governments in power during the 1970s' (Wheaton et al., 1997: 84). These controls were in place during the later 1960s but there was a Conservative government during 1970–4, the period of concern. A more plausible explanation is that the crashes in the stock and property markets led to expectations of low future demand for offices. This suggests these expectations are poorly modelled.

Another problem may lie in the use of data covering very different spatial scales. The analysis uses employment data for the whole of the South East

236

(roughly a 40 mile radius of Central London); new construction orders for Greater London (the main conurbation and a much smaller area) and vacancy data for Central London. The spatial scale of the rental data is unclear. Construction activity in areas of the South East beyond Greater London, and the decentralisation of office activity to these areas is, therefore, excluded from the analysis.

A further unusual feature about the chosen estimated equation is the absence of a lag in the vacancy rate. This is in contrast to Wheaton's earlier work, which included a five period (two and a half year) lag in the vacancy rate. This lag was used to explain the length of the development cycle. This new formulation without lags suggests a more plausible responsiveness of development to vacancy rates, and may suggest problems with the data used for the earlier formulation. This again indicates the flexibility researchers have when determining the precise formulation of a model.

The third behavioural equation is for rental adjustment. As rent data are available for London, (headline) rents are included in the other equations, rather than being proxied by vacancy rates as in Wheaton's US study. The rental adjustment model is developed as follows. First, the equilibrium rent is taken to be a linear function of the lagged vacancy and absorption rates:

$$RR^n = \beta_0 - \beta_1 VR_{t-1} + \beta_2(A_{t-1}/OS_{t-1}) \qquad (9.27)$$

As in previous studies discussed above, the failure to link equilibrium rent to the capital market implies that rents are endogenous to the property market. Next, actual (headline) rent adjusts partially to the difference between equilibrium (natural) rent and actual rent, thus:

$$RR_t - RR_{t-1} = \beta_3(RR^n - RR_{t-1}) \qquad (9.28)$$

Substituting equation (9.27) in (9.28) gives:

$$RR_t = \beta_3[\beta_0 - \beta_1 VR_{t-1} + \beta_2(A_{t-1}/OS_{t-1})] - (1 - \beta_3)RR_{t-1} \qquad (9.29)$$

where RR_t is the real rent; RR^n is the equilibrium rent; A_t is absorption; OS_t is the occupied space; VR_t is the vacancy rate; and β_i are constants.

In the estimation, R^2 is 0.89 but there is a problem of autocorrelation. All coefficients are correctly signed but β_0 is not quite significant at 95 per cent. The fact that β_0 is insignificantly different from zero is a concern, as one interpretation of the specification is that β_0 subsumes the natural vacancy rate (as in Chapter 8).

Within the above model framework, rents affect property demand and, therefore, the vacancy rate which, in turn, determines a stable level of rents. Thus, there exists a short-run market equilibrium which results from a given level of total space and office employment. This equilibrium has the following characteristics (Wheaton *et al.*, 1997):

1   For a given level of office employment and total stock, the absorption equation eventually produces a stable occupied stock with zero absorption and, hence, a stable vacancy rate. Equation (9.29) takes this vacancy rate and adjusts rents until they are also stable. When rents have the same value in equations (9.25) and (9.29), the market is in equilibrium: rents lead to a level of tenant demand that produces a vacancy rate which in turn leads to stable rents.

2   If office employment increases, absorption becomes positive and, with a fixed stock, vacancies fall. The lower vacancy rate causes rents to rise which partially reduces absorption. Eventually a new stable equilibrium is reached with higher rents, zero absorption and a lower vacancy rate. Total occupied space will have increased but space per worker will be less.

3   If stock increases, while demand remains constant, the vacancy rate rises and rents fall. Lower rents generate positive absorption which helps bring down the vacancy rate. Eventually a new stable equilibrium is reached at which real rents are lower, absorption is zero and the vacancy rate is higher. Total occupied space has increased through new supply and lower rents mean greater space per worker.

The model was used to produce forecasts under three scenarios. These involve forecasts of the three exogenous variables: office employment, interest rates and real construction costs. The results were plausible, but dynamic forecasts, that is period by period forecasts where the inputs are also forecasts from the equations, are not provided.

The model suffers from a number of problems. First, it fails to provide a link to the financial asset market through the capital markets. Second, the use of data from very different levels of spatial aggregation means caution is necessary in interpreting the results. Third, in order to get a reasonable fit for the development equation it is necessary to omit several years without convincing justification. Fourth, the analysis, as it uses headline rent rather than effective rent, omits the large incentives available to new tenants during the early 1990s. Finally, the rental adjustment equation allows the interpretation that the natural vacancy rate is zero, which is unlikely.

Data compatibility and links to the capital markets are addressed in the final multi-equation model considered.

Hendershott, Lizieri and Matysiak (1997)

Hendershott *et al.* (1997) produce an alternative model to that of Wheaton *et al.* (1997). It considers only the City of London (the main financial centre of

London rather than a wider area) for the period 1977–96. The most important difference from earlier models is a direct link to the capital markets through a time varying equilibrium rent derived from the conventional gilt yield. As with Wheaton *et al.* (1997), there are three behavioural equations (for development, absorption and rental adjustment), but now there are four, rather than three identities (for the capital stock, the vacancy rate, occupied space and equilibrium rent). The seven equations (three behavioural and four identities) link two exogenous variables (employment and real interest rates) with six endogenous variables (absorption, real rent, completed development, vacancy and total and occupied floor space). Except for the exclusion of construction costs, the variables are the same as in Wheaton *et al.* (1997).

Three of the identities (for the capital stock, the vacancy rate and occupied space) are:

$$K_t = K_{t-1}(1-\delta) + CD_t \tag{9.30}$$

$$VR_t = (K_t - OS_t)/K_t \tag{9.31}$$

$$OS_t = OS_{t-1} + A_t \tag{9.32}$$

where K_t is the total stock; CD_t is total completed development; VR_t is the vacancy rate; OS_t is the occupied space; A_t is the absorption; and δ is the rate of depreciation of the existing stock.

Two of these identities are the same as those of Wheaton *et al.* but equation (9.30) is different in two ways. First, it uses completed developments rather than lagged new construction. This is a more logical and accurate measure of the total stock, as development starts will be completed over a number of periods. Second, the depreciation rate is applied to the total stock rather than the new developments.

Hendershott *et al.* then add a fourth identity providing a direct link to the capital markets:

$$RR^n_t = (RC_t + \delta + OE_t)CR_t \tag{9.33}$$

where RR^n_t is the time varying equilibrium rent; RC_t is the real gross redemption yield on 20 year government stocks (gilts); δ is the depreciation rate, taken as a constant; OE is the operating expenses ratio, taken as a constant; and CR_t is the replacement cost.

This can also be expressed as:

$$RR^n_t/CR_t = (RC_t + \delta + OE) \tag{9.34}$$

As δ and OE are taken to be constant at assumed values, the equilibrium rental rate varies only with the long gilt redemption yield. Note that the RP premium is omitted. However, as the estimations including the rental rate include a constant term, this specification is equivalent to the assumption of a constant risk premium. Although this is unlikely to hold, there is, unfortunately, no obvious way to measure the risk premium to introduce it into the specification. Note, also, that this specification omits the expected rate of change in value set out in equation (9.5) above, although expectations of its average long-term rate are unlikely to change much from period to period.

There are also three behavioural equations, for rental adjustment, development and absorption. The rental adjustment equation is:

$$\Delta RR_t / RR_{t-1} = \lambda(VR^n - VR_{t-1}) + \beta(RR_t^n - RR_{t-1}) \tag{9.35}$$

where ΔRR_t is the change in real rent; RR_{t-1} is real *effective* rent (not the headline rent); VR^n is the natural vacancy rate; VR_{t-1} is the vacancy rate at $t-1$; λ, β are adjustment factors; and RR_t^n is the equilibrium rent.

The rent used in this analysis is effective rent, that is, it takes into account incentives such as rent free periods available to new tenants particularly in the early 1990s. The estimated model has correct signs on the coefficients and an adjusted R^2 of 0.69. It implies a natural vacancy rate of around 7 per cent, a plausible figure and the same as Rosen's.

The preferred formulation for the development equation, following Grenadier (1995), is based on development being linked to the ratio of value to replacement costs plus the value of the option to wait for an improvement in profitability (see above). However, there are data problems in estimating such a model. First, data on property values are from valuations which are likely to be smoothed estimates of true value (see Chapters 10 and 11). Second, data are not available for the land component in replacement value. Instead, therefore, they propose the following general form for the development equation:

$$CD_t = f(VR^n - VR_{t-n}, RR^n - RR_{t-n}) \tag{9.36}$$

where CD_t is completed developments; VR^n is the natural vacancy rate; VR_{t-n} is the vacancy rate with an appropriate lag; RR^n is the real equilibrium rent; and RR_{t-n} is the real rents with an appropriate lag.

The real equilibrium rent is taken as the average for the period 1977 to 1985 when real effective rents changed little and it is assumed that rents were in equilibrium.

In the estimation, a dummy variable is included for 1989. This is justified by developer momentum not related to rent or vacancy signals and suggests a degree of irrationality in behaviour (see Chapter 8). The vacancy term is not significant and the coefficients on rent and its lag are not significantly different from each other, so can be combined with a common coefficient. The estimated equation is thus:

$$CD_t = \alpha_0 + \alpha_1(GR_{t-1} + GR_{t-2}) + \alpha_2 D_{89} \tag{9.37}$$

where GR_t takes the value of $[RR^n_t - RR_{t-1}]$ if it is negative, and zero if it is positive, so no new development is triggered if rents are below equilibrium; and D_{89} is a dummy variable for 1989.

In the estimation, the coefficient on the rental gap term is correctly signed and the equation has an adjusted R^2 of 0.824.

This equation suffers from three problems. First, while development starts might be plausibly hypothesised as a function of the 'gap' variable, it is less easy to see why completions (which are likely to include starts from a number of previous periods) should be. Second, one interpretation of α_0 is that it is the amount of development which meets average new demand and replaces depreciated stock, and so keeps rents in equilibrium. This would mean a constant *amount* of replacement and so a stock which is constant or growing slowly. Given changes in technology and space use, this may not be unrealistic. Third, the formulation does not allow development to be triggered when rents are *expected* to rise above their equilibrium.

The third equation is for net absorption. It has the following general specification:

$$A_t/OS_{t-1} = g(\%\Delta E_{t-n}, RR_{t-n}) \tag{9.38}$$

where A_t is absorption; OS_{t-1} is the occupied space; $\%\Delta E_{t-n}$ is the percentage change in business and financial services with appropriate lags; and RR_t is the real effective rent.

However, the actual estimation is rather more complex. It involves an equilibrium demand equation and an absorption adjustment equation:

$$K_t^* = \gamma_0 + \gamma_1 E_t + \gamma_2 RR_t \tag{9.39}$$

$$A_t/OS_{t-1} = \mu_1 A_{t-1}/OS_{t-2} + \mu_3 \Delta RR_{t-1}/RR_{t-2} + \mu_2 \varepsilon_{t-1} \tag{9.40}$$

where K_t^* is the desired space; and ε_t is the error from the demand equation, used as a correction term.

The logic behind the formulation is that the *desired* level space rises as employment rises, but falls as real rents rise. However, *actual* absorption is 'sticky' and takes time to adjust to the long-term equilibrium defined in equation (9.39). Actual absorption adjusts to its lagged value, the lagged rental growth, and the *difference* between the desired level and the actual level of occupied space (the error term in equation 9.39). Although the method is different, this is, in essence, a stock adjustment process like that of Wheaton *et al.* (1997). Like all such specifications, this model implies a constant floor space/employment ratio, an assumption which is at variance with reality.

Having considered the three equations, the overall model was tested dynamically, using change in employment and the real interest rate as the exogenous variables. The estimation began in 1986, and the process was repeated using, in each period, the results of the endogenous variables generated by the model in the previous period. This is a useful test of a multi-equation model, as errors between actual and estimated values are compounded over the estimation period, and the model performs well.

The model was used to generate forecasts under three scenarios: constant employment growth and real interest rates; an employment boom; and a fall in real interest rates. Under the first, rents and vacancy rates converge on equilibrium levels. In the second, there is a sharp decrease in the vacancy rate and a rise in rents. Over time these are dampened by increased construction, but supply lags increase the adjustment period. Under the third, there is a less dramatic effect: rents fall, and demand increases and vacancy falls to its natural rate.

In summary, the model has a number of advantages over that of Wheaton *et al.* (1997): it has a direct link to the capital markets, has a generally more logical specification of the equations, performs well dynamically and uses data for the same geographical area (the City of London).

However, this model, like that of Wheaton *et al.* does not allow interaction with other submarkets which might be expected to be substitutes for users, depending on rental differences. The most notable of these is the Docklands area which grew rapidly during the 1980s and attracted City users, but also important are the much longer established Mid-town and West End markets. As such the model can be seen as a partial equilibrium model, that is, part of a larger system. This is a general problem when modelling local property markets and is discussed in the section on local modelling below.

The main features of multi-equation models

Although all of the multi-equation modelling frameworks considered above deal with the office market, it is clear that there is no consensus view on the appropriate detailed form. Nonetheless, some common features can be discerned:

- A basic system has emerged containing three behavioural equations (for demand, development and rental change) and a number of identities linking endogenous variables (absorption, rent, completed development, vacancy, occupied and total floor space) to exogenous variables (employment, interest rates and construction costs).
- Desired demand is taken as a function of the level of economic activity (measured by employment rather than output, because of data availability) and the costs of occupancy (real rents). The actual take-up of space follows a stock adjustment process but the form of this varies.

- A number of variables have been modelled for development: permissions; construction orders; and completed development. It is driven by either the profitability of construction or by vacancy rates. In the profitability formulations: rent rather than capital value is used and is generally significant; construction costs are significant only in one model; the interest rate, always nominal rather than real, is never significant; and land prices are never included because of lack of data. Where the vacancy rate is used, it is significant.
- Rental change, perhaps because of the US domination of the literature, is always modelled using some variant of the vacancy gap. The most recent models also include some form of adjustment based on the difference from equilibrium rent. The variables are always significant.
- Only one model has a direct link to the capital markets through the gilt yield.
- No model includes a land market equation.
- With the exception of the interest rate, the variables are usually in real terms, although this is not always clear from the papers. In general, the descriptions of the models tend to be less full than would be preferred by someone wishing to replicate the procedures.

SINGLE EQUATION MODELS

In general, multi-equation models of the type discussed above are theoretically better. Single equation, reduced form models, although they can be more difficult to interpret, are easier to formulate and require fewer variables to estimate. Accordingly, they may be the best practical modelling strategy. This section considers such models of development (the development market), yields (or capitalisation rates) and investment (the financial asset market) and rents (the user market). Returns are not usually modelled in their own right but are derived from rent and yield forecasts. Some of these models are primarily historical while others can be used for forecasting.

Development

The multi-equation models of development discussed in Chapter 8 include a variant of the flexible accelerator principle in their formulation. The models considered in this section do not; instead, like some of those considered in the previous section, they are based on the profitability of development. Thus, they contain explanatory variables which measure the expected value and costs of development.

The following models come from Key *et al.* (1994a), who modelled construction starts for each of the three main property types in the UK, that is retail, office and industrials. The same basic model structure was used for retail and offices but a different formulation was required for industrials. The retail and office models are based on the profitability of development. Thus, they include the capital value of completed development, capital values in the past (proxying for land costs), building costs and the cost of finance. This basic formulation is set out in equation (9.41). Note that it also includes the lagged dependent variable (TD_{t-1}).

$$TD_t = \alpha_0 + \alpha_1 TD_{t-1} + \alpha_2 CV_{t-n} + \alpha_3 CC_{t-n} + \alpha_4 NC_t \qquad (9.41)$$

where TD_t is total development starts; CV_{t-n} is the real capital value in the current and previous periods; CC_{t-n} is current and previous real construction costs; NC_{t-n} is the interest rate in the current and previous periods; and α_i are constants.

1 *Retail* The preferred version of the retail equation includes current retail capital values and values lagged two years, the rate of change in building costs over two years and the interest rate lagged two years. It does not contain the lagged dependent variable. All variables are correctly signed and significant and the adjusted R^2 is 0.85. The model fits the exceptionally large upturn and downturn in development in the late 1980s. The model can be interpreted as follows (Key *et al.*, 1994a: 61). Construction starts rise with the current value of property, but rise less if land prices were high two years ago. The higher is the cost of construction and the higher is the interest rate, the lower is the level of new construction.

2 *Offices* The preferred version of the office equation includes the lagged dependent variable, current office capital values and values lagged two and three years, the rate of change in building costs and the interest rate. All variables are correctly signed and the adjusted R^2 is 0.97. All variables except the interest rate are significant at 5 per cent; although the latter is significant at 10 per cent. Again, the model fits during the late 1980s. The model can be interpreted as follows (Key *et al.*, 1994a: 62). Rising capital values generate development while higher construction costs and the interest rate rises inhibit it.

3 *Industrial* In contrast to the retail and office sectors, a profit-driven development model did not work for the industrial sector. For that sector, indicators of real activity in the economy are required in the model to make it track industrial development.

$$TD_t = \alpha_0 + \alpha_1 TD_{t-1} + \alpha_2 RR_{t-1} + \alpha_3 CC_{t-n} + \alpha_4 NC_t + EF_t + IN_t \quad (9.42)$$

where EF_t is the employment–floor space ratio (used as a measure of demand pressure); and IN_t is the inflation rate.

The preferred version of the industrial model contains the lagged dependent variable, rents lagged one year, construction costs, the interest rate lagged two years, the employment–floor space ratio and the inflation rate. All variables are correctly signed and significant and the adjusted R^2 was 0.86. Key *et al.* (1994a: 64) argue that the inclusion of the last three of these variables shows that industrial development responds to broad cyclical movements in the economy as well as to profitability. This may be because of the higher proportion of owner-occupiers in the industrial sector compared to the retail and office sectors. Owner-occupiers are more driven by levels of activity than by development profitability. The shorter development period for industrial property also means a faster response is possible to demand changes. These findings are in line with the arguments of Wheaton and Torto (1990) and Barras (1994) that there is less speculative development in the industrial sector and that development is more driven by user demand.

4   *Regional estimates* The same authors also estimate regional equations for the sectors using a panel approach. This procedure involves estimating a common equation for all regions by combining time series data for all of the regions. The broad structures of the regional models are similar to those estimated at the UK level but the lag structures vary and the models have poorer explanatory power. This illustrates a common problem in practical model building, particularly where data accuracy may be a problem. The preferred model combines prior theory with the results of the estimations. There is likely to be a range of lags which would conform with a sensible interpretation of the theory but the chosen lags are likely to come from the best statistical fit.

The above equations were not estimated with the intention of using them for forecasting. The national equations for the retail and office sectors both include current capital values: so in order to produce a forecast from them, a forecast is required of capital values or of rents and yields (capitalisation rates). Similarly, the industrial equation contains current construction costs.

A general concern with the above specifications is the use of levels without tests for stationarity or co-integration (see section above on issues in model building). This is typical of many such analyses.

Yields

The following paragraphs consider modelling of the initial yield (or capitalisation rate). This is the mechanism by which rent in the user market is converted to value in the financial asset market. It is more difficult to model than either rents or supply. One modelling problem is that property yields are relatively stable. This lack of variation contrasts with the high variations in the variables which could be used to explain yield movements. The stability of the series is, in part, because yields are forward looking. They do not reflect only current information but, more importantly, contain expectations about future cash flows and risks. Chapter 10 shows that the initial yield on property can be decomposed into a number of component parts:

$$k_P = RF_N + RP - g_P + d \tag{9.43}$$

where k_P is the initial yield, that is the ratio of current income to current value; RF_N is the nominal risk free rate derived from the conventional gilt market; RP is the risk premium (RF_N and RP together make up the target return from an investment: see Chapter 10); g_P is the expected average rental growth in perpetuity of a hypothetically continually new building; and d is the expected average depreciation rate in perpetuity.

Movements in initial yields are the result of changes in any of these variables. Yields also move because of investor sentiment rather than economic fundamentals. As investor demand increases, prices (capital values) rise and yields fall. One way to explain this is as a reduction in the risk premium. Given the forces driving yield movement, modelling yields is not easy. There are two approaches, one based on regression and the other on cash flow analysis.

Hetherington (1988) proposes a regression yield model that includes the following independent variables: the yield on long dated gilts; institutional investment in property (smoothed, that is, averaged over several periods); and bank lending to property companies. The gilt yield produces RF_N in equation (9.43) while the other two are linked to both RP and g. While this provides a reasonable fit on historical data, it has limited value as a forecasting model because a forecast of yields requires, as inputs, forecasts of the independent variables which are extremely difficult to produce. Key *et al.* (1994a) adopt a broadly similar approach.

An alternative way to forecast yields is to construct an expected cash flow model derived from forecasts of rental change and depreciation and to discount it at the target or required return (see Chapter 10 for details). The required return comprises the risk free rate, taken from the gilt market, plus the risk premium, derived from the investor's research. This can then be solved to give the 'correct' value of the initial yield in each period. However, it may still be necessary to impose a view of how the market yield will adjust to the correct value. This ultimately depends on the speed at which the market adjusts to the available information. Evidence in the property market suggests it may be slow to react during periods of rapid change.

New investment

Key *et al.* (1994a) consider financial investment allocations to property. These are driven by the expected returns and risk of property relative to other asset classes and by expectations of rent (the user market) and yield change (the financial asset market). There is also a feedback into the financial asset market through the influence investment allocations have on the required return and so on current yields (see Chapters 10 and 11). In essence, other things being equal, an increase in investment demand raises the price of property and lowers the initial yield (the capitalisation rate).

They suggest that investor behaviour can be divided into two contrasting periods: one, from the early 1960s to the early 1980s, when the property share in total investment rose from 7 per cent to 18 per cent; and a second, from the early 1980s to the early 1990s, when it fell back to 7 per cent.

This strong upward then downward movement trend is difficult to model with plausible explanatory variables. Instead of modelling either *total* property investment as a proportion of total Institutional investment, or *net* property investment as a proportion of net Institutional investment, *net* property investment is modelled as a proportion of *total* Institutional investment assets.

Allocations to property rise with strong returns in the previous year, the current inflation rate and the current (nominal) long gilt yield, but fall as the (nominal) value of property assets increases. The positive influences suggest a response to property investment returns (see discussions of adaptive expectations in Chapter 6) and a move to property in times of high inflation and economic uncertainty. Property is traditionally seen as a hedge against inflation, although the empirical evidence for this is poor (see Chapters 10 and 11). The negative influence suggests a target range for property exposure because, as the value of the property portfolio increases, the proportional increase falls.

Barras (1994) considered real Institutional investment in property. He argues that it follows the ratio of property to equity returns. He suggests the observable lag may indicate that the direction of causality is from relative return to levels of investment. However, he cautions that the reverse causality may operate: switches in market sentiment, and thus investment allocations, influence capitalisation rates and, thus, total returns.

Rents

The basic framework for published rent models is provided by the interaction of supply and demand in the user market. These models do not, as has been argued above, provide a direct link to the capital markets. The approach set out below, that is reduced form estimation of rents, differs from the rental adjustment models commonly used in the US and discussed above and in Chapter 8. Antwi and Henneberry (1995: 220) assert, without citing supporting evidence, that 'Support for this case [the importance of a rental adjustment process based on the vacancy rate] in the British property market is not strong.' Both approaches, nonetheless, consider the interaction between supply and demand.

Published work on rent forecasting is limited, mainly because the models have commercial value. What there is often considers only demand and omits supply variables in the estimations because the supply variable is insignificant, lack of supply data or for some theoretical consideration. At the UK level, total supply is relatively stable and shows much less variation than either demand or rents. Supply responds only slowly to changes in demand and new development does not take place everywhere at the same time. The UK figures represent the aggregation and averaging of supply changes in many locations. In contrast, at the local level, supply can change substantially in a short space of time with the development of new space. Accordingly, it is not surprising that, at the aggregate level, the low level of variation in the supply series is unable to explain the substantial variations in the rent series. The problem is exacerbated by the poor quality of the data for current stock.

Hetherington (1988) finds supply insignificant for the UK retail sector and Giussani et al. (1993) do not have supply data for European office markets. Dobson and Goddard (1992) incorporate supply by proposing, without convincing explanation, that the total stock of commercial property available depends on the ratio of the price of commercial property to the price of housing.

Gardiner and Henneberry (1991) also exclude supply from one of their formulations of a regional office model for the UK, but justify this by a 'habit persistence' model which incorporates adaptive expectations and partial adjustment (see Chapter 6). In this, expectations of demand adapt only partially to new information about actual demand and the rent occupiers are willing to pay adjusts only partially to actual demand. The model works well in depressed regions but not for growing regions, while the opposite is true for their standard reduced form demand and supply model (Gardiner and Henneberry, 1988). In practice, the estimations require the inclusion of a lagged dependent variable and values of the adjustment parameters can be derived from the coefficients. This is the basic framework considered below.

As models which omit supply are theoretically weak, the following discussion is restricted to ones which incorporate both demand and supply as explanatory variables. Key et al. (1994a) estimate models for the three main property sectors. These have the form:

$$RR_t = \beta_0 + \beta_1 RR_{t-n} + \beta_2 D_{t-n} + \beta_3 K_{t-n} + \beta_4 TD_{t-n} + \beta_5 RC_t \qquad (9.44)$$

where RR_t is the real rent; D_{t-n} is the demand proxy in the current and previous periods; K_{t-n} is the total stock in the current and previous periods; TD_{t-n} is new development in the current and previous periods; RC_{t-n} is the real interest rate in the current and previous periods; and β_i are constants.

The demand for space cannot be measured directly and has to be proxied by a measure of user output in the relevant sector of the economy. Consumer expenditure is used for the retail sector, GDP for offices and both manufacturing output and GDP for industrials.

The preferred versions of the models show the strong influence of demand, with current demand featuring in the retail and office equations but lagged manufacturing output and the GDP growth rate in the industrial equation: Floor space with various lags features in the retail and office equations but not in the industrial. Construction starts with two or three lags feature in the retail and office models: this is at the maximum plausible (with annual data) for a building lag converting starts into new supply. The lagged interest rate appears only in the retail equation; so the other sectors have no link to the capital markets (see previous sections).

The adjusted R^2 is 0.97 for the retail and office equations and 0.9 for the industrial equation. However, with the estimation undertaken in levels, high values are to be expected.

The models were also estimated for the regions using a panel approach. In order to obtain reasonable results, the office regions had to be split into those in the south (London, the South East, East Anglia and the South West) and the rest of the UK, and separate panel estimations undertaken. The justification is the domination of London influences such as financial services in the southern regions. Neither the retail nor the 'rest of the UK' office model contains supply as none of the supply variables was significant. It is possible that these markets are primarily demand driven and little speculative development occurs, but it is also possible that the problem lies in the poor quality of the supply data at the regional level or in the model specification.

The main features of single equation models

It is likely that as commercial property research has developed, confidentiality and potential commercial advantage has prevented the publication of many of the single equation models which have been developed. Despite this, there are more published studies which take a single equation approach rather than a multi-equation approach and there is, accordingly, a wider variety of approaches. Nonetheless, some common features can be identified:

- Demand in the user market is not estimated but is taken as an exogenous variable.
- Development models are based on profitability and, in common with those used in multi-equation frameworks, the nominal interest rate is not significant.
- The investment market has been the subject of modelling. Yields models contain some form of expectations and are, accordingly, difficult to use for forecasting. New investment models are consistent with shifts in asset allocation based on current returns.

249

- Rents are modelled using reduced form supply and demand equations. Demand usually features strongly but supply is not always significant.
- There are no formal quantitative models of the land market.
- Much of the modelling is done in levels and the consequent high values of R^2 can be misleading.

MODELLING AT THE LOCAL LEVEL

The lower the level of aggregation, the more difficult forecasting becomes. Some of the issues involved have been touched on above in considering town level office market models. The problems of local market forecasting are now illustrated by the example of retail rents. The issues include: defining appropriate boundaries for the area of study; overlapping demand and supply from proximate centres; the availability and quality of data; the 'lumpiness' of supply; and the importance of specific local factors which are difficult or impossible to incorporate within a formal model.

The shopping catchment area of a town, that is, the area within which supply and demand should be considered, is not easy to define. In many places, shoppers are able to choose among competing towns, between in-town and out-of-town shopping and between local and city centre shopping. In such circumstances, towns do not have easily defined and exclusive market areas but, rather, there is a probability that a shopper will go to a particular centre. Moreover, the attractiveness of a particular town, and so the probability of a shopper visiting it, will change when new development takes place either in the area or in an adjoining area. The competition between the city centre and an out-of-town centre within the same locality also creates problems. (See Chapter 4 for a fuller discussion.)

While reasonable quality data are available for many key variables at the UK level and the UK regional level, local level data pose problems. Rent data are more difficult to obtain, are typically for a shorter time series, are not corrected for differing incentive packages, and are of poorer quality. Moreover, they are often valuers' estimates of open market rents rather than actual rents paid. Demand proxies, such as retail sales, are not available at the local level. Other variables are collected for administrative areas and not for specially defined local market areas. It can be difficult to apportion data from the areas for which they are collected to the areas for which they are required for a modelling or forecasting study. Such local market areas are likely to vary over time and to differ from one sector of the property market to another.

Data may not be collected at sufficient frequency to enable models to be constructed. In such circumstances, it may be appropriate or necessary to use cross sectional analysis to compare several centres at one time rather than one centre through time. A panel analysis, that is, one which combines cross sectional and time series analyses, may be possible.

Supply creates problems at the town level. Markets can be segmented according to quality and it is likely that the rent being modelled would be for 'prime' property and not for small secondary shops. In contrast, supply data, unless specially collected, cover all retail space. Most development is prime. Assumptions may be required about the relationship between prime and total space. This problem also applies to the demand variables but to a lesser extent.

At the local level, supply is often stable for long periods and then changes in relatively large steps as new developments are completed. This contrasts with the UK level, where supply increases at a small and reasonably stable rate. Further, such an increase in local supply may change the attractiveness of a centre and so attract demand from other areas. A final problem at the town level is the importance of variables which are not easy to model. These include changes to the relative accessibility of particular areas by, for example, pedestrianisation or new roads, and changes to planning policy.

Despite these difficulties, reasonable local market models are one of the most important requirements in property investment, as forecasts of local markets are fundamental to stock selection. Without such forecasts, the use of discounted cash flow models is seriously restricted and valuations must rely on traditional implicit comparable methods (see Chapter 10).

SUMMARY AND CONCLUSIONS

This chapter has considered the construction of commercial property market models, some of which can be used for forecasting. It first covered the general principles involved in model building and the theoretical basis for the model specifications. This used the framework provided in Chapter 2 of the four submarkets. Next, multi-equation models of US office markets and the London office market were examined. These incorporate demand, supply and rent equations. Then, single equation models of development, yields, new institutional investment and rents were discussed. Finally, some of the issues involved in forecasting at the local level were considered.

Forecasts are a central part of any investment decision. Forecasts of total return are used in asset allocation at the level of the multi-asset portfolio; forecasts of individual sectors and regions of the property market are used to construct and rebalance property portfolios; and forecasts for towns and individual buildings can be used for stock selection.

In general, the decision between different specifications of a model combines prior theory with the results of specific estimations. One practical problem is that available data may provide poor empirical measures of the theoretical concepts being modelled. Another is that theory may have little to say about the appropriate lag structures. There is likely to be a range of lags which conform to a theory and the chosen lag structure will come from the statistical features of the estimations.

251

Multi-equation models of office markets typically focus on the user and development markets and contain three behavioural equations for development, demand and rental adjustment. The endogenous variables include absorption, rent, new construction orders, vacancy, total floor space and occupied floor space. The exogenous variables include interest rates, office employment and real construction costs. These models assign an important role to a rent adjustment process, whereby rents adjust slowly to vacancy rates. Only one of those considered had a direct link to the financial investment market through the capital markets. This was argued to be an important link. None considers the land market.

Single equation models discussed were mainly from the user and development markets, a few were from the financial asset market but none was from the land market. Models of demand in the user market are based on the user requirement for space and the cost of the space. Those in the development market are based on the profitability of development and include variables representing value and costs.

The basic framework for rent models is provided by the interaction of supply and demand. UK models of rents tend to be single equation, reduced form models. This contrasts with US models (discussed as part of the multi-equation frameworks) which use an adjustment process by which rents adjust to vacancy rates. The differences in focus are partly explained by data availability in the two countries.

Yields (capitalisation rates) can be modelled using variables measuring, or proxying, the risk free rate, the risk premium, expected income growth and depreciation. These include the yield on long dated gilts, net property investment, the interest rate, office and retail construction starts, expected property returns and the rate of inflation. Such models are of little value for forecasting.

The difficulties associated with forecasting increase with the level of disaggregation and, while robust models can be constructed at the UK level, the town level creates many problems. For example, the problems associated with local rent models include: defining appropriate boundaries for area of study; overlapping demand and supply from proximate centres; the availability and quality of data; the 'lumpiness' of supply; and the importance of specific local factors which are difficult or impossible to incorporate within a formal model.

No modelling in the property market is without difficulties, not least of which is the availability of suitable and reasonable quality data. The approach of most models is strongly influenced by the availability of data. Nonetheless, with caution, it is possible to build property models derived from sound economic theory and with reasonable explanatory power. The difficulty arises when using these for forecasting. For this, forecasts of exogenous economic variables are necessary, and such forecasts are subject to well-known problems. Turning points are the most difficult to forecast, yet these are of most interest.

252

Part 3

FINANCIAL ECONOMICS AND COMMERCIAL PROPERTY

INTRODUCTION AND
COMMENTARY

This section groups together in its four chapters a variety of topics that fit broadly under the heading of financial economics. They provide the background for an understanding of the theory and practice of property investment. The linkages between the financial asset market and the user, development and land markets depend upon investment decisions that form the subject matter of financial economics.

Three broad trends in investment practice have influenced the contents of this part of the book. *First*, the investment management of property is increasingly integrated into multi-asset portfolios comprising shares, bonds and property. Most prime property investments in the UK are now held by insurance companies and pension funds as part of portfolios containing a majority of other asset classes. Decisions, therefore, are made about the allocation of funds across the different asset classes based on information about expected returns and risk to allow comparison of property with the other asset classes.

Second, there has been an expansion, in many countries, of indirect property investments, that is, paper assets backed in some way by direct property assets. The main reason has been the problems associated with direct investment in property. Indirect vehicles have grown in importance, particularly in the US since the 1980s.

Third, as the organisation of economic activity has become increasingly global, investment markets and investment strategies in all assets have become increasingly international in perspective, although these trends have been slower to develop in property investment.

With these developments, there has been a change in the skills required of those who manage property investment portfolios, and an understanding of financial economics has become essential. Accordingly, the integration of the property investment market with other capital markets, including international markets, is the general theme of this section.

Traditionally in the UK and in former British Commonwealth countries, the education of property professionals has paid very little attention to the principles of financial economics and almost none to comparative analysis of

255

other investment classes. More recently, finance has expanded in the syllabus but still represents a relatively small part. In contrast, in parts of mainland Europe and in the US, property academics and professionals tend to come from a business and finance background.

The integration of property into multi-asset portfolios is not without difficulty, as property has characteristics that are very different from other asset classes. Thus, Chapter 10 considers the financial investment characteristics of property. It compares the basic cash flow characteristics of fixed interest gilts, index-linked gilts, shares and property. Property is shown to exhibit some of the investment characteristics of both shares and bonds. Discounted cash flow analysis is then used to construct frameworks which should form the basis of pricing models for the assets.

Other characteristics of property that create difficulties for comparative analyses are then considered. These include heterogeneity, large lot size, the absence of a central trading market with up-to-date price information, cost structures, illiquidity and management requirements, rights and costs. One fundamental consequence is that, unlike the share and gilt markets, current price information for identical investments is unavailable. The likely selling price of a property is estimated by comparison with previous transactions of similar properties. The seller and potential buyers of each property negotiate a price based on these estimates rather than, as in the share market, accepting the market price of frequently traded identical investments with many buyers and sellers.

Such difficulties, and the historical separation of the property investment market from other investment markets, have given rise to property valuation techniques where discount rates and income growth expectations are derived implicitly from comparable properties. This approach is contrasted with explicit discounted cash flow analysis which considers links to other financial markets and to the wider economy. Although traditional property valuation techniques can be derived from the principles of financial mathematics, the links are not obvious and comparison with other asset classes is difficult. One consequence of the characteristics of property and the reliance on implicit valuation techniques is that the property market may not be price efficient. Specifically, differences may occur between the valuation, the price achieved in the market and an assessment of the investment worth of a property. This has implications for the role of the price mechanism in adjustment processes, as explored in Parts 1 and 2.

Chapter 11 then considers property in a portfolio context. The basics of Modern Portfolio Theory (MPT) and the Capital Asset Pricing Model (CAPM) are first set out. The practical application of these theories requires information on expected return and risk which is typically derived from return or performance indices. The characteristics of property, including heterogeneity and infrequent trading, lead to problems in constructing a property capital value or returns index. The most important is that there is insufficient price information: so valuation estimates of price have to be used. Such valuations are, at best, undertaken monthly but are most commonly undertaken annually, in contrast to price information on the main share market which is available as trades take place.

Valuation indices typically suffer from serial correlation, that is, returns from one period are correlated with those from previous periods. The consequent smoothing of returns results in an understatement of the volatility risk of property investment. This leads to difficulties in comparing investment performance across asset classes. In particular, the application of MPT produces theoretical allocations to property which are much higher than actual allocations. Reasons for the difference, other than valuation smoothing, are also discussed. There are also problems in the practical implementation of portfolio strategies to multi-asset portfolios containing property. The most important is the relative illiquidity of property.

Property portfolio strategies are then explored. One strategy in other asset markets is a passive one: to replicate the market portfolio in an index tracking fund. For property, since each building in an index is unique, it is impossible to replicate, and thus track, a property index exactly. Active management of property portfolios is much more common than passive management. Fund managers seek to exploit perceived market inefficiency in three ways: taking positions relative to a benchmark depending on whether a category of property is expected to underperform or outperform; buying and selling of mispriced stocks; and active management of properties already in the portfolio. Each of these requires some forecasting ability.

For small funds, large lot size means that it is difficult to construct a diversified portfolio. For large funds, illiquidity means it is difficult to restructure quickly and there is an additional risk that a large volume of sales or purchases might significantly affect market price. Nonetheless, despite the difficulties it is possible to adapt strategies used in other asset markets to the particular requirements of direct property investment.

Chapter 12 considers a variety of indirect property investments. Such investments do not involve the direct ownership of actual properties but, rather, the ownership of a paper asset backed by direct property. These have grown in significance in recent years as witnessed by the expansion of the Real Estate Investment Trust (REIT) market in the United States. One of the main reasons for the development of such assets has been the problems associated with direct investment as considered in Chapters 10 and 11. In particular, large lot size, illiquidity, transaction and management costs, and lack of market information deter many investors. Indirect vehicles seek to overcome these difficulties and provide investors with low entry cost exposure to property markets.

There are two broad categories of indirect property investment: those based on equity and those based on debt. The former includes shares in property companies, US Real Estate Investment Trusts, UK Property Units Trusts

(PUTs), managed funds and securitised single property vehicles; while the latter includes mortgages and securitised debt vehicles. Equity investments provide returns based on the returns on the underlying direct property investment while debt vehicles provide returns based on agreed interest rates independent of returns on the underlying investment. Hybrid vehicles include a combination of equity and debt returns.

The fundamental issue is whether these indirect vehicles provide returns similar to those of direct property. Clearly, debt vehicles do not, although the risk associated with them will vary according to property market conditions. For equity vehicles, it depends on whether the units are traded in a secondary market and returns are based on traded price, or whether units are traded only with the issuer and the transaction prices are derived from valuations. In general, the former provide investments with returns similar to those of shares while the latter provide returns similar to direct property. This distinction has important consequences for the role of such vehicles in a multi-asset portfolio. In the long term, there should be linkages between returns in the indirect assets and returns in the underlying property market. Whether the long-term or short-term characteristics are most important depends on the individual investor's time horizon.

Chapter 13 then considers the globalisation of investment, in general, and of property investment in particular. Overseas investment in the UK, and UK investment overseas have seen major growth in recent years. These international investments can take the form of direct property investment or indirect property vehicles. Investment based on operational business needs of multinational companies is distinguishable from the requirements and objectives of institutional and other investors. A distinction can also be drawn between short-term objectives based on higher expected returns and longer-term strategies based on low correlation between returns in different countries. The low correlations between property markets in different countries have to be considered in the context of the economic drivers of returns and growing international economic convergence which reduce diversification opportunities.

International diversification strategies can be considered within a MPT framework as set out in Chapter 11. It is also possible to apply the CAPM and Arbitrage Pricing Theory (APT). The related issues of currency risk and currency hedging strategies add an important and practically difficult dimension to international investment.

There are other disadvantages of international diversification. One important problem is the cost of obtaining market information which is generally much less available than in the UK. Obtaining comparable data is made difficult by definitional differences and by distinct market structures. Cultural differences and different regulatory frameworks and political risk are also important. All of these mean additional costs and risk for the international investor.

In conclusion, the underlying theme of this part of the book is the need to consider the particular characteristics of property investment within the framework of other asset classes and their links to the economy, both nationally and internationally. Such a context is essential for an understanding of property investment both in theory and in practice.

10

PROPERTY'S FINANCIAL INVESTMENT CHARACTERISTICS

INTRODUCTION

This chapter is the first of four which consider the financial economics of property. It considers the financial characteristics of direct property investments. Direct investment means ownership of the physical asset rather than of a paper asset backed by property. This latter case, which is termed indirect property investment, and which includes property company shares, unit and investment trusts, mortgages and loans, is considered in Chapter 12.

The management of both investment and owner-occupied commercial property has undergone substantial change since the early 1980s. Property investment management has shifted from a focus on individual buildings to a more strategic and quantitative approach, which sets property in the context of other investments and the wider economy. In the owner-occupied commercial market, there is now a greater realisation that an occupier has the choice to rent or buy, and that owner-occupied commercial property also has to be managed as an investment. Investment ownership in the property market accounts for £120bn while owner-occupation accounts for approximately £160bn (see Table 10.2).

The most important investors in the property market, as in all UK investment markets, are the 'Institutions', the collective name for insurance companies, pension funds, investment trusts and unit trusts (see Rutterford, 1993). Together, in 1997 they controlled 51 per cent of the share market, 55 per cent of the government bond (gilt) market and (in 1995) 54 per cent of the investment property market. The insurance companies and pension funds are by far the most important of the Institutions and together control over 90 per cent of Institutional investment holdings.

The influence and importance of the Institutions has grown, in part, as a result of government regulation, such as: the prewar introduction of compulsory car insurance; the current tax advantages of life assurance policies; and obligations, since 1975, on employers to provide pension schemes. The Institutions are now the intermediaries through which most people invest.

Data on long-term property investment have been compiled by Scott

(1996). Figure 10.1 shows the long-term role of different types of Institution from 1954 to 1995. Historic data on other types of investor is far less accurate. Net investment represents purchases minus sales. The role of insurance companies and pension funds is overwhelming; while unit and investment trusts, which are vehicles enabling wider types of investors to participate, are comparatively small. The peak decade of Institutional property net investment can be seen to be the 1970s. Since then it has declined overall by about a half on trend, with far more sales than acquisitions. Moreover, up until the mid-1980s the pattern of investment was similar for insurance companies and pension funds.

Since the mid-1980s pension funds have moved from property at a greater rate, and the holdings of both insurance companies and pension funds have become markedly more volatile. In terms of insurance company and pension total assets, according to Scott (1996), property peaked with a 15 per cent share in the late 1970s. By the early 1990s, the shares had fallen to 6 per cent for insurance companies and 3 per cent for pension funds. Higher returns in the share market, the expansion of overseas investment in share markets, perceived problems with property investment and more emphasis on short-term trading probably explain most of these changes (see Chapter 11).

Figure 10.2 shows that, since the mid-1980s, financial institutions have been replaced in property investment by property companies (see Chapter

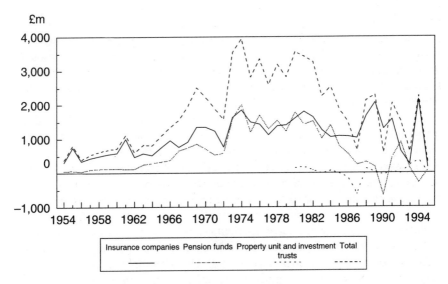

Figure 10.1 Real net property investment by category of financial institution, 1954–95

Note: Property unit trust data includes all unit trusts.
Source: Adapted from Scott (1996) and Office for National Statistics (1996)

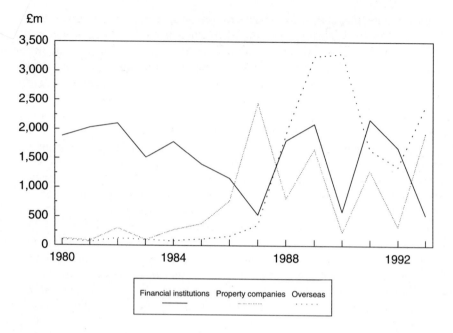

Figure 10.2   Real net property investment by financial institutions, property companies and overseas investors, 1980–93
Source: Scott (1996)

12) and, especially, overseas investors (see Chapter 13). Property companies,
in turn, borrow from banks and others; whereas the Institutions tend to use
their own funds for property investment. Overseas investors now control
approximately 10 per cent of the investment property market and about 20
per cent of the ordinary share and gilt markets.

Property types have also been changing. From the 1980s, new user
requirements and changes to planning controls have led to a blurring of the
distinction between some types of office and industrials, the expansion of
warehousing and the development of a variety of types of retail, including
out-of-town shopping centres and retail warehouse parks. Some of these
property types now form distinct subsectors of the investment market. New
sectors, such as leisure, are also emerging.

The sectoral and geographical distribution of investment property by value
is shown in Table 10.1. The retail and office markets are the largest while the
industrial market is considerably smaller. The geographical dominance of
London and the South East, particularly the London office market is clear.
One-fifth of all UK property investment, by value, is in the Central London
Office market and over half of the total market is in London and the South
East. These markets are dominated by prime property owned by the Insti-

Table 10.1 The sectoral and geographical distribution of the UK investment property market by value, December 1996 (percentages)

Region	Retail	Office	Industrial	Total
Central London	3.3	19.0		22.3
of which:				
City	0.5	9.1		
Mid Town		2.5		
West End	2.8	7.0		
Central London Fringe		0.4		
Rest of London	5.7	3.2	2.4	11.3
London total	9.0	22.2	2.4	33.6
South East	10.3	7.8	5.7	23.9
South West	4.3	1.3	1.2	6.7
East Anglia	2.1	0.6	0.3	3.0
East Midlands	2.5	0.3	1.1	4.0
West Midlands	4.3	1.4	1.2	6.9
North	1.5	0.2	0.1	1.8
North West	4.4	1.6	1.0	7.0
Yorkshire and Humberside	2.8	0.8	0.7	4.4
Scotland	4.1	2.1	0.5	6.7
Wales	1.4	0.1	0.2	1.7
Northern Ireland	0.2	0.1	0.0	0.3
Total	47.0	38.6	14.4	100.0

Source: Investment Property Databank

tutions and it is in these markets that most international investment takes place.

There is also a secondary market, consisting of poorer quality property, which is much less important to the Institutions. The definitions of prime and secondary are not precise and change over time with new occupier requirements. There is substitution at the margin. Properties, which were once regarded as prime, can 'filter' through users to become secondary and then obsolete.

The following sections consider various aspects of the investment characteristics of commercial property. First, the cash flow characteristics of the main assets (bonds, shares and property) are discussed and a simple, explicit framework for price analysis is developed. Second, the characteristics of the property investment market are examined in detail, in particular, the need for valuations to estimate capital value and returns. Third, traditional implicit valuation methods, used in the UK commercial market to estimate likely selling price, are explained. Fourth, issues linked to the predominance of traditional implicit methods are considered. These are market efficiency, price determination, mispricing and valuation accuracy. Finally, there is a summary and conclusions.

THE CASH FLOW CHARACTERISTICS OF INVESTMENTS

A decision to invest can be viewed as an exchange of present capital for future income and capital. These future cash flows have a variety of characteristics depending on the investment:

- *Variability of income* All the main investment assets generate regular income. This income may be fixed in nominal or real terms, or change with economic growth or inflation.
- *Variability of capital value* The capital value of an investment may similarly be fixed in nominal or real terms, or variable.
- *Security of income* The income may be secure or there may be some risk of non-payment through, for example, bankruptcy.
- *Security of capital value* The capital may be secure or there may be some risk of loss.

Some investors require guaranteed real income, some require guaranteed nominal income and some aim for long-term growth linked to the economy. Accordingly, they have different investment objectives and the main asset classes have varying attractions for them. Before considering the cash flows of the asset classes, it is necessary to introduce the notion of a trade-off between the expected return and the risk of an investment.

The mean–variance criterion

At the core of financial investment theory and practice is a trade-off between risk and return. The higher the risk of an investment, the higher is the return required by an investor. An investor must expect to receive the required (or target) return in order to make the investment. This return is analogous to the user cost of capital discussed in Parts 1 and 2 above.

The trade-off can be expressed in the mean–variance criterion. The mean is the average return; and the variance (or its positive square root, the standard deviation), which gives a range of possible returns, is a measure of risk. Strictly, both return and risk should be expected values but, for convenience, they are often proxied from historical data.

For any given level of return, a rational investor chooses the investment with the lowest risk; and for any given level of risk, chooses the investment with the highest return. In Figure 10.3, an investor should choose, for example, A rather than D, as it offers a lower risk for the same return, and B rather than A, as it offers a higher return for the same risk. The choice between A and C is not so straightforward: C offers higher return but also higher risk.

Assets A and C are *mean–variance efficient*, that is, higher expected return comes with higher risk. The choice between them depends on the trade-off

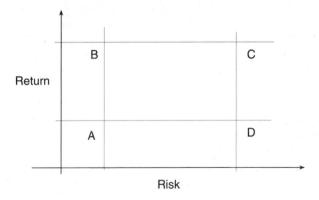

Figure 10.3 The mean–variance criterion

an investor makes between return and risk. In theory, it is possible to determine combinations of risk and return among which any given investor is indifferent, and so construct risk–return indifference curves. These issues are developed later in the context of Modern Portfolio Theory in Chapter 11.

Discounted cash flow (DCF) methods

Discounted cash flow (DCF) methods can be used to develop models for the analysis of price in the main asset classes. The present value of the income stream from an investment is the sum of the present values of the individual cash flows, A_t, which includes the capital value at some future time. Thus:

$$PV = \Sigma A_t/(1 + R)^t \qquad (10.1)$$

where A_t is a future amount at time t; and R is the discount rate.

The discount rate is the same as the target or required return; so it increases with the risk of the investment. It comprises a risk free rate, that is the return available for no risk, and a risk premium, dependent on the risk of the investment. Both the cash flows and the required return can be expressed in nominal or real terms, and appropriate models to analyse price can be developed from either. For the following analysis, a nominal framework is adopted. The nominal required return is:

$$R_N = RF_N + RP \qquad (10.2)$$

where R_N is the required nominal return or discount rate; RF_N is the nominal risk free rate; and RP is the risk premium.

The first is common to all investments while the latter varies from investment to investment according to its risk. Risk free rates are discussed below in the context of the gilt markets.

The PV of an investment estimated in this way can be compared with the market price, P. The investment is considered to be correctly priced if the PV is equal to the price. The net present value (NPV) is the difference between the two:

$$NPV = \Sigma A_t/(1 + R_N)^t - P \geq 0 \qquad (10.3)$$

This type of analysis allows investment decisions to be made by comparing the market price with an estimate of worth (the PV) derived from the expected cash flows, discounted at a rate which takes account of the risk of an investment. Thus, an investment is made only if the present value of the expected future income stream is greater than or equal to the current price, P, that is, if the net present value (NPV) is greater than or equal to zero.

The internal rate of return (IRR) of an investment is the discount rate, r, such that the NPV is zero, thus:

$$\Sigma A_t/(1 + r)^t - P = 0 \qquad (10.4)$$

It is also possible to base investment decisions on an IRR analysis by comparing the IRR with the required return. The NPV and IRR methods give the same investment decision. If the IRR is equal to the required return, the NPV is zero. If the IRR is greater than the required return, the NPV is positive, and if the IRR is less than the required return, the NPV is negative.

The above analysis can now be used to consider the cash flows of major investments and to show how models to analyse price can be developed for the main asset classes. These are fixed interest or conventional gilts, index-linked gilts, shares and property. The market capitalisations of the main UK investment markets are shown in Table 10.2. The share market is by far the largest at £1,234bn, followed by the fixed interest gilt market at £264bn. The investment property market (£120bn) and index-linked gilt market (£54bn) are much smaller.

Table 10.2 Market capitalisation of the main UK asset classes

Asset	Market capitalisation (£bn)
Shares	1,234
Fixed interest gilts	264
Index-linked gilts	54
Property (investment)	120
Property (including owner occupation)	280

Sources: Datastream; Greenwells; Investment Property Databank, 1997

Fixed interest securities

The simplest investment is a fixed interest security or bond, purchased at issue at the *par value*. In return, the holder receives each year (usually in two equal instalments in arrears), a fixed nominal amount of money, known as the *coupon* and, at the end of the contract, *the redemption date*, receives the par value.

The period of a bond is usually from 5 to 25 years. Some bonds are undated, that is, they have no redemption date and income is receivable in perpetuity. For such bonds, and assuming, for simplicity, a single annual payment in arrears, the present value is given by:

$$PV_B = \Sigma C/(1 + R_N)^t \qquad (10.5)$$

where PV_B is the present value of the bond income stream; C is the constant nominal income, the coupon; and R_N is the nominal required return.

Using the formula for the sum to infinity of a geometric progression, this simplifies to:[1]

$$PV_B = C/R_N \qquad (10.6)$$

Using (10.5) and (10.6), equation (10.4) may be rewritten as:

$$C/r_B = P \qquad (10.7)$$

or

$$C/P = r_B \qquad (10.8)$$

where r_B is the internal rate of return of the bond.

This leads to a simple investment rule for bonds, derived from the present value analysis: if the worth to the investor (C/R_N from 10.6) is equal to or greater than the market price (P), the investment is worthwhile. An alternative, but equivalent, rule can be derived for the internal rate of return from equations (10.6) and (10.7). Thus, if the IRR of the bond (r_B) is greater than the required return (R_N), the investment is worthwhile.

The ratio of current income to current price (C/P) is known as the *income yield* and is usually denoted by 'k'. It is a measure of initial income return. The internal rate of return of the bond is known as the *gross redemption yield*. It is a measure of total return. For an undated bond, the two are equal; for long bonds, that is, of around 25 years, the two yields are approximately equal.

If the bond is *correctly priced* for an investor, that is, if price equates to present value, then from equation (10.6):

$$C/P \,(\equiv\, k_B) \,=\, R_N \tag{10.9}$$

Both income and gross redemption yields are common to the main asset markets but have different names in each market. In the share market, they are known, respectively, as the dividend yield and holding period return and, in the property market, as the initial yield and the equated yield.

As all the future cash flows are known in nominal terms, if the bond is held to redemption, the nominal IRR is known exactly. The only risk in nominal terms is that the issuer may default. UK government fixed interest bonds, known as *gilts*, are regarded as riskless. Bonds are also issued by local authorities and by companies, but government bonds are by far the most common in the UK and account for around 99 per cent of the market. In the US, company bonds are more common than in the UK.

A conventional gilt provides a riskless nominal rate of return, its *gross redemption yield*, which can be used as a building block to consider pricing in other asset markets. It is a measure of total return, derived from explicit analysis of expected cash flows and can be considered as a reward for loss of liquidity. Any other investment which involves risk must be expected to provide a higher return. Recalling equation (10.2), the higher the risk, the higher the risk premium:

$$R_N \,=\, RF_N \,+\, RP$$

where R_N is the required nominal return from an investment; RF_N, the nominal risk free rate, is the gross redemption yield, r_G, for conventional gilts of a maturity comparable to the investment being considered; and RP is the appropriate risk premium.

Index-linked gilts

Index-linked gilts (ILGs) are a relatively new form of investment, having been introduced in 1981. An ILG is a security issued by the UK government for which there is compensation for inflation.[2] Thus, the cash flows (the coupons) and redemption value (the par value) are guaranteed in *real* terms, so ILGs offer a guaranteed *real* return if held to redemption. The nominal income varies according to inflation. Whereas, for conventional gilts, the compensation is *ex ante* and for *expected* inflation which has to be estimated, for ILGs it is *ex post* and for *actual* inflation. The estimation of inflation bears risk: and so, strictly, an additional return, a risk premium, is required for a conventional gilt.

Until redemption, both index-linked and conventional gilts trade on a secondary market in which price changes to ensure the IRR equates to the market's new required returns, respectively real and nominal. The index-linked IRR reflects changes in the real risk free rate while the conventional gilts IRR adjusts both to changes in the real risk free rate and to changes in expected inflation. A conventional gilt can reflect only expected inflation: even if held to redemption, it cannot protect against unexpected inflation. In contrast, ILGs provide protection against expected and unexpected inflation.

'Protection' is a looser term than a 'hedge against inflation'. The former is intended to mean a positive real return over a 'reasonable' holding period while the later means full compensation for inflation from period to period. Thus, ILGs do not provide a complete inflation hedge *unless held to redemption*. Although income is fully hedged, the capital value, and so the capital return, varies from period to period according to market conditions.

Market prices for both types of gilt adjust to supply and demand. The government issues gilts as part of its economic policy to provide funds for expenditure programmes. Prices adjust to actual and expected changes in government borrowing. If the government issues more gilts, other things being equal, the price will fall and the risk free real rate will rise. Interest rate changes also affect gilt prices as such changes imply either a change in the risk free rate or expected inflation.

The gross redemption yields on conventional gilts and ILGs can be compared:

$$RF_N = RF_R + I_E + IRP \qquad (10.10)$$

where RF_N is the gross redemption yield on conventional gilts; RF_R is the gross redemption yield on index linked gilts; I_E is expected inflation; and IRP is an inflation risk premium.

Equation (10.2) can, therefore, be rewritten as:

$$R_N = RF_R + I_E + RP \qquad (10.11)$$

where RP is the total risk premium, including an inflation risk premium.

This basic equation, known as the *Fisher equation*, can be used to decompose any required return into three components: a real risk free rate, a reward for expected inflation and a risk premium. The risk free rate can be viewed as a return for loss of liquidity or for delaying consumption.

Changes in gilt yields have an impact on other markets as they are used as part of the discount rate in discounted cash flow analyses of pricing. An understanding of gilt yields is, therefore, important in investment analysis. A simple nominal analysis, using conventional gilt yields, is now applied to shares and to property.[3]

Shares

Both fixed interest and index-linked gilts are termed money investments and are a form of *debt*. They contrast with shares (also known as equities or stocks) which are a form of *equity*. Ordinary shares give voting rights in the management of a company and a share of the company's capital assets (its equity) and provide income in the form of dividends. Income is not known in advance as dividends are linked to profits which in turn are linked to the level of activity in the real economy.

Shares do not have a redemption date and so, to realise the capital, it is necessary to sell them on the secondary market where prices vary according to expectations of the future cash flows and perceptions of risk. This risk includes profits being other than expected, for example, because of changes in interest rates, as well as the risk of bankruptcy and, therefore, loss of capital and future income. Thus, the IRR of a share, in either nominal or real terms, is unknown and has to be estimated. Accordingly, shares carry a risk premium.

If it is assumed that dividends grow at a constant rate, g_S, using the same procedure as for equation (10.6), it can be shown that:

$$PV_S = D/(R_N - g_S) \tag{10.12}$$

where PV_S is the present value of the share; D is the current dividend; g_S is the (assumed) constant rate of nominal growth in dividend; and R_N is the required nominal return.

The equivalents of equations (10.7) and (10.8) are:

$$D/(r_S - g_S) = P \tag{10.13}$$

and:

$$D/P \ (\equiv k_S) = (r_S - g_S) \tag{10.14}$$

where P is the market price; D/P is the dividend yield, k_S, for shares; g_S is the (assumed) constant rate of nominal growth in dividend; and r_S is the internal rate of return, equal to the required return when the share is correctly priced.

As for bonds, simple decision rules can be derived, comparing the worth to an investor ($D/(R_N - g_S)$) with the price (P), or the IRR (r_S) with the required return (R_N). These provide the basis for an analysis of price in the share market. For a *correctly priced* share:

$$k_S = (R_N - g_S) \tag{10.15}$$

This is known as Gordon's growth model. It can be expanded to:

$$k_S = RF_N + RP - g_S \tag{10.16}$$

where RF_N is the risk free nominal rate from conventional gilts; and RP is the risk premium of the share.

Property

The patterns of cash flows of property vary from country to country and can have the characteristics of both debt and equity. In the UK, leases have, until recently, typically been for periods of 25 years and rents are reviewed every 5 years.[4] Between reviews, gross income (excluding management costs), in the form of rent, is fixed in nominal terms. Thus, property has the income characteristics of a conventional bond between reviews. Rents on review are set to market levels and so reflect the level of market demand. However, the typical UK lease has an 'upward only' review condition which means that, even when occupier demand and market rents fall, contract (or passing) rents do not. This protects against a fall in income and means there is an equity component to the *rise* in income.

In circumstances where the rent for a property has been set in a strong market and is above open market rents, there will be no rent rises until open market rents rise above the contract rent. Such a property has all the income characteristics of a conventional bond: income is fixed in nominal terms for long periods and its security depends on the tenant. When let to a government tenant, this type of property has many of the features of a conventional gilt.

In addition to default risk, there may be a break clause in the lease which allows the tenant to discontinue the lease at specified dates. A similar problem arises when the lease ends and the tenant chooses not to renew it. In either case, the owner is faced with the costs of reletting and a temporary loss of income. In some market conditions, such as those of the early and mid-1990s, there was a high risk of being unable to relet at the previous rent, or in extreme circumstances not being able to relet at all.

As property is traded, its capital value can rise or fall in nominal and real terms. As with shares, the general state of the economy affects the capital value. Property is also subject to under or over supply which creates additional risk (see Chapter 8).

In periods of strong economic growth and demand for property, when rents are rising in line with economic activity and there is no oversupply, property has greater equity characteristics. In contrast, when economic growth is weak, when there is oversupply and when market rents are below passing rents, property has stronger bond characteristics.

Assuming annual, in arrears, cash flows, present value and internal rate of return decision rules can be derived for property investment. In this case g_P represents rental growth. A further complication is the introduction of depreciation (d) in the rent-earning capacity of a building as it ages and as it becomes obsolete (see the following section for a brief discussion). The decision rules compare the worth to an investor $(I/(R_N - g_P + d))$ with price (P), or the IRR (r_P) with the required return (R_N).

For a *correctly priced* property (approximately):

$$k_P \, (\equiv I/P) = RF_N + RP - g_P + d \qquad\qquad (10.17)$$

where I is the current rental income; P is the market price; k_P ($\equiv$ I/P) is the initial yield for property; d is the expected average rate of depreciation in perpetuity; and g_P is the expected average rental growth in perpetuity for continuously new property in perpetuity. (Note that the last two terms could be combined as (g_P − d), the rental growth for actual, depreciating properties.)

In practice, this is no more than a starting point and full cash flow analyses are required which take into account the distinctive cash flows of property. In the UK, rents are held constant between five-yearly rent reviews and are paid quarterly in advance. Nonetheless, the basic principles of a model to analyse price can be established from explicit cash flow analysis linking property to the gilt market through the gilt yield, and to the real economy through rental growth (Baum and MacGregor, 1992; Baum et al., 1996). These methods, rather than the traditional implicit property valuation methods considered later in this chapter, provide the proper basis for consideration of estimates of worth in the property investment market.

The above discussion has focused on UK property. In other countries, occupational lease contracts and cash flow patterns are different. Outside the UK, leases are typically shorter: 3 years in Hong Kong and Singapore; 3 to 10 years in the US; and 5 to 10 years in most of Western Europe. The shorter the lease, the greater are the costs of renegotiation or tenant search, and the greater is the risk of vacancy.

There are usually no reviews in a three-year lease. Some overseas leases have rents indexed to a measure of inflation (such as a building cost index) or to a measure of economic activity (such as the turnover of a tenant's business in the retail property). The former investment has index-linked gilt features while the latter, linked to the real economy, has equity features.

Another important difference from market to market is the availability of suitable land. This can be affected by physical factors, ownership patterns or planning controls. These last two are institutional factors (see Chapter 5). For example, in the US where planning controls are relatively relaxed, supply may be produced quickly to meet demand. Long-term real rental growth is, therefore, close to zero. In countries with more restrictive planning, supply can be restricted, and so there can be long-term real rental growth.

THE PROPERTY INVESTMENT MARKET

The last section considered and compared the cash flow characteristics of property and the other main types of investment and showed how these can be used to construct a simple pricing model. This section examines other features of property which affect its investment characteristics and management. These issues provide necessary background for an understanding of the continuing use of traditional implicit valuation methods in the property market. The consequences, for market efficiency, of the use of these methods are discussed in the subsequent section. Chapter 11 considers related issues in the measurement of returns.

Heterogeneity and lot size

Whereas two shares in the same company or two gilts of a particular issue are identical, no two properties are the same: that is, property is heterogeneous. Two shops of identical construction close to each other are likely to have different values depending on pedestrian flows. In contrast, identical offices in reasonable proximity are likely to have similar values as micro-location is less crucial. More generally, properties vary according to size, construction, design, use, tenant and lease terms, all of which affect value.

The lot size, or unit cost, is much greater in the property market than in the other main investment markets because direct property investment means ownership of the whole property.

These two features, heterogeneity and lot size, have important consequences for property investment. These are discussed in more detail in Chapters 11 and 12, and are considered only briefly here. First, as each property is different, it is impossible to hold a portfolio which is identical to either competitors or a market average. In contrast, in the share and security markets, it is possible to hold an identically structured portfolio and so to achieve an identical return (ignoring management costs). Second, the large lot size means that a substantial investment is required in property to achieve a reasonably diversified portfolio: even a portfolio of £100m in the late 1990s cannot be regarded as well diversified.

The trading market, cost structures and illiquidity

Partly because the investment is heterogeneous and immobile, no central trading market, equivalent to the stock market, has developed for property. Property is traded locally and sellers have to seek potential buyers, typically with the help of professional advisers. The uniqueness of each individual property means the potential buyers have to undertake a substantial amount of checking of the physical structure and legal documentation.

As there is no central trading market for homogeneous investments, there is no market price which buyers and sellers must take. The likely selling price has to be estimated by reference to what information is available on similar properties – the *comparables*. This forms the basis for negotiation between the seller and potential purchasers. However, property is infrequently traded and information is not generally published on either rents or prices. Buyers and sellers, therefore, require specialist advice on likely price (as well as on marketing, letting and management).

In the UK, this is provided by the surveying profession although, in other countries, it may be provided by accountants, lawyers or architects. Typically, surveyors act as appraisers of likely selling price for both buyers and sellers but, as information is not publicly available, it is likely that they will have access to different but overlapping information sets for comparables. Property is infrequently traded, so these appraisals, rather than actual traded prices, are used in evaluating fund and market performance. This raises important issues in the measurement of property returns which are discussed in detail in Chapter 11.

Trading in the property market is costly. Baum and Crosby (1995) estimate the total trading costs of property in the UK to be 5.5 per cent compared to 0.5 per cent for shares and less for gilts. There are also taxes on trading which vary substantially from country to country and can create a disincentive to trade. The overall effect is to make the trading of property slow and costly; so property is an illiquid investment. This is in contrast to the share and gilt markets which typically have high liquidity.

Management

Investment in direct property means ownership of a physical asset. This brings direct responsibility for its management and, consequently, direct costs. One important consequence is that depreciation, caused by deterioration and obsolescence, requires explicit consideration and management.

Other management *obligations* include buying and selling, letting, rent reviews, rent collection and management and maintenance of the physical fabric. Major investors may have large in-house teams responsible for the management of their property or may contract this out to firms of surveyors.

Property ownership also offers rights, such as deciding when to refurbish or redevelop, to whom to let the property and under what terms. This permits active management and may allow those with property management skills to generate additional returns by exploiting market inefficiencies (see below).

To counter the disadvantages of direct property investment, attempts have been made to produce more liquid tradable paper assets backed by property. These indirect vehicles are discussed in Chapter 12.

Traditional valuation methods are examined in the next section and the consequences of using them, rather than the explicit cash flow techniques discussed above, are considered in the subsequent section.

TRADITIONAL VALUATION METHODS

The basic principles of an assessment of value or worth based on discounted cash flow techniques were set out above. Such techniques permit a logical and explicit approach in the bond and share markets; and could be applied to the property market. In practice, in the property market, traditional implicit techniques prevail. In part, this can be explained by the particular character-istics of the property market set out in the last section.

In the UK, the term 'valuation' is used to refer to an estimate of the most likely selling price of a property, usually termed its open market value (OMV).[5] In other countries, this is known as appraisal. The traditional methods used in the UK property market are not proper discounted cash flow techniques, as outlined in the section above. They are implicit methods that involve capitalisation of the income at a rate derived from comparable market transactions. Four widely used methods are now considered.[6]

The fully let method

A fully let property is one which has just been let at, or the rent has just been reviewed to, (estimated) open market rental value. The income is capitalised at a rate usually referred to as the all risks yield (ARY) and often denoted by 'k'. It is determined from the yields on similar properties which have been sold recently – the comparables. Market information on comparables is col-lected and adjusted, subjectively, to take into account factors such as differ-ences in location, lease terms, tenant, size, condition and date of sale (to take account of market movements).

The income is treated as if it were fixed in perpetuity and the capitalisation rate (the ARY) is chosen to incorporate the income growth at rent reviews. Indeed, the ARY is supposed to reflect, albeit implicitly, expected income growth, risk and depreciation. Its inverse (1/k) is know as the 'years purchase in perpetuity' (YP).[7] At the simplest, the valuation is:

$$OMV = I/k = I.YP \qquad (10.18)$$

where OMV is the open market value; I is the rental income (which should be net of management costs); k is the capitalisation rate or initial yield; and YP is the years purchase (= $1/k$).

This is analogous to equation (10.6) for an investment with a fixed income in perpetuity. In that case, the capitalisation rate was simply the required return. In the UK, until the 1950s, property was let on long leases with a fixed income, and value could be estimated by capitalising the income at the required return. The required return was typically the gilt yield plus a 2 per cent risk premium. Contemporary property valuation has developed as an elaboration of this method, rather than from the principles of financial math-ematics, and does not consider growth and risk explicitly.

EXAMPLE 10.1

Suppose a property has just been let at a market rent of £100,000 each year and the yield on comparable properties is 5 per cent, giving a YP of 20. The 'block' of income to be valued is as shown in Figure 10.4.

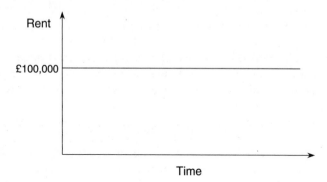

Figure 10.4 Valuation of a fully let property

The valuation is as follows (ignoring costs of acquisition):

Rent	£100,000	
YP in perpetuity at 5%	20	
Capital value		£2,000,000

Management costs should also be considered, either by reducing the income to make it net of such costs, or the yield should be adjusted. For simplicity, these are ignored here.

If the initial letting or most recent rent review were some time ago, the open market rent has to be estimated from comparables. If the open market rent is greater than the passing rent, the property has *reversionary potential*, that is, at the next rent review, an increase in rent can be expected. This expected increase in income has to be taken into account in the valuation. In this case, the traditional valuation can take three forms (Baum and Crosby, 1995): term and reversion; the layer method; and the equivalent yield method.

Term and reversion

This method involves splitting the income into two components: the first (the term) is the passing rent fixed from the present to the next rent review; and the second (the reversion) is the estimated (current market) rental value (ERV). The latter is treated as if it were fixed in perpetuity (see Figure 10.5).

The yield applied to the reversion is taken from a comparable fully let property, the logic being that the reversion is equivalent to a fully let property, as both have income growth every 5 years on review. The capitalised income of the reversion then has to be discounted back to the present. Conventionally, this is at the same rate as the yield applied to the reversionary income although, as ERV may be subject to annual growth until the review, the rate should be lower than a yield derived from a comparable with growth every 5 years.

The yield applied to the term is typically 1 per cent lower than that applied to the reversion as the term income is regarded as more secure. However, as there is no income growth, it could be argued that the yield should be higher. Baum and Crosby (1995: 90) suggest that the low yield applied to the term tends to cancel the high discount applied to the reversion but that the method is 'logically incorrect and practically difficult to understand'.

EXAMPLE 10.2

Suppose a property were let 3 years ago at £100,000 each year and with rent reviews every 5 years. The estimated rental value (ERV) in the current market is £125,000 and the yield on comparable fully let properties is 5 per cent. The blocks of income to be valued are shown in Figure 10.5.

The valuation is as follows:

Term rent	£100,000	
YP 2 years at 4%	1.886*	
Capital value of term		£188,600
Reversion to ERV	£125,000	
YP perpetuity at 5%	20	
PV 2 years at 5%	0.907	
Capital value of reversion		£2,267,500
Total capital value		£2,456,100

* This is the present value of £1 received in arrears for 2 years and discounted at 4%.

Three yields, which summarise the analysis, are commonly used in traditional valuations of reversionary properties: the *initial yield* is the ratio of current income to capital value; the *reversionary yield* is the ratio of the ERV to the capital value; and the *equivalent yield* is the internal rate of return of the cash flow assuming a rise to ERV at next review but with no further rental growth. For this analysis, these are:

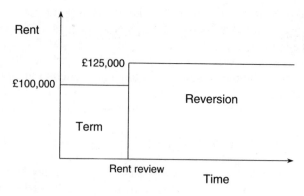

Figure 10.5 A term and reversion valuation

Initial yield: £100,000/£2,456,100 = 4.07%
Reversionary yield: £125,000/£2,456,100 = 5.09%
Equivalent yield: the IRR of the cash flow: −2,456,100;
100,000; 100,000; 125,000 in perpetuity
= 4.99%

(Note that the equivalent yield must always lie between the initial and the reversionary yields.)

Layer method

While the term and reversion method can be viewed as splitting the cash flows *vertically* at the time of the next rent review, the layer method splits the cash flow *horizontally*. There are two parts: a constant income from the present in perpetuity; and a constant income from the review date in perpetuity.

A low yield, typically derived from a fully let comparable, is applied to the (fixed) bottom slice income as it is regarded as secure. There are two reasons for this supposed security: rent reviews do not permit downward revision of rents; and rental growth should ensure that the rent paid by any new tenant on reletting is at least as high as the current rent. However, default risk applies equally to both the bottom and top slices. A further problem is that the fully let comparable property has income growth potential, as reflected in the yield, but the bottom slice income does not.

The top slice is capitalised at a higher yield because it is regarded as more risky. It is calculated as the difference between the estimated ERV and the passing rent, so any error in the calculation of the ERV is 'geared' and will result in a proportionally higher error in the top slice rent. On the other hand, the top slice income contains growth (which is highly geared) which suggests a lowering of the yield, other things being equal.

278

EXAMPLE 10.3

Consider the property in Example 10.2. The blocks of income to be valued are shown in Figure 10.6.

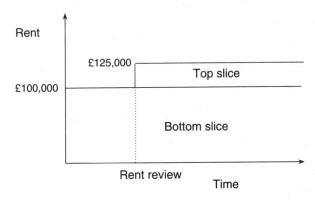

Figure 10.6 A layer valuation

The valuation is as follows:

Term rent	£100,000	
YP in perpetuity at 5%	20	
Capital value of bottom slice		£2,000,000
Reversion to ERV	£125,000	
Less bottom slice	£100,000	
Top slice rent	£25,000	
YP perpetuity at 6%	16.667	
PV 2 years at 6%	0.890	
Capital value of top slice		£370,841
Total capital value		£2,370,841

The yields in this case are:

Initial yield:	4.22%
Reversionary yield:	5.27%
Equivalent yield:	5.17%

This answer is different from the term and reversion valuation. The difference is the result of the adjustments of the yield on the common comparable. Such adjustment is a combination of convention and subjectivity. Clearly, different adjustments to yields could have produced similar answers.

Equivalent yield

This method applies a common (equivalent) yield to both parts of the valuation. It does not matter whether a term and reversion or a layer approach is used to split the income. Baum and Crosby (1995) suggest that a horizontal split is more common in practice. For illustration, this approach is used in the example below.

The equivalent yield is used because the IRR can be calculated from the comparable and then applied to the subject property with adjustments, as necessary, for differences between the comparable and the subject property. It is supposed to remove the subjectivity in yield choice in the term and reversion and layer methods. However, the adjustments to the comparable are still subjective.

EXAMPLE 10.4

Using the same property as above, the valuation is as follows:

Term rent	£100,000		
YP in perpetuity at 5.5%	18.182		
Capital value of bottom slice		£1,818,200	
Reversion to ERV	£125,000		
Less bottom slice	£100,000		
Top slice rent	£25,000		
YP perpetuity at 5.5%	18.182		
PV 2 years at 5.5%	0.8985		
Capital value of top slice		£408,413	
Total capital value			£2,226,613

The yields in this case are:

Initial yield:	4.49%
Reversionary yield:	5.61%
Equivalent yield:	5.50%

(Note that the equivalent yield in the valuation is simply the average of the bottom and top slice yields in the layer valuation and not from any analysed comparable.)

It should be stressed that such methods predominate in modern practice: in a survey of 203 valuations, Adair et al (1996) found that 202 were undertaken using one of the above methods. Baum and Crosby (1995: 95) criticise the above methods as lacking logic, being irrational and 'devoid of reality'.

They show how the methods have been unable to deal with short leaseholds and 'over-rented' properties, that is, where the contract rent exceeds the ERV.

Readers familiar with financial mathematics or investment theory, and unfamiliar with traditional property valuation practice, may find the above methods bewildering and sympathise with the judgement of Baum and Crosby. However, such criticism of traditional growth implicit techniques has to be put in context. The practical application of explicit DCF techniques to the analysis of property, would require the development of explicit forecasts of rent and analysis of risk. Neither is well developed, particularly at the level of an individual property. Further, despite the availability of DCF techniques, the use of traditional techniques has been backed by law and they are an established set of heuristics by which the market operates. If price efficiency (see below) were to exist, these heuristics would result in valuations identical to those produced by a fully explicit cash flow analysis.

The next section considers some of the consequences of the reliance on traditional valuations techniques in the property market. It considers market efficiency and the related issues of pricing and mispricing.

MARKET EFFICIENCY, PRICING AND MISPRICING

The *Efficient Markets Hypothesis* (EMH) requires that prices fully reflect all available information and so future price changes are unpredictable.[8] In practice, the questions arise of what information should be reflected in price and how efficient is the market. Fama (1970) defined three levels of market efficiency.

- *Weak form* efficiency requires prices to reflect the information in all past prices.
- *Semi-strong* efficiency requires that prices reflect all publicly available information, such as company accounts and reports, broker's reports and economic forecasts.
- *Strong form* efficiency requires that prices reflect all information whether publicly available or not, including insider information.

Tests for strong and semi-strong efficiency are difficult and involve techniques such as event studies. Tests for weak form efficiency mainly involve consideration of price movements or returns. One way is to consider if prices are a 'fair game' (Brown, 1991; Rutterford, 1993). Let the expected return for an investment, j, for period $t + 1$, with respect to a particular information set at time t, Φ_t, be $E(R_{j, t+1}/\Phi_t)$. The excess return, $\varepsilon_{j, t+1}$, is the difference between the actual return and the expected return:

$$\varepsilon_{j, t+1} = [R_{j, t+1} - E(R_{j, t+1}/\Phi_t)] \qquad (10.19)$$

If the expected value of $\varepsilon_{j,\,t+1}$ is zero, that is, if:

$$E(\varepsilon_{j,\,t+1}) = 0 \qquad\qquad (10.20)$$

the process is defined as a fair game and the market is efficient with respect to the information set. This does not mean that excess returns are never large, merely that, on average, excess return is zero. Thus, it is not possible to out-perform the market consistently except by taking an above average level of market risk. In this case, the risk adjusted returns could not be consistently above average.

A development of the basic concept of efficiency considers a market to be efficient if investors are unable to profit once information search and trans-actions costs are taken into account. Thus, serial correlation (that is, correlation between returns in one period and previous periods) may be consistent with weak form efficiency, even though it means that information about returns in one period provides information about subsequent returns.

Empirical results in the 1960s and 1970s for share markets provided sup-port for the EMH. Although inconclusive, tests in the UK tend to support semi-strong efficiency for the share market. However, more recent work has disputed such findings and there is some controversy over the EMH. Some researchers argue that behavioural aspects, such as investor sentiments and market psychology, rather than rationality, play important roles in pricing.

There has been little empirical work to test the efficiency of the commer-cial property market: Gatzlaff and Tirtiroglu (1995) identify only five stud-ies, only one of which (Brown, 1985) was for the UK. The work tends to provide evidence in support of the weak form of the EMH in the commercial property market: only one study, by Evans (1990), reports results which are inconsistent. However, these findings do not preclude periods of systematic mispricing in particular markets. As Adams (1989: 267) suggests, in the con-text of studies of the UK share market, the main problem is that the tests do not help 'in assessing whether the market is *valuing* a share efficiently'. Put another way, the tests do not enable mispricing to be assessed. Mispricing in the property market is now considered.

Price, valuation and worth

Issues of efficiency in the property market are inextricably linked to valua-tion. Property valuations do not involve the explicit DCF techniques outlined above but rather a set of traditional methods determined by professional guidance and legal precedent. Such methods create particular problems for price determination in the property market. These problems and some of their consequences are examined in the following paragraphs.

At the outset, it is important to distinguish among four related concepts (see Baum *et al.* 1996):

- *Market price*   This is simply the observed exchange price for a property.
- *Valuation*   This is an estimate of the most likely market price of a property using particular professional rules. The estimation of this selling price, known in the UK as *open market value* (OMV), is an important part of a valuer's or appraiser's professional activities.
- *Individual worth*   This is the maximum bid price of an individual purchaser who takes into account the information and analytical tools available to him/her.
- *Market worth*   This is the price at which a property would sell in a competitive market where buyers and sellers were using all the available information.

In a homogeneous product market, with good information and transparent transactions, market price and market worth would be equal in expectations and the valuation would be a good estimate of both. Individual worth might differ from market worth but the equilibrium price would prevail (see Chapter 3). In a product-differentiated, heterogeneous market, with information asymmetry and lack of transparency (see Chapter 5), market price and market worth may diverge, not least because valuations might influence individual worth and hence market price (see below).

Baum *et al* (1996) argue that, in the property market, at any time, the four (price, valuation, individual and market worth) need not be the same. Individual worth varies from individual to individual according to the information to which they have access, the way in which they are able to use the information, their individual views of expected cash flows, and their views and preferences of risk. It is unlikely that all market participants will have the same view of worth: indeed, it could be argued that such differences are essential for the functioning of the market. Only for the successful purchaser can individual worth equate to price. In practice, the majority of others are likely to have similar views. It is also possible that the successful purchaser may have been able to buy below his/her assessment of worth. Individual worth will only equate to market worth or valuation if the market is trading efficiently and if the valuation is accurate.

The different views of worth among interested purchasers will set the price of an individual property; and, among market participants, will set the general level of prices in a property submarket.[9] For an individual property, price may differ from market worth if the successful purchaser's estimate of individual worth is higher. For a submarket as a whole, this will occur only if there is a systematic difference between individual and market worth. In such circumstances, price does not equate to market worth and there is systematic mispricing.

This leaves the relationships between valuation, on the one hand, and on the other, market worth and price. Valuation is supposed to be an estimate of the most likely selling price: so unless price equates to market worth, a valuation will not equate to market worth. Indeed, it might be argued that, given its purpose, if a market is mispriced, valuation should reflect this mispricing rather than true market worth. This raises the issue of who is able to advise an investor on the individual or market worth of a property, and how that compares with likely market price. An estimation of worth requires explicit cash flow analysis, as set out above, with forecasts of the expected cash flows, discounted at an appropriate rate to take account of the risk of the investment.

Valuations and mispricing

Baum *et al* (1996) argue that, as a valuation is undertaken for a potential seller or buyer to determine the most likely market selling price, valuations may influence market prices, particularly in the short term. This raises the issue of whether valuations can cause mispricing.

Traditional valuation methods, as has been illustrated above, do not explicitly link the property market to the capital markets (through, for example, the choice of a discount rate linked to gilt yields) or to the wider economy (through, for example, explicit forecasts of rental growth based on economic forecasts). Rather, they are backward looking and restrict the valuation context to the local property market by assessing the most likely selling price by reference to past comparable sales. Valuations can, therefore, be slow to incorporate new information. In fairness, there are institutional constraints on a valuer, who may be called upon to defend a valuation in court, and so must wait for clear market signals of market movement to adjust his or her views.

Baum and Crosby (1995) argue that systematic mispricing occurred in the City of London office market in the early 1990s and can, in part, be explained by the prevalence of traditional valuation methods. A lack of information or inadequate analysis are other possible causes.

Valuation accuracy and variation

The purpose of a valuation is to *estimate* likely selling price and so valuations might be expected to produce a range of possible answers. Two issues arise: bias and efficiency. The former refers to any systematic difference between the correct answer and the average (the expected value in a statistical sense). In this case, the estimator (valuations) is unbiased if its average is the true selling price. The latter refers to the range or spread of possible answers. In research on valuation, these concepts have been termed valuation *accuracy* and valuation *variation*.

Comparisons of valuations with eventual selling price tend to show a high degree of correspondence and have been used to argue that valuations are 'accurate'. The work has, however, been criticised both for its statistical robustness and for the positive interpretation. It is possible to interpret the results as valuers acting for sellers and buyers, using the same ineffective techniques and obtaining the same, incorrect estimates. (For a fuller discussion of the issues, see, for example, Brown, 1992; Drivers Jonas/IPD, 1988; 1990; Lizieri and Venmore-Rowland, 1991; 1993; Matysiak and Wang, 1995; Webb, 1994.)

The use of traditional techniques, the variety of comparables used and the subjective adjustment of yields, as outlined above, mean that a wide range of estimates of most likely selling price can be produced by valuers operating in the same market. Adair *et al.* (1996) considered properties in a number of different towns and sectors, some let at open market value and some with reversionary potential. Each property was valued by a number of valuers practising in the locality. The differences between the average valuation of a particular property and individual valuations of that property were calculated. The results were aggregated into categories of properties in a particular sector and with and without reversionary potential. For the separate categories, between 25 per cent and 45 per cent of valuations were more than 10 per cent from the average.[10]

Thus, the existence of a heterogeneous product and the central importance of valuation gives the commercial property market a distinctiveness and creates particular problems for investors. The particular issue of the measurement of return and risk is considered in Chapter 11.

SUMMARY AND CONCLUSIONS

This chapter has considered the investment characteristics of property. It began by considering the cash flow characteristics of the main investment classes. A decision to invest is an exchange of present capital for future income and capital. Important features of the cash flows of an investment include variability and security of both income and capital. Consideration of future cash flows, discounted at an appropriate rate to take account of risk, produces the present value of an investment and is the price at which the investment should trade. Such explicit cash flow analysis allows consideration of mispricing.

Fixed interest government securities (conventional gilts) and index linked gilts, if held to redemption, provide, respectively, a risk free nominal return and a risk free real return. These provide a base return against which to compare returns on other assets. They are debt instruments and contrast with shares which are an equity investment, that is, the cash flows depend on the success (or failure) of the company. Property combines both debt and equity characteristics which depend on the lease structure and the prevailing state of the property market.

Other property investment characteristics include heterogeneity, large lot size, depreciation, management obligations and rights, the absence of a central trading market, high transactions costs, illiquidity and the need for valuations to assist in price determination. These features add to the investment costs and create problems when constructing property portfolios.

Traditional implicit valuation methods in the UK rely on the capitalisation of income at rates based on market comparables. From a simple approach of capitalisation of the current income, methods have evolved to accommodate more frequent rent reviews. The purpose of these methods is to estimate price and they tend to be backward looking and rely on recent comparable transactions. None of the methods involves an assessment of worth. This would require an explicit consideration of future cash flows generated by an analysis of links between the property market and the economy, and discounted at a rate derived from the gilt market and adjusted for risk.

While there is some limited evidence to suggest the UK property market meets the criteria for weak form efficiency, there is no suggestion that it is as efficient as other investment markets. Such analyses do not preclude systematic mispricing, and case studies of short leases and over-rented offices suggest that this does occur in particular markets over a long enough period for knowledgeable investors to exploit.

Property market characteristics of heterogeneity, lack of a central market and shortage of market information make valuation a difficult and imprecise procedure. The use of traditional methods does not help. Research shows that valuers operating in the same market can make a wide range of estimates of likely selling price. The influence of valuations on price and the focus on price estimation, rather than worth, can lead to systematic mispricing.

The consequences of these characteristics of the property market, for property portfolio strategy, are considered in the next chapter.

11

PROPERTY IN INVESTMENT PORTFOLIOS

INTRODUCTION

This chapter considers portfolio theory and applications to property investment. It examines the effects of property's characteristics on the measurement of property portfolio returns and risk, the construction of multi-asset portfolios, containing shares, gilts and property, and the management of property portfolios.

There are two ways to manage an investment portfolio. The first is *passive* management and stems from the view that it is not possible to outperform the market consistently or, at least, that attempting to do so is too costly. This is consistent with the Efficient Markets Hypothesis outlined in Chapter 10. A passive strategy involves constructing a portfolio with particular characteristics, such as the same composition as the market, and maintaining that characteristic. A portfolio with the same structure as a market index is known as an index fund. It will have a return below that of the market because of management costs. The second is *active* management and stems from the belief that, through research and management expertise, above average returns are achievable consistently. Whatever the merits of the different viewpoints, active management dominates and active fund managers seek to buy and sell assets in order to add value to portfolios, over and above that possible from a passive strategy.

Active management requires information on the performance of assets, not only the return but also the variability of that return and the co-variability with other assets. This co-variability is what enables diversification, the central purpose of portfolio construction. Modern investment markets are dominated by major Institutional investors who are able to hold substantial portfolios in the share, gilt and property markets. In such markets, the performance of any asset class is important only in the context of what it contributes to a multi-asset portfolio, and the performance of any single asset, whether a share, a gilt or a property, is important only in the context of the respective asset portfolios.

The measurement of market performance is well established for shares and gilts, with data available from the early part of this century, but did not begin in property until the 1960s with the development of the modern direct property investment market. Measurement of the performance of individual property portfolios is even more recent and did not start in a systematic and standardised way, and on an industry-wide basis, until the establishment of the Investment Property Databank (IPD) in 1985. Property performance analysis was a costly and time-consuming activity and, as property was infrequently traded, there was no compelling need for such information to be regularly available.

The development of property performance measurement was part of a wider series of changes affecting the property investment market. These included: the expansion of Institutional investment in the 1970s; efforts to compare property with other assets and to apply portfolio construction and financial appraisal techniques developed in the share market; and consideration of the links between the property market and the economy.

The measurement of market performance is important as it provides information about the return and risk characteristics of assets. This information is used to forecast returns (see Chapter 9), to estimate risk and to assist in portfolio construction. The measurement of the performance of individual portfolios allows comparison with the market as a whole and with competitors. It also enables fund managers to be assessed against their portfolio objectives which are typically expressed in terms of out-performing the market.

The next section sets out the basic principles of portfolio theory. This is followed by a section on the property indices used to measure property returns and to compare property with other assets. The two subsequent sections consider property in the multi-asset portfolio and property portfolio construction. Finally, there is a summary and conclusions.

PORTFOLIO THEORY

Modern Portfolio Theory[1]

Before consideration of property indices and of practical aspects of property in a portfolio context, it is necessary to set out the theoretical context provided by Modern Portfolio Theory (MPT). This is then extended to the Capital Asset Pricing Model (CAPM). Both MPT and CAPM analyses are used in Chapter 13 on international property investment.

MPT was introduced by Markowitz (1952, 1959) for analysis of the share market. The basic notion of MPT is that the return and risk of any individual asset are important not in their own right but rather because of what they contribute to the return and risk of the portfolio. When assets are combined in a portfolio, its expected return is simply the weighted average return of the individual assets and is given by:

$$E(R_p) = \Sigma w_i E(R_i) \tag{11.1}$$

where $E(R_p)$ is the portfolio expected return; w_i is the weight or proportion of total funds invested in asset i and $\Sigma w_i = 1$; and $E(R_i)$ is the expected return of asset i.

Risk in this context is the volatility of returns. The portfolio risk is more complex than the portfolio return and involves the correlations among the returns of the assets. It is given by:

$$\sigma_p^{\,2} = \Sigma\Sigma w_i w_j \sigma_i \sigma_j \rho_{ij} \tag{11.2}$$

where $\sigma_p^{\,2}$ is the total portfolio risk as measured by the variance (the square of the standard deviation); w_i, w_j are the individual asset weights; σ_i, σ_j are the standard deviations of the returns to individual assets; and ρ_{ij} is the correlation coefficient between returns to assets i and j.

If the returns for all assets are perfectly positively correlated, that is, if they always move up and down together, the expression simplifies to:

$$\sigma_p = \Sigma w_i \sigma_i \tag{11.3}$$

So, the portfolio standard deviation is the weighted average of the standard deviations of the individual assets. If the returns are not perfectly correlated, the portfolio risk is less than the weighted average: this is the principle of diversification.

If the expected return and risk of each individual asset and the correlation coefficients are known, all possible combinations of *portfolio* risk and return can be calculated from equations (11.1) and (11.2) using all possible weights. A typical set of possible combinations of risk and return for five assets is shown in Figure 11.1. Of these possible combinations, it is clear that some are sub-optimal as it is possible to obtain either higher expected return

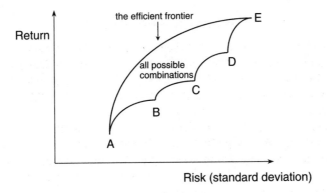

Figure 11.1 Possible and efficient risk/return combinations

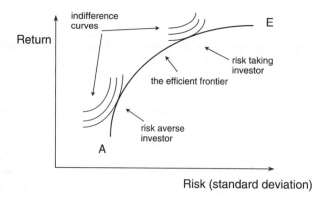

Figure 11.2 Indifference curves and the efficient frontier

for the same risk or lower risk for the same expected return. The optimal or efficient combinations of risk and return are given by the line AE in Figure 11.1. This is known as the *efficient frontier*. Along this line, higher risk is rewarded by higher expected return so the choice investors make depends on their risk/return indifference (see Chapter 10).

Upwardly sloping indifference curves, showing combinations of expected return and risk between which an investor is indifferent, can be drawn. The highest possible one is the tangent to AE. It defines the optimal portfolio choice for the investor. Investors would choose their optimal portfolios according to their risk/return trade-offs: those for a risk averse and a risk taking investor are shown in Figure 11.2. Associated with the optimal point on the efficient frontier are the optimal combination of return and risk, and the portfolio weights. In practice, it is more likely that an investor would define a maximum risk tolerance or a minimum expected return requirement and structure the portfolio to achieve this.

The Capital Asset Pricing Model (CAPM)

The Capital Asset Pricing Model (CAPM) was developed in the 1960s as an extension of MPT. It considers the risk–return trade-off in a portfolio context to determine if an asset is correctly priced for its risk. Some of its basic notions are used later in this chapter and the framework is used in Chapter 13.

A starting point for the development of CAPM is the observation that the returns on most shares are positively correlated, that is, they tend to move up and down together. Thus, a simple hypothesis is that there is a single common market response, with the expected return on a security expressed as a linear function of the expected return on the market as a whole. This is the *market model* (or single index model):

$$E(R_i) = \alpha_i + \beta_i E(R_m) \tag{11.4}$$

where $E(R_i)$ is the expected return on an asset; $E(R_m)$ is the expected return on the market; and α_i and β_i are constants.

The Capital Asset Pricing Model is estimated using the market model and provides the theoretical justification for it. The analysis requires a large number of simplifying assumptions.[2] Assume a risk free asset and unlimited borrowing or investing at the (same) risk free rate. Any investor can then move to a higher indifference curve (and so improve their risk–return combination) by combining an investment in a common portfolio, known as the *market portfolio* (M), with investment in, or borrowing at, the risk free asset (RF). The new optimal combinations of risk and return are on the straight line from the risk free asset, and tangent to the previous efficient frontier at M. This is known as the *Capital Market Line* (CML) (see Figure 11.3).

The CML represents linear combinations of the market portfolio and the risk free asset. Its equation is:

$$E(R_p) = RF(1 - \sigma_p/\sigma_m) + E(R_m)\sigma_p/\sigma_m \tag{11.5}$$

where $E(R_p)$ is the return on the portfolio; $E(R_m)$ is the return on the market; RF is the risk free rate; σ_p is the risk of the portfolio; and σ_m is the risk of the market.

This represents a linear relationship between the risk (σ_p) and the expected return ($E(R_p)$) of a portfolio. It can be rewritten as:

$$E(R_p) = RF + [(E(R_m) - RF)/\sigma_m]\sigma_p \tag{11.6}$$

This shows that the expected return of a portfolio comprises the risk free

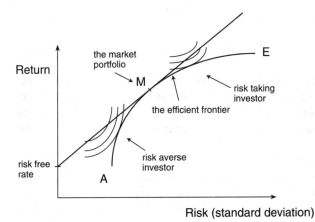

Figure 11.3 The Capital Market Line

return (RF) plus a risk premium which increases with the risk of the portfolio (σ_p).

The analysis can be developed and applied to an individual asset. It shows that the expected return on an asset can be expressed as the risk free rate plus a risk premium which varies with the volatility of the asset *relative to the market*. Thus:

$$E(R_i) = RF + [E(R_m) - RF]COV_{im}/\sigma_m^2 \qquad (11.7)$$

where COV_{im} is the covariance of the asset with the market.

This is known as the Capital Asset Pricing Model or the *Securities Market Line*. The term COV_{im}/σ_m^2 is known as the beta of an asset (β_i) and measures its volatility relative to the market. Equation (11.7) can then be written as:

$$E(R_i) = RF + [E(R_m) - RF]\beta_i \qquad (11.8)$$

Thus, as β_i increases, the expected return increases. This equation can be re-ordered as:

$$E(R_i) = (1 - \beta_i)RF + \beta_i E(R_m) \qquad (11.9)$$

This is a form of the market model (equation 11.4), that is, a linear relationship between the expected return of an asset and the expected return on the market. An asset with a β of unity has the same risk as the market, so the expected return is the same as the expected return on the market. If β is zero, there is no risk and the return is the same as for the risk free asset. If β is less than unity, the return is less than the market; and if β is greater than unity, the return is greater than the market. Figure 11.4 presents these relationships graphically.

This is a different measure of risk: rather than the total risk, as measured

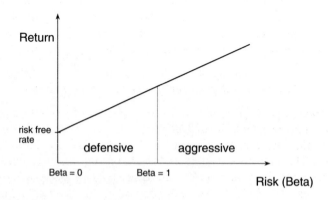

Figure 11.4 The Securities Market Line

by the standard deviation of returns, β measures only the volatility of returns relative to the market. Under CAPM, risk is divided into two components: market risk (measured by β, and also known as systematic or non-specific risk) and specific risk (also known as non-market or non-systematic risk). The first is a general market risk borne by all assets and cannot be diversified; the second is specific to an individual asset and can be diversified away in a portfolio. It is possible to extend the above statistics to derive equations for each component of risk. In the property market, specific risk is a higher proportion of total risk than in other major asset markets.

The market and the non-market components of risk have to be considered separately. The risk of an asset for which an investor is compensated is determined by its volatility relative to the market. The remaining risk (non-market or specific) will not be compensated by a higher return because, in an efficient market, it will be diversified away within a portfolio.

βs for individual shares are calculated using historical data as a proxy for expectations. They are available for all quoted shares on all major stock exchanges and are regularly updated. However, CAPM is not generally used in the direct property market for individual properties because of the problems, outlined below, with valuation-based measures of return and because of the absence of sufficiently long returns series to estimate reliable values for βs.

PROPERTY RETURN INDICES

Many analyses of the property investment market use historical returns data from property indices to estimate its risk and diversification characteristics. Such information is used to determine the weighting of property in multi-asset portfolios and also to assist in the construction of property portfolios. Indices also enable the performance of individual funds to be measured and compared with the market as a whole or with a group of competitors. Such analyses are often published in league tables. It is also possible to use the returns information to identify and explain the causes of portfolio performance. This section considers index construction in the property market. The next two sections then consider practical portfolio construction.

The issues in property index construction

The construction of property indices raises a number of general issues which create particular problems in the property market. These are: defining the population; the selection of a sample; and sample size and information on the sample. The *first* important issue is defining the property market. The major investment portfolios consist predominantly of prime offices, shops and industrials.[3] Accordingly, the main property indices comprise such property types to the virtual or total exclusion of others.

A *second* issue is sample selection which is more difficult in a heterogeneous market. The property type composition of the main UK property indices varies. For example, Morrell (1991) shows that the office component, by value, varies from 34 to 65 per cent. Thus, even if all the indices measured the same property type returns, the total property return would differ according to the composition of the index.

If the indices contained the same proportions of each property type and in each geographical region and, if the sampling took account of other characteristics such as age and size, the indices would still be likely to produce different answers, unless they were to comprise the same samples. This is the result of the specific characteristics of each property in the samples. The extent of the differences depends on the sizes of the samples.

A *third* and related issue is the effect of the size of the sample used to construct the index. Suppose, for simplicity, that the return of an individual property comprises two parts, one a return attributable to the broad category to which the property belongs (such as City of London offices or Scottish retail), and the other a return attributable to the specific characteristics of the property (as in the CAPM). By construction, these two components must be independent; and the specific components for any two properties must be independent (as they are specific to the individual properties). The variance or investment risk of the total return is, therefore:

$$\sigma_i^2 = \sigma_{mi}^2 + \sigma_{si}^2 \tag{11.10}$$

where σ_i^2 is the total risk of a property; σ_{mi}^2 is the variance attributable to the category; and σ_{si}^2 is the variance attributable to the specific characteristics of a property and is known as the specific risk.

Then, using MPT, for a portfolio used to construct an index:

$$\sigma_p^2 = \Sigma\Sigma w_i w_j \sigma_{mi} \sigma_{mj} \rho_{ij} + \Sigma w_i^2 \sigma_i^2 \tag{11.11}$$

$$= \sigma_{mp}^2 + \Sigma w_i^2 \sigma_i^2 \tag{11.12}$$

where σ_p^2 is the total portfolio risk; ρ_{ij} is the correlation between returns for categories i and j; σ_{mp}^2 is the portfolio's market risk; and $\Sigma w_i^2 \sigma_i^2$ represents the remaining specific risk of the index portfolio.

For illustration only, assume that the specific risks are equal for all properties and that the properties are of equal capital value. Thus, $\sigma_i = \sigma_s$ and $w_i = 1/n$, for all i. Then:

$$\sigma_p^2 = \sigma_{pm}^2 + \sigma_s^2/n \tag{11.13}$$

As the sample size increases, the second term tends to zero, and the risk of the index falls and approaches the market component. Table 11.1 shows the

Table 11.1 Property portfolio risk

Number of properties	Total risk (market risk = 12, specific risk = 30)	Percentage of average specific risk diversified away
10	15.30	72.5
30	13.19	90.0
100	12.37	96.9
500	12.07	99.4
1000	12.04	99.7

total portfolio risk (σ_p) when market risk (σ_{pm}) is 12 per cent (taken from Table 11.2) and specific risk (σ_s) is 30 per cent (Brown, 1991, suggests a range of average property risk of 15–47 per cent depending on market conditions). It also shows the percentage of specific risk which is diversified away with a particular number of properties. With 30 properties, 90 per cent of specific risk is diversified. In contrast, in the equity market, according to Solnik (1974b), only ten properties are needed for this level of diversification.

Thus, any index based on a sample contains property specific risk: the smaller the sample, the greater is this component. Only an index comprising the total market has no such risk. The main UK property index, the Investment Property Databank (IPD) annual index, has by far the largest sample and comprises over 12,000 properties, valued at over £51bn at the end of 1996, and making up 42 per cent of the total investment (as opposed to owner-occupied) market. Other UK property indices are much smaller (see Morrell, 1991).

The IPD annual index has become established as the market benchmark against which funds measure their performance. However, it represents a particular segment of the property market: prime property, predominantly in the office, retail and industrial sectors, and owned by major investors. It serves a similar function to that of the FT-SE Actuaries All-Share Index in the stock market.

The existence of asset specific risk has implications for property portfolio construction. It means that it is impossible to track an index exactly and that small property portfolios have substantial risk, attributable to individual properties and not to the market. As no two investors can hold identical properties, they are unlikely to achieve the same performance.

The *fourth* issue is the lack of price information. Each property is bought and sold infrequently, and at different times. Thus, unlike the share market, it is not possible to compare the prices of a sample on either a regular or a frequent basis.

The above issues make the construction of a price index in any property market difficult and, in the commercial property market, probably impossible.

Valuation indices

Property market indices are based on valuations because these are required by law for most investment funds and so are more readily available.[4] Most funds are valued annually but some are valued quarterly, and Property Unit Trusts require monthly valuations. The reliance on valuations creates problems for comparison of property with other asset classes which have price indices. The fundamental problem is the *smoothing* and the consequent low volatility of valuation-based indices. Smoothing results in the observed value of a valuation-based series being a weighted average of the current true value and historical values.

Several authors (see for example, Blundell and Ward, 1987; Brown, 1991; and MacGregor and Nanthakumaran, 1992) have shown that returns generated by indices constructed from valuations suffer from first order serial correlation, that is, the return in any period is correlated with the return in the previous period. Serial correlation in the main UK property indices is shown in Table 11.2. It can be seen that the problem is worse for monthly and quarterly series than for annual series.

There are two causes of valuation smoothing:[5]

1   Valuers respond slowly to new public information, either from caution or because it is not immediately available to them, and so take some time to incorporate it fully into valuations. Thus, the information set used in the valuation is not the true information set. The use of historic comparables in conventional valuations is a major factor.

2   Valuations used in an index do not all take place at the same time. This is a simple logistic problem which increases with the size of the index: without great cost it is impossible to have all valuations undertaken at exactly the same time. Typically, valuations ascribed to a particular date are undertaken during the preceding and succeeding month. The published index, therefore, comprises a moving average of valuations undertaken over a period of up to two months.

A valuation-based index can be seen as a weighted average of the correct

Table 11.2 Serial correlation in UK property indices

Index	Frequency	First order	Second order	Third order	Fourth order
IPD	Annual	0.45	−0.18	−0.53	−0.31
JLW	Quarterly	0.77	0.61	0.47	0.30
Richard Ellis	Monthly	0.75	0.68	0.58	0.57

Sources: Calculated from Investment Property Databank Annual Index, 1981–95; Jones Lang Wootton Property Index 1977 q3 to 1995 q4; Richard Ellis Monthly Index, January 1979 to December 1995

price based on the full information set and of the previous period's valuation, thus (Brown, 1991):[6]

$$V_t = (1 - A)P_t + AV_{t-1} \qquad (11.14)$$

where V_t is the valuation at time t; P_t is the true market worth at time t; and A is the smoothing parameter, such that $0<A<1$. If $A = 0$, there is no smoothing; if $A = 1$, no new information is incorporated into the current valuation.

Some consequences of smoothing can be seen by using desmoothing models to estimate an underlying price series from a valuation index. Thus, using the above model:[7]

$$R_t = (1 - A)Rm_t + AR_{t-1} \qquad (11.15)$$

or

$$Rm_t = (R_t - AR_{t-1})/(1 - A) \qquad (11.16)$$

where R_t is the capital return observed from the valuation series in period t; Rm_t is the true underlying capital return in period t; and A is the smoothing parameter.

A is estimated as the β coefficient in the regression model:

$$R_t = \alpha - \beta R_{t-1} \qquad (11.17)$$

If it is assumed that the underlying returns series follows a random walk (so that the market is weak form efficient – see Chapter 10), then it can be shown (see Brown, 1991, for a proof) that:

$$E(Rm) = E(R) \qquad (11.18)$$

and

$$\sigma^2(Rm) = \sigma^2(R)[(1 - A^2)/(1 - A)^2] \qquad (11.19)$$

where E is the expectation; and σ^2 is the variance.

As the smoothing parameter, A, is less than unity, this means that the variance of underlying series is greater than the variance of the observed series. The increase has been estimated by various studies in the UK and the US to be from twofold to fivefold (see Brown, 1991; MacGregor and Nanthakumaran, 1992; Ross and Zisler, 1987). Thus, the desmoothing of a valuation-based series has the effect of increasing the risk of property.

The next section considers property in multi-asset portfolios. In particular, some of the problems resulting from the use of valuation indices are discussed.

PROPERTY IN A MULTI-ASSET PORTFOLIO

It is possible to apply basic MPT analysis to determine the optimal weights of the major assets classes in a multi-asset portfolio. Typical inputs for risk and return of the main asset classes are shown in Table 11.3; and asset correlations are shown in Table 11.4 below. The property figures are derived from a valuation index.

These figures are typical of those calculated from valuation indices of UK direct property.[8] They show that the average historical return for property has been similar to that for gilts but lower than for shares; while the standard deviation for property has been lower than for either shares or gilts. This appears to suggest that property offers equivalent return to, and lower risk than, gilts. The correlations indicate that property offers good diversification opportunities within a multi-asset portfolio.

Numerous studies, which have used such figures in an MPT analysis, conclude that the proportion of property in a multi-asset portfolio should be high.[9] Even high risk portfolios should contain substantial amounts of property. For example, MacGregor and Nanthakumaran (1992: 23–4) calculate allocations to property in excess of 68 per cent for low risk portfolios and from 10–20 per cent for high risk portfolios. However, they caution that the results are 'of limited value' because of the unreliability of the property data.

Actual allocations to property in the UK have varied but have generally been falling. Scott (1996) suggests a fall from 15 per cent to around 5 per cent from the late 1970s to the early 1990s (see also Baum and Schofield,

Table 11.3 Annual return and risk of UK asset classes, 1971–95

Asset	Return	Risk	Risk-adjusted return
Shares	21.0	34.2	0.6
Gilts	13.1	16.0	0.8
Property	12.5	11.5	1.1

Source: Calculated from figures provided by the Investment Property Databank
Notes: (a) Returns are the average historical returns; risk is the standard deviation of the historical returns. All figures are nominal.
(b) The risk-adjusted return is expressed as return/risk.

Table 11.4 Annual correlations between UK asset classes, 1971–95

	Shares	Gilts	Property
Shares	1.0		
Gilts	0.67	1.0	
Property	0.18	0.04	1.0

Source: As for Table 11.3

1991; Key *et al.*, 1994a). The allocations vary by fund size: generally the smaller the fund the smaller the property holding, with many smaller funds holding no property because of the difficulties of constructing a properly diversified property portfolio as discussed above.

The difference between the hypothetical and actual allocations requires some explanation. The following are possible reasons:

1 *Estimation error* There is a general problem in mean–variance optimisation (such as MPT) which arises from the errors in the estimates of return and risk. Such errors are a particular problems in property returns. Michaud (1989: 33) suggests that the procedures are '. . . in a fundamental sense, estimation error maximisers . . .' which '. . . significantly overweight (underweight) those securities that have large (small) estimated returns, negative (positive) correlation and small (large) variances. These securities are, of course, the ones most likely to have large estimation errors.'

2 *Valuation smoothing* When appropriate adjustments are made, the actual risk of property is greater. However, as MacGregor and Nanthakumaran (1992) show, increasing the risk of property has only limited impact on hypothetical allocations to property as the low correlation of property with other assets ensures high allocations to property.

3 *Correlations* As the correlation coefficient is an average of the product of the deviations of two assets from their means, it is possible to consider the contributions of individual periods to this average. Such analysis shows that the low average figures are attributable chiefly to a small number of years, mainly in the mid-1970s. Thus, the estimated correlations depend on whether these years are in the sample.

The period of the mid-1970s was one when all asset markets rose and fell sharply but the property market lagged the shares and gilt markets. This suggests either, that during these periods valuations were slow to react to new economic conditions, or that the correlation coefficients are likely to vary according to the economic environment.

A further possible explanation of the low correlations between property and other assets lies in the low correlations between the business cycle and the property cycle as discussed in Chapter 7.

4 *Specific risk* Only large property portfolios can diversify away specific risk: so smaller investors are subject to higher risk in their property portfolios and should not hold property. It is, therefore, appropriate to compare the MPT results only with actual allocations of large funds. This goes some way to explaining the differences between actual and theoretical allocations.

5   *Illiquidity* The risk measure used in the analysis is the standard deviation
    of historical returns and no allowance is made for the differential liquid-
    ity of the assets. It is likely that there is an illiquidity premium for prop-
    erty. This could be seen as reducing the return or increasing the risk. Both
    would change the level of the risk-adjusted return for property but nei-
    ther would affect its correlations with other assets.

    The time taken to transact in the property market also creates practical
    problems for active fund management as changes in allocations take
    much longer to implement. Accordingly, such changes are made less fre-
    quently. This may deter some investors.

6   *Transactions costs* The analyses using MPT tend to ignore transactions
    costs which are much higher in the property market. Active fund man-
    agement, with frequent adjustments to asset allocations makes such costs
    important as they reduce returns.

7   *Historical data* In practice, portfolio construction is not undertaken
    using returns generated from historical data but rather from forecasts,
    although historical risk and correlation measures are used. This sets
    actual allocations in a rational expectations framework. However, it
    would tend to affect short-term tactical positions rather than longer-term
    strategic allocations.

8   *Other assets* The analyses typically exclude overseas shares which have
    low correlations with UK assets. At the same time as allocations to prop-
    erty have been falling, those to overseas shares have risen from 9 per cent
    in 1980 to 25 per cent in 1995. Including overseas shares in the analysis
    has the effect of reducing hypothetical allocations to property.

9   *Competitor risk* Portfolio strategies are typically developed in relation to
    a benchmark against which fund performance is measured. This may be
    a market benchmark or competitors in the same business area. Poor rel-
    ative performance is likely to mean loss of business. This is an example
    of the principal–agent problem (see Chapter 8): the interests and objec-
    tives of the principal (the investor) are not necessarily coincident with
    those of the agent (the fund manager).

    An appropriate strategy for the fund manager in these circumstances
    is to measure return relative to the benchmark. Risk, then, is the standard
    deviation of this expected return relative to the benchmark and is known
    as the tracking error. With this notion of return and risk, the inputs to
    MPT are:[10]

$$RE(R_p) = \Sigma(w_i - W_i)E(R_i) \qquad (11.20)$$

$$R\sigma_p^2 = \Sigma\Sigma(w_i - W_i)(w_j - W_j)\sigma_i\sigma_j\rho_{ij} \qquad (11.21)$$

where $RE(R_p)$ is the expected *relative* return for the portfolio, P; w_i, w_j

are the portfolio weights in each asset; W_i, W_j are the benchmark weights in each asset; $E(R_i)$ is the expected return for each asset; $R\sigma_p^2$ is the portfolio's *relative* variance (the standard deviation ($R\sigma_p$) is the tracking error); σ_i, σ_j are the asset standard deviations; and ρ_{ij} is the correlation coefficient between assets i and j.

An index fund is one with the same structure as the benchmark, that is, $w_i = W_i$ for all i. For such a fund, the expected relative return is zero, that is, the portfolio has an identical return to the market. The tracking error is also zero, that is, no matter what happens, the portfolio is guaranteed the same return as the benchmark. This is a form of passive fund management.

Other things being equal, the larger are the differences between the portfolio weights and the benchmark weights, the larger is the expected relative return and the larger the tracking error. Active fund strategies involve taking positions relative to the benchmark: above average in an asset expected to do well and below average in one expected to do badly (see below).

As the conventional benchmarks comprise both large and small funds, they tend to have low weights allocated to property. Thus, funds which consider tracking error risk are likely to hold low weights in property.

10 *Liabilities* Institutional investors must also consider their liabilities, and must hold assets which are likely to allow them to meet these. Liability matching is subject to statutory regulation.[11] From this perspective, an important additional dimension of risk is not being able to meet liabilities. Accordingly, investments are not made purely on the basis of the annual return and volatility risk of assets. The long-term fund strategy of matching liabilities with appropriate assets provides a long-term strategic position for a fund around which it can take tactical positions based on short-term forecasts.

Differences in liabilities help to explain fund structures. For example, a pension fund with obligations to pay out pensions based on final salaries many years in the future, will seek assets, the values of which are likely to rise and fall with those of its liabilities. In general, in the UK at least, both wages and share values have been linked to economic growth, so investing in the share market is to be preferred. Property is also a real asset, that is, its returns are linked directly to the economy; so it too has a role in the portfolio of an immature pension fund but this tends to be a role secondary to that of shares.[12]

Taken together, the above issues help to explain why the hypothetical allocations to property differ from the actual allocations.

In addition to the return and risk arguments for holding property, it is often argued that property is an inflation hedge (see Chapter 10). There is every reason to expect that property, like all the other main asset classes, will provide long-term protection against inflation, that is, real returns over a reasonable period are likely to be positive. However, there is little evidence to support the contention that there is full compensation for expected and unexpected inflation on a period to period basis (see Hoesli *et al.*, 1997b for a full discussion of the issues).

There are other factors which mitigate against property holdings in multi-asset portfolios. An important one is the institutional separation of property investment from other investment markets, both in professional training and organisational structures within investing organisations. This has led to a lack of understanding of property among other investment professionals. There is also a general suspicion about the reliability of valuation-based property performance information and concerns about illiquidity, periodically exacerbated by property market crashes and long-lasting over-supply.

In summary, although its importance is overstated by conventional MPT analyses, property has a role in larger multi-asset portfolios for investors with longer-term objectives. However, as long as performance information is valuation-based and property remains illiquid, suspicion is likely to remain among other investment professionals.

PROPERTY PORTFOLIO INVESTMENT STRATEGY

As discussed in the introduction to this chapter, management can be classified as passive or active. The most common form of passive management involves the generation of market returns from a portfolio with the same structure as the market. This is easy for shares and gilt portfolios and index funds are common in the share market, but heterogeneity and the consequent specific risk makes it difficult in the property market. Even with an identical structure, but different buildings, a property portfolio has specific risk which depends on the number and value distribution of the buildings it comprises.

Active management of property portfolios is long established. There are two broad forms: a newer strategic or 'top down' approach; and a more traditional individual building or 'bottom up' approach. Property fund management has always contained an element of both but the emphasis shifted substantially to strategic management in the mid- to late-1980s, when property fund managers began to adopt approaches and techniques developed in the share market. The strategic approach views the portfolio as having its own characteristics, separate from those of its component properties, and sets property in the context of the economy and other asset markets. This approach is now considered.

Active management of any asset portfolio has to be seen in the context of a competitive market place for new business which will depend not on a fund's absolute performance but on its performance relative to its competitors. This means that strategies are set relative to a benchmark. Liability matching is dealt with by allocations at the multi-asset level; whereas, in the property portfolio, tracking error risk is important.

The achievement of consistently above market returns requires the existence of market inefficiencies which can be exploited. There are three ways in which active managers seek to achieve above market returns. The first two involve buying and selling and are common to other asset classes; the third is a specific feature of property portfolios and involves the active management of the properties within the portfolio. Each should require some element of forecasting and explicit cash flow analysis, although neither has been a feature of the traditional property approach.

- *Set the structure* to have more than the market average in sectors and geographical areas which are expected to perform well; and less than the average in sectors and areas expected to do badly. This requires forecasts of the income streams (see Chapter 9) which can be put into a cash flow analysis (see Chapter 10) to assess over- or under-pricing. The forecasts of expected return are used within a tracking error framework.

- *Buy and sell stock* to improve portfolio return. This is the traditional approach to property fund management. Note that the analysis of specific risk presented in previous sections requires that the expected return due to specific risk is zero. For all properties, this must be true by construction; here the objective is to buy and sell properties which individually will produce above average returns. However, the larger the portfolio, the more difficult it is to generate above average stock specific returns as this would require identifying large numbers of mispriced properties.

- *Actively manage* the properties in the portfolio to improve portfolio return. This exploits one of the characteristics of property investment: the need for management of individual properties. It includes aspects such as the timing of refurbishment and redevelopment to coincide with rises in the market, and the phasing of new lettings to take advantage of market changes. For example, at rent review, a property's rent is raised to 'open market rent' which is derived from comparables based on actual open market lettings and from other rent reviews. If the market has risen but the only evidence is historic rent reviews, there will be no market evidence to prove a high rent. A new letting will provide such evidence. Thus, the phasing of the rent reviews and lease expiries may allow market evidence to be exploited to add value to a portfolio.

The following paragraphs now consider the first of these three approaches in more detail.

Setting the structure

Since the mid-1980s, the conventional way to structure a property portfolio has been as shown in Table 10.1: the three main property sectors of office, retail and industrial (perhaps extended to subsectors such as high street shops, shopping centres and retail warehouses); and the standard regions used for government statistical purposes (with more detailed geographical divisions within London). The underlying assumption is that there is a high degree of similarity within these sector/region combinations and a low degree of similarity between them.

The justifications for the sectoral divisions are that office, retail and industrials are distinct property types driven by different sectors of the economy, respectively, the office services sector, retail sales and manufacturing output. However, changes to planning legislation and the growth of warehousing have led to a blurring of the office/industrial border and to different types of industrials.

The justifications for the geographical divisions are the existence of distinctive regional economies and the availability of data which makes some regional forecasting possible (see Chapter 9). However, the usefulness of the region as a unit of analysis has been the subject of much debate in economic geography. There exist a wide range of town types and sizes within a region and it has been argued that town function and size offer a better means of classification.

Hoesli et al. (1997) consider town-based property market performance data. They argue in favour of a distinct retail sector but note that, outside London, office and industrial markets tend to have similar return and risk features. They also suggest a broad north–south divide in the office and industrial markets. However, they note that such classifications are unlikely to be stable over time. In the US, where the spatial scale under consideration is much larger, researchers have suggested either economic regions or groups of similar conurbations rather than geographical regions.[13]

Thus, although recent research has challenged the sector/region classification, no new classification has yet emerged in UK practice, although subsectors are increasingly used. The continuing use of this classification in property portfolio management is based as much on data availability and convenience as on the efficacy of the classification.[14]

The sector/region structure of a portfolio is considered in relation to the structure of a benchmark portfolio, now typically the IPD annual index (see Table 10.1). However, some funds have a customised benchmark, for example, of large life funds or occupational pension funds, according to their business requirements. One reason is that the value of some individual properties, such as central London offices or shopping centres, is too large to enable smaller funds to acquire them, either at all or without creating too much specific risk. When these large value markets do well, funds with exposure to them do well, but when they do badly so do the funds. As this is a result of the characteristics of the property market and is beyond the control of the fund manager, appropriate benchmarks have to be chosen.

Positions are taken relative to the index: above benchmark weights in sector/regions expected to perform well and below in those expected to perform poorly. The size of these positions is controlled by the risk tolerance as measured by the tracking error: other things being equal, the larger the positions, the larger the tracking error risk. However, the smaller the portfolio, the more difficult it is to get exposure, let alone benchmark weights, in every sector/region combination. Thus, typically, small portfolios have no exposure to many of the smaller markets.

Using equations (11.13), (11.20) and (11.21), it is possible to calculate the probability distribution of the expected relative return of the portfolio and so the probability of achieving a particular relative return objective. The structure may have to be adjusted in order to achieve return or risk objectives: this provides a context for the buying and selling of property and for refurbishment and redevelopment in order to achieve the new desired structure.

So far, with the exception of specific risk and the opportunities for active management of individual properties, this is little different in principle from the setting of strategy in other asset portfolios. The biggest difference is the illiquidity of the property market which means that the strategy cannot be implemented quickly. Significant restructuring takes three to six months for anything other than very small portfolios and creates particular problems for very large portfolios. Restructuring of large portfolios creates the additional problem that buying and selling on such a scale may affect market prices. Any strategy must also take account of market liquidity which varies from period to period according to market conditions as owners are rarely willing to sell at prices below valuation.

If new money is allocated to property, it is likely to be easier to achieve restructuring; but if money is to be withdrawn from the property portfolio, this imposes substantial constraints on the property strategy as sales may have to be concentrated on the more liquid properties. Illiquidity, and the consequent differences in the timescale for implementation of buying and selling strategies, means that it is difficult to integrate property strategy with those of other assets.

Portfolio analysis allows performance to be analysed and attributed to the structure and stock of a portfolio. It also allows the effects of buying and selling and developments to be isolated. Such analyses allow the property fund managers to assess weaknesses and strengths and to improve their portfolio management.

SUMMARY AND CONCLUSIONS

This chapter has considered property in a portfolio context. It has examined the basics of portfolio theory and the problems of constructing property indices to measure returns. It has also considered the active management and the construction of multi-asset and property portfolios.

Modern Portfolio Theory (MPT) is a technique to determine the optimum combination of risk and return for a portfolio and the appropriate portfolio structure. Whereas the expected portfolio return is simply the weighted average of the individual asset expected returns, the portfolio risk is a function both of the individual asset risks and their correlation structure. Lowly correlated assets give substantial opportunities for diversification and risk reduction. The Capital Asset Pricing Model (CAPM), although not used in practical property portfolio analysis, introduces the important notions of market and asset specific risk.

The application of portfolio theory to property investment is hindered by the data available on property returns. While it is simple to construct indices of frequently traded homogeneous assets, such as shares and gilts, property poses a number of problems:

- *Defining the property market* This is generally taken to be the investment market as measured by the Investment Property Databank (IPD). It excludes most owner occupation, most secondary property and contains very little housing, hotels, pubs, agricultural land and forestry land.
- *Sample selection* As no two properties are identical, property indices based on distinct samples produce different performance results.
- *Sample size of the index* As this increases, the building specific risk gets smaller, and the risk measure from the index approaches that of the market. It is impossible to track an index exactly as any property portfolio contains risk attributable to individual buildings.
- *Price information* This is linked to the heterogeneity of property, the lack of a central trading market with price information, and infrequent trading of individual properties. Commercial property indices are based on valuations and not prices. The result is smoothing, both within individual valuations and when these are combined in an index, and to an understatement of the risk of property when compared to other assets. This is particularly important in the context of MPT.

Figures derived from valuation indices for property suggest it has low risk and low correlations of returns with other assets, suggesting investment portfolios should have large proportions in property. This is in contrast to practice. The differences may be explained thus:

- estimation errors in property returns result in the hypothetical allocation to property being too high;

- valuation smoothing reduces the apparent risk of property;
- the slowness of valuations to react in fast rising and falling markets and so the apparent low correlations of property with other assets;
- measured average allocations are affected by the inclusion of many small funds which have no property;
- measuring risk by the volatility of expected returns ignores illiquidity;
- higher transaction costs;
- the use of historical averages to estimate expected returns;
- the omission of other assets, such as overseas equities from the analysis;
- the use of benchmarking in practical fund management and the consequent importance of tracking error risk; and
- the omission from the analysis of any consideration of Institutional liabilities.

For property portfolios, even a passive strategy requires substantial management input because of ownership of the physical asset. All active management requires forecasting and analysis of mispricing. Property portfolios in the UK are conventionally structured by sector and region. While there is some theoretical justification for this, it is also a data convenience. Classifications based on towns rather than regions have been suggested but the associated problems mean that none has been properly developed in practice.

A strategy to produce above market returns has three parts:

- having more than the market average in a sector/region expected to do well and less than the average in one expected to do badly;
- good stock selection in buying and selling; and
- active management of existing stock.

It is difficult to integrate property strategy with those of other assets. Illiquidity in the property market means that strategy cannot be implemented quickly. Buying and selling of individual properties takes three to six months, so restructuring creates particular problems for very large portfolios. There is also a risk that buying and selling large amounts of property may affect market prices.

Finally, portfolio analysis allows performance to be analysed and attributed to the structure, stock, buying and selling and development. This assists with subsequent portfolio strategy.

12

INDIRECT INVESTMENT IN PROPERTY

INTRODUCTION

Chapters 10 and 11 considered direct investment in property markets – the acquisition of buildings in order to receive the rental income stream and to benefit from any capital appreciation. This was shown to be beneficial in terms of diversification in the mixed asset portfolio. However, those benefits may be offset by the specific characteristics of investment property, uncertainty as to performance statistics and the difficulties associated with implementing formal portfolio allocation strategies in property. As a result, investors might seek to identify assets which provide exposure to property performance without possessing the adverse features of direct ownership. In the UK, these assets are termed *indirect property vehicles*. They are paper assets backed by direct property rather than bricks and mortar. In US real estate markets, direct property ownership is termed the *private* real estate market while indirect investments such as Real Estate Investment Trusts (REITs) are referred to as the *public* real estate market. This reflects the nature of trading of the assets.

UK Institutional involvement in property prior to the 1970s was largely indirect. Insurance companies and pension funds provided long-term financing of property through mortgages or purchased long leases with ground rents – an investment with bond-like qualities of low-risk, stable income but with little or no growth potential. Institutional direct ownership increased during the 1970s and into the 1980s (boosted, following the mid-1970s property slump, when Institutions were able to acquire 'distressed' property from property companies). Institutional direct investment has subsequently declined as a proportion of total assets as funds have sought more liquid investments such as corporate bonds and shares and as they have increasingly invested overseas (see Chapter 13).

In considering indirect property, a distinction must be made between debt instruments and equity instruments. Mortgages are an example of a debt instrument. The underlying property provides security for the loan but the return the investor receives is specified in the loan agreement. With a conventional loan, the investor does not participate in any capital growth in the property asset. However, the risk of loss through default on the loan reduces as the capital value increases and as the income stream increases relative to interest payments. Property owners may also issue bonds secured on their property assets. Since the mid-1980s a number of debt instruments have been created which enable the lender to participate in growth. Some of these instruments are hybrid debt–equity assets (see below).

Property company shares are an example of an equity-type indirect property vehicle. The performance of the property company is dependent on the performance of the property markets in which it owns property. This should be reflected in the share price and the dividend stream. Share owners are, thus, exposed to, or participate in, property performance. However, they have a liquid asset that is traded in a public equity market. This means they are also exposed to the volatility of the stock market. A critical issue is the extent to which property company shares behave like shares or like property. Other equity-type assets include property unit trusts and investment trusts. These may have performance which is closer to the underlying direct market than property company shares since they are 'priced' based on valuations rather than in a secondary market place. More recently, there have been attempts to securitise single properties.

Most asset markets have seen the development of derivative investments: forwards, futures, options, swaps and 'exotics' – hybrids of these. A *forward* contract is an agreement between two parties to buy (or sell) something at a later date at a price agreed today; a *future* is a forward contract traded on an exchange and subject to a daily settlement procedure. An *option* is the right, but not the obligation, to buy or sell something at a future date at a price agreed today. An option to buy is a *call* option; a *put* is an option to sell. A *swap* is a contract under which two parties agree to swap cash flows. Hybrid forms of these instruments include options on futures, options to enter into a swap – a 'swaption' – and other complex structures.

Such developments have been slow to arrive in property markets. During the 1980s some derivative products were utilised in the funding of major developments and it has been possible to trade in futures on Land Securities – the largest listed UK property company. However, attempts to establish a futures market in property on the Futures and Options Exchange (FOX – now absorbed into the London International Financial Futures Exchange) failed – as did similar attempts in Chicago. More recently, a number of derivatives based on property indices have been launched in London.

A further development has been the securitisation of debt instruments. In the United States, residential mortgage debt has been subject to securitisation, aided by the existence of federal mortgage bodies and insurance schemes. It has been estimated that 35–50 per cent of residential mortgages in the US are securitised.[1] Experience in the residential field led to the development of commercial mortgage-backed securities. Portfolios of commercial property loans are assembled and used to secure bond issues: the loan payments providing an income flow to meet the bond coupon payments and the returned loan capital permitting redemption of the bonds.

In the next section, the investment characteristics, advantages and disadvantages of different indirect vehicles are described. Next, the behaviour of indirect equity assets is considered. Are they a property investment? What can they tell us about the underlying property market? The fourth section examines debt instruments and considers how risks are assessed. Finally, the implications of growth in the market for indirect vehicles are discussed.

INDIRECT PROPERTY VEHICLES

In this section, the advantages and disadvantages of various forms of indirect property investments are considered. Given the vast variety of investments available, there is no attempt to provide a comprehensive or complete listing. However, the major types of indirect property assets are described. The investment characteristics of the vehicles are viewed in the context of the characteristics of direct ownership of property. This involves consideration of risk and return, the pricing models employed, market structure and the relationship between the behaviour of indirect assets and the underlying property assets. Most attention is paid to the major investment vehicles: property company shares and Real Estate Investment Trusts (REITs).

The investment characteristics of direct property were outlined in Chapters 10 and 11. For an investor, direct ownership of property has a number of adverse features. To recap, these include:

- *Lot size and heterogeneity* The lumpiness of commercial real estate assets makes it difficult for all but the largest of funds to create fully diversified property portfolios, leaving the investor exposed to specific risk. This problem is exacerbated by the heterogeneity of property, leading to high levels of specific risk.

- *Trading market* Thin trading, the lack of a transparent public market, heterogeneity of product and uncertainties surrounding valuations lead to information asymmetries and high information costs (in part imposed by the need to employ intermediaries).

- *Cost structures* Direct property assets have higher transaction costs than publicly-traded assets and higher management costs. These serve to depress achieved returns and impose a constraint on active portfolio management.

- *Illiquidity* Difficulties in trading property add a timing risk to uncertainties surrounding the cash flow and cause problems in implementing an active portfolio management strategy. The length of time taken to transact is an associated disadvantage.

- *Management* The higher management costs of owning investment property represent a cash outflow and act as a disincentive to investment.

The attractiveness of indirect property investments is, in large part, determined by the extent to which they solve these problems.

Equity vehicles

In this section, the investment characteristics of property company shares, Real Estate Investment Trusts, property unit trusts and single property securitised investments are examined.

Property company shares

The characteristics of shares as investments were discussed in Chapter 10. Property companies have long formed part of the London Stock Exchange. There are, broadly, two types of property company. The first type, property investment companies, such as Land Securities or MEPC, acquire or develop properties and then retain them. The rental income is used to cover running costs, interest charges and to pay dividends. The value of the properties underpins the company's market price. The second type of company, developer-traders such as Helical Bar, construct or acquire properties then sell them following completion or refurbishment. The difference between sale price and development costs from those sales provide company profits and dividend payments. As a result, such companies' shares tend to be priced according to their (expected) earnings growth. Property companies may specialise in a particular sector of the property market or concentrate their activity geographically. Others hold diversified portfolios of property, some having international holdings.

For property investment companies, the share price is generally related to the net asset value (NAV) of the properties, that is, the open market valuation of the properties owned along with other assets, adjusted for liabilities and other claims on the company. Since the valuations should reflect anticipated rental cash flow (see Chapter 10) which, in turn, determines the ability to pay dividends, the NAV basis should be equivalent to the value arrived at by a dividend discount model. However, property companies generally trade at a discount to NAV (that is, the share price times the number of shares is less than NAV). This discount may reflect contingent capital gains tax liability, the fact that the amount realisable from a forced sale of properties would be less than open market value and adjustments for illiquidity in the underlying market (see Adams and Venmore-Rowland, 1990).

Market capitalisation as a share of the overall equity market has varied over time, although not as markedly as US REIT data. Analysis is complicated by changing compositions but the average share of the total stock market for a consistent subsample of major companies over the period 1980–95 was 2.85 per cent In mid-1995, the estimated market capitalisation of property companies in the Financial Times-Stock Exchange Property sector was approximately £16.1bn.

The major advantages of property company shares as an investment are a mirror image of those disadvantages of directly held property listed above. Investors gain from greater liquidity since property company shares are publicly traded and the time taken to make trades is far shorter than the time taken to buy or sell real property. Investors can create diversified portfolios of property company shares at relatively low cost and are, in many cases, buying into diversified portfolios of properties in acquiring those shares. Transaction costs are lower than for direct purchase. Finally, since the stocks are publicly traded, the share price is known at any time, with none of the uncertainties associated with valuation.

These advantages must be set against certain disadvantages of property share ownership. First, the prices of property shares move up and down with the stock market (see below). Accordingly, property stocks are more volatile. Between 1970 and 1992, the annualised standard deviation of UK property company shares was 27 per cent compared to 11 per cent for direct property as measured by the Jones Lang Wootton index (Barkham and Geltner, 1995). It should be noted that when the impact of gearing was removed from property share prices and when the JLW series was desmoothed, the standard deviations were much closer in magnitude. Since, according to finance theory, risk-adjusted returns should equalise, property companies should offer higher average performance to compensate investors for this volatility. Second, since property companies are taxed on their profits, there is not full tax transparency. This is a major disadvantage for tax-exempt investors such as pension funds who cannot claim back corporation tax (Brett, 1990).

A further disadvantage of property shares over direct ownership is the lack of management control. The shareholder has little influence over the acquisition and disposal decisions made by the company, nor over financing decisions (the amount of borrowing – gearing or leverage – and the issuing of new shares which dilute the value of existing shares). Since share prices should reflect judgements about the quality of management, the equity market provides some form of discipline. The shareholder may also find it difficult to obtain full information on the property assets and development schemes of the company, particularly where there exist complex ownership structures with joint ventures and off balance sheet holdings.

Real Estate Investment Trusts

Real Estate Investment Trusts (REITs) are US publicly traded investment companies which own real estate assets. The REIT structure was approved in 1960. 'Qualified' REITs provide major tax benefits. To be qualified, a REIT must:

1   have 75 per cent of its assets invested in real estate, real estate equities, mortgages or government securities;
2   distribute 95 per cent of its taxable income to shareholders each year;
3   earn at least 95 per cent of its taxable income from rents, mortgages or the sale of real estate; and
4   not hold property primarily for the purpose of sale.

Qualifying REITs pass through income untaxed to their shareholders. The National Association of Real Estate Investment Trusts classifies REITs into equity REITs (having direct ownership of income-producing property), mortgage REITs (holding property-related debt instruments) and hybrids of the two.

REIT growth was relatively slow until the late 1960s. In the early 1970s, mortgage REITs grew rapidly. However, the bankruptcy and liquidation of a number of REITs in the mid-1970s curtailed growth. The 1986 Tax Reform Act allowed greater management flexibility and established a less restrictive tax environment, creating the conditions for growth in the REIT market. This emphasises how critical the tax structure is to the success of indirect property instruments.

As many researchers have pointed out, there has been an explosive growth of the REIT market and, in particular, the equity REIT market, in the 1990s (for example, see Pagliari and Webb, 1995; Han and Liang, 1995; and Corgel et al., 1995). As detailed in Figure 12.1, below, the market capitalisation of the industry has gone from $1.88 billion in 1972 to $44.31 billion in 1994 for the total index with a substantial amount of that growth in the equity index (without healthcare).[2] The NAREIT equity index has increased in nominal terms from $377 million in 1972 to $35.59 billion in 1994.

As at 1994, total balance sheet asset values reported by NAREIT were $88.17 billion, an increase of $27.09 billion, or 44 per cent, from the previous year. The breakdown between types of REITs in the index was as follows: 205 equity REITs with a reported value of $62.06 billion (70.4 per cent of total asset value); 32 mortgage REITs with a reported value of $21.78 billion (24.7 per cent); and 23 hybrid REITs with a reported value of $4.34 billion (4.9 per cent). Equity REITs are those REITs whose primary investment (over 75 per cent) are in direct ownership of the property asset; mortgage REITs are those publicly traded REITs which are invested in real estate predominantly (again over 75 per cent) through mortgages and other forms of loan; and the hybrids are REITs invested in property as both an equity position and on a loan basis. Figure 12.1 shows these relationships graphically.

313

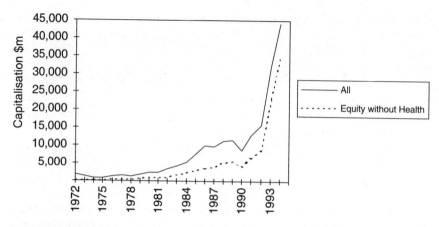

Figure 12.1 REIT capitalisation
Source: 1995 REIT Handbook

REITs, then, possess many of the advantages of property company shares in terms of lot size, liquidity, public trading and price information, with the added advantage of tax transparency. Similar structures exist in other developed economies (for example in Australia and in Belgium). REITs have generally outperformed both direct property investments and real estate operating companies (REOCs) – the nearest equivalent to UK property companies – in terms of returns, presumably due to their tax status. However, in common with property company shares, they exhibit higher volatility than the direct market.

The growth of the REIT market in the United States has generated considerable research.[3] Much of this has focused on the equity characteristics of REIT price performance. Researchers have examined REIT performance series attempting to detect pricing anomalies and the existence of a distinct 'property' factor generating returns. This research question is discussed further below. REIT-like investments are not available in the UK market due to the lack of tax transparency, although US REITs are increasingly active.

Other collective investment vehicles[4]

In the United Kingdom, Institutions may invest in property through Property Unit Trusts and Managed Funds. Property Unit Trusts, first established in the mid-1960s, are pools of property investments held in the name of a trust. The manager, appointed by the trustee, issues units. The price of the units is determined by regular (generally monthly) valuations. Most trusts provide a regular income distribution and are open-ended (that is, the size of the fund may increase or decrease as units (and properties) are bought/issued or sold. Units must be traded with the trust's manager (there is only a limited secondary market).

Managed Funds are similar in objective to Property Unit Trusts. They consist of unitised property funds managed for occupational pension schemes by insurance companies. Both property unit trusts and managed funds confer tax advantages on tax exempt investors. Since 1991, Authorised Property Unit Trusts have been permitted and may be advertised to the general public. Only a small number of APUTs have been issued. The scrapping of the proposed Hermes/Dusco APUT in October 1997 following the ending of advanced corporation tax benefits in the July 1997 budget further eroded confidence in APUTs as an investment asset.

These unitised vehicles offer the advantage of relatively low unit costs, allowing investors to acquire an interest in a diversified property portfolio without excessive commitment of capital. They are clearly property investments since the unit price is determined by the valuation of the assets in the trust or fund. Regular benchmark performance measures are available. However, there are potential disadvantages in terms of lack of management control and illiquidity. In theory, there is some liquidity in that units may be redeemed on a monthly basis. In practice, in a poor market or when a high proportion of unit holders are attempting to sell, the manager may defer redemption. Furthermore, the spread – the gap between unit purchase and redemption prices – tends to increase when there is selling pressure, harming performance. Finally, since selling pressure tends to occur in falling markets, sales take place in poor conditions and are, in effect, forced rather than open market sales. These disadvantages temper the benefits in terms of lot size and diversification.

Securitised single asset vehicles

A disadvantage of property company shares, REITs and other collective vehicles is that the investor must rely on the stock selection decisions of the asset's managers. More control would be obtained if an investor could acquire an interest in individual properties. This would enable investors to tailor a property portfolio to their specific needs bearing in mind their holdings of other assets and the pattern of their liabilities. However, existing UK property laws make it difficult to establish tax-efficient multiple ownership of commercial properties. Various schemes have been proposed to create publicly traded securitised single asset vehicles. Property Income Certificates (PINCs) aimed to provide investors with a specified share of rental income stream from a property; Single Property Ownership Trusts (SPOTs) were to operate as single asset unit trusts; while Single Asset Property Companies (SAPCOs), as the name implies, were structured like a conventional listed property company but with only one property under ownership. These have, at the time of writing, failed to become established, either due to their lack of tax transparency or to market conditions at the time of their launch.

Adams and Baum (1989) point out that the success of single property securitisation or unitisation depends on the achievement of liquidity in the secondary market. This requires prices in the secondary market to be at a sufficient level to encourage further securitisation until market capitalisation reaches sustainable levels. For the property owner, the price levels must be superior to those achievable by a sale of the direct asset after allowing for the costs of both transactions. Yet, since investment trusts and property companies trade at a discount to asset value, how could this be achieved?

They suggest one possible mechanism. Large buildings in a market, because of their value, have fewer potential purchasers than smaller buildings of the same quality. As a result, yields may be higher for larger properties, perhaps as a result of a higher illiquidity premium (see Chapters 10 and 11). The vendor may, thus, achieve a higher price for a property by breaking it up into smaller units even allowing for a discount to asset value in the securitised market. This is akin to the profit realised in converting a residential property into flats, or in the 'break up' of mansion blocks of tenanted flats for sale into owner-occupation.

They illustrate this with reference to yields in the London office market in 1986. As Table 12.1 shows, yields on the smallest properties were some 80 per cent of yields on large buildings, although it is not clear how comparable the buildings were in terms of quality or location. A fully-let 100,000 square foot (c. 9,290 square metre) property with a rent of £30/sq ft would be valued at:

$$£3,000,000 / 0.0648 = £46.3\text{million},^{5} \text{ approximately}$$

Split into units, it might have a value of:

$$£3,000,000 / 0.0524 = £57.4\text{million, approximately}$$

assuming that investors would pay the lower yield. This would allow a discount and additional costs of:

$$(£57.4\text{m} - £46.3\text{m})/£57.4\text{m} = 19\%$$

The investor might be prepared to accept the lower return implied in the yield, trading off return against liquidity (assuming the development of a

Table 12.1 Property size and initial yields, City of London offices, 1986

Size of property (sq. ft)	Average initial yield %
< 20,000	5.24
20,000 – 50,000	5.84
50,000 – 100,000	6.08
> 100,000	6.48

Source: Adams and Baum (1989)

secondary market) and the opportunity for portfolio diversification and active management (as a result of the smaller lot size). Difficulties in establishing tax efficient vehicles, the property recession of the late 1980s and the elimination of the yield gap as a result of large capital inflows from mainland European investors (in many cases seeking to purchase large units) precluded practical tests of these theoretical benefits.[6]

Debt vehicles

Conventional debt instruments – mortgages, mortgage debentures, bonds – are property-related investments in that the risk of the investment is dependent on the performance of the property which acts as security for the debt or underpins the corporate strength of the borrower. The return for the lender is not influenced by the behaviour of the property market, except where a property crash leads to default on the part of the borrower. However, the lender does not benefit from any growth in rents or capital values: there is downside, but no upside, risk. The *risk-adjusted* return will, therefore, change with conditions in the property market.

Innovative forms of debt funding have similar characteristics. Deep discount bonds are sold below par (that is, at less than their face and redemption value) so that the investor obtains capital growth on redemption. A zero coupon bond pays no dividend and is again issued at a considerable discount to the redemption value. A developer may attempt to fund a project using deep discount or zero coupon bonds anticipating that the development will experience sufficient capital growth to redeem the debt issue and provide a profit. In the absence of capital growth, default is much more probable. Mortgage-backed bonds are used in similar fashion, but are secured with mortgages on one or more properties.[7]

A number of hybrid debt–equity instruments have been developed which enable the investor to participate in market performance. Convertible mortgages are loans secured on a property (or, possibly, a portfolio of properties). The lender, however, has an option to convert some or all of the loan into a direct or indirect equity interest in the property. Thus, the lender, as an investor, can benefit from greater than anticipated growth in the property market. The borrower benefits from lower interest rates or from the lender permitting a higher loan to value ratio, thus reducing the borrower's own equity input. A participating mortgage is similar in structure. The lender receives a premium related to the sale price (or agreed valuation) at redemption. There are tax and accounting advantages in such structures for both borrower and lender. However, a legal problem – the fact that the lender's call option acts as 'a clog on the equity of redemption', preventing a borrower from clearing debt and thus owning the asset unencumbered – has, at the time of writing, not been decisively resolved and has been the subject of Law Commission deliberations in the UK.

In the 1980s, many US residential mortgages were pooled and securitised. The rapid development of mortgage-backed securities created a market infrastructure and knowledge base that permitted risk assessment and pricing. This, in turn, led to the securitisation of pools of commercial property mortgages and growth of commercial mortgage-backed securities (CMBS) as a investment asset. The returns on mortgage-backed securities do not directly relate to market performance of the underlying property. However, the risk of prepayment and default is a function of property prices. In contrast to a conventional loan, specific risk is diversified away in the mortgage pool. In terms of risk and cash flow profile, a CMBS has similarities to a mortgage REIT, although there are differences in tax structure. Commercial mortgage-backed securities and other aspects of debt markets are discussed further in the fourth section of this chapter.

Property derivatives

Derivatives are instruments whose returns are derived from those of other investments – that is their performance depends on how another asset performs (Chance, 1995). The rapid growth of futures, forwards, options, swaps and other innovative forms of investment has altered the nature of capital markets across the 1980s and 1990s (Chance, 1995). Derivatives have been at the heart of a number of highly public financial 'disasters' such as the collapse of Barings or the Sumitomo copper scandal and there have been warnings from regulatory authorities that the growth of derivatives has destabilised markets. Ironically, the original rationale for many derivative instruments was risk management. Forward and future contracts were originally created to stabilise commodity prices, exchange rate futures were designed to insulate businesses from currency fluctuations, swaps developed to reduce the risk of interest rate (or currency) shocks.[8] The explosive growth of derivatives has followed their use as a pure investment vehicle (benefiting from a gearing effect that enables investors to make large gains – or losses – from low initial investment) and the development of financial derivatives based on stock and bond market indices.

Although the property industry has utilised derivatives in funding and financing and adopted option pricing frameworks in investment appraisal, the development of property derivatives has been slow. There have been a number of attempts to establish futures markets based on property performance. In the 1990s, UK property futures contracts were established on London FOX. These were to be based on movements of the Investment Property Databank's monthly index. The experiment failed due to lack of investor interest and trading irregularities. In the late 1990s, further attempts to introduce derivative instruments were made, with the launch of Barclays Property Index Certificates (PICs) and Property Index Futures (PIFs), again based on IPD indices.[9]

The principal advantages of such assets relate to their low unit costs, the ability to gear up investment and the ability to gain exposure to the property market without incurring high levels of specific risk (for example, a PIC enabled an investor to track the IPD portfolio – then valued at some £40bn) for just £250,000. However, there are a number of drawbacks. These include questions about the information content of commercial property indices (see Chapter 11), lags in the publication of the indices and the fact that the investor is buying into average performance and cannot hope to 'outperform' the market.

The key condition for successful development of property derivatives is the establishment of an active secondary market. This requires sufficient market capitalisation, investors prepared to trade actively in the market (as opposed to buying the initial offering and holding it to redemption) and, critically, differences in opinion as to future trajectories of the underlying assets or index. There must be buyers *and* sellers. Once established, it is possible that price movements in the derivative market will, as in other capital markets, have implications for pricing in the underlying direct property market.

ARE INDIRECT VEHICLES PROPERTY INVESTMENTS?

If investors opt to invest in indirect property in place of direct holding of property assets, then they would expect those assets to behave in a similar fashion to the underlying real assets; that is, indirect and direct property assets are substitutes. If, however, the performance of securitised property is driven by non-property factors then, by holding indirect vehicles, the investor may forgo diversification benefits. The extent to which the returns for indirect property follow the behaviour of the property market will depend on the type of vehicle.

The returns on a conventional loan will not depend on the performance of property – except that default risk will increase if the property market performs badly (this is discussed further below). By contrast, property unit trust performance is directly tied to the property market since the unit prices are determined by the valuation of the assets held in the trust. Furthermore, the state of the market affects the liquidity of those units. In a falling market, many unit holders seek to cash in their units and there are few purchasers, leading to delays in receipt of payment.

The performance of property company shares and Real Estate Investment Trusts has been the subject of much research. The underlying process generating prices and dividends should be linked to the performance of the properties owned by the property company or REIT since:

- Property investment company shares are valued on a net asset value basis (Adams and Venmore-Rowland, 1990). Rises or falls in the value of properties should be reflected in changing share prices.

- Rental income from tenanted property forms the cash flow for property investment companies and determines those companies' ability to pay dividends. Anticipated rental growth should, therefore, be linked with anticipated dividend growth.
- The share price performance of trader-developer companies is linked to their profits (that is, they are valued on a price-earnings basis). Profits are dependent on capital growth in the property markets in which they operate.
- REIT pricing reflects anticipated dividend growth. Since 95 per cent of taxable income must be distributed, dividends are fundamentally linked to property cash flows.

However, it is clear that property company and REIT returns exhibit patterns common to those of the wider equity market. There are high contemporaneous correlations between property stocks and other shares and the variances of property share returns are comparable to those of other shares and far higher than those reported in the direct property market. Direct equity property indices (as noted in Chapter 11) appear to have low contemporaneous correlation with stock market indices.[10] This has led many commentators to conclude that property company and REIT shares do not represent a property investment.

Two notes of caution should be sounded at this point. First, there is a difference between a contemporaneous relationship and a long-run relationship. On a month to month (quarter to quarter) basis, property company shares and reported property market performance may diverge. This may reflect differences in the way that information is processed in the two markets. However, in the long run, prices in both markets may be linked. Analysis which examines the underlying pricing process or which seeks to determine long-run dynamics through cointegration or error correction mechanism models, for example, may thus produce a different picture. Matysiak et al. (1996) and Wang et al. (1997) provide examples. In the long run, both direct and indirect markets may be more closely integrated with other asset markets than appears from contemporaneous analysis, casting some doubt on the existence of a clear property factor.

Second, the data series may not be comparable. Direct market property performance is typically measured by valuation (appraisal) based indices. As noted in Chapter 11, the capital returns reported in such indices may be subject to smoothing. In similar fashion, property company (or REIT) performance may be affected by the financial structure of the company. One particular factor that will affect volatility of their share prices is the balance between capital raised as equity and capital raised as debt (see below). Such factors need to be accounted for in any analysis of the relationship between securitised and unsecuritised property assets.

Barkham and Geltner (1995) analyse the relationship between securitised and unsecuritised (that is indirect and direct) property return performance in the US and in the UK.[11] Their study covers the period 1970 to 1992. For the US, they compare the NCREIF index (an appraisal-based portfolio index similar in construction to the IPD index) to the National Association of Real Estate Investment Trusts (NAREIT) equity REIT price index. In the UK, their direct property measure is the Jones Lang Wooton (JLW) index. This is compared to the Financial Times property company share index (FTProp).

Barkham and Geltner attempt to correct for valuation smoothing by using an unsmoothing procedure similar to that of Blundell and Ward (1987). The unsmoothed return R_{mt} is estimated (using the Chapter 11 notation) as:

$$R_{mt} = (R_t - AR_{t-1})/(1 - A) \tag{12.1}$$

where R_t is the observed, smoothed, return in period t; R_{mt} is the 'true', unobserved or unsmoothed, market return in period t; and A is the smoothing parameter.

Based on an earlier study (Barkham and Geltner, 1994), they use A = 0.60 for the US NCREIF index and 0.37 for the UK JLW index.[12] Thus, if the observed return at time t−1 were 10 per cent and at time t were 8 per cent then, for the UK, the unsmoothed value at time t will be:

$$R_{mt} = [8\% - (0.37)\ 10\%]/0.63 = 6.83\%$$

The property company and REIT share price data are also adjusted to account for the impact of gearing or leverage. As discussed further below, gearing may increase the volatility of returns. To remove gearing, a simple weighted average cost of capital model is used:

$$R_{pt} = \{R_{et} - (1 - P/E_t)\ R_{dt}\}/(P/E_t) \tag{12.2}$$

where R_{pt} is the degeared return to the property portfolio; R_{et} is the observed equity return; R_{dt} is the return on debt (taken as the long bond yield); and P/E_t is the value of the property portfolio as a ratio of shareholder equity.

Thus, if the observed return is 16 per cent, the long bond yield is 10 per cent and the property to equity ratio is 1.25 then the degeared return is:

$$R_{pt} = \{16\% - (1 - 1.25)\ 10\%\}/1.25 = 14.8\%$$

The degearing process has the effect of reducing the volatility of securitised property while the unsmoothing process increases the volatility of the valuation-based indices. Barkham and Geltner next compare the adjusted series. In both the US and the UK, they believe that the indirect and direct series exhibit similar patterns of behaviour over time 'suggesting a strong fundamental link across the two market structures' (Barkham and Geltner, 1995: 31). It should be noted that returns are nominal: with inflation as a common component it would be surprising if there were no common patterns. In the UK, the unsmoothed JLW index has a correlation of 0.61 with the degeared FTProp series. In the US the NAREIT index has a lower correlation of 0.19 with the unsmoothed NCREIF index.

Barkham and Geltner suggest that there is graphical evidence that securitised property prices 'lead' unsecuritised prices. They test this formally using a Granger causality testing framework.[13] For the UK, this confirms that the JLW index lags property company share prices. They suggest that this indicates that information is impounded into prices faster in the securitised market than in the direct market – that there is a 'price discovery' effect. This would imply violation of semi-strong form market efficiency in the direct market (see Chapter 11). Whether the price discovery effect could be profitably exploited is not tested.

Wang *et al.* (1997) examine the long-run relationships between direct and indirect property assets in the UK using co-integration analysis and Granger causality testing. Their results, confirming those of Barkham and Geltner, suggest that there is a long-run relationship between the underlying, direct market and property shares and that the indirect market 'leads' the direct market in price formation. This study provides evidence that there *is* a long-run link between the direct and indirect markets. Given the strong correlations between property company share price movement and that of the general equity market, this may suggest that property performance is not as distinct from other asset classes as is often argued.

Gyourko and Keim (1992) arrive at a similar conclusion in an examination of US property stock prices against the NCREIF index. They suggest that the infrequent revaluations of the NCREIF index leads to securitised property prices impounding information in a more timely manner than appraisal prices. By contrast, Seck (1996) has argued that direct property assets and securitised property assets are not substitutes. Seck asserts that two assets are substitutes if the same information sets produce the best estimates or forecasts of the price of each asset. This implies that the processes underlying the pricing of both assets can be linked through some mathematical transformation. Seck concludes that appraisal based returns have a different stochastic process to property equities, the latter conforming to a random walk process.

McCue and Kling (1994) regress REIT returns (the NAREIT index) on the Standard and Poors 500 equity index. They argue that the residuals represent a separate property industry effect. They then use a vector autoregressive approach to examine the impact of the macroeconomy on property. The results show that macroeconomic variables explain some 60 per cent of the variation in property returns. Inflation (property prices are in nominal terms) and interest rates have the most significant impact. Upward shocks to interest rates have a significant negative effect on the property series. Lizieri and Satchell (1997) similarly find that high interest rates result in falls in indirect property prices in the UK. This last study suggests that in high interest rate environments, price falls are steeper than the rises in low interest rate regimes.

The evidence on the nature of property company shares and REITs as investment assets is mixed. The high contemporaneous correlations with equity market indices and the pattern of returns and volatility suggest that such assets have many similarities with other shares. However, when the effects of smoothing and gearing are reduced or when a long-run perspective is adopted, indirect property assets are seen to be more closely related to the underlying direct property market, and returns in the underlying market are more closely aligned with those of other asset classes. There is some evidence of a distinct property industry effect. However, it may be that property is not as distinct an asset class as has sometimes been asserted.

DEBT INSTRUMENTS, FUNDING AND FINANCING OF PROPERTY

The traditional interface between the property industry and financial services markets has been through lending. Lending takes many forms. It is necessary to distinguish between short-term borrowing for development (project finance) and longer-term funding; between corporate borrowing (full-recourse lending where the lender can draw on all the borrower's assets in the event of non-payment of the loan) and borrowing secured on properties (limited-recourse lending); and between fixed interest rate and variable interest rate borrowing. Some debt instruments are private contracts between borrower and lenders, others result in tradable securities. In this section, three aspects of lending are considered. First, modes of conventional borrowing are considered. Second, the growth of mortgage-backed securities is discussed. Finally, the impact of lending on the property cycle – and of property debt on the economy – is examined.

Property lending

The traditional long-term borrowing instrument used by the property industry is the mortgage debenture. A firm borrows money and secures its lending against the title of one or more properties. These may be held in trust. The loan may be a fixed or variable rate mortgage. The amount of the loan is normally limited to a proportion of the value of the property – the *loan-to-value* (LTV) ratio. The reciprocal of the loan to value ratio is the *capital cover*. This is to protect the lender against falling capital values. Borrowers lose some flexibility in their portfolio management since they cannot trade those properties held as security. A conventional mortgage secured against a single property has a similar structure. However, much of the surge in bank lending on property which took place in the 1980s was corporate lending, that is loans to property companies secured on the firm and not on specific properties or developments.

As investments, property loans are subject to a number of sources of risk. The nature and significance of the risk depends on the structure of the loan. Risk is dependent on the type of security. A *full-recourse* loan has the security not only of the relevant property but also the borrower's assets. A *limited-recourse* loan has only the property as security; these are sometimes referred to as 'non-recourse' loans. The nature of interest payments affects the risk profile. For the lender, a *fixed rate mortgage* is subject to interest rate risk and inflation risk (there are strong cash flow similarities with a fixed interest bond). Inflation erodes the value of the capital advanced, while general interest rate increases do not result in an increasing cash flow. A *variable rate mortgage* makes the borrower vulnerable to interest rate rises. Traditionally, property loans have been individual transactions between borrowers and lenders. With increasing loan size, commercial loans are frequently *syndicated* amongst a pool of lenders, thus spreading the specific risk and reducing balance-sheet exposure to single assets.

While such risks are general to bank lending, there are risks that are specific to the characteristic of property loans. The typical commercial property loan is a 'balloon' or 'bullet' loan, where the borrower pays only interest during the life of the loan, repaying all capital advanced at maturity. Given the cyclical nature of property markets, it is possible that the value of the property securing the loan will have fallen to a level at which it is not possible to refinance or sell the property and return the capital. Interest payments depend on rental income: falling rents, tenant default and high vacancy levels may, thus, create difficulties for the borrower. In either case, the borrower might default on the loan.

Given these property-related risks, lenders would be expected to assess the level of risk inherent in a loan and both price that risk (through higher interest rates) and seek additional security. The principal risk-control measures are the *loan-to-value ratio* and the *income cover*. The loan to value ratio (LTV) is the proportion of the value of the property the lender is prepared to advance. A typical commercial property LTV ratio is 70 per cent. If property values fall by less than 30 per cent and the borrower defaults, the lender may foreclose, sell the property and still recover its capital. Furthermore, borrowers, utilising their own equity, are assumed to have more commitment to the scheme.

When capital value increases are anticipated, a property developer or investor may well seek to increase the amount of borrowing relative to its own equity invested. Consider a building that can be acquired today for £10m and will increase in value to £15m in five years time. If the investor acquires it with own equity then the capital growth is (£15m − £10m)/£10m or + 50 per cent, a compound growth of approximately 8.5 per cent p.a.

Now suppose the investor acquires the building by borrowing £5m and investing £5m of own capital. At the end of five years, the debt remains fixed at £5m, while the property has increased in value to £15m. Equity then has increased to £10m (the £15m less the £5m debt) and the capital growth is (£10m − £5m)/£5m or +100 per cent, a compound rate of 14.9 per cent per annum.

The situation becomes more complex when interest payments are considered. Suppose the interest rate is 7 per cent and interest payments are 'rolled up' to the end of the loan period, as might be the case with a development project. Then the amount outstanding will become:

$$£5m \ (1.075)^5 = £7.18m.$$

The equity increase, then, is £7.82m (that is £15m − £7.18m) and so growth is (£7.82m − £5m)/£5m, +56 per cent, or 9.35 per cent per annum. Gearing will increase profitability if the annualised growth in the property value exceeds the interest rate. For an income producing property, the relationship between the interest payments and the rental income would also need to be considered to ensure that rental income is available and sufficient to meet periodic repayments.

Gearing (the ratio of debt to equity) thus affects profitability. When property values rise, gearing increases the capital return. Should property values fall, the losses will be magnified. As a consequence, gearing increases volatility of returns. It is for this reason that it is necessary to remove the impact of gearing from property company or REIT returns to recover the underlying property market performance. If the borrower is publicly-listed, shareholders are likely to demand higher returns as a compensation for that extra volatility, affecting the share price of the property company.

Income cover (or debt service coverage) is the ratio of rental income to interest rate payments. Pressure to lend sometimes leads to erosion of prudent lending criteria. For example, the difference between value and the amount lent under LTV criteria may be met not through equity but through another loan – known as mezzanine funding. With mezzanine funding, a lender agrees to part fund that investment not covered by the first or senior debt. Since this is more risky, a higher rate of interest is charged and, often, some form of additional security or credit enhancement is sought. Although the underlying loan (senior debt) has a prior claim on the property, mezzanine funding may make default more likely. As the borrower has less personal commitment to the project, it is more likely that the value of the property will fall below the level of debt outstanding and there are now two parties able to foreclose on the loan. Similarly, interest payments may be deferred or stepped in anticipation of future rental growth – which may not materialise.

The factors influencing mortgage default have been extensively analysed by US researchers.[14] The key ratio appears to be the current value of the property to the loan outstanding. When current value falls below loan outstanding, default becomes much more likely: the borrower is 'out of the money'. The LTV at loan origination acts as a buffer against default, but current market conditions are critical. Default, however, is not 'ruthless', that is, not all out of the money borrowers default. Inertia, transaction costs, recourse structure and intangible factors (such as concern about reputation and creditworthiness) limit the extent of default.

Figures 12.2 and 12.3 show the rapid growth in bank lending on commercial property in the UK and in the US during the 1980s. The sharp property downturns in both countries resulted in loan defaults, extensive bank provisions and bankruptcy for many property companies. Lenders, faced with 'distressed' debt, either sought to swap the debt for equity (thus, many banks became significant property owners 'by accident') or to securitise the debt (see below) to take it off balance sheet. Before examining the impact of the property downturn on banks and other financial institutions, the growth of debt securities as investment assets is considered.

Mortgage-backed securities

Mortgage-backed securities are paper assets usually in the form of fixed rate bonds or notes. A pool of mortgages is collected together and the loan

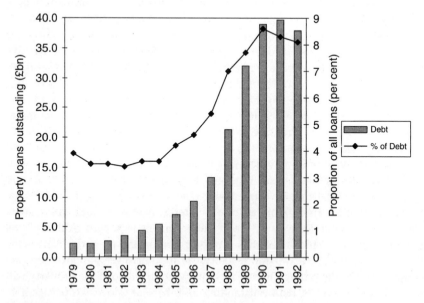

Figure 12.2 Bank lending to property companies, UK, 1979–92
Source: *Bank of England Quarterly Bulletin* (various)

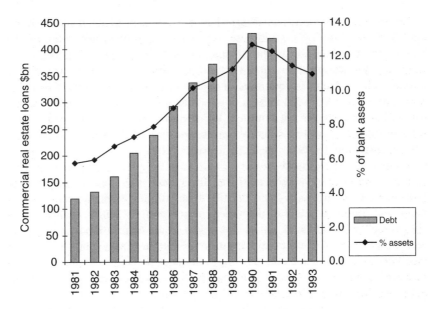

Figure 12.3 Lending on commercial real estate, US, 1981–93
Source: Federal Reserve Bank; Cole and Fenn (1996)

repayments of capital and interest are used to pay the dividends of the security holders and redeem the securities. The cash flow may be split and allocated to different classes of securities. For example, one class of securities may have a prior claim to receive dividend payments and redemption value over another. The second class of securities would, thus, be more risky and receive a higher dividend payment to compensate investors. The value of mortgages in the pool normally exceeds the size of the issue ('over-collateralisation') and other credit enhancement measures, for example insurance guarantees, may be required. Different structures are possible, depending on treatment of the cash flow and the tax and regulatory environment.

In the US, mortgage-backed securities have grown rapidly in significance since the establishment of residential mortgage-backed securitisation in the early 1970s. Commercial mortgage securitisation developed from the mid-1980s. The first securitisation is generally acknowledged to be Olympia and York's $970m floating rate note secured by mortgages on three Manhattan office buildings brokered by Salamon Brothers. Commercial property debt securitisation is more complex than residential mortgage securitisation since the loans (and the underlying assets) are much more heterogeneous and hence it is more difficult to assess the risk. Rating by a credit agency, such as Moody's or Standard and Poors, is critical to the success of securitisation and the establishment of an active secondary market. However, the motivation for securitisation comes from the financial and investment positions of lending institutions.

Banks and other credit institutions have traditionally acted as financial intermediaries funding illiquid assets (like property) by way of loans from liquid liabilities (deposits). The financial intermediary reduces agency costs (such as monitoring the borrower and matching borrowers to lenders) through administrative economies of scale and through risk diversification. The loan assets were seen as non-marketable and held until maturity on the banks' balance sheets. By contrast, the deposits used to fund lending are short-term and volatile. Reliance on short-term, liquid deposits makes a lender vulnerable to a run on those deposits. This, in part, helps to explain the growth of debt securitisation.

Securitisation allows lenders to tap the capital markets for cheaper, or broader, sources of funds. Securitisation takes illiquid assets and transforms them into liquid assets (as discussed in relation to equity securitisation above). Securitisation also allows a lender to readjust the risk and maturity of its loan portfolio. A final factor lies in the regulatory framework. Following the 1988 Basle Accord, banks must hold funds equivalent to a minimum of 8 per cent of the 'risk-weighted' volume of loans made – the *Solvency Ratio*. Commercial property loans have a 100 per cent risk weighting (while residential mortgages carry a 50 per cent risk weighting). By securitising loans, the financial institution both reduces the size of its loan portfolio and brings in additional capital, helping it meet the Basle targets.

The profitability of the security is given by:

$$\Pi = P_I - P_L - C_S \tag{12.3}$$

where P_I is the price paid by the investor in the security; P_L is the price the lender must receive to initiate the securitisation; and CS is the cost associated with the securitisation. This implies that $P_I > P_L$. Investors may be prepared to pay more for the security than the price required by the original lender since they gain a liquid asset, benefit from risk diversification (by comparison to a property specific loan) and may well benefit from competitive returns in comparison to other fixed-interest investments. Since interest rates on (risky) loans are higher than the coupon on fixed interest securities, the original lender and the investor may share the margin.

The rating of a mortgage-backed security requires careful analysis of three aspects. The rating agency (or investor) must consider the following aspects.

- *Mortgage collateral* the interest rates payable, the profile of repayments of principal, the characteristics of the borrowers (likelihood of default) and the quality of the underlying properties – market conditions, tenant covenant, lease structures and building components.
- *Cash flow adjustments* any techniques used to reshape the cash flow: liquidity provisions; reserve funds; use of swaps to control interest rate risk; and segmentation of the cash flow.

- *Credit enhancement* credit support from the seller or from a third party in the form of guarantees or insurance.

The growth of mortgage-backed securitisation has encouraged parallel developments in the property field. UK examples include the securitisation of rents by British Land in order to refinance its commercial paper (short maturity) debt and the asset-backed bonds proposed by Nomura as a result of the privatisation of Ministry of Defence housing. The experience of rating and marketing mortgage-backed securities has been translated into a more general securitisation of property cash flows and may well lead to equity-type property securitisation.

Property debt, the property market and banking

In discussing property-related debt as an investment asset, it is important to recall the macroeconomic role played by property, addressed in Chapters 6, 7 and 8. It has been suggested that over-enthusiastic or imprudent bank lending played an important role in the over-supply of commercial property that contributed to the property slumps experienced in the UK and the US (and in many other developed economies – see Chapters 7, 8 and 13). Hendershott and Kane (1992) attribute much of the over-building in the US in the 1980s to too much finance at too low interest rates. This, they suggest, resulted from artificially boosted competition from Savings and Loans institutions which were not properly assessing the riskiness of their lending. This forced the banks into competition. Market segmentation meant that commercial mortgage markets were not fully integrated into the broader capital markets. Loans were underpriced with interest rates charged not reflecting the riskiness of the lending. Thus, property debt, as a financial asset, has macroeconomic impacts.

The 1980s saw rapid increases in lending in the UK and the US (see Figures 12.2 and 12.3 above). In the UK, bank lending to property companies peaked in 1991 at some £40bn, while in the US commercial property loans reached $429bn in 1989. Default, delinquency (failure to make payments) and foreclosure rates increased in the late 1980s and, in the US, there were many failures of Savings & Loans companies and banks. In the UK, banks' provisions for bad debts affected their profitability and performance. Warnings about the extent of property lending were issued at national level (by the Bank of England and the Federal Reserve Board) and more generally by international regulatory bodies such as the World Bank and the IMF concerned about the possibility of systemic risk.[15] These warnings led to a tightening of regulation and a reduction in the supply of credit – the so-called 'credit crunch' (Fergus and Goodman, 1994; Hancock and Wilcox 1993; Peek and Rosengren, 1994).

Whether the restriction of credit adversely affects the property market depends on the market environment, as discussed in Chapters 6 and 7. There would be no adverse effect if alternative sources of capital (from the stock market or from overseas investors, for example) were available, or if demand for loans were low. Hancock and Wilcox (1994) investigate this question for the United States by regressing commercial property activity variables (construction starts, contracts let, planning permits) on national and local economic conditions, on property market conditions and on commercial banking conditions. If the credit crunch has no effect then economic conditions alone should explain property market behaviour. They found instead that rates of real estate loan delinquency and bank capital shortfalls had significant negative impacts on subsequent levels of property activity.

The mirror of banking impacts on real estate is the effect of property markets on banking performance. Cole and Fenn show that US bank failures between 1987 and 1990 were strongly influenced by exposure to commercial property loans – particularly to construction loans. Allen *et al.* (1995) suggest, using a capital asset pricing framework (see Chapter 11), that bank stock returns respond to the extent of property exposure. In similar vein, Ghosh *et al.* (1994), using an event study methodology, show the impact of the failure of Olympia and York on the performance and profitability of international banks. Thus, it is not easy to distinguish cause and effect in the relationship between bank performance and the property market.

These studies emphasise that the growing sophistication of commercial property market financing and funding, the securitisation of property assets and the rapid product innovation in commercial property have resulted in the closer integration of property markets and other capital markets. The behaviour of property markets is not only influenced by the events in bond, equity and money markets. It has a reciprocal influence on the behaviour of those markets. This has implications for the diversification gains possible from investment in commercial property. If national capital markets are more closely integrated, it may be necessary for investors to look towards international markets to achieve risk diversification. This is the subject of the next chapter.

SUMMARY AND CONCLUSION

Indirect property vehicles are paper assets which are backed in some way by commercial property. The investment returns on these assets, or the risks associated with those returns, are linked to the underlying real property market. Indirect property investments encompass equity vehicles, debt vehicles, hybrid debt–equity vehicles and derivatives. The relationship between indirect and direct market behaviour varies according to the type of vehicle.

Indirect property vehicles reduce many of the disadvantages of direct ownership: large lot size; illiquidity; high transaction and management costs; and lack of public information. However, they have their own disadvantages. These include generally higher levels of volatility and closer correlations with other asset markets, reducing the degree of risk diversification.

In the UK, property company shares are the best known indirect investment. Property companies may be property investment companies or trader-developers. These two forms are valued differently: the former in relation to the net asset value of the property owned, the latter in terms of earnings growth. Property company shares possess greater liquidity but are subject to greater volatility than direct holdings of property.

The US has seen rapid expansion of Real Estate Investment Trusts. They are (generally) publicly traded collective forms of property investment which offer tax advantages to investors. Collective investment vehicles in the UK, such as Property Unit Trusts, are yet to offer similar tax benefits and are valuation-based with no secondary market.

Empirical evidence as to whether indirect property assets are property investments is mixed. Indirect equity vehicles experience higher volatility than the direct market and have higher correlations with stock market prices. More recent research examining long-run relationships or correcting for the smoothing in property indices and the effect of gearing on property company and REIT performance suggest a closer link between indirect and direct markets.

Debt vehicles such as mortgages, mortgage debentures, bonds and mortgage-backed securities may not seem to exhibit returns that are related to the underlying property market. However, the risk associated with those returns (and hence the risk-adjusted returns) is strongly linked to property market conditions. In adverse market conditions, borrowers are more likely to default on their obligations; when capital values fall sharply, lenders may not be able to recover their capital by selling the property held as security.

Bank lending has a significant impact on property markets, as noted earlier in Chapter 6. The boom–slump conditions of the 1980s and early 1990s illustrate the close relationship between property and financial markets. In turn, property has an impact on banking and financial service performance.

The rapid growth of securitisation (particularly mortgage-backed securitisation) has served to increase the linkage between property and other capital markets. The development of derivative markets is likely to increase the degree of linkage still further. This closer integration has implications for the correlation between property and other assets and hence for portfolio strategy.

Closer integration of national markets may drive international diversification. Indirect property assets are more suitable as vehicles for international investment than the underlying property asset, due particularly to lot size, liquidity and lower information costs. This is the subject matter of Chapter 13.

13

INTERNATIONAL PROPERTY INVESTMENT

INTRODUCTION

The international ownership of property is scarcely a new phenomenon. Colonial expansions in the sixteenth and seventeenth centuries set in place a pattern of international ownership that had profound implications for international trade. More recently, firms active in different world markets would seek, where local regulations permitted, to own their operational property. However, the 1980s and 1990s saw a rapid expansion in the ownership of overseas property as an *investment* asset. This chapter examines aspects of that expansion. In gaining exposure to international property, investors may hold direct equity stakes in land and buildings alone or with a local partner through a joint venture scheme. For indirect exposure, they may purchase shares in firms that develop or invest in property – Real Estate Investment Trusts, property companies and similar vehicles. These shares may be traded publicly or acquired through private placement. Investors may also gain exposure to international property through direct funding or financing of property schemes, through purchase of debt instruments such as bonds secured on property or by acquisition of securitised property debt. Finally, in more developed markets, it may be possible to invest in property derivatives (see Chapter 12). The choice of vehicle affects the extent to which the investment is influenced by geographically localised property factors or broader national economic factors. The chosen vehicle also determines the investment characteristics of the asset – volatility, return, liquidity for example. It is difficult to measure the extent of international investment in property. For direct property, most countries maintain records of foreign ownership. However, property may be acquired through a special purpose vehicle, through nominee purchase or other means that mask the nature of ownership. Similarly, corporate acquisitions are recorded as domestic whatever the share ownership. For example, a well-known UK property company trading in retail property is owned 72 per cent by a South African firm. Nonetheless, its property trading counts as UK domestic, not international. Records of indirect investment and debt based instruments are still harder to obtain. As a result, reported statistics on international activity understate the extent of exposure. The trend towards greater international involvement, however, is clear.

DTZ (1997) reports on direct purchase of UK property by overseas firms. As Figure 13.1 shows, investment did not exceed £0.33bn until 1988. Thereafter, despite the troubled state of the UK commercial property market, it has never fallen below £1bn, with direct purchases exceeding £3bn in 1989 and 1990. In the US, Bureau of Economic Affairs statistics (BEA, various) show international ownership in 1980 at $2.4bn, increasing dramatically to a local peak of $35.9bn in 1989 before falling back to $28.4bn in 1994. Of this, Japanese ownership rose from $57m in 1979 to $15.4bn in 1990 – a compound growth rate of 66 per cent per annum in nominal terms, before falling thereafter (see Holsapple *et al.*, 1996).

For indirect investment, it is harder to obtain statistics. Eichholtz and Op 't Veld (1997) suggest that the market capitalisation of property securities increased from £9bn in 1983 to £198bn in 1996 – a rate of growth of 27 per cent per annum. This growth has been accompanied by growing liberalisation of share ownership regulations permitting investors to build international equity portfolios. In terms of debt financing, outstanding commercial property loans to UK residents by overseas banks rose from £1.12bn in 1983 – 25 per cent of total bank lending on commercial property – to £17.3bn in 1991 – 43 per cent of the total (Bank of England, various). This figure is an under-estimate since it includes only loans to property companies and not loans to the property arms of firms classified to other sectors. Adding construction loans, overseas bank exposure to UK property in 1991 was £21.8bn. The

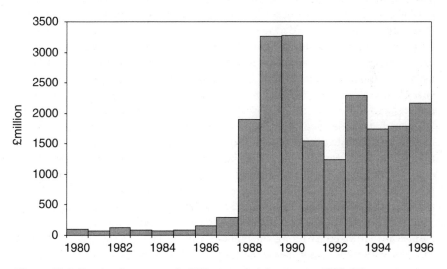

Figure 13.1 Foreign investment in UK commercial property, 1980–96
Source: Office of National Statistics; DTZ Debenham Thorpe (various)

expansion of international property investment in part results from deregulation and liberalisation of global markets with erosion of currency controls and regulations which limited foreign ownership of assets. These moves permitted the development of a global market for international financial services, facilitated by rapid advances in information and communications technologies. Growth in property investment may initially follow direct corporate investment before developing its own momentum. As in domestic markets, international investors may be short-term traders or long-term investors and range from wealthy individuals through corporations to institutional investors and international property funds.

The motivations for international property investment vary according to the players involved. For the corporate sector, investment may be for operational or strategic reasons. Short-term traders may be seeking higher returns than are available in their domestic markets, either due to local market conditions or currency factors. Longer-term investors may seek portfolio diversification and higher risk-adjusted returns. For institutional investors from small countries, the size of the local market may be insufficient in relation to available capital – a reported motive for Dutch and Swedish pension funds' overseas investment strategies. Wealthy individuals may be seeking politically or economically more stable environments for their capital.

An international direct investor faces disadvantages when competing with domestic firms. These are essentially information costs: cultural barriers to understanding the market; the cost of information acquisition; monitoring costs; and the risk of adverse currency movements. In a properly functioning international capital market, it is unlikely that a firm would invest in foreign property unless possessed of some advantage over local firms. The advantage may well be based on the cost of capital – a firm may have access to cheaper capital in its domestic market (an argument made by Bacow, 1990, to explain Japanese real estate investment in the US) or domestic firms may be restricted from investing in property due to poor recent domestic performance in that asset class. Such advantages are transitory and, in the case of cost of capital, may be eroded by exchange rate movements. This is explored further below.

Since the motivating factors vary across time and space, international property investment may be characterised by particular national waves of activity. In addition to Japanese investment in US real estate noted above, over the period 1988–90, Japanese investors purchased some £3.5bn of UK property. In the mid- to late-1990s, the UK experienced considerable direct investment from German open ended funds seeking high income returns and a destination for the rapid inflow of domestic capital. International investment was facilitated by removal of investment restrictions on those funds and the relatively poor performance of the German economy following reunification. Earlier Swedish acquisitions were similarly driven by relaxation in investment restrictions on Institutional funds. Canada and the UK both experienced high levels of investment from Hong Kong in the years preceding the 1997 reversion of the colony to the People's Republic of China.

The next section explores portfolio diversification as a rationale for international investment. The third section examines the key issue of currency movement. The fourth section (echoing the discussion in Chapter 11) discusses difficulties associated with implementing an international property investment strategy. Next, the economic factors that may drive differential market performance are considered. The possibility of a convergence in international property markets performance is discussed, leading to a summary and set of conclusions.

PORTFOLIO STRATEGY AND INTERNATIONAL INVESTMENT

The underlying principles of portfolio theory were outlined in Chapter 11. The essential features of a formal portfolio strategy are that investors seek to maximise the utility of their terminal wealth and hence base allocation strategies on expectations of risk and return. The expected return on a portfolio is simply the weighted average of the expected returns on the individual assets. However, since the risk of a portfolio is a function both of the individual standard deviatiations (as a measure of volatility) and of the correlations between assets, risk diversification may be achieved by constructing diversified portfolios of assets whose correlations are less than unity.

As noted in the discussion of the Capital Asset Pricing Model in Chapter 11, it is possible to diversify away specific risk related to the individual assets. However, since assets within an asset class tend to exhibit some positive covariance, there remains a layer of asset class risk that cannot be diversified away. In property, for example, this might be common movements in prices related to the property cycles discussed in Part 2 of the book. Constructing mixed asset class portfolios may further reduce risk by diversifying away asset class risk. However, there will remain a level of risk – systematic or market risk – that is undiversifiable. This risk relates to economic and financial factors that have an effect on all assets and asset classes. Formally, this is equivalent to the unweighted average covariance between assets (Brown, 1991).

The systematic risk of a portfolio within a single country may relate to factors that are unique to that country: policies that affect macroeconomic variables, national monetary policy affecting interest rates, inflation and hence the cost of capital, business and political (election) cycles and institutional, social and demographic factors. These are, in effect, *national* specific risk factors. The underlying theory behind international diversification is that a global portfolio strategy of investment in markets which have different economic drivers or are at different stages of the economic cycle will diversify away national risk resulting in portfolios that are more efficient in terms of risk–return (that is, in an efficient frontier lying to the left and above a nationally-constrained frontier). As Solnik (1991: 40) remarked, 'in a fully efficient, integrated international capital market, buying the world market portfolio would be the natural strategy' (as holding the 'market portfolio' is the natural strategy under CAPM).

Figure 13.2 shows graphically the principle behind international diversification. Investing domestically, risk will fall (*ceteris paribus*) with increasing portfolio size. However, a limit will be reached beyond which further diversification gains are not possible. This is shown as $cov_{ij|D}$, the average covariance between assets given domestic investment.[1] If the international average asset covariance $cov_{ij|I}$ is lower than $cov_{ij|D}$, then greater risk diversification will occur as portfolio size increases.

It is generally likely to be the case that the average domestic asset covariance $cov_{ij|D}$ will be higher than the average international asset covariance $cov_{ij|I}$. National economic policies tend to have some systematic influence on the variables affecting asset returns. It may well be that, as asset markets become more integrated internationally, $cov_{ij|D}$ and $cov_{ij|I}$ will converge. This might occur within regional blocs – for example, the behaviour of asset classes within the European Union may converge. In practice, international portfolios of direct property are likely to be small, increasing the importance of specific risk at the level of the individual property.

Formal analysis of diversification benefits from international investment can be traced to the work of Grubel (1968), Levy and Sarnatt (1970) and Solnik (1974a, 1974b). These works used Markowitz mean–variance analysis

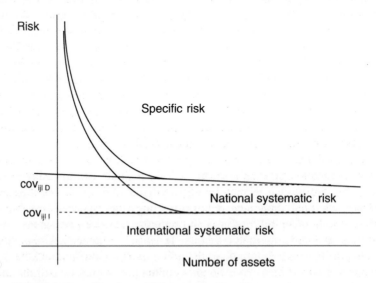

Figure 13.2 Risk diversification with international assets

to examine the potential benefits of diversifying a portfolio of shares and bonds by investing outside the United States. Solnik used individual shares while Grubel and Levy and Sarnatt analysed stock indices. All three analyses showed that international portfolios dominated US domestic portfolios in terms of risk-adjusted return. In Levy and Sarnatt's study, the efficiency gains for a US investor relate largely to a reduction in the portfolio variance as a result of negative covariance between Japanese and US shares (-0.26) and, to a lesser extent, to the low or negative correlations between the stock markets in South Africa and other countries included in efficient portfolios. This may, in part, result from widespread national restrictions on capital flows at that time that would limit the actual implementation of an international diversification strategy. Madura (1985) suggests that there is evidence both of higher long-term positive correlations between countries and of temporal instability in correlation patterns (such that analysis over short periods may produce unreliable results). It is also possible that global capital market integration may result in an upward trend in correlations. This is explored further below.

These early studies were carried out in an era when most institutional investors had a highly constrained domestic focus and there existed considerable barriers to movements of capital. Subsequent deregulation and liberalisation have made global investment strategies feasible. However, subsequent published work has concentrated on refining – or challenging – the models using *ex post* data (for reviews see Madura *op. cit.*; Solnik, 1991; Lizieri and Finlay, 1995). Studies that test the risk–return performance of actual portfolios are largely lacking in the literature.

Another common feature of the early research on international investment was the use of the Markowitz mean–variance optimiser framework for analysis. Development of analysis based on asset pricing models was constrained by the lack of representative global indices of asset performance. This has increasingly been resolved for shares with the widespread availability of the Morgan Stanley Capital International and FTA World Indices which have enabled the formulation of international capital asset pricing models (see, for example, Drummen and Zimmerman, 1992). Formally, however, a CAPM framework demands a benchmark index containing the full universe of investable assets rather then one composed only of shares.

The use of the mean–variance optimisation framework is problematic. Optimal portfolios generated from *ex post* data are highly sensitive to individual observations which may be subject to uncertainty and error. As Jorion (1985) notes, optimisation programmes tend to overselect assets that have experienced high relative returns in the past and thus generate suggested portfolios that are imprudent. Mean–variance 'optimisers' have a general tendency to generate extreme results where many assets/markets have zero weighting while others have large weightings (unrelated to their market capitalisation) – characterised by Black and Litterman (1992) as 'corner solutions'. This concentration of investment in a small number of assets does not conform to an intuitive idea of diversification. It leaves the portfolio vulnerable to unexpected poor performance in the small number of selected assets (or markets). This tendency to produce extreme solutions may be exacerbated in international studies beset with data problems leading to unrealistically low correlations between assets.

The international diversification literature has tended to ignore property as a direct asset. Solnik's 1991 review mentions property only in passing: 'as a rule, foreign real estate is seldom considered by institutional investors'. However, property is a sizeable asset class and one with apparent negative covariance with other assets. It was, thus, likely that attention would turn to the diversification potential of global property.

In the UK, the most cited work on international property diversification is that of Sweeney (1988b, 1989). Using a standard, *ex post* data, Markowitz optimiser approach, Sweeney analysed office market rental growth between 1976 and 1988 for a range of world cities. She constructed efficient frontiers and concluded (1989; 30) that 'international real estate diversification can be a viable strategy . . . international property investment does provide significant diversification benefits . . .'.

Despite serious methodological shortcomings, Sweeney's analysis, represented the first published attempt in the UK to analyse the potential for international property diversification formally.[2] Around the same time, a number of institutional investors – notably the Prudential Realty Group – were advancing the concept of a globally diversified property portfolio (see Baum and Schofield, 1991; PICA/JLW, 1988; Prudential Real Estate Investors, 1990).

A series of papers by Ziobrowski and co-workers has questioned the effectiveness of diversification gains from international property investment.[3] It is argued that the additional volatility that results from currency fluctuations outweighs any reduction in risk due to low correlations between markets. A variety of currency hedging strategies are employed and it is suggested that these do not remove the problem. Worzala *et al.* (1997) contend that the assumptions of the Ziobrowski model may be unrealistic.[4] Nonetheless, exchange rate issues are critical in analysing the investment potential of international diversification. Currency risk is discussed in more detail in the next section.

CURRENCY RISK

In making international property investments, direct or indirect, the risks of exchange rate movements must be considered alongside those associated with the underlying asset. Investors may thus seek to *hedge* their currency exposure, that is, to use a range of financial instruments that ensure that investment returns are not affected by adverse currency movements. As Black and Litterman (1992) demonstrate, it may be suboptimal, from a portfolio diversification perspective, to hedge currency variability away completely. Some of the differential price movement which leads to superior risk-adjusted returns results from (or is linked to) exchange rate movements. The situation is complicated by linkages between prices and expected investment returns in one country and expected exchange rate shifts.

A number of theoretical models exist that attempt to explain currency movements. The most cited are the theories of Purchasing Power Parity (PPP) and Interest Rate Parity (IRP), reviewed in Eaker *et al.* (1996) or Kim (1993). Purchasing Power Parity is based on the idea of a long-term relationship between the inflation rates of two countries and the exchange rate of those countries' currencies. The theory holds that currencies are valued according to what they can purchase. The Law of One Price suggests that a commodity should sell for the same price regardless of the currency of denomination. So if gold is priced at \$320 an ounce and the dollar–sterling exchange rate is 1.60 (that is, £1 buys \$1.60) then the price of gold in sterling should be \$320/1.60 = £200. If this were not the case, an arbitrage opportunity would exist. Suppose the exchange rate were actually 1.55. An investor could sell an ounce of gold for \$320, exchange the dollars for £206.45, purchase an ounce of gold for £200 and make a profit of £6.45. Since all investors should do this, the price of gold in the US should fall, the value of the dollar fall relative to the pound and the price of gold should rise in the UK. This would serve to eliminate any arbitrage opportunities. Such an analysis assumes away transaction costs.

While PPP might not apply to individual commodities, due to transportation barriers, segmented markets and non-standardised goods (Eaker *et al.*, 1996), it might be expected to hold for prices in general. Absolute PPP holds that there is a direct relationship between prices and currency in the form $Price_i = Price_j (Currency_i/Currency_j)$ where the subscripts i and j indicate the two countries. Relative PPP suggests that exchange rate *movements* relate to movements in prices (that is differential inflation rates). A country with a high inflation rate is expected to see a relative decline in the value of its currency in relation to a country with a lower rate of inflation, since the purchasing power of the high inflation currency is eroding at a faster rate. Unfortunately, empirical evidence for either version of PPP is weak. In part, this results from methodological problems including the difficulty of identifying appropriate comparable indices of prices, the time span for analysis and determination of a base year.

Interest Rate Parity theory relates exchange rates to nominal interest rates and the returns on financial assets. Again, the basis is the Law of One Price. Investment returns on assets with the same amount of risk and with the same maturity should be equal. Consider government bonds with a maturity of one year in France and the United Kingdom. Suppose the French bond offered a return of 10 per cent and the UK bond a return of 8 per cent. The current exchange rate (the spot rate) is S_0. The spot rate in a year's time will be S_1 and this is forecast by the forward rate F_0 which is the market's expectation of the exchange rate in the future. A French investor may either buy a French bond for 100FF and receive 100(1.1) or 110FF in one year, or exchange francs for pounds and receive $(100/S_0)$ (1.08) F_0 in one year. These two investments should give equal returns, that is:

$$100 (1.1) = (100/S_0)(1.08) F_0 \qquad (13.1)$$

or, by rearrangement

$$(1.1)/(1.08) = F_0 / S_0 \qquad (13.2)$$

This states that the ratio of interest rates should be equivalent to the ratio of forward to spot rates. In this case, the forward rate should be around 2 per cent higher than the spot rate, indicating that the franc is expected to depreciate against the pound. Once again, if the interest rate–exchange rate relationship is out of line, arbitrage opportunities will exist which, once exploited, will result in a return to an equilibrium position.

Empirical evidence for IRP is somewhat stronger than for PPP. It appears to hold closely in the eurocurrency markets where there are few constraints to capital movements. Between countries, a variety of factors including differential taxation and transaction costs, restrictions on currency movements and differences in liquidity reduce the strength of the relationship. IRP and PPP are linked through the Fisher interest rate model discussed in Chapter 10, where the nominal interest rate consists of a real interest rate and an amount for anticipated inflation. IRP and PPP would be equivalent if real interest rates were constant for comparable assets across countries. The links between inflation, interest rates and exchange rates are shown diagramatically in Figure 13.3.

Extending these ideas, Krugman (1991) suggested that countries with positive current account surpluses are likely to experience currency appreciation while those with current account deficits are likely to experience downward exchange rate movement. Large current account surpluses are likely to be associated with net capital outflows. Holsapple et al. (1996) suggest that this should have reduced the extent of Japanese investment in US property in the late 1980s since an expected appreciation in the value of the Yen would erode any cost of capital advantages. In practice, large scale investment in US real estate, attracted by higher apparent yields, led to exchange rate losses that were compounded by weak US property market performance.

Most of the available hedging instruments have been designed for use with short time horizon assets – shares, bonds, cash. As a result, while they may be well suited to hedging indirect property investments, such as shares in

340

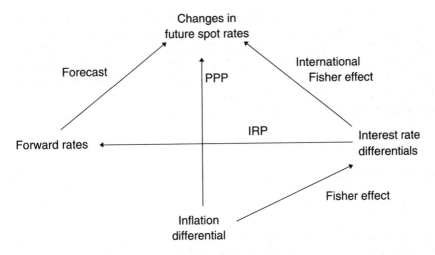

Figure 13.3 Exchange rates, interest rates and inflation
Source: Adapted from Eaker *et al.* (1996) with permission from The Dryden Press

Real Estate Investment Trusts or property companies, they may be less appropriate for direct equity ownership of foreign property. Given its high transaction costs and relative illiquidity, directly held property tends to have longer holding periods than more liquid assets. The long holding period adds uncertainty to the investment, since the final sale price (exit value) is unknown making it hard to hedge the capital appreciation. Furthermore, few of the available hedging instruments have long settlement periods, typically months rather than years, making the task of hedging more complex. In developing a currency strategy, an investor must consider transaction risk (the risks associated with the actual purchase of the asset in the foreign currency) and translation risk (the impact of currency movements on the repatriation of funds, both of income and of the uncertain terminal value).

Early research into international property investment tended to gloss over currency effects, at best converting all returns into the domestic currency. It was implicitly assumed that exchange rate risk could be hedged away. More recent studies have dealt more explicitly with hedging (see, for example, Ziobrowski and Boyd 1991; Ziobrowski and Curcio, 1991; Ziobrowski and Ziobrowski, 1993; 1995; Ziobrowski *et al.*, 1997; Worzala, 1995; Worzala *et al.*, 1997). The results obtained are very sensitive to the assumptions made. For example, the Ziobrowski studies have assumed single period investments and have not dealt explicitly with the costs of the varying hedging instruments. However, the majority of studies cast some doubt on more extravagant claims about the advantages of 'going global'. The range of possible hedging instruments includes forward contracts, futures contracts, currency options, back-to-back loans and currency swaps. The main features of these instruments were discussed in Chapter 12.

Forward contracts

Forward contracts are the negotiated, over the counter purchase of a right and obligation to take delivery of a sum of foreign currency at a specified price (in domestic currency) on a specified date. Most forwards have a term of one year or less, although there are longer-term contracts which are, generally, less liquid, and hence more risky. They would enable an investor to lock in the purchase or sale price of a property where the price is known but closure (completion) is in the future. Their use for hedging the income cash flow is more complex. A number of contracts with maturities of less than the expected holding period of the property investment could be taken out ('stacked up') at the onset of the investment, and gradually converted into longer maturity contracts over time. This generates both high carrying costs and additional transaction costs (Chance, 1995). Alternatively, the hedge could be rolled over. This entails closing out the contract on maturity by purchasing foreign currency at the spot rate and then purchasing a new forward (Madura and Reiff, 1985).

The investor is exposed to currency risk at the roll-over point, depending on the spot rate at that point and the forward contracts on offer. Suppose the forward contract allowed the investor to sell £1m for dollars in six months at a forward rate of $1.60/£. At the end of that period, if the investor wishes to continue the hedge, they must fulfil the contract, then purchase a new contract. If the spot rate has increased to £1.65, then the investor must pay $1.65m to purchase £1m and receive only $1.6m in settlement – a loss on settlement of 3 per cent.

Ziobrowski and Ziobrowski (1995) analyse the hedging of international property using forward contracts. Their analysis assumes away transaction and hedging costs and is based on an annual contract. Making more realistic assumptions, Worzala (1995) examines the use of forward contracts for a US investor purchasing UK property. She shows that forward contracts appear to improve the risk-adjusted return (measured by the coefficient of variation) for the US investor. However, when the transaction and roll-over costs of the three-month forward contracts are included, the volatility increases sharply: the investor would have obtained superior results by 'going naked' – that is not attempting to hedge at all (see Table 13.1).

Futures contracts

Futures contracts operate in similar fashion to forwards, except that they are traded and regulated on exchanges, carry a brokerage fee and are 'marked to market', that is, there are daily transfers of cash to account for the changing settlement price. The impact of currency movements on a forward contract is only experienced when the contract matures. By contrast, with a currency futures contract, there are regular cash flow adjustments as

Table 13.1 The impact of forward contracts for a US investor in UK property

	UK returns 1981–91 (%)	$ Returns unhedged (%)	$ Returns with forward contract (%)	$ Returns, forward contract and costs (%)
Mean return	3.0	2.6	2.4	2.3
Standard deviation	2.6	6.4	2.9	7.7
Coefficient of variation	0.9	2.5	1.2	3.4

Source: Worzala, 1995

the exchange rate, and hence the settlement price, changes. The secondary market in futures provides liquidity and makes it easier to adjust exposure. Futures tend to have standardised amounts and delivery dates, so it may be difficult to tailor a futures hedging strategy to an international property investor's requirements. Although a hedging strategy based on futures could be used to handle exchange rate risk for regular and stable income flows, futures do not seem an appropriate instrument for hedging direct property holdings.

Currency options

Currency options are the right, but not the obligation, to buy (call) or sell (put) an amount of foreign currency at a particular price on a particular day. As with forwards, options can be used to lock in capital value to the domestic currency at a particular exchange rate. They have the advantage that, should the exchange rate shift in the investor's favour, the option would not be exercised. Thus, downside risk is hedged without constraining upside potential. This comes at a price, of course: the up front premium payable to acquire the option. Currency options suffer similar drawbacks to forwards in that the absence of liquid long-term contracts would require an investor to stack up a number of short-term options at the start of the holding period or roll over the contract, accepting the additional risk incurred. Ziobrowski and Ziobrowski (1993) examine the potential use of options in international property investment but avoid the roll-over problem by assuming annual holding periods and repatriation of funds.

Back to back loans

Back to back, or parallel, loans involve firms in two countries agreeing to borrow capital for the other firm in their home market. The foreign firm makes interest payments (presumably from their foreign asset income) and repays the loan on maturity (perhaps from sale of assets). Back to back loans developed in the 1970s to circumvent exchange rate controls. They result in lowered currency exposure. Any surplus capital after repayment of the loan is subject to currency risk. Back to back loans have accounting implications in that they create a balance sheet asset and liability and they have default risk. As an alternative, the foreign investor could simply borrow on their own account in the overseas country (the situation analysed by Ziobrowski and Boyd, 1991). However, a foreign firm may be at a disadvantage in terms of obtaining long-term fixed rate debt. Use of annual loans and hence exposure to variable interest rates adds a financing risk to the investment risk of the underlying asset.

Currency swaps

Currency swaps operate in a similar manner to parallel loans, although they are financial contracts generally handled through an intermediary dealer. They have accounting advantages and low credit risk (Madura, 1992). As Figure 13.4 shows, the investor agrees to swap principal and payments. Thus, the initial principal and fixed cash flows are locked into the domestic currency. This makes them potentially suitable as a property hedging instrument where the rental income is known with some certainty, as might be the case with the UK institutional lease where rents are fixed between rent reviews, typically for five years.

Worzala et al. (1997) examine the potential for hedging using currency swaps for a US investor purchasing a UK property investment. They take a typical UK office building and analyse the cash flows from the perspective of a US investor. The investor may either accept the currency risk (that is, not hedge) or hedge the rental income using a straightforward ('plain vanilla') currency swap. The cost of the swap is built into the analysis. To account for uncertainty of exchange rates, Worzala et al. run a series of simulations with different currency scenarios. They show that hedging reduces the expected return (due to costs) but results in superior risk-adjusted returns as the volatility due to currency movements is eliminated. They conclude that it might be feasible to hedge partially against adverse exchange rate shifts. Ziobrowski et al. (1997) argue that currency swaps counteract exchange rate volatility for UK and Japanese property investors purchasing US real estate, although they suggest that this does not generate obvious diversification gains over purely domestic portfolios or US financial assets for such investors.

The foregoing assumes that investors would hedge at the individual property level or on a country by country basis for their property investments. While this might be a valid assumption for an individual investor or a property company with exposure to just one or two foreign property markets, it may not be an optimal strategy for a large corporate or institutional investor with a diversified international portfolio. Here it is more likely to be efficient

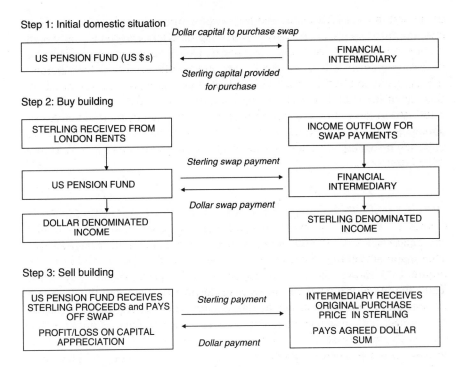

Figure 13.4 Possible structure for a currency swap
Source: Worzala *et al.* (1997)

for the investor to manage currency exposure over the whole of the portfolio. Currency assets and liabilities would be netted out to reveal the net exposure to particular exchange rate movements and that risk managed centrally. This maximises economies of scale in carrying out hedges.

There is evidence that a number of firms investing in international property as part of a wider mixed asset portfolio have such portfolio-level currency management procedures. The firms set up a 'currency grid' that shows their assets and liabilities in different currencies. Where there is high exposure to a currency that is expected to depreciate (perhaps on the basis of an interest rate parity model), hedging will take place, generally using forward contracts. The price of the forward contract will reflect the anticipated depreciation. In this way, the currency is treated as an additional asset class. This does cause some difficulty in assessing the investment performance of particular international assets as these give rise to currency exposure but any cost of hedging is not charged to the asset's cash flow. Performance is usually assessed in the firm's domestic currency ignoring any hedging activity.

In summary, exchange rate risk must be considered in assessing the potential for an international property strategy. The investment characteristics of commercial property (large lot size, long holding period, uncertain timing of disposal and uncertain future capital value) make many of the financial hedging instruments developed for more liquid assets like shares and bonds inappropriate for directly held property. However, some of the risk of adverse currency moves can be hedged, particularly where rental cash flows are comparatively stable. For firms with diversified mixed-asset portfolios of international assets, it is more efficient to manage currency risk at the over-all portfolio level. However, performance measurement of individual assets and asset classes should strictly reflect their contribution to the costs of currency management. There is little published evidence that this takes place in practice.

PROBLEMS IN INTERNATIONAL PROPERTY INVESTMENT

Solnik (1991) sets out five major difficulties associated with international investment strategies.

- *Familiarity* An investor may not know or fully understand the trading practices or actors involved in an overseas market and may have diffi-culty in obtaining and assessing information on market opportunities and market performance.
- *Regulations* There may be restrictions or prohibitions on foreign owner-ship, constraints on the repatriation of capital and profits and a restrictive regulatory framework.
- *Market efficiency* Smaller markets may exhibit liquidity problems, there may be pricing inefficiencies or manipulation and obstacles to capital flows. These may not be impounded into return data.
- *Risk perception* Investment may be discouraged by concerns over polit-ical and currency stability – particularly in the light of uncertainties con-cerning performance, correlation structures and hence the gains possible from diversification.
- *Cost structures* International property may generate higher costs in terms of information gathering and monitoring, management fees and currency transmission costs. These costs are compounded by differences in transaction costs which may not be fully reflected in available perfor-mance statistics.

These difficulties are largely related to information costs, apply to commer-cial property and are compounded by property's specific characteristics and the institutional structure of property markets. Some of them may be over-come through joint ventures with local partners.

Directly held property has high relative management and monitoring costs compared to paper assets. This problem is exacerbated in a globally-scattered portfolio where no scale efficiencies in managing the assets can be obtained.

Where local management agents are used, there are additional costs imposed in monitoring their activities. As a result, firms engaging in international investment strategies are likely to concentrate on a small range of target countries (or, more likely, target cities) and, possibly, on larger-size units. While such a strategy lowers the unit costs, it sacrifices diversification benefits. Diversification gains may be more easily obtained where the overseas property is held as a small part of a domestic property portfolio than for a fully international property portfolio.

This strategy of concentration may divert attention away from smaller markets. In addition, low market capitalisation in relation to fund size may restrict market access. The total value of investment-quality property in a smaller city or an emerging market may be small relative to target allocations. For example, Sweeney's (1993) 'optimal' European portfolio gives a weighting of 13 per cent to Lisbon. However, she estimates that the total office stock was only 1.1 million sq. ft with a value of around £3.2 billion. An international portfolio of £2bn would have an allocation of £252m for Lisbon – around 8 per cent of the total market. Since only a small proportion of the stock will be on sale at any one time, such an allocation would have a distorting effect. A purchase of a 200,000 sq. ft office development in Lisbon would have represented 18 per cent of the investment market. Such smaller markets often exhibit low correlations to the global portfolio. In part, this may reflect lack of research and performance statistics and restrictive market practices, or the lack of integration of local capital markets to the global financial system.

Paucity of data makes the formalisation of an international direct property investment strategy problematic. Even in developed markets, there are problems in measuring performance. In some markets, there are indices of commercial property performance. Most of these benchmark indices rely on appraisals (valuations) to estimate capital appreciation (see Chapter 11 for a discussion of index construction). However, differences in valuation procedures may mean that the indices are not comparable across countries. In Germany, for example, valuations were traditionally carried out on a depreciated replacement cost basis. It is only recently that income-based approaches have assumed a greater significance (Thomas, 1995). In other markets, there may be little data of good quality or with a long time series. Often, the only data available are headline rents for prime property. These need to be adjusted for variations in landlord's costs and typical incentives to tenants to produce a comparable effective rent. Furthermore, there are compatibility problems that relate to differences in terminology, in appraisal methodology, in ownership, lease contract terms and taxation (see Adair *et al.*, 1996). Unless these are accounted for in analysis, a direct comparison of nominal returns may mislead more than illuminate.

To some extent, these disadvantages may be overcome through investment in indirect, publicly traded vehicles such as property companies or Real

Estate Investment Trusts. Chapter 12 discussed whether such vehicles represent property or equity market investment, concluding that in the long run they are linked to property market performance but that they exhibit short-run behaviour that is similar to share prices. Since these are paper assets traded (generally) on public markets, information is more readily available and transaction, management and monitoring costs are reduced considerably. As with most publicly traded assets there are liquidity benefits that permit the development of a more active portfolio strategy. There are still additional information costs associated with stock selection and portfolio management, with (outside the theoretical realm of strong-form market efficiency) local analysts holding advantages in terms of market knowledge.

In an attempt to show the advantage of local knowledge, Eichholtz et al. (1997) compare the performance of public traded property companies which concentrate on domestic investment with those that trade internationally. They have data on eighteen companies with capitalisations of greater than $50m that hold 25 per cent or more or their properties outside their domestic market. These included companies from the Far East (for example, City Developments from Indonesia), from North America (for example, Markborough, Canada) and from Europe (Rodamco, Netherlands or MEPC, UK for example). The performance of these firms is compared to that of firms with purely national portfolios in the GPR-LIFE Global Real Estate Securities database.

Unadjusted results suggest that internationally diversified firms are at a considerable disadvantage relative to domestic firms. In the period 1983–95, domestic firms had produced compound average returns of 14.1 per cent per annum compared to just 7.7 per cent for international firms. This stark difference is not compensated by reduced risk: the international firms had only a slightly lower standard deviation (4.98 per cent to 5.33 per cent). When the data are segmented into time periods, the results remain broadly consistent. This implies that, within a CAPM framework, underperformance does not result from lower systematic risk: if this were the case, international firms would have had lower betas and should have performed less badly in the 1988–91 period of negative returns. Eichholtz et al. suggest that this provides evidence of an information advantage for domestic firms. Another possibility might be that the firm types are not strictly comparable.

To investigate this further, they construct a synthetic index for each international stock. The synthetic index uses the portfolio composition of the international firm but calculates returns based on the performance of equivalent domestic property companies. This allows correction for differences in the types of asset held by the two types of firms. The synthetic and actual indices are used within a CAPM framework to calculate two performance measures, the Sharpe ratio and Jensen's alpha. The former measures the ratio of return (actual return less the risk free rate) to the total risk of the asset (measured by its standard deviation). The greater the Sharpe ratio, the greater the risk-adjusted reward. Jensen's alpha measures whether a company 'outperforms' the market in terms of its security market line expected return.[5] A positive alpha indicates that the asset outperformed its benchmark market in terms of return.

Their results again consistently show superior performance by domestic firms. Mean compound return on domestic firms exceeds that of the international firms (10.4 to 7.7 per cent per annum). In terms of Sharpe ratio, only four of the 18 firms outperform their customised index (two of these are Swedish firms whose international holdings may have protected them from the sharp fall in value of Swedish property). Similarly, in terms of alpha, five firms had positive alphas, but only one of these is statistically significantly higher than zero. Alpha appears to be positively related to size of firm which suggests that a property company can benefit from scale advantages (and possibly the ability to diversify more fully). From their analysis, Eichholtz et al. conclude that an investor would make a higher risk adjusted return by acquiring shares in property companies or REITs from different countries with a domestic portfolio than by investing in either internationally-diversified property companies or REITs or by making direct property investments. They attribute this to information costs: the fact that the direct property market is a non-public market with information privately held. Establishing contacts, obtaining information and overcoming barriers is costly. This is reflected in the lower returns. This can, in part, be compensated for by increasing market capitalisation, resulting in scale economies, or by merger and acquisition activity to obtain local expertise, as for example, in the UK acquisition of CIN Properties by US firm La Salle in 1996.

The Eichholtz results might also be attributable to the fact that individual investors can acquire an internationally diversified portfolio by making a single purchase and hence are prepared to accept (or are unable to avoid) lower returns for the convenience and from avoiding search and transactions costs. Such 'one-stop shopping' advantages will be eroded with the growth of mutual funds investing worldwide in domestic property companies.

Kruijt et al. (1996) obtain similar results in comparing the performance of Dutch public real estate investment trusts (which are highly diversified internationally in terms of geographical holdings) to the GPR-LIFE Global Real Estate Securities index over the period 1984–94 in Dutch guilder terms. Since the majority of firms in the LIFE database have purely domestic portfolios, this represents a test of the value of international diversification. The Dutch REITs were seen to underperform the LIFE index by some 7 per cent per annum. The performance difference attributable to portfolio composition (that is the extent to which the lower returns resulted from being in the 'wrong' region of the world) was around 4.3 per cent. The remaining 2.7 per cent is explained in terms of regional investment peformance – that is outperformance by local firms. These studies suggest that a strategy of international diversification into directly held property may be ill advised.

Information and monitoring costs (and, as discussed earlier, currency factors) may erode any risk diversification benefits. The gains from pursuing an international strategy based on indirect property investment may be more easily realised, although, as noted in Chapter 12, this exposes the investor to the higher volatility of the stock market.

There may still be strong economic reasons for investing in international markets. The returns available may still exceed those obtainable in a firm's domestic market, even if the properties may underperform those held by local investors. Alternatively, international firms may possess advantages over domestic firms in terms of market access or cost of capital that offset the higher information and monitoring costs. This might occur where domestic firms or funds have restrictions on the portfolio mix and type of assets they can hold. This was the case with German pension funds, which faced restrictions on the location of their investment and the proportion of funds that could be invested in 'risky' assets such as commercial property. It might also occur where domestic firms' access to capital for property investments is restricted by regulations imposed on banks and by negative views of property by the capital markets in general, as was reportedly the case in the United States 'capital crunch' in the 1980s, discussed in Chapters 6 and 12. This could happen in the aftermath of a property slump and may give overseas firms a timing advantage.[6]

A third set of reasons for 'going international' relates more to the country than the asset: investment as a currency play or to provide a haven against political or economic instability. In the former case, the investment is made for return rather than its risk diversifying properties, while, in the latter case, avoiding political instability is a particular form of risk avoidance. Such considerations are more likely to inform the investment strategies of wealthy private individuals, while institutional investors may be more mindful of portfolio considerations.

ECONOMIC DRIVERS AND ECONOMIC CONVERGENCE

The 1980s advocates of international property diversification identified a number of markets as being suitable for investment. These markets were mainly in the centres of large global cities and the emphasis was predominantly on office property. Cities cited included the three 'world cities', London, New York and Tokyo with Paris and Frankfurt in Europe and Sydney and Toronto as second order cities. Lizieri and Finlay (1995) examined the office returns in those cities from 1989. As Table 13.2 demonstrates, returns were consistently poor in those cities. Any portfolio based on offices in those markets would have performed badly. It could be argued that property is a long-term investment and that four years of returns are insufficient to judge strategic success. However, it is unlikely that many firms would have an investment horizon of ten years or more. Even with strong later growth, the negative returns of the 1989–93 period would result in poor performance for an investor. As discussed in Part 2, the early 1990s saw a world-wide property slump that might make this analysis period exceptional. More concrete evidence is provided by the demise of Olympia and York. At its peak, the largest private property investment company in the world, Olympia and York had major office holdings in its Canadian base, Toronto, in Manhattan and in London through the Canary Wharf development. This internationalisation of ownership provided no protection against economic downturn. Specific risk had not been diversified away or was small relative to market risk.

Lizieri and Finlay (*op. cit.*) suggest five reasons for the apparent failure of global property strategies:

- technical problems with portfolio theory;
- data problems – garbage in, garbage out;
- *ex post* analysis rather than use of expectations;
- omitted asset categories (analysis of property alone); and
- failure to consider economic fundamentals.

With regard to formal portfolio models the use of optimiser techniques and quantitative investment analysis directs attention to those markets with good research coverage and time series performance data. These tend to be similar types of market – major city centre markets often dominated by financial and business services. Even within economies with a well established commercial property market, coverage of smaller centres and regional markets tends to be patchy. This leads to the key question of economic fundamentals.

Property performance is driven, to a large extent, by occupational demand

Table 13.2 Prime office performance, 1990–2 (estimated nominal returns as a percentage, domestic currency)

| City | Period | | | |
	1989/90	1990/91	1991/92	1992/93
London	−20	−22	−31	−3
Tokyo	+10	−8	−11	−49
New York	+0	+6	−11	+2
Paris	+12	−12	−15	−4
Frankfurt	+15	+11	−7	−7
Sydney	+3	−16	−14	−4
Toronto	+1	−9	−15	−1
Geometric mean	+2	−8	−15	−12

Source: Adapted from Hillier Parker International Property Bulletins

and by investment demand. If diversification is to occur then the markets should be driven by different economic fundamentals (or be at different points in the economic cycle). However, office markets in the cities cited in the global property literature are driven largely by *international* financial services demand. With the development of an integrated 24 hour global financial services industry, economic activity in those cities is likely to be increasingly coordinated.[7] This, in part, may explain the simultaneous downturn.

The coincidence of demand cycles would not necessarily produce simultaneous booms and slumps in the absence of common supply cycles. However, it seems that in many major cities large capital flows occurred into property development at much the same time, producing supply-side booms. This may be related to financial liberalisation in the 1980s.[8] Lizieri (1995) argues that, additionally, there is strong linkage between occupation, ownership and investment activity in financial centre office markets, citing evidence from Toronto. This potentially exacerbates the property cycle in those markets. This links to concerns about systemic risk – the risk to the whole financial system from failure of one element – related to property lending as expressed by the World Bank and the Bank for International Settlements.[9] As an example, Ghosh *et al.* (1994) demonstrate, using an event-study methodology, the impact of the Olympia and York collapse on the global banking system.

The idea of a convergence of financial services has generated most interest in relation to the rapid transmission of shocks in global equity markets – notably the sharp falls in stock prices in October 1987 – 'Black Monday' – and in 1990 following the Iraqi invasion of Kuwait. Speidell and Sappenfield (1992) argue that historic correlations between equity markets may increase over time. They show an average correlation of 0.62 between stock markets in developed economies and the US Standard and Poors 500 index between 1986 and 1991 (with correlations of over 0.8 for the London, Toronto and Singapore indices). Correlations between the shares indices of the US and emerging markets are far lower, averaging just 0.22. They raise the spectre of 'correlation risk' – that 'seemingly diversified portfolios will prove to be undiversified in the future because assets will begin to move uniformly rather than independently'. Four main reasons for such a phenomenon can be advanced:

- institutional portfolios increasingly dominate investment: institutional decision makers may use the same analysis tools and data, thus arriving at very similar investment decisions;
- increasing use of index tracking methodologies binds markets together and acts to coordinate investment timing;[10]
- growth of regional economic and currency blocs such as the European Union and NAFTA drive regional convergence; and
- major events, shocks, are increasingly transmitted around the global system, facilitated by information and communications technology.

Some analysts have argued that it is misleading to impound the impact of shocks in comparing markets. Certainly, Speidell and Sappenfield's correlations with the US equity market fall sharply when the impact of the fourth quarter of 1987 and the third quarter of 1990 are removed. In similar vein, Sorensen and Mezrich (1989) argue that outliers should be trimmed from the data and that, with shocks removed, average correlations between stock markets are no more than 0.30 and may be falling. However, shocks *do* occur and *do* affect stock returns. It may be more informative to consider whether or not stock markets are linked together in the long run and whether the degree of integration has increased over time.[11]

That equity and bond market movements may converge does not necessarily imply property convergence, although, given evidence on the relationship between stock prices and indirect property market prices, some convergence would be expected. Some evidence of a global property market factor is provided by Goetzmann and Wachter (1995). Analysing returns in a number of global office markets, their analysis suggests the presence of a common property factor, although the data used is somewhat questionable.[12] In contrast, Eichholtz and Lie (1995) examine property equity correlations and argue that there is only weak evidence for increasing global correlations. However, *within* continental markets (Europe, North America and Asia) they observe high and increasing correlations.

Another approach to the question of convergence comes from the new economic growth literature that developed from neo-classical models where convergence should occur due to diminishing returns to capital (see Cheshire and Carbonaro, 1995). Baumol (1986) and Baumol and Wolff (1988) found evidence for convergence of national incomes. Empirically, convergence may be tested using the methods set out initially by Barro (Barro and Sala-i-Martin, 1991; 1992). This defines two forms of convergence. Sigma (σ) convergence occurs when the variance (or coefficient of variation) of the chosen indicator falls over time. Beta (β) convergence relates to growth rates, which are assumed to converge to a steady state equilibrium.

In its simplest form, a Barro beta-convergence regression is in the form:

$$\Delta Y_i = \alpha + \beta Y_{0i} + u_i \qquad (13.3)$$

where ΔY_i is the average growth rate over the period; Y_{0i} is the initial value; u_i is a random error or noise factor; and subscript i indicates the country or region. The Y variable might be national income, per capita GDP or some similar macroeconomic variable. If there is convergence, β is expected to be negative. This is because countries with low starting incomes (low values of Y_{0i}) must grow faster than those with higher initial values for convergence to occur. Thus Y_{0i} is negatively correlated with ΔY_i.

Barro regressions have been adapted to include a set of explanatory variables (human capital, propensity to save, regional dummies) which imply conditional convergence, that is, that countries converge to different steady state equilibrium points. A further extension has been provided by Chatterji (1993), who suggests that there might exist 'convergence clubs', groups of economies with similar rates of convergence or economic equilibrium, with no convergence between the groups. This implies persistence of inequalities between economies, which seems plausible.

The translation of Barro style convergence analysis to international property markets is made complex by the lack of long time series of compatible data. For most markets where data exist, analysis rarely extends back beyond the 1980s. Thus, the data are influenced by the pronounced global property cycle of the mid- to late-1980s. Analysis is made more complex by the need to adjust for currency effects, as noted above.

If macroeconomic convergence does occur, a number of predictions may be made. First, with rents driven by macroeconomic variables such as GDP, one might expect, *ceteris paribus*, that rental growth would be fastest in countries with low initial GDP (as national income catches up). Rents in *levels* might be expected to equalise as firms have greater mobility and flexibility over locational choices.[13] However, certain cities possess similar advantages (notably agglomeration economies – see Chapters 3 and 4) and may thus retain higher rental levels, forming convergence clubs. Finally, yields and returns on similar properties should converge with capital mobility.[14]

Some weak evidence of convergence is provided in an analysis by Worzala *et al.* (1996) for the period 1984–94. While the time series is too short to provide conclusive results, the research showed some evidence of sigma convergence in yields and, to a lesser extent, in rental growth for the office markets of European cities and financial services cities. The return correlations shown in Table 13.3 indicate continent-specific effects and the possible existence of similarities between financial services cities, giving some confirmation to the studies discussed earlier.

A final convergence factor might be the harmonisation of institutional factors in the market.[15] Major differences exist in terms of lease length, lease contract details, rent fixing procedures and landlord–tenant obligations. As occupational and investment markets become more international, a convergence of lease terms might be anticipated. One measurable indicator of this

Table 13.3 Average correlations between property returns, 1984–94

	Office	*Retail*
European cities	0.38	0.27
Asian cities	0.13	0.08
Financial cities	0.44	0.37
Full sample	0.30	0.23

Source: Worzala *et al.* (1996)

might be a convergence of lease lengths. Thus, the 25 year lease term which dominated the UK market has reduced in length since the 1980s while in a number of European markets, lease lengths on prime buildings have increased.

International dispersal of property investment alone, then, is insufficient to guarantee risk diversification. The trend towards economic deregulation and financial liberalisation means that many of the economic drivers of property market performance (and urban growth) are not confined within national boundaries. While the examples in this chapter relate mainly to office markets, similar arguments could be made in relation to industrial and, to a lesser extent, retail property.

SUMMARY AND CONCLUSIONS

There has been a rapid growth in cross-border investment in commercial property. This enhanced activity includes direct foreign investment in private property markets, indirect investment in public-traded vehicles such as property company shares, funding and financing of property projects and purchase of securitised debt.

Cross-border investment in commercial property may be motivated by different factors. Investors may invest because the returns are superior to those available in their domestic market, to obtain risk diversification, as a currency play, to seek a safe haven for capital or in response to the size of their domestic market. The nature of the investment strategy varies depending on the motivation.

There are theoretical diversification gains to be made by including international property in a mixed asset portfolio. Lower covariance between property assets across national borders should enable a reduction in the amount of systematic risk carried and, hence, superior risk adjusted returns to be achieved. These theoretical advantages of international diversification must be set against the difficulties involved in implementing a global strategy. These difficulties relate principally to information and monitoring costs. Research suggests that international investors are at a disadvantage when competing with domestic firms. This may be overcome through economies of scale, although this may entail concentrating in a few markets rather than spreading investment more widely.

The global property slump affected many urban property markets in developed economies. Office markets in large cities specialising in financial services were particularly badly hit. This emphasises that it is not geography alone that creates risk diversification but the fact that markets are driven by different economic factors. The near-simultaneous downturns in the office markets of major financial service centres such as New York, London and Toronto that occurred in the late 1980s illustrate this point.

International investment strategies must consider currency risk – and the cost of managing that risk – explicitly. High expected returns in the foreign market may be eroded by adverse exchange rate movements. Although there are many vehicles for hedging currency risk, few are appropriate for direct investment in property. Larger institutional investors can hedge their currency exposure at the portfolio level, thus reducing costs.

Although there are many difficulties in developing international property strategies, the size of the commercial property markets make it likely that further growth will be seen in cross-border investment. Given the difficulties involved in directly owning and managing properties, notably illiquidity and large lot size, much of that growth is likely to be in the indirect property vehicles examined in Chapter 12. This may have implications for market behaviour and pricing in the underlying asset market as the indirect market grows in size and significance relative to direct ownership.

NOTES

2 A MODEL OF COMMERCIAL PROPERTY MARKETS

1 Such stickiness is associated with several interrelated characteristics of real property markets. They include expectations formation (this chapter and Chapter 6); behaviour in the land market (Chapters 3 and 5); institutional structures (Chapter 5); the efficiency of price determination (Chapters 7 and 10); and, finally, capital flows (Chapter 13).
2 See Fisher *et al.* (1993), Harvey (1986) and DiPasquale and Wheaton (1996) for alternative treatments.
3 Chapters 5 and 12 examine the national and international characteristics of property development.
4 Other costs, such as marketing, professional advice and taxation are assumed to be constant, but would, of course, shift the supply schedule if they changed.
5 These forecasts vary in their degree of sophistication from simple, poorly articulated, 'gut' beliefs to sophisticated rational expectations views. Theories of expectations are examined in more depth later in this chapter and in Chapter 6.
6 Commercial building surveyors and commercial agents also provide such information in their market reviews.

3 USER DEMAND AND THE LAND MARKET

1 US studies have contained a larger housing element, since residential property forms part of the typical Institutional real estate investment portfolio. There has been growing interest in investment in residential property amongst UK Institutional investors but, as yet, housing makes up a very small part of their portfolios.
2 75 per cent of London jobs were in service occupations in 1990, compared to 60 per cent nationally.
3 Call centres are offices dedicated to the administrative processing of telephone enquiries for an organisation. These are physically separate from the main operations of the firm and need not even be in the same country. For example, a number of firms have established their European call centres in the area around Dublin.
4 Use Class 4 in Scotland.
5 An (unexpected) increase or decrease in the level of exports in the economy in question perhaps due to cyclical behaviour in the national or global economy.
6 See McNulty (1995) for a review.
7 These US studies and other research on land-use impacts of transportation improvements are reviewed in Antwi and Henneberry (1995).

8 An *externality* exists where an individual or firm's consumption or production decision directly affects the consumption or production decisions of other individuals or firms other than through the price mechanism.

9 Sunk costs are costs of production that do not vary with output or scale and which cannot be recovered by selling part of the plant, capital or equipment to another firm. A discussion of the relevance of sunk costs in economic geography may be found in Clark and Wrigley (1995).

10 Developed like Ricardo's in the early nineteenth century, Von Thunen's (1826) agricultural rent model assumes such transportation differences and, for simplicity, land of the same fertility. This generates a concentric ring pattern of land-use.

11 For reviews see Imrie and Thomas (1993) and Brownhill (1990).

12 As noted in Chapter 2, any decrease in total occupation costs should lead to an increase in the demand for space, other things being equal.

13 The relevant legislation is the Town and Country Planning (Assessment of Environmental Effects) Regulations 1988, the UK's implementation of the European Community directive 85/337.

14 See Feldstein (1977) and Prest (1981) for detailed discussions.

15 See Needham (1992) for a description of the Dutch land planning system and analysis of the resultant pricing mechanisms.

16 The idea of an optimum amount of planning is embedded in the balance-sheet approach to planning suggested by Lichfield (1988) and others.

4 THE LOCATION OF COMMERCIAL PROPERTY

1 For further discussion in a property context see Lizieri (1991; 1994). Gertler (1992) provides a comprehensive review from a geographer's perspective. Piore and Sabel's *The Second Industrial Divide* (1984) is one of the seminal works in this area.

2 For a review of store choice research, see Eppli and Benjamin (1994).

3 By direct analogy to the gravitational attraction of bodies, proportional to mass, in Newtonian physics.

4 A more detailed discussion of gravity models may be found in Field and MacGregor (1987).

5 The minimum size for a regional shopping centre is usually put at around 50,000 square metres of retail floor space (Schiller, 1986; McGoldrick and Thompson, 1992).

6 A literature review of the impact of out-of-town retail development may be found in BDP/OXIRM (1992).

7 Miles (1990) discusses the potential growth of teleshopping in the UK. His paper barely touches on the potential of Internet shopping, reflecting the rapid advances in information technology and communications in the 1990s.

8 An alternative view is provided by Crampton and Evans (1992) who suggest that the operation of the Location of Offices Bureau, Office Development Permits and regional employment policy, in part, explain the relatively poor economic performance of the London economy in a European context.

9 Precise definitions differ. Both hot desking and office hotelling involve employees being allocated workspace on arrival at the office, rather than having a permanent base. See Lizieri *et al.* (1997) for a discussion.

10 A review of business space trends and their impact on the commercial property market can be found in Lizieri *et al.* (1997).

5 PROPERTY SUPPLY AND INSTITUTIONAL ANALYSIS

1 The absence of property examples in this list is because there is no literature on strategic behaviour in property markets, although, as this chapter argues, institutionalism can be interpreted as a particular theoretical approach to strategic behaviour.

2 Punter's diagram is available in a conference paper (Punter, 1985), but is reproduced in Gore and Nicholson (1991).

3 See Ball (forthcoming) for more detailed analysis of this.

4 Similar arguments could apply to REITs in the USA – see Chapter 13.

5 Chapters 5 and 12 examine moral hazard and commercial property lending in more detail.

6 This situation highlights the difference between institutions and organisations. The community is an institution and protest groups are organisations aiming to represent its interests.

7 These cited references illustrate that underlying theories are not always good indicators of views about property markets. Massey and Catalano wrote from within a 1970s style Marxist perspective, whereas the later writers cited did not; yet, the conclusions about landowners are common to all of them.

8 In practice, the ASH treatment of economic dynamics, following general sociological tradition, tends to be cursory. Its structural characteristics are derived from classifications of economic and other social systems, which give rise to sweeping generalisations about supposed epochs of capitalism, such as 'post-Fordist'.

9 The approach was originally formulated as part of research on British housing (Ball, 1981; 1983), and then argued to be applicable to other forms of building and to the interpretation of issues such as urban rent and the development of the construction industry (Ball, 1985; 1986a; 1986b; 1988; Ball *et al.*, 1988 and Ball and Harloe, 1992).

10 See the references cited in note 9.

6 PROPERTY MARKETS AND THE MACROECONOMY

1 Good macroeconomics textbooks abound. Dornbusch and Fischer (1994) is still one of the best and regularly updated. See also Begg, Dornbusch and Fischer (1995) for a more UK-oriented, simpler approach, while Barro and Grilli (1994) provide a European perspective. Romer (1996) is an advanced modern treatment.

2 Potential growth is the long-term, full employment, trend growth rate.

3 Empirical evidence on the relationship between UK business and property market cycles is considered in Chapter 7.

4 The real exchange rate is the nominal exchange rate times the ratio of foreign to domestic prices, where foreign prices are calculated on the basis of the importance of other countries in a country's overseas trade.

7 LONG-RUN SUPPLY, STABILITY AND EFFICIENCY

1 This section is based on detailed information provided in Ball and Grilli (1997).

2 Most economic data are presented diagramatically in log form because of the exponential growth trend within them.

3 Note that commercial here, following the convention of the DOE statistical series, does not include industrial building.

4 The income share data are derived by dividing *Housing and Construction Statistics* commercial output data by NSO UK national income data. The share is consequently marginally lower than it really is because the very small commercial market in Northern Ireland is excluded.

5 Barras' theory is examined in detail in the next chapter.

6 Spectral density tests produced no evidence of cycles in construction orders, but four to five year cycles were found when the series for construction starts was detrended and deviations from that trend were considered.

7 Maddison (1991) provides a good critical review of the cycle literature; van Duijn (1983) is a more enthusiastic supporter.

8 Harvey (1978) suggests an alternative view that these cycles are produced by the switch of capital from the primary to the secondary circuit and so are related to the supply of capital and not the demand for buildings. This theory is criticised in Ball (1986b) and Beauregard (1994).

9 Commercial orders data are available only from 1964.

10 Tests of significance of these volatility results were made by comparing the sequential time periods (for example, 1955–72 and 1973–96) in order to check for heteroskedasticity. The tests are not reproduced here but the standard deviations in bold in Table 7.2 indicate that the volatility is significantly different from that in the previous period at the 1 and 5 per cent significance levels.

11 There is no perfect measure of volatility, only approximate indicators of theorised key characteristics can be derived. ARCH and other statistical techniques have been used in financial markets, where data are available for very short time periods, to examine market stability and changes within it. The characteristics and availability of data make such techniques inapplicable in many property market contexts, including development activity.

12 Where work-in-progress is funded by interim payments, and falls into the definition: 'The amount chargeable to customers . . . in the relevant period'. *Housing and Construction Statistics*, Notes and definitions, *passim*.

13 Persistent criticisms of the accuracy of construction data tend not to receive much official response, as they require more public expenditure and legal coercion to rectify.

14 Most of these arguments, it should be noted, equally apply to economic base theory, considered in Chapter 3, and reinforce the criticisms of the approach made there.

15 See Chapter 6 for detailed analysis of these potential transmission routes.

16 See also Baum and Schofield (1991); Key *et al.*, 1994a; and Scott, 1996.

8 PROPERTY CYCLES

1 However, as UK institutional leases typically contain upward-only rent review clauses, rents received for let properties do not fall. This leads to overrenting and a change in the investment characteristics of property from an equity to a bond where tenant risk assumes great importance (see Chapter 10).

2 The approach is not without problems. The estimated value for μ is 0.18 which the authors use to suggest that 18 per cent of the desired long term stock is constructed each six months. However, the demand variables used are information sets comprising both output and employment and it may be that the coefficients should not be interpreted in this way. The value of 0.18 contrasts dramatically with Barras' figure of 0.9 which, despite the differences in country and property sector, suggests caution is required when interpreting such models.

3 An early use of the accelerator principle to model commercial property building

cycles is to be found in Bischoff (1970). An earlier and more complex variant using a lag structure was proposed by Nicholson and Tebbutt (1979). They note that not all firms are able to complete the ordering process at the same rate and different projects will have different completion times. Consequently, there is a lagged distribution with changes in output generating new construction over a number of subsequent periods but at a decreasing rate.

4 Barras also introduces another term which represents a long-term investment demand for new development which is autonomous from short-term changes in user demand. Thus:

$$TD_t = ND_t + \delta K_{t-1} + A_t$$

For ease of exposition, this is ignored here.

5 Two second order difference equations can be derived to represent total new development and the capital stock:

$$TD_t - (1 - \delta)TD_{t-1} + (\mu - \delta)TD_{t-2} = \alpha\mu[Q_t - (1 - \delta)Q_{t-1}]$$

$$K_t - (1 - \delta)K_{t-1} + (\mu - \delta)K_{t-2} = \alpha\mu Q_{t-1}$$

The detailed mathematics is beyond the scope of this book and is an unnecessary diversion in the exposition.

6 Note that rents are exogenous as they are not being modelled. This approach contrasts with the conceptually much simpler approach adopted in the US literature and outlined later in this chapter and in Chapter 9. In this, rental adjustment plays a central part.

7 This is not inconsistent with a capital switching analysis: see Beauregard (1994) for the contrary view, and Lizieri and Satchell (1997) for a discussion.

8 Note that it might be expected that the longer the lease, the less responsive rents would be to changes in the vacancy rate.

9 Operating expenses consist of cleaning, electricity costs, heating and cooling, administration, minor alterations and normal periodic maintenance and decorating and total fixed charges, such as real estate taxes and insurance.

There is a related literature on the apartment market. Eubank and Sirmans (1979) argue that operating expenses are also important in determining rents. They estimate a version of equation (8.18) using nominal data. In general, neither vacancy nor lagged vacancy are significant and change in operating expenses is. This is perhaps not surprising as both rents and operating costs contain inflation and thus might be expected to be highly correlated: so expenses would be significant in the regression. Rosen and Smith (1983) estimate a similar model, also with nominal data, both with pooled data and with a city dummy variable to allow the natural vacancy rate to vary from city to city. In both analyses, the vacancy rate and lagged vacancy are significant but operating expenses are not.

10 It is more difficult to make a plausible case that the third issue, adverse selection, should be relevant to this discussion.

9 MARKET MODELLING AND FORECASTING

1 $\log(CV_t) - \log(CV_{t-1})$

$= \log(CV_t/CV_{t-1})$

$= \log(1 + g)$ where g is the growth rate

$\approx g$ for small values of g.

2 One of the simplest tests for the 'goodness-to-fit' of an equation is the R^2. This is the ratio of the variation explained by the equation (the model) to the total variation in the dependent variable. Strictly, the R^2 should be adjusted for the number of variables, although some studies report only the 'raw' R^2.

3 Rent (the price of occupation) is determined by the interaction of supply and demand in the user market. Supply is a function of both demand and price; and demand is a function of both supply and price: $S = f(D,P)$ and $D = g(S,P)$. The reduced form is: $P = h(D,S)$.

4 This estimation appears not to be in logs although this is not clear. No explanation is given why the demand equation is estimated in logs while the others are not.

5 The explanation in the paper is terse: it is unclear whether the four periods for the vacancy rate calculation end at t or $t-1$; no explanation is given of how the expected rent variable is derived; and no explanation is given of the tax laws variable.

6 Rosen (1984) uses the smoothed vacancy rate and the expected rent in his specification but does not find rent to be significant.

7 Note that this suggests the estimation is in logs as $\log (E_t/E_{t-1}) \approx$ the growth rate of E_t.

8 The coefficients μ and $\mu\gamma_i$ are estimated and γ_i calculated by division.

9 The coefficients τ_1 and $\tau_1\gamma_i$ are estimated and γ_i calculated by division.

10 PROPERTY'S FINANCIAL INVESTMENT CHARACTERISTICS

1 A geometric series is: a, ar, ar^2, ... ar^i, ... The formula for the sum to infinity is $a/(1 - r)$ where a is the first term and r is the common ratio. In this case, the first term is $C/(1 + R)$ and the common ratio is $1/(1 + R)$.

2 Strictly, the compensation is based on inflation lagged by 8 months; so there is some residual risk of over or under compensation.

3 The entire analysis could also be presented in real terms using index-linked gilt yields.

4 During much of the early 1990s, with substantial oversupply in many local markets, potential tenants were in a strong position to bargain for shorter leases often with other incentives such as rent free periods.

5 This 'most likely selling price', referred to as the open market value (OMV), is determined under a set of conditions established by the Royal Institution of Chartered Surveyors (RICS). These include a willing seller, a reasonable period to negotiate a sale, a reasonable period for marketing, values remaining static during this period and the absence of a special purchaser. In 1995, new guidance was issued by the RICS to professional valuers on additional and different bases for valuation, depending on the purpose of the valuation. It remains to be seen which of these clients will wish to use.

6 The versions presented here are for property owned in perpetuity (freehold in England and Wales and feuhold in Scotland). The methods can be adjusted to accommodate leasehold properties.

7 This is equivalent to the standard concept in financial mathematics of the present value (PV) of £1 in perpetuity discounted at the capitalisation rate. This, of course, holds only if cash flows are in arrears and if the period of the interest rate (here the discount rate) is the same as the period between successive payments. Although the capitalisation rate is an annual rate, property cash flows are typically quarterly and in advance. Accommodating such cash flows makes the mathematics a little more tedious although tables exist. The conventional response of the property profession is that such differences are already reflected in the ARY.

8 Note that an efficient market is different from a perfect frictionless market as required by the Capital Asset Pricing Model (CAPM) (see Chapter 11). The latter requires, among other features, that there are no taxes, no transaction costs, information is free and simultaneously available to all investors, assets are infinitely divisible, no individual can affect price and all investors are rational expected utility maximisers.

9 It is not possible to offer a precise definition of 'submarket'. It is a group of properties which are 'reasonable' substitutes and may be defined by property type and locality.

10 The authors acknowledge that the valuers were undertaking the valuations without payment. They suggest it is possible that the valuers might have taken greater care and researched the market more fully if they had been paid. They also acknowledge that there was a lack of good comparable data available at the time of the study. Nonetheless, the results do indicate the difficulties of price determination in the property market.

11 PROPERTY IN INVESTMENT PORTFOLIOS

1 More detailed expositions of MPT and CAPM can be found in many texts, such as Alexander and Francis (1986), Elton and Gruber (1984), and Rutterford (1993).

2 It is necessary to assume: (1) a perfect securities market (that is: no taxes; no transaction costs; no restrictions on selling short; all information is free and simultaneously available to all investors; securities are infinitely divisible; no individual can affect the market by buying and selling; investors are rational maximisers); (2) all investors agree on the period under consideration and have identical expectations about risk (this is not needed for MPT); (3) unlimited amounts of money can be borrowed or lent by all investors at the risk-free rate; and (4) if inflation exists it can be fully anticipated in interest rates (Rutterford, 1993: 261–2). Some of these can be relaxed without affecting the most important results.

3 As suggested in Chapter 10, the definition of 'prime' and 'secondary' is imprecise. Further, the classification of an individual property can change through time as a result of wear and tear and obsolescence.

4 One variant is the Hillier Parker Index which includes information on estimated open market rents and yields for defined, standardised properties in specified locations. In some locations, rents refer to actual properties but in others rents refer to a typical property. The index represents valuers' views of market conditions rather than that provable from lettings and rent reviews. It is argued to be more responsive to market movements than normal valuations indices.

5 Strictly, the problem is more complex. First, volatility varies according to the liquidity of the market and any analysis should take account of changes in liquidity. Secondly, the observed price of any individual property (which comprises both a market component and a specific component) may differ from the true market worth for a number of reasons other than valuation smoothing. These have been discussed in Chapter 10 and include: random errors in valuations; asymmetric information sets or negotiating skills; and special purchasers with particular individual requirements.

6 This model of the smoothing process was suggested by Blundell and Ward (1987) and is only one possible model of the smoothing process (see also Barkham and Geltner, 1994; Geltner, 1991, 1993; MacGregor and Nanthakumaran, 1992). It is also possible that the smoothing parameter A is not constant over time but

depends on the state of the market, for example, whether prices are rising, failing or stable (see Chaplin, 1997 and Matysiak and Wang, 1995).

7 Strictly, this is for capital returns only but the procedure can be adapted for total return, including income return. From (11.14):

$$V_t = (1 - A)P_t + AV_{t-1}$$

and

$$V_{t-1} = (1 - A)P_{t-1} + AV_{t-2}$$

so

$$V_t - V_{t-1} = (1 - A)(P_t - P_{t-1}) + A(V_{t-1} - V_{t-2})$$

If the series are expressed in natural logarithms, then the log of the difference is approximately equal to the rate of change, so:

$$R_t = (1 - A)Rm_t + AR_{t-1}$$

See Brown (1991: 228–30) for a fuller derivation.

8 Indirect property holdings are considered in Chapter 12. Their characteristics depend on a number of factors including whether the returns are valuation or price based and the extent to which their performance is based on property and debt. Many property company shares are highly geared and are strongly correlated with the share market. In contrast, Property Unit Trusts are valuation-based and have return and risk characteristics very similar to those of direct property.

9 For the UK, see Fraser (1985), Sweeney (1988), Lee (1989) and Howells and Rydin (1990), and for the US, Fogler (1984), Firstenburg et al. (1988) and Webb et al. (1988).

10 Strictly, for a property portfolio, specific risk must also be included in the formulation for the tracking error risk.

11 There are technical difficulties in the calculation of assets and liabilities. The benchmark used contains only shares and gilts, so that holding property may induce greater volatility in the solvency ratio and hence require greater management activity (see Booth et al., 1996, for a discussion).

12 An immature pension fund is one which is receiving in contributions from members more than it has to pay out in pensions. A mature fund pays out more than it receives. The latter requires larger weights in liquid assets with guaranteed returns, such as gilts, while the former is interested in real assets, such as shares and property.

13 See, for example, Corgel and Gay (1987), Hartzell et al. (1987), Shulman and Hopkins (1988), Malizia and Sirmans (1991), Mueller and Zierling (1992) and Mueller (1993).

14 A recent development has been the further division of a portfolio according to overrenting, that is, when the passing rent is higher than the market rent because of upward-only rent reviews and a fall in the market. Highly overrented properties are unaffected by rental growth and have bond rather than equity characteristics.

12 INDIRECT INVESTMENT IN PROPERTY

1 For reviews, see Manolis and Meistrich (1986) and Pryke and Whitehead (1991).
2 Healthcare REITs invest in private retirement homes and similar ventures. The

behaviour of such REITs differs from that of equity and mortgage REITs. US real estate analysts have thus tended to exclude them from research into REIT performance.

3 For a review, see Corgel et al. (1995).

4 See Investment Property Forum (1993) for a discussion.

5 See Chapter 10 for more detail on valuation methodologies.

6 The elimination of the yield gap between large and small units through overseas investment may indicate that financial liberalisation served to eliminate capital market inefficiencies.

7 For a description of the structure of mortgage-backed bonds, see Manolis and Meistrich (1986).

8 See Chapter 13 for a further discussion.

9 PICs are certificates which offer capital and income return linked to the reported returns on the Investment Property Databank portfolio. They could be purchased in lots as small as £250,000 and thus offer access to 'average' returns on a fully diversified property portfolio less management costs. PIFs are futures contracts based on the value of the IPD capital growth index.

10 For evidence in US markets see, for example, Brueggeman et al. (1984), Mengden and Hartzell (1987) and, for UK markets, MacGregor and Nanthakumaran (1992), Campeau (1995).

11 For a Hong Kong example, see Chau et al. (1997).

12 Note that this implies that UK valuation based returns are less smoothed than US returns. In the original article, the smoothing parameter reported, a, is equivalent to $(1-A)$ in the version presented here.

13 The Granger causality model tests whether one of a pair of variables 'leads' the other, thus implying that knowledge of the leading variable would help in forecasting the value of the lagging variable. For discussions in a property context see Barkham and Geltner op. cit. and Lizieri and Satchell (1997).

14 See Vandell (1993) for a comprehensive review.

15 BIS (1994), Goldstein and Folkerts-Landau (1993).

13 INTERNATIONAL PROPERTY INVESTMENT

1 Equation 11.2 in Chapter 11 gave the portfolio variance as $\sigma_p^2 = \Sigma\Sigma w_i w_j \sigma_i \sigma_j \rho_{ij}$. For all pairs of assets, $i \neq j$, the term $\sigma_i \sigma_j \rho_{ij}$ is the covariance cov_{ij}. As noted in Chapter 11, where the assets are perfectly correlated, risk simplifies to $\sigma_p = \Sigma w_i \sigma_i$. Where this is not the case, the risk is given by $\sigma_p^2 = \Sigma w_i \sigma_i^2 + \Sigma\Sigma w_i w_j \sigma_i \sigma_j \rho_{ij}$ $(i \neq j)$. For equally weighted assets, the first term can be represented as $\Sigma\sigma_i^2/n$ and tends to zero as n increases. The second term, in covariance form, is $\Sigma\Sigma w_i w_j cov_{ij}$. Averaging the covariances, this term reduces to $[(n-1)/n] cov_{ij}$. This implies that, as n increases, the risk in the portfolio tends to cov_{ij}.

2 The paper makes the contentious assumption that rental growth could be used as a proxy for overall returns, ignoring temporal variations in yields across countries. Data is nominal not real. The analysis does not account for differential tax and transaction costs, nor does it consider the feasibility of portfolios in the light of market capitalisations. It does tentatively examine currency effects by separately analysing correlations for UK, US and Japanese investors.

3 Ziobrowski and Boyd, 1991; Ziobrowski and Curcio, 1991; Ziobrowski and Ziobrowski, 1993, 1995; Ziobrowski, Ziobrowski and Rosenberg, 1997.

4 In particular, the returns are calculated on an annual basis that implicitly assumes repatriation of capital gains.

5 Standard finance texts such as Alexander et al. (1993) will provide derivations

of these performance measures. Chapter 11 discussed the key features of CAPM.

6 Overseas acquisitions of London office properties in the early 1990s may be explained in this way, although German purchases are generally attributed to the flow of capital into German open ended funds (Thomas, 1995).

7 The integrated global financial system has resulted from a combination of economic liberalisation (deregulation of financial services, removal of barriers to capital flow and currency rules), rapid advances in information and communications technology and innovation in financial products that emphasise liquidity.

8 See, for example, Ball (1994), Pryke (1994), Coakley (1994).

9 Goldstein and Folkerts-Landau, 1993; Bank for International Settlements, 1993.

10 Rule-based investment strategies lead to a large number of firms reacting in the same way to new information, magnifying its impact.

11 The econometric technique of cointegration analysis has been used to examine this question. Empirical results are mixed but generally support a thesis of increased linkage either globally or across broad regions.

12 Goetzmann and Wachter (1995) apply principal components analysis – a data analysis technique that aims to extract the underlying patterns in the data. The first component extracted explained 44 per cent of the variation in returns. Since all the cities loaded (in effect, correlated) strongly with this component, they use this as evidence of a global property factor.

13 After correcting for currency effects by taking purchasing power parity into account.

14 Capitalisation rates (initial yields) represent a combination of required return and implied rental growth (see Chapter 10). If required returns are similar across countries, initial yield differentials will relate to implied rental growth in real terms. This will relate to real rental growth, which is expected to converge. As noted above, inflation differences between countries should lead to currency movements (as implied in the purchasing power parity model).

15 For a discussion see Worzala and Bernasek (1996).

REFERENCES

Abramowitz, M. (1968) The Passing of the Kuznets Cycle, *Economica*, 45–8.

Adair, A., Downie, M-L., McGreal, S. and Vos, G. (editors) (1996) *European Valuation and Practice: Theory and Techniques*, London: E & FN Spon.

Adair, A., Hutchison, N., MacGregor, B. D., McGreal, S. and Nanthakumaran, N. (1996) An analysis of valuation variation in the UK commercial property market, *Journal of Property Valuation and Investment*, 14, 5: 34–47.

Adams, A. (1989) *Investment*, London: Graham and Trotman.

Adams, A. and Baum, A. (1989) Property Securitisation: Premium or Discount?, *The Investment Analyst*, 91: 31–8.

Adams, A. and Venmore-Rowland, P. (1990) Property Share Valuation, *Journal of Valuation*, 8 122–42.

Adams, A. and Venmore-Rowland, P. (1991) Proposed Property Investment Vehicles: Will They Work?, *Journal of Property Valuation and Investment*, 9: 287–94.

Adams, D. (1994) *Urban Planning and the Development Process*, London: UCL Press.

Adams, D. and May, H. G. (1991) Active and passive behaviour in landownership, *Urban Studies*, 28: 687–705.

Adams, D., Baum, A. E. and MacGregor, B. D. (1985) The influence of valuation practices on the price of vacant inner city land, *Land Development Studies*, 2: 157–73.

Adams, D., Baum, A. E. and MacGregor, B. D. (1988) The availability of land for inner city development: a case study of inner Manchester, *Urban Studies*, 25: 62–76.

Akerloff, G. (1970) The market for 'lemons': quality, uncertainty and the market mechanism, *Quarterly Journal of Economics*, 89: 345–64.

Alexander, G. J. and Francis, J. C. (1986) *Portfolio analysis*, (third edition), New Jersey: Prentice Hall.

Alexander, G., Sharpe, W. and Bailey, J. (1993) *Fundamentals of Investments*, Englewood Cliffs NJ: Prentice Hall.

Allen, M., Madura, J. and Wiant, K. (1995) Commercial Bank Exposure and Sensitivity to the Real Estate Market; paper presented to the American Real Estate Society conference, Hilton Head, S.C.

Alonso, W. (1964) *Location and Land Use,* Cambridge: Harvard University Press.

Ambrose, P. and Colenutt, P. (1975) *The Property Machine*, London: Penguin Books.

367

Antwi, A. and Henneberry, J. (1995a) Developers, non-linearity and asymmetry in the development cycle, *Journal of Property Research*, 12, 3: 217–39.

Antwi, A. and Henneberry, J. (1995b) The Impact of Public Transport Infrastructure on House Prices, *Proceedings, RICS Cutting Edge Research Conference*, 1: 433–45 London: RICS.

Archer, W. (1981) Determinants of Location for General Purpose Office Firms Within Medium-Sized Cities, *Journal of the American Real Estate and Urban Economics Association*, 9: 283–97

Aschauer, J. (1989) Is Public Expenditure Productive?, *Journal of Monetary Economics*, 23: 177–200.

Axelrod, R. (1990) *The Evolution of the Corporation*, Harmondsworth: Penguin.

Bacon, R. (1984) *Consumer Spatial Behaviour*, Oxford: Oxford University Press.

Bacow, L. (1990) Foreign Investment, Vertical Integration and Structure in the US Real Estate Industry, *Real Estate Issues*, 15: 1–8.

Ball, M. (1981) The development of capitalism in housing provision, *International Journal of Urban and Regional Research*, 5: 145–77.

Ball, M. (1983) *Housing Policy and Economic Power: the Political Economy of Owner Occupation*, London: Methuen.

Ball, M. (1985) The urban rent question, *Environment and Planning A*, 503–25.

Ball, M. (1986a) Housing research: time for a theoretical refocus?, *Housing Studies*, 147–65.

Ball, M. (1986b) The built environment and the urban question, *Society and Space*, 4: 447–64.

Ball, M. (1988) *Rebuilding Construction: Economic Change and the British Construction Industry*, London: Routledge.

Ball, M. (1990) *Under One Roof. Retail Banking and the International Mortgage Finance Revolution*, Hemel Hempstead: Harvester Wheatsheaf.

Ball, M. (1994) The 1980s property boom, *Environment and Planning A*, 26: 671–95.

Ball, M. (1996) *Housing and Construction: a Troubled Relationship*, Bristol: Policy Press.

Ball, M. (1998) Institutions in British property research: a review, *Urban Studies*, 35: 1501–18.

Ball, M. (forthcoming) *Changing Construction. Firms and Professions in the UK Construction Industry*, forthcoming.

Ball, M. and Grilli, M. (1997) UK commercial property investment: time series characteristics and modelling strategies, *Journal of Property Research*, 14, 4: 279–96.

Ball, M. and Harloe, M. (1992) Rhetoric barriers to housing research. What the provision thesis is and is not, *Housing Studies*, 8: 3–15.

Ball, M. and Wood, A. (1996) Trend growth in post-1850 economic history: the Kalman filter and historical judgement, *The Statistician, Journal of the Royal Statistical Society Series D*, 45: 143–52.

Ball, M. and Wood, A. (1998) Housing investment: long-run international trends and volatility, *Housing Studies*, vol. 13, (forthcoming).

Ball, M., Harloe, M. and Martens, M. (1988) *Housing and Social Change in Britain and the USA*, London: Routledge.

Ball, M., McDowell, L. and Gray, F. (1989) *The Transformation of Britain: Contemporary Economic and Social Change*, London: Fontana Press.

Ball, M., Morrison, T. and Wood, A. (1996) Structures investment and economic growth: a long-term international comparison, *Urban Studies*, 33: 1687–706.

Bank for International Settlements (1993) *63rd Annual Report*, Basle: Bank for International Settlements.

Bank of England (various) *Bank of England Quarterly Bulletin*, London: Bank of England.

Barkham, R. and Geltner, D. (1994) Unsmoothing British Valuation-Based Returns Without Assuming an Efficient Market, *Journal of Property Research*, 11: 81–95.

Barkham, R. and Geltner, D. (1995) Price Discovery in American and British Property Markets. *Journal of the American Real Estate and Urban Economics Association*, 23: 21–44.

Barras, R. (1983) A simple theoretical model of the office development cycle, *Environment and Planning A*, 15: 1361–94.

Barras, R. (1994) Property and the economic cycle: building cycles revisited, *Journal of Property Research*, 11, 3: 183–97.

Barras, R. and Ferguson, D. (1985) A spectral analysis of building cycles in Britain, *Environment and Planning A*, 17: 1369–91.

Barras, R. and Ferguson, D. (1987a) Dynamic modelling of the business cycle: 1. Theoretical framework, *Environment and Planning A*, 19: 353–67.

Barras, R. and Ferguson, D. (1987b) Dynamic modelling of the business cycle: 2. Empirical results, *Environment and Planning A*, 19: 493–520.

Barrett, S., Stewart, M. and Underwood, J. (1990) *The land market and the development process: a review of research and policy*, Occasional Paper 2, School for Advanced Urban Studies, University of Bristol.

Barro, R. and Grilli, V. (1994) *European Macroeconomics*, Basingstoke: Macmillan.

Barro, R. and Sala-i-Martin, X. (1991) Convergence Across States and Regions, *Brookings Papers in Economic Activity*, 1: 107–82.

Barro. R. and Sala-i-Martin, X. (1992) Convergence, *Journal of Political Economy*, 100: 223–51.

Bassett, K. (1996) Partnerships, Business Elites and Urban Politics: New Forms of Governance in an English City?, *Urban Studies*, 33: 539–55.

Baum, A. E. (1990) *Property investment depreciation and obsolescence*, London: Routledge.

Baum, A. E. (1995) Can Foreign Investment be Successful?, *Real Estate Finance*, 12: 81–9.

Baum, A. E. and Crosby, N. (1995) *Property investment appraisal*, 2nd edition, London: Routledge.

Baum, A. E. and MacGregor, B. D. (1992) The initial yield revealed: explicit valuations and the future of property investment, *Journal of Property Valuation and Investment*, 10, 4: 709–27.

Baum, A. E. and Schofield, J. A. (1991) Property as a global asset, in Venmore-Rowland, P., Brandon, P. and Mole, T. (editors) *Investment, procurement and performance in construction*, London: E and F N Spon (pp. 103–55).

Baum, A. E., Crosby, N. and MacGregor, B. D. (1996) Price formation, mispricing and investment analysis in the property market, *Journal of Property Valuation and Investment*, 14, 1: 36–49.

Baumol, W. (1986) Productivity Growth, Convergence and Welfare: What the Long-Run Data Show, *American Economic Review*, 76: 1075–85.

Baumol, W. and Wolff, E. (1988) Productivity Growth, Convergence and Welfare, *American Economic Review*, 78: 1155–9.

BDP/OXIRM (1992) *The Effects of Major Out of Town Retail Development: A Literature Review for the Department of the Environment*, BDP Planning and the Oxford Institute of Retail Management, London: HMSO.

Beauregard, R. (1994) Capital switching and the built environment: United States, 1970–89, *Environment and Planning A*, 26: 715–32.

Begg, D., Dornbusch, R. and Fischer, S. (1995) *Economics*, Maidenhead: McGraw-Hill.

Berndt, E. (1991) *The Practice of Econometrics*, Reading, MA: Addison Wesley.

Berry, J., Deddis, W. and McGreal, W. (1992) Town regeneration schemes: an evaluation of project initiatives, *Journal of Property Research*, 9: 161–71.

Binmore, K. (1992) *Fun and Games. A Text on Game Theory*, Lexington MA: D.C. Heath.

BIS (1993) *63rd Annual Report*, Basle: Bank for International Settlements.

Bischoff, C. (1970) A model of non-residential construction in the United States, *American Economic Review: Papers and Proceedings*, pp. 10–17.

Black, F. (1989) Universal Hedging: Optimizing Currency Risk and Reward in International Equity Portfolios, *Financial Analysts' Journal*, July–August, pp. 16–22.

Black, F. and Litterman, R. (1992) Global Portfolio Optimization, *Financial Analysts Journal*, September–October 1992 pp. 28–43.

Blundell, G. F. and Ward, C. W. R. (1987) Property portfolio allocation: a multifactor model, *Land Development Studies*, 4, 2: 145–56.

Booth, P., Lizieri, C. M. and Matysiak, G. A. (1996) Property Investment and the Pensions Bill, *Proceedings of the 1995 Institute/Faculty of Actuaries Investment Conference*, pp. 149–58, London: Institute of Actuaries.

Brendt, E. R. (1992) *The Practice of Econometrics*, London: Addison-Wesley.

Brett, M. (1990) *Property and Money*, London: E & F N Spon.

Brown, G. R. (1985) The information content of property valuations, *Journal of Valuation*, 3: 350–62.

Brown, G. R. (1991) *Property investment and the capital markets*, London: E & F N Spon.

Brown, G. R. (1992) Valuation accuracy: developing the economic issues, *Journal of Property Research*, 9: 199–207.

Brownhill, S. (1990) *Developing London's Docklands*, London: Paul Chapman Publishing.

Brownhill, S. (1993) The Docklands Experience, in Imrie, R. and Thomas, H. (editors) *British Urban Policy and the Urban Development Corporations*, London: Paul Chapman Publishing.

Brueggeman, W., Chen, A. H. and Thibodeau, T. (1984) Real Estate Investment Funds: Performance and Portfolio Considerations, *Journal, American Real Estate and Urban Policy and the Urban Economics Association*, 12: 333–54.

Cameron, G., Monk, S. and Pearce, B. J. (1988) *Vacant Urban Land. A Literature Review*, London: Department of the Environment.

Campeau, F. (1995) *A microstructure analysis of the information on securitized and unsecuritized commercial real estate markets*. Unpublished PhD thesis, University of Cambridge.

370

Canova, F. (1993). Detrending and business cycle facts. *Centre for Economic Research Discussion Paper*, (782), London.

Carbonaro, G. and d'Arcy, É. (1994) Key issues in property-led urban restructuring: a European perspective, *Journal of Property Finance and Investment*, 11: 339–53.

Case, K. (1992) The real estate cycle and the economy: consequences of the Massachusetts boom of 1984–7, *Urban Studies*, 29: 171–83.

Case, K. and Schiller, R. (1989) The efficiency of the market for single family homes, *American Economic Review*, 79: 125–37.

Case, K. and Schiller, R. (1990) Forecasting prices and excess returns in the housing market, *Journal of the American Real Estate and Urban Economics Association*, 18: 253–73.

Chance, D. (1995) *An Introduction to Derivatives*, 3rd edition, Fort Worth: The Dryden Press.

Chandler, A. (1977) *The Visible Hand. The Managerial Revolution in American Business,* Cambridge MA: Belknap Press.

Chandler, A. (1990) *Scale and Scope. The Dynamics of Industrial Capitalism*, Cambridge MA: Belknap Press.

Chaplin, R. (1997) Unsmoothing valuation based indices using multiple regimes, *Journal of Property Research*, 13, 3: 189–211.

Chatterji, M. (1993) Convergence Clubs and Endogenous Growth, *Oxford Review of Economic Policy*, 8: 57–69.

Chau, K., MacGregor, B. D. and Schwann, G. (1997) Price discovery in Hong Kong property markets; paper presented to the RICS Cutting Edge Research Conference, Dublin, 1997.

Cheshire, P. and Carbonaro, G. (1995) Convergence–divergence in regional growth rates: an empty black box?, in Armstrong, H. and Vickerman, R. (editors) *Convergence and Divergence Among European Regions*, London: Pion.

Chirinko, R. (1993) Business fixed investment spending: modelling strategies, empirical results, and policy implications, *Journal of Economic Literature*, 31, 1875–911.

Christaller, W. (1933) *Die zentralen Orte in Süddeutschland*, Jena: Fischer; translated by Baskin, C. as *The Central Places of Southern Germany*, Englewood Cliffs NJ: Prentice Hall.

Church, A. (1988) Urban regeneration in London; a five year policy review, *Environment and Planning C*, 6: 187–208.

Clapp, J. (1980) The Intra-Metropolitan Location of Office Activities *Journal of Regional Science*, 20: 387–99.

Clapp, J. (1993) *Dynamics of Office Markets*, Washington DC: The Urban Institute Press.

Clark, G. and Wrigley, N. (1995) Sunk costs: a framework for economic geography, *Transactions, Institute of British Geographers*, N.S.20: 204–33.

Coakley, J. (1994) The integration of property and financial markets, *Environment and Planning A*, 26: 697–713.

Cole, R. and Fenn, G. (1996) The Role of Commercial Real Estate Lending in the Banking Crisis of 1987–1992, Working Paper, Board of Governors of the Federal Reserve System, Washington DC.

Cooke, P. (1988) Flexible Integration, Scope Economies and Strategic Alliances, *Society and Space*, 6: 281–300.

Corgel, J. and Gay, G. (1987) Local economic base, geographic diversification and risk management of mortgage portfolios, *Journal of the American Real Estate and Urban Economics Association*, 15: 256–67.

Corgel, J., McIntosh, W. and Ott, S. (1995) Real Estate Investment Trusts: A review of the Financial Economics Literature, *Journal of Real Estate Literature*, 3: 13–43.

Crampton, G. and Evans, A. (1992) The Agglomeration Economy of London, *Urban Studies*, 29: 259–71.

Cullingworth, J. B. (1992) *Town and Country Planning in Britain*, London: Allen and Unwin.

D'Arcy, E. and Keogh, G. (1994) Market maturity and property market behaviour: a European comparison of mature and emergent markets, *Journal of Property Research*, 11: 215–35.

Daniels, P. (1977) Office Locations in the British Conurbations: Trends and Strategies, *Urban Studies*, 14: 261–74.

Daniels, P. (1991) *Services and Metropolitan Development*, London: Routledge.

Daniels, P. and Holly, B. (1983) Office Location in Transition, *Environment and Planning A*, 15: 1293–98.

Department of the Environment (1980) *Enterprise Zones: A Consultation Document*, London: HMSO.

Department of the Environment (1987) *An Evaluation of the Enterprise Zone Experiment*, London: HMSO.

Dicken, P. (1992) *Global Shift: The Internationalization of Economic Activity*, 2nd edition, London: Paul Chapman Publishing.

DiPasquale, D. and Wheaton, W. (1996) *Urban Economics and Real Estate Markets*, Englewood Cliffs N.J.: Prentice Hall.

Dobson, S. M. and Goddard, J. A. (1992) The determinants of commercial property prices and rents, *Bulletin of Economic Research*, 44, 4: 301–21.

Dornbusch, R. and Fischer, S. (1994) *Macroeconomics*, New York: McGraw-Hill.

Drivers Jonas/IPD (1988) *The variation in valuations*, London: Drivers Jonas/IPD.

Drivers Jonas/IPD (1990) *The variation in valuations – 1990 update*, London: Drivers Jonas/IPD.

Drummen, M. and Zimmerman, H. (1992) The Structure of European Stock Returns, *Financial Analysts' Journal*, July/August, pp. 15–26.

DTZ (annual) *Money into property*, London: DTZ Debenham Thorpe.

Dunning, J. and Norman, G. (1983) The Theory of the Multinational Enterprise, *Environment and Planning A*, 15: 675–92

Dunning, J. and Norman, G. (1987) The Locational Choice of Offices in International Firms, *Environment and Planning A*, 19: 613–31

Eaker, M., Fabozzi, F. and Grant, D. (1996) *International Corporate Finance*, Fort Worth TX: Dryden Press.

Economist (1996) Monetary-policy mysteries, *Economist*, 28 September, p. 134.

Edwards, M. (1992) A microcosm: redevelopment proposals at Kings Cross, in Thornley, A. (1991) (editor) *The Crisis of London*, London: Routledge.

Eichholtz, P. and Lie, R. (1995) Globalization of Real Estate Markets?; paper presented to the American Real Estate Society annual meeting, Hilton Head S.C., March 1995.

Eichholtz, P. and Op 't Veld, H. (1997) Property turns up trumps, *Estates Gazette*, 9704: 128–30.

Eichholtz, P., Koedijk, K. and Schweitzer, M. (1997) Testing International Real Estate Investment Strategies; paper presented to the Real Estate Research Institute Annual Seminar, Chicago.

Elton, E. and Gruber, M. J. (1984) *Modern portfolio theory and investment analysis*, New York: John Wiley and Sons.

Eppli, M. and Benjamin, J. (1994) The Evolution of Shopping Center Research: A Review and Analysis, *Journal of Real Estate Research*, 9: 5–32.

Eubank, A. A. and Sirmans, C. F. (1979) The price adjustment mechanism for rental housing in the United States, *Quarterly Journal of Economics*, 93, 1: 163–83.

Evans, A. (1983) The determination of the Price of Land, *Urban Studies*, 20, 2: 119–29.

Evans, A. (1990) No Room! No Room! The Costs of the British Town and Country Planning System, *Institute of Economic Affairs Occasional Papers*, 79, London: IEA.

Evans, A. (1995) The property market: ninety per cent efficient?, *Urban Studies*, 32: 5–29.

Evans, M. K. (1969) *Macroeconomic activity: theory, forecasting and control*, New York: Harper and Row.

Evans, R. D. (1990) A transfer function analysis of real estate capitalization rates, *Journal of Real Estate Research*, 5: 371–9.

Fainstein, S. (1992) *The City Builders*, Oxford: Basil Blackwell.

Fama, E. F. (1970) Efficient capital markets: a review of theory and empirical work, *Journal of Finance*, 25: 383–420.

Feldstein, M. (1977) The Surprising Incidence of a Tax on Pure Rent: A New Answer to an Old Question, *Journal of Political Economy*, 85, 2.

Fergus, J. and Goodman, J. (1994) The 1989–1992 Credit Crunch for Real Estate: A Retrospective, *Journal of the American Real Estate and Urban Economics Association*, 22: 5–32.

Field, B. and MacGregor, B. D. (1987) *Forecasting Techniques for Urban and Regional Planning*, London: Hutchinson.

Firstenburg, P. M., Ross, S. A. and Zisler, R. C. (1988) Real estate: the whole story, *The Journal of Portfolio Management*, Spring: 23–32.

Fisher, J., Hudson-Wilson, S. and Wurtzebach, C. (1993) Equilibrium in commercial real estate markets: linking the space and capital markets, *Journal of Portfolio Management*, Summer: 101–7.

Fogler, H. R. (1984) 20% in real estate: can theory justify it?, *The Journal of Portfolio Management*, Winter: 6–13.

Foreman, C. (1989) *Spitalfields. A Battle for Land*, London: Hilary Shipman.

Fraser, W. D. (1985) The risk of property to the institutional investor, *Journal of Valuation*, 4, 1: 45–59.

Friedmann, J. (1986) The World City Hypothesis, *Development and Change*, 17: 69–84.

Galbraith, J. K. (1990) *A short history of financial euphoria*, Harmondsworth: Penguin.

Gardiner, C. and Henneberry, J. (1991) Predicting regional office rents using habit-persistence theories, *Journal of Property Valuation and Investment*, 9, 3: 215–25.

Garreau, J. (1991) *Edge City*, New York: Doubleday.

Gatzlaff, D. H. and Tirtiroglu, D. (1995) Real estate market efficiency: issues and evidence, *Journal of Real Estate Literature*, 3, 2: 157–92.

Gatzlaff, D., Sirmans, C. and Diskin, B. (1994) The Effect of Anchor tenant Loss on Shopping Center Rents, *Journal of Real Estate Research*, 9: 99–110.

Geltner, D. (1991) Smoothing in appraisal based returns, *Journal of the American Real Estate and Urban Economics Association*, 13, 1: 15–31.

Geltner, D. (1993) Estimating market values from appraised values without assuming an efficient market, *Journal of Real Estate Research*, 8, 3: 325–45.

Gertler, M. (1992) Flexibility Revisited, *Transactions, Institute of British Geographers*, N.S.17: 259–78.

Ghosh, C., Guttery, R. and Sirmans, C. (1994) The Olympia and York Crisis, *Journal of Property Finance*, 5: 5–46.

Giuliano, G. (1986) Land Use Impacts of Transportation Investments, in Hanson, S. (editor) *The Geography of Urban Transportation*, New York: Guildford Press.

Giussani, B., Hsia, M. and Tsolacas, S. (1993) A comparative analysis of the major determinants of office rental values in Europe, *Journal of Property Valuation and Investment*, 11, 2: 157–73.

Goddard, J. (1973) *Office Linkages and Location*, Oxford: Pergamon Press.

Goddard, J. (1975) *Office Location in Urban and Regional Development*, Oxford: Oxford University Press.

Goetzmann, W. and Wachter, S. (1995) The Global Real Estate Crash: Evidence From An International Database, in *Proceedings of the International Congress on Real Estate*, vol. 3 (unpaginated) AREUEA, Singapore.

Goldstein, M. and Folkerts-Landau, D. (1993) *International Capital Markets Part II: Systemic Issues in International Finance*, Washington: International Monetary Fund.

Goodchild, R. and Munton, R. (1985) *Development and the Landowner,* London: Allen and Unwin.

Gordon, M. (1993) The neo-classical and a post-Keynesian theory of investment, in Davidson, P. (editor) *Can the Free Market Pick Winners?*, Armonk, New York: M.E. Sharpe.

Gordon, R. J. (editor (1986)) *The American business cycle*, Chicago: University of Chicago Press.

Gore, T. and Nicholson, D. (1991) Models of the land-development process; a critical review, *Environment and Planning A* , 23: 705–30.

Graham, D. and Spence, N. (1995) Contemporary Deindustrialisation and Tertiarisation in the London Economy, *Urban Studies*, 32: 885–911.

Gravelle, H. and Rees, R. (1992) *Microeconomics,* Harlow: Longman.

Greenwell, W. and Co. (1976) A call for new valuation models, *Estates Gazette*, 7638: 481–4.

Grenadier, S. R. (1995) The persistence of real estate cycles, *The Journal of Real Estate Economics and Finance*, 10, 2: 95–120.

Grubel, H. (1968) Internationally Diversified Portfolios, *American Economic Review*, 58: 1299–314.

Gyourko, J. and Keim, D. (1992) What Does the Stock Market Tell Us About Real Estate Returns?, *Journal of the American Real Estate and Urban Economics Association,* 20: 457–85.

Han, J. and Liang, Y. (1995) The Historical Performance of Real Estate Investment Trusts, *The Journal of Real Estate Research*, 10: 235–62.

Hancock, D. and Wilcox, J. (1993) Has There Been a 'Capital Crunch' in Banking?, *Journal of Housing Economics,* 3: 31–50.

Hancock D. and Wilcox, J. (1994) Bank Capital and the Credit Crunch: The Roles of Risk-Weighted and Unweighted Capital Regulation, *Journal of the American Real Estate and Urban Economics Association*, 22: 59–94.

Hartzell, D., Shulman, D. and Wurtzebach, C. (1987) Refining the analysis of regional diversification for income-producing real estate, *Journal of Real Estate Research*, 2: 85–95.

Harvey, A. C. (1989) *Forecasting, Structural Time Series Models and the Kalman Filter*, Cambridge: Cambridge University Press.

Harvey, A. C. and A. Jaeger (1993). Detrending, Stylized Facts and the Business Cycle, *Journal of Applied Econometrics*, 8: 231–41.

Harvey, D. (1978) The urban process under capitalism: a framework for analysis, *International Journal of Urban and Regional Research*, 2: 101–31.

Harvey, J. (1986) *Urban Land Economics*, 4th edition, Basingstoke: Macmillan.

Healey, P. (1992) An institutional model of the development process, *Journal of Property Research*, 9: 33–44.

Healey, P. and Barrett, S. (1990) Structure and agency in land and property development processes: some ideas for research, *Urban Studies*, 27: 89–104.

Healey, P. and Nabarro, R. (editors) (1990) *Land and Property Development in a Changing Context*, Aldershot: Gower.

Healey, P., Davoudi, S., O'Toole, M., Tavsanoglu, S. and Usher, D. (1992) *Rebuilding the City: Property-Led Urban Regeneration*, London: E & F N Spon.

Heilbrun, J. (1987) *Urban Economics and Public Policy*, New York: St Martin's Press.

Hekman, J. S. (1985) Rental adjustment and investment in the office market, *Journal of the American Real Estate and Urban Economics Association*, 13, 1: 32–47.

Helsley, R. and Strange, W. (1991) Agglomeration Economies and Urban Capital Markets, *Journal of Urban Economics*, 29: 96–112.

Helsley, R. and Sullivan, A. (1991) Urban Subcenter Formation, *Regional Science and Urban Economics*, 21: 255–75.

Hendershott, P. (1995) Real effective rent determination: evidence from the Sydney office market, *Journal of Property Research*, 12, 2: 127–35.

Hendershott, P. and Kane, E. (1992) Causes and consequences of the 1980s commercial construction boom, *Journal of Applied Corporate Finance*, 5: 61–70.

Hendershott, P., Lizieri, C. and Matysiak, G. (1997) *The workings of the London office market: model estimation and simulation*, Real Estate Research Institute, WP-63.

Henderson, J. (1985) *Economic Theory and the Cities*, Orlando: Academic Press.

Henderson, J. (1988) *Urban Development*, Oxford: Oxford University Press.

Hepworth, M. (1989) *Geography of the Information Economy*, London: Bellhaven Press.

Hetherington, J. (1988) Forecasting of rents, in MacLeary, A. and Nathakumaran, N. (editors), *Property Investment Theory*, London: E & F N Spon (pp. 97–107).

Hickman, B. G. (1973). What became of the building cycle? *Nations and Households in Economic Growth: Essays in Honor of Moses Abramovitz.* New York: Academic Press.

Hillier Parker (various) *International Property Bulletin*, London: Hillier Parker May and Rowden.

Hirst, P. and Thompson, G. (1996) *Globalization in Question*, Cambridge: Cambridge University Press.

Hoesli, M., Lizieri, C. and MacGregor, B. D. (1997) The spatial dimensions of the investment performance of UK commercial property, *Urban Studies*, 34, 9: 1475–94.

Hoesli, M., MacGregor, B. D., Matysiak, G. A. and Nanthakumaran, N. (1997) The short-term inflation-hedging characteristics of UK real estate, *Journal of Real Estate Finance and Economics*, 15, 1: 27–58.

Holloway, S. and Wheeler, J. (1991) Corporate Headquarters Relocation and Changes in Metropolitan Corporate Dominance, *Economic Geography*, 67: 54–74.

Holsapple, E., Olienyk, J. and Ozawa, T. (1996) Japanese Investment in US Real Estate in the 1980s: A Current Account Recycling Analysis; paper presented to the American Real Estate Society Annual Meeting, South Lake Tahoe CA.

Hooper, A. (1992) The construction of theory; a comment, *Journal of Property Research*, 9: 45–8.

Hoover, E. (1926) *The Location of Economic Activity*, New York: McGraw-Hill.

Hotelling, H. (1929) Stability in Competition, *Economic Journal*, 39: 41–57.

Howells, P. G. A. and Rydin, Y. J. (1990) The case for property investment and the implications of unitised property market, *Land Development Studies*, 7, 1: 15–30.

Huff, D. (1963) A Probability Analysis of Shopping Centers' Trade Areas, *Land Economics*, February 1963: 81–90.

Huff, D. (1964) Defining and Estimating a Trade Area, *Journal of Marketing*, 28: 34–8.

Imai, M. (1986) *Kaizen*, New York: McGraw-Hill.

IMF (1996) Policy challenges facing industrial countries in the late 1990s, International Monetary Fund *World Economic Outlook*, May: 42–56.

Imrie, R. and Thomas, H. (1993) *British Urban Policy and the UDCs*, London: Paul Chapman Publishing.

Ingham, G. (1984) *Capitalism Divided? The City and Industry in British Social Development,* Basingstoke: Macmillan.

Investment Property Forum (1993) *Property Investment for UK Pension Funds*, London: IPF.

Isard, W. (1942). A neglected cycle: the transport-building cycle, *Review of Economic Statistics*, 24: 149–58.

Isard, W. (1956) *Location and Space-Economy*, Cambridge MA: MIT Press.

Jacobs, J. (1969) *The Economy of Cities*, New York: Vintage Books.

Jacobson, D. and Andreosso-O'Callaghan (1996) *Industrial Economics and Organisation: A European Perspective*, Maidenhead: McGraw-Hill.

Jenkins, S. (1975) *Landlords to London*, London: Constable.

JLW (1990) *The Decentralisation of Offices from Central London*, London: Jones Lang Wootton.

Jorgenson, D. (1971) Econometric studies of investment behaviour: a survey, *Journal of Economic Literature*, 9: 1111–47.

Jorion, P. (1985) International Portfolio Diversification with Estimation Risk, *Journal of Business*, 8: 259–278.

Kaiser, E. J. and Weiss, S. F. (1970) Public policy and the residential development process, *Journal of American Institute of Planners*, 36: 30–7.

Kane, E. (1985) *The Gathering Crisis in Federal Deposit Insurance*, Cambridge MA: Ballinger.

Kennedy, N. and Andersen, P. (1994) *Household Saving and Real House Prices*, Basle: Bank of International Settlements.

Keogh, G. and Evans, E. (1992) The Private and Social Costs of Planning Delay *Urban Studies* 29: 687–99.

Key, T., MacGregor, B. D., Nanthakumaran, N. and Zarkesh, F. (1994a) *Economic cycles and property cycles*, Main report for Understanding the property cycle, London: RICS.

Key, T., MacGregor, B. D., Nanthakumaran, N. and Zarkesh, F. (1994b) *The availability and adequacy of data*, Working Paper One, Understanding the property cycle, London: RICS.

Key, T., MacGregor, B. D., Nanthakumaran, N. and Zarkesh, F. (1994c) *A literature review*, Working Paper Two for Understanding the property cycle, London. RICS.

Kim, T. (1993) *International Money and Banking*, London: Routledge.

Kindleberger, C. (1978) *Manias, Panics and Crashes*, Basingstoke: Macmillan.

Kivell, P. (1993) *Land and the City: Patterns and Processes of Urban Change*, London: Routledge.

Knight, R. and Trygg, L. (1977) *Land Use Impacts of Rapid Transit: Implications of Recent Experience*, Final Report No. DOT-TPC-10–77–29 San Francisco: U.S. Department of Transportation.

Krabben, E. van der and Lambooy, J. (1993) A Theoretical Framework for the Functioning of the Dutch urban property market, *Urban Studies*, 30: 1399–1408.

Krabben, E. van der (1996) *Urban Dynamics: A Real Estate Perspective*, Tilburg: University Press.

Krabben, E. van der and Boekma, F. (1994) Missing iinks between urban economic growth theory and the functioning of property markets: economic growth and building investments in the City of 's-Hertongenbosch, *Journal of Property Research*, 11: 111–29.

Krugman, P. (1991) *Geography and Trade*, Cambridge MA: MIT Press.

Kruijt, B., van Wetten, P. and Goetmakers, D. (1996) Real Estate Shares and International Diversification; paper presented to the AREUEA International Real Estate Conference, Orlando FL.

Kuznets, S. (1930) *Secular Movements in Production and Prices*, New York: Houghton Mifflin.

LaSalle (1996) *Investment Strategy Annual 1996*, Chicago: LaSalle Advisors.

Lawless, P. (1994) Partnerships in Urban Regeneration in the UK: the Sheffield Central Area Case Study, *Urban Studies*, 31: 1303–24.

Lazonick, W. (1991) *Business Organisation and the Myth of the Market Economy*, Cambridge: Cambridge University Press.

Lee, S. L. (1989) Property returns in a portfolio context, *Journal of Valuation*, 7, 3: 248–58.

Leitner, H. (1994) Capital markets, the development industry, and urban office dynamics: rethinking building cycles, *Environment and Planning A*, 26: 779–802.

377

Levy, H. and Sarnatt, M. (1970) International Diversification of Investment Portfolios, *American Economic Review*, 60: 668–75.

Leyshon, A., Thrift, N. and Daniels, P. (1990) The operational development and spatial expansion of large commercial property firms, in Healey, P. and Nabarro, R. (editors), *Land and Property in a Changing Context*, Aldershot: Gower.

Lichfield, N. (1988) *Economics in Urban Conservation*, Cambridge: Cambridge University Press.

Lizieri, C. (1991) The Property Market in a Changing World Economy, *Journal of Property Valuation and Investment*, 9: 201–14.

Lizieri, C. (1994) Property Ownership, Leasehold Forms and Industrial Change, in Ball, R. and Pratt, A. (editors) *Industrial Property: Policy and Economic Development*, London: Routledge.

Lizieri, C. (1995) Real Estate Ownership, Finance and Risk: Evidence From The Toronto Office Market, Proceedings, *RICS Research Conference The Cutting Edge*, 1: 13–28.

Lizieri, C. and Finlay, L. (1995) International property portfolio strategies: problems and opportunities, *Journal of Property Valuation and Investment*, 13, 1: 6–21.

Lizieri, C. and Palmer, S. (1997) Environmental Legislation, Real Estate Appraisal and Investment in the UK, *Growth and Change*, 28: 110–29.

Lizieri, C. and Satchell, S. (1997) Interactions between property and equity markets: an investigation of the linkages in the UK, 1972–1992, *Journal of Real Estate Finance and Economics*, 15, 1: 11–26.

Lizieri, C. and Venmore-Rowland, P. (1991) Valuation accuracy: a contribution to the debate, *Journal of Property Research*, 8, 2: 115–22.

Lizieri, C. and Venmore-Rowland, P. (1993) Valuations, prices and the market: a rejoinder, *Journal of Property Research*, 10, 2: 77–84.

Lizieri, C., Crosby, N., Gibson, V., Murdoch, S. and Ward, C. (1997) *Right Space, Right Price? A Study of the Impact of Changing Business Patterns on the Property Market*, London: RICS.

Llewellyn-Davies (1996) *Four World Cities: A Comparative Study of London, Paris, New York and Tokyo*, London: Llewellyn-Davies.

Lloyd, M. and Black, S. (1993) Property-Led Urban Regeneration and Local Economic Development, in Berry, J., McGreal, S. and Deddis, W. (editors) *Urban Regeneration, Property Investment and Development*, London: E & F N Spon.

Logan, J. and Molotch, H. (1987) *Urban Fortunes*, Berkeley CA: University of California Press.

London Planning Advisory Council (LPAC) (1991) *London: World City*, London: HMSO.

Lösch, A. (1954) *The Economics of Location*, New Haven CT: Yale University Press.

Lyons, D. (1994) Changing Patterns of Corporate Headquarter Influence 1974–1989, *Environment and Planning A*, 26: 739–47.

MacGregor, B. D. and Nanthakumaran, N. (1992) The Allocation to Property in the Multi-Asset Portfolio: the Evidence and Theory Reconsidered, *Journal of Property Research*, 9: 5–32.

Macho-Stadler, I. and Perez-Castrillo, D. (1997) *An Introduction to the Economics of Information*, Oxford: Oxford University Press.

Maddala, G. (1994) *Econometrics*, Maidenhead: McGraw-Hill.

Maddison, A. (1991) *Dynamic Forces in Capitalist Development: a Long-run Comparative View*, Oxford: Oxford University Press.

Madura, J. (1985) International Portfolio Construction, *Journal of Business Research*, 13: 87–95.

Madura, J. (1992) *International Financial Management,* 3rd edition, St. Paul MN: West Publishing Company.

Madura, J. and Reiff, W. (1985) A hedge strategy for international portfolios, *Journal of Portfolio Management*, 12: 70–4.

Malecki, E. (1991) *Technology and Economic Development*, Harlow: Longman.

Malizia, E. and Sirmans, R. (1991) Comparing regional classifications for real estate portfolio diversification, *Journal of Real Estate Research*, 6: 53–67.

Manolis, J. and Meistrich, S. (1986) The Development of Rated Nonrecourse Mortgage-Backed Bonds, *Real Estate Finance*, 3: 17–26.

March, J. and Simon, H. (1958) *Organisations*, New York: Wiley.

Markowitz, H. M. (1952) Portfolio selection, *The Journal of Finance*, 12: 77–91.

Markowitz, H. M. (1959) *Portfolio selection: efficient diversification of investments*, Yale CT: Yale University Press.

Marriot, O. (1967) *The Property Boom*, London: Hamish Hamilton.

Marshall, A. (1893) *Principles of Economics*, 1920 edition, London: Macmillan.

Marshall A. (1919) *Economics of Industry*, London: Macmillan.

Martin, R. and Rowthorn, R. (editors) (1986) *The Geography of Deindustrialisation*, London: Macmillan.

Martin, S. (1993) *Advanced Industrial Economics*, Oxford: Basil Blackwell.

Marvin. S. and Guy, S. (1997) Infrastructure Provision, Development Processes and the Co-production of Environmental Values, *Urban Studies*, 34: 2023–36.

Massey, D. (1984) *Spatial Divisions of Labour*, London: Macmillan.

Massey, D. and Catalano, A. (1978) *Capital and Land*, London: Edward Arnold.

Matysiak, G. and Wang, P. (1995), Commercial property market prices and valuations: analysing the correspondence, *Journal of Property Research*, 12, 3: 181–202.

Matysiak, G., Hoesli, M., MacGregor, B. D. and Nanthakumaran, N. (1996) The Long-Term Inflation Hedging Characteristics of UK Commercial Property, *Journal of Property Finance*, 7: 50–61.

McCue, T. and Kling, J. (1994) Real Estate Returns and the Macroeconomy: Some Empirical Evidence, *Journal of Real Estate Research*, 9: 277–87.

McGoldrick, P. and Thompson, M. (1992) *Regional Shopping Centres*, Aldershot: Avebury.

McMillan, J. (1992) *Games, Strategies and Managers*, Oxford: Oxford University Press.

McNulty, J. (1995) Overbuilding, Real Estate Lending Decisions and the Regional Economic Base, *Journal of Real Estate Finance and Economics*, 11: 37–53.

McWilliams, D. (1992) Commercial property and company borrowing, *Research Paper 22*, London: Royal Institute of Chartered Surveyors.

Mengden, A. and Hartzell, D. (1987) *Real Estate Investment Trusts - Are They Stocks or Real Estate?*, New York: Salomon Bros.

Michaud, R. (1989) The Markowitz optimisation enigma: is 'optimised' optimal?. *Financial Analyst Journal*, September–October, 31–4.

Mieszkowski, P. and Mills, E. S. (1993) The causes of suburbanisation, *Journal of Economic Perspectives*, 7: 135–47.

Miles, D. (1994) *Housing, Financial Markets and the Wider Economy*, Chichester: John Wiley.

Miles, I. (1990) Teleshopping: Just Around the Corner? Proceedings, Britain in 2010: Future Patterns of Shopping, *RSA Journal*, February: 180–9.

Mills, E. S. (1987) *Handbook of Regional and Urban Economics. Volume 2: Urban Economics*, North-Holland, Amsterdam.

Mills, E. S. and Lubuelle, L. S. (1997) Inner Cities, *Journal of Economic Literature*, 35, June: 727–56.

Mills, T.C. (1991) *Time Series Techniques for Economists*, Cambridge: Cambridge University Press.

Minns, R. (1980) *Pension Funds and British Capitalism*, London: Heinemann.

Moore, B., Tyler, P. and Elliot, D. (1991) The Influence of Regional Development Incentives and Infrastructure on the Location of Small and Medium sized Companies in Europe, *Urban Studies*, 28: 1001–26.

Morrell, G. D. (1991) Property performance analysis and performance indices: a review, *Journal of Property Research*, 3, 4: 29–57.

Moscovitch, E. (1990) The Downturn in the New England Economy: What Lies Behind It?, *New England Economic Review*, July/August 1990: 53–65.

Mueller, G. (1993) Refining economic diversification strategies for real estate portfolios, *Journal of Real Estate Research*, 8: 55–68.

Mueller, G. and Zierling, B. (1992) Real estate portfolio diversification using economic diversification, *Journal of Real Estate Research*, 7: 375–86.

NAREIT (1995) *1995 REIT Handbook*, National Association of Real Estate Investment Trusts.

Needham, B. (1992) A Theory of Land Prices When Land is Supplied Publicly, *Urban Studies*, 29: 669–86.

Needham, B., Jassen, J. and Krujit, B. (1994) The Honeycomb Cycle in Real Estate, *Journal of Real Estate Research*, 9: 237–52.

Nicholson, R. and Tebbutt, S. (1979) Modelling of new orders for private industrial buildings, *The Journal of Industrial Economics*, 28, 2: 147–60.

North, D.C. (1990) *Institutions, Institutional Change and Economic Performance*, Cambridge: Cambridge University Press.

Noyelle, T. and Stanback, T., Jr (1984) *The Economic Transformation of American Cities*, Totawa NJ: Rowman and Allanheld.

NSO (1996) *Annual Abstract of Statistics*, National Statistical Office, London.

NSO (1997) *Annual Abstract of Statistics*, National Statistical Office, London.

O'Brien, R. (1992) *Global Financial Integration: The End of Geography*, London: Chatham House Papers.

Ó hUallacháin, B. (1990) The Location of US Manufacturing: Some Empirical Evidence on Recent Geographical Shifts, *Environment and Planning A*, 22: 1205–22.

Pagliari J., Jr and Webb, J. (1995) A fundamental examination of securitized and unsecuritized real estate, *Journal of Real Estate Research*, 10: 381–426.

Peek, J. and Rosengren, E. (1994) Bank Real Estate Lending and the New England Capital Crunch, *Journal of the American Real Estate and Urban Economics Association*, 22: 32–58.

Peet, R. (1991) *Global Capitalism*, London, Routledge.

Piore, M. and Sabel, C. (1984) *The Second Industrial Divide: Possibilites for Prosperity*, New York: Basic Books.

380

Plender, J. (1984) *That's the Way the Money Goes*, London: Weidenfeld and Nicholson.

Pollakowski, H. O., Wachter, S. M. and Lynford, L. (1992) Did office size matter in the 1980s? A time series cross-sectional analysis of the metropolitan area office markets, *Journal of the American Real Estate and Urban Economics Association*, 20, 2: 303–24.

Porter, M. (1990) *The Competitive Advantage of Nations*, New York: Free Press.

Poterba, J. (1984) Tax subsidies to owner-occupied housing: an asset markets approach, *Quarterly Journal of Economics*, 729–52.

Poterba, J. (1991) House price dynamics: the role of tax policy and demography, *Brookings Papers in Economic Activity*, 143–203.

Pred, A. (1967) *Behavior and Location: Foundations for a Geographic and Dynamic Location Theory, Part I*, University of Lund, Lund Studies in Geography B, 27.

Pred, A. (1969) *Behavior and Location: Foundations for a Geographic and Dynamic Location Theory, Part II* University of Lund, Lund Studies in Geography B, 28.

Prest, A. (1981) *The Taxation of Urban Land*, Manchester: Manchester University Press.

Prudential Insurance Company of America/JLW (1988) *A Comparison of International Real Estate Returns*, London and New York: Prudential Insurance Company of America/Jones Lang Wootton.

Prudential Real Estate Investors (1990) *Global Watch Report*, Newark NJ: Prudential Real Estate Investors.

Pryke, M. (1994) Looking back on the space of a boom: (re)developing spatial matrices in the City of London, *Environment and Planning A*, 26: 235–64.

Pryke, M. and Whitehead, C. (1991) *Mortgage-Backed Securitisation in the UK*, Land Economy Research Monograph 22, University of Cambridge.

Punter, J. (1985) Aesthetic control within the development control process: a case study; paper given to conference on local land-use planning, Oxford: Oxford Polytechnic.

Rauch, J. (1993) Does History Matter Only When It Matters Little? The Case of City-Industry Location, *Quarterly Journal of Economics*, CVIII: 843–67.

Reilly, W. (1929) *Methods of the Study of Retail Relationships*, University of Texas, Austin TX, Bulletin 2944.

Romer, D. (1996) *Advanced Macroeconomics*, New York: McGraw-Hill.

Rosen, K. T. (1984) Towards a model of the office building sector, *Journal of the American Real Estate and Urban Economics Association*, 12, 3: 261–69.

Rosen, K. T. and Smith, L. B. (1983) The price adjustment process for rental housing and the natural vacancy rate, *American Economic Review*, 73: 779–86.

Ross, S. and Zisler, R. (1987) A Close Look at Equity Real Estate Risk, Research Paper, New York: Goldman Sachs.

Rowlinson, M. (1997) *Organisations and Institutions*, Basingstoke: Macmillan.

Rubenstein, W. (1986) *Wealth and Inequality in Britain*, London: Faber and Faber.

Rutterford, J. (1993) *Introduction to stock exchange investment*, (2nd edition), London: Macmillan.

Salway, F. (1986) Building depreciation and property appraisal techniques, *Journal of Valuation*, 5, 2: 118–24.

Sassen, S. (1991) *The Global City*, Princeton NJ: Princeton University Press.

Schiller, R. (1986) Retail Decentralisation – the Coming of the Third Wave, *Planner*, (July): 13–15.

Schinasi, G. and Hargraves, M. (1993) 'Boom and bust' in assets market since the 1980s: causes and consequences, *Staff Studies for the World Economic Outlook*, World Economic and Financial Survey, pp. 1–27, International Monetary Fund, Washington D.C.

Schoenberger, E. (1987) Technical and Organisational Change in Automobile Production, *Regional Studies*, 21: 199–214.

Scott, A. (1986) Industrial Organization and Location: Division of Labour, the Firm and Spatial Process, *Economic Geography*, 62: 215–31.

Scott, P. (1996) *The property masters*, London: E & F N Spon.

Seck, D. (1996) The Substitutability of Real Estate Assets, *Journal of the American Real Estate and Urban Economics Association*, 24: 75–96.

Shilling, J. D., Sirmans, C. F. and Corgel, J. B. (1987) Price adjustment process for rental office space, *Journal of Urban Economics*, 22: 90–100.

Shulman, D. and Hopkins, R. (1988) Economic diversification in real estate portfolios, *Bond Market Research: Real Estate*, November, New York: Salomon Brothers Inc.

Sirmans, C. and Guidry, K. (1993) The Determinants of Shopping Center Rents, *Journal of Real Estate Research*, 8: 107–116.

Smith, D. (1981) *Industrial location: an economic geographical analysis*, London: Wiley.

Smith, L., Rosen, K. and Fallis, G. (1988) Recent developments in economic models of housing markets, *Journal of Economic Literature*, 26: 29–64.

Solnik, B. (1974a) Why not diversify internationally rather than domestically?, *Financial Analysts' Journal*, 30, 4: 48–54.

Solnik, B. (1974b) An Equilibrium Model of the International Capital Market, *Journal of Economic Theory*, 8 July/August.

Solnik, B. (1991) *International Investments*, Reading MA: Adison Wesley.

Sorensen, E. and Mezrich, J. (1989) Changing global stock markets: the world is getting larger, New York: Salomon Bros.

Speidell, L. and Sappenfield, R. (1992) Global Diversification in a Shrinking World, *Journal of Portfolio Management*, 19: 57–67.

Stiglitz, J. (1992) Capital markets and economic fluctuations in capitalist economies, *European Economic Review*, 36: 269–306.

Sweeney, F. (1988a) 20 per cent in real estate: a viable strategy, *Estates Gazette*, 13, February: 26–8.

Sweeney, F. (1988b) International Real Estate Diversification – A Viable Investment Strategy, *Property Management*, 5, 317–26.

Sweeney, F. (1989) Investment Strategy: A Property Market Without Frontiers, *Estates Gazette*, 8935: 20–30.

Sweeney, F. (1993) Mapping a European Property Investment Strategy, *Journal of Property Valuation and Investment*, 11: 259–67.

Thomas, M. (1995) The Performance of the German Property Market Between 1989 and 1994, *Journal of Property Valuation and Investment*, 13, 5: 67–84.

Thornley, A. (1991) *Urban Planning under Thatcher*, London: Routledge.

Thunen, J. H. von (1826) *Der Isolierte Staat in Beziehung auf Landwistschaft und Nationalötonomie*, Berlin.

Tiebout, C. (1956) A Pure Theory of Local Expenditures, *Journal of Political Economy*, 64: 416–24.

Tukey, J. W. (1977) *Exploratory Data Analysis*, Reading MA: Addison-Wesley.

Turok, I. (1992) Property-Led Urban Regeneration: Panacea or Placebo?, *Environment and Planning A*, 24: 361–79.

Uthwatt Report (1942) *Expert Committee on Compensation and Betterment, Final Report*, Cmnd. 6386, London: HMSO.

Vandell, K. (1993) Handing Over The Keys: A Perspective on Mortgage Default Research, *Journal of the American Real Estate and Urban Economics Association*, 21: 211–46.

Vandell, K. and Carter, C. (1993) Retail Store Location and Market Analysis: A review of the Research, *Journal of Real Estate Literature*, 1: 13–45.

van Duijn, J. J. (1983) *The Long Wave in Economic Life*, London: George Allen & Unwin.

Verdict (1991) *Out of Town Retailing*, London: Verdict Research Ltd.

Wang, P., Lizieri C. and Matysiak, G. (1997) Information Assymetry, Long Run Relationship and Price Discovery in Property Investment Markets, *European Journal of Finance*, 3: 261–75.

Webb, J. R., Curcio, R. J. and Rubens, J. H. (1988) Diversification gains from including real estate in mixed asset portfolios, *Decision Sciences*, 19: 434–52.

Webb, R. B. (1994) On the reliability of commercial appraisals, *Real Estate Finance*, 11, 1: 62–5.

Webber, M. (1972) *The Impact of Uncertainty on Location*, Cambridge MA: MIT Press.

Weber, A. (1909) *Über der Standort den Industrien,* translated C. Freidrich (1929) as Theory of the Location of Industry, Chicago: University of Chicago Press.

Weber, B. A. (1955) A New Index of Residential Construction 1838–1950, *Scottish Journal of Political Economy*.

Wheaton, W. C. (1987) The cyclic behavior of the national office market, *Journal of the American Real Estate and Urban Economics Association*, 15, 4: 281–99.

Wheaton, W. C. and Torto, R. G. (1988) Vacancy rates and the future of office rents, *Journal of the American Real Estate and Urban Economics Association*, 16, 4: 430–6.

Wheaton, W. C. and Torto, R. G. (1990) An investment model of the demand and supply for industrial real estate, *Journal of the American Real Estate and Urban Economics Association*, 18, 4: 530–47.

Wheaton, W. C., Torto, R. G. and Evans, P. (1997) The cyclic behavior of the Greater London office market, *The Journal of Real Estate Finance and Economics*, 15, 1: 77–92.

White, L. J. (1991) *The S&L Debacle. Public Policy Lessons for Bank and Thrift Regulation*, Oxford: Oxford University Press.

Williamson, O. (1985) *The Economic Institutions of Capitalism*, New York: Free Press.

Wiltshaw, D. G. (1985) The supply of land, *Urban Studies*, 22: 49–56.

Wise, M. (1949) On the Evolution of the Jewellery and Gun Quarters in Birmingham, *Transactions, Institute of British Geographers*, 15: 57–72.

Witten, G. R. (1987) Riding the real estate cycle, *Real Estate Today*, August: 42–8.

Worzala, E. (1994) Overseas property investments: how are they perceived by the institutional investor?, *Journal of Property Valuation and Investment,* 12: 31–47.

Worzala, E. (1995) Currency risk and international property investments, *Journal of Property Valuation and Investment,* 13: 23–28.

Worzala, E. and Bernasek, A. (1996) European Economic Integration and Commercial Real Estate Markets: An Analysis of Trends in Market Determinants, *Journal of Real Estate Research,* 11: 159–81.

Worzala, E., Johnson, R. and Lizieri, C. (1997) A Comparison of Alternative Hedging Techniques for International Equity Investment, *The Journal of Property Finance,* 8: 134–51.

Worzala, E., Lizieri, C. and Newall, G. (1996) The Convergence of International Real Estate Markets; paper presented to the AREUEA International Real Estate Conference, Orlando FL.

Ziobrowski, A. and Boyd, J. (1991) Leverage and foreign investment in US real estate, *Journal of Real Estate Research,* 7: 33–58.

Ziobrowski, A. and Curcio, R. (1991) Diversification benefits of US real estate to foreign investors, *Journal of Real Estate Research,* 6: 119–42.

Ziobrowski, A. and Ziobrowski, B. (1993) Hedging foreign investments in US real estate with currency swaps, *Journal of Real Estate Research,* 8: 27–54.

Ziobrowski, A. and Ziobrowski, B.(1995) Hedging foreign investments in US real estate with forward contracts, *Journal of Property Valuation and Investment,* 13: 22–43.

Ziobrowski, A., Ziobrowski, B. and Rosenberg, S. (1997) Currency Swaps and International Real Estate Investment, *Journal of the American Real Estate and Urban Economics Association,* 25: 223–51.

AUTHOR INDEX

SUBJECT INDEX

Note: Page numbers in *italics* refer to tables or figures where these are separated from the textual reference